INDIA IN EMERGING ASIA

INDIA IN EMERGING ASIA

Edited by

SUDHIR SINGH

ASSOCIATION WITH SOCIETY FOR SOCIAL EMPOWERMENT,
NEW DELHI

PENTAGON PRESS

INDIA IN EMERGING ASIA
Sudhir Singh (Editor)

ISBN 978-81-8274-806-4

First Published in 2015

Published by
PENTAGON PRESS
206, Peacock Lane, Shahpur Jat,
New Delhi-110049
Phones: 011-64706243, 26491568
Telefax: 011-26490600
email: rajan@pentagonpress.in
website: www.pentagonpress.in

Branch:
Flat No.213, Athena-2,
Clover Acropolis,
Viman Nagar,
Pune-411014.
Email: pentagonpresspune@gmail.com

Printed at Aegean Offset Printers, Greater Noida, U.P.

Contents

About the Contributors

Dr. Alok Kumar Gupta is Associate Professor, Central University of Bihar, Gaya, Bihar.

Dr. Alokka Dutta is Assistant Professor, Aditi College, University of Delhi.

Dr. Bibhuti Bhusan Biswas is associated with Southern Studies Programme, Pondicherry Central University, Pondicherry.

Dr. Chandra Mohan Upadhaya is Associate Professor, Kisan P.G. College, Bahraich, Uttar Pradesh.

Dr. Deepak Yadav is Assistant Professor, Kalindi College, University of Delhi, New Delhi.

Prof. Ganganath Jha is Professor, School of International Studies, Jawaharlal Nehru University, New Delhi.

Dr. Geetha Govindasamy is Senior Lecturer, Department of East Asian Studies, Faculty of Arts and Social Sciences, University of Malay, Kuala Lumpur, Malyasia.

Dr. Koushiki Dasgupta is Assistant Professor, University of Gour Banga, West Bengal.

Dr. Krishan Gopal was formerly with Jawaharlal Nehru University, New Delhi.

Dr. Manan Dwivedi is Assistant Professor, Indian Institute for Public Administration, New Delhi.

Dr. Mahesh Ranjan Debata is Assistant Professor, School of International Studies, Jawaharlal Nehru University, New Delhi.

Ms. Mithila Bagai is Assistant Professor, Bharti College, University of Delhi.

Dr. M. Pragaya is Assistant Professor, Centre for Southeast Asian & Pacific Studies, Sri Venkateswara University, Tirupati.

Dr. Ravindra Sharma is Associate Professor, Dun University, Dehradun.

Mr. Ramakrishnan Ramani is Research Scholar, Department of Defence and Strategic Studies, University of Madras

Dr. Satish Kumar is Associate Professor, Central University of Haryana, Mahendragarh.

Dr. Suresh R is Associate Professor, University of Kerela.

Dr. S. Prabhakar is Joint Director, Lok-Sabha, New Delhi.

Prof. S.N. Singh is Dean, School of Political Science & Public Adminstration, MDS University, Ajmer, Rajasthan.

Dr. Sudhir Singh is Assistant Professor, Dyal Singh College, University of Delhi, New Delhi.

Dr. S. Utham Kumar Jamadhagni is Associate Professor, Defense Department, University of Madras, Chennai.

Dr. S. Manivasakan is the Director, Centre for the South and Southeast Asian Studies, University of Madras, Chennai.

Prof. Tridib Chakraborti is Professor, Jadavpur University, Kolkata.

Prof. Tej Pratap Singh is Professor, Banaras Hindu University, Banaras.

Introduction

The end of the Cold War has altered the contours of the international relations. The process of globalization has become the backbone of the new system. Asia in particular and developing south in general is gaining at the economic front. The 2013 Global Human Development Report is indicating towards this economic shift. By 2020, according to projections developed for this report, the combined economic output of three leading developing countries alone—Brazil, China and India—will surpass the aggregate production of Canada, France, Germany, Italy, the United Kingdom and the United States. Much of this expansion is being driven by new trade and technology partnerships within the South itself, as this report also shows.[1] The bitter rivalry of South and North is going on but South has gained a lot at the outset of 21st century which will propel the North to make a justice based international economic order with the South. The headline story of a resurgent South is both uplifting and in some ways misleading. The South needs the North, and increasingly the North needs the South. Recent years have seen a remarkable reorientation of global production, with much more destined for international trade, which, by 2011, accounted for nearly 60 per cent of global output. Developing countries have played a big part between 1980 and 2010, they increased their share of world merchandise trade from 25 per cent to 47 per cent and their share of world output from 33 per cent to 45 per cent. Developing regions have also been strengthening links with each other: between 1980 and 2011, South-South trade increased from less than 8 per cent of world merchandise trade to more than 26 per cent.[2]

> The global mantra CCC (Conflict, Competition and Cooperation) of globalization has propelled the nations to cooperate at least on the points where there are convergences of interests.
>
> To quote President Obama about commerce and trade in Asia, "economic ties and commercial ties that are taking place in this region are helping to lower a lot of the tensions that date back before you were born or I was

born....there's something about when people think that they can do business and make money that makes them thinks very clearly and not worry as much about ideology. And I think that that's starting to happen in this region".[3]

Former US President, George W. Bush described the exchange of many handshakes of friendship and commerce between the American and Chinese people as enhancing understanding and therefore peace.[4]

Financial interdependence and cooperation among Asian countries is growing as well. The idea also has strong historical roots in the work of thinkers such as Montesquieu, Immanuel Kant and Adam Smith. Moreover, the structure of economic interdependence is not intra Asian, but also transpacific. Four Asian countries rank among the top ten nations holding US treasury securities (as of May 2009), with China topping this list at US$ 801.5 billion, Japan 2nd at $ 677.2, Hongkong 7th at $ 93.2 and Taiwan at $ 75.7 biilion.[5] Asian countries have also kept the legacy of Bandung Asia-Africa Conference held at 1955. Between 1955 to 2005 trade among the Asian countries have nearly doubled. Intra East Asia trade today is higher than in the NAFTA region (46%).[6] Bilateral trade between Japan and China was $ 300 billion in 2011. China has also become global investor; from 2005 to mid 2013, it spent $ 57.8 billion in the United States and $ 157.2 billion in East and Southeast Asia, with Australia, Indonesia and Vietnam being the top recipients.[7] Though both China and Taiwan are bitter rivals in 2012 two way trades between them was valued at $ 169 billion, over one third of Taiwan's GDP that year. [8]

Critics says that the growing economic interdependence has a poor record in preventing conflict in the past (two world wars) and that it can create new forms of competition and conflict now, such as competition over resources and markets. Although trade interdependence imposes some level of caution on country's behavior but it has its own limit. China has dangerous territorial disputes with gamut of bigger Asian countries. China's bilateral relations with Vietnam, the Philippines, India, Japan and the United States have soured considerably over the past five years, even as trade has grown impressively.[9] This is largely the result of China's increasingly assertive behavior in its territorial disputes.[10]

Japan's Prime Minister Shinzo Abe caused a stir in Davos, Switzerland, when he noted in January 2014 that Britain and Germany went to world war in 1914 even though they had close economic ties much as China and Japan have now.[11]

At the outset of 21st century it is predicated by many pundits of the international system that future of global governance will be decided by Asia. But the problem is that Asia has yet to achieve that status but in anticipation major Asian players are indulged in Prisoner's Dilemma due to baggage of history. The disputes over South China Sea, East China Sea, Water sharing issues on transnational rivers, North Korea nuclear issue, Tibet, Taiwan, etc. have propelled trust deficit among major Asian powers. This situation has created the situation of balance of power and propelled major Asian countries to be part of balance of power within Asia.

The terror attacks of 9/11 have further complicated the situation. Interestingly this process has manifested that the balance of global power system is changing. It is shifting from Europe-American to Asia. As from Keshore Madhubani to many known pundits of the international system have insisted that 21st century will be an Asian century. The second decade of the 21st century has already in the middle but supremacy of Asia has not been established yet. It cannot happen till all aspirants of Asian power will adopt the mentality of mutual understanding but instead of this they are fighting with each other with the baggage of history. It is true that the process of globalization has facilitated the economic relationship among all these powers but it could not minimize the level of divergences in security and strategic level.

The end of the Cold War and rise of China has triggered a new debate of new architecture of power in Asia. Many views China growth of regional expansion is the Monroe Doctrine in the western hemisphere, this view foresees China seeking a regional hegemony over it neighbors. Amitabh Acharya argues that the rise of China will differ not only from the images of a Hobbesian anarchy, but also from the benign visions of a Confucian hierarchy or a Kantian community.[12] According to him Asian security was shaped by economic nationalism, security bilateralism, and political authoritarianism. These have gradually but unmistakably given way to market liberalism and economic interdependence, security multilateralism (coexisting with U.S. centric bilateralism), and growing domestic political pluralism. Together they mitigated those factors of impending anarchy.[13] The billion dollor questions remain answered about the relationship between rising powers and regional players. It is a fact that in the South China Sea dispute, which has emerged critical test of Chinese restraint because of asymmetrical military balance between China and rival ASEAN disputants. Despite this prevailing tensions over SCS, China has not invaded any islands by force since 1974, only occupied islands that were previously unnoticed.[14] For Mearsheimer, rising powers tend to seek regional hegemony and China is heading in this direction.[15] The Chinese have refused to be adhered by international laws to resolve South China Sea and East China Sea dispute with ASEAN and Japan respectively. In Tibet case too, China has violated all norms of the international standards to respect human rights. To vindicate the prevailing situation in the Asia-Pacific the following statement of the Philippines President is self explanatory .

The Philippines is one of the disputant countries against China over South China Sea. Philippines President Benigno S. Aquino III called for nations around the world to do more to support the Philippines in resisting China's assertive claims to the seas near his country, drawing a comparison to the West's failure to support Czechoslovakia against Hitler's demands for Czech land in 1938.

Like Czechoslovakia, the Philippines faces demands to surrender territory piecemeal to a much stronger foreign power and needs more robust foreign support for the rule of international law if it is to resist.

"If we say yes to something we believe is wrong now, what guarantee is there that the wrong will not be further exacerbated down the line?" he said. "At what point do you say, 'Enough is enough'? Well, the world has to say it—remember that the Sudetenland was given in an attempt to appease Hitler to prevent World War II."[16] Tokyo and Manila are even more expressive about their willingness to uphold territorial claims, no matter the cost. On many occasions, Abe has vowed publicly that he will 'never make concessions' over the sovereignty of the Diaoyus/Sankakus and will defend 'Japanese territory at all costs.'[17]

> Right from Kautilaya to Morgenthau the realist school of thought has insisted that foreign policy is based on convergences of interests and other kinds of convergences could not be the basis for cordial bilateral relations between the states.
>
> The trust deficits among the Asian powers are growing rapidly. India and China have good relationships on economic fronts but they didn't have convergences on security issues. Despite high voltage bilateral trade at the eve of Chinese Premier New Delhi visit in May 2013, Chinese made a provocative incursions 19 KM inside of the LAC in the western sector of Laddakh, which has lasted for three weeks, when the PLA withdrawn.[18] Ties also soured because of reported dam construction over Tibetan river (Brahmaputra) near the border to divert the water towards arid Chinese landmass.[19] In majority of the cases despite growing economic interdependence of major Asian countries over China the fact remains that almost all cases surplus is tilted towards China. For an example, in India public increasingly believes that China is benefiting more from the country's increasing trade. The value of India's export to China is one third of those moving in the opposite direction.[20] As a result India had a trade deficit of $ 40 billion in 2012 from just $ 1 billion in 2002.
>
> China wanted multi-polar global system with itself as an important power but wanted uni-polar Asia dominated by her. India, Japan, South Korea, Vietnam, Indonesia, Iran and Australia which is an extended Asian country wanted both the global as well as Asian system multi-polar not dominated by any single power.
>
> In India as well there is a verbal consensus among security community that China's assertive postures in many regional issues are a matter of utmost concern. Managing the assertive China is one of the biggest propelling elements of convergences among major Asian powers. They are thinking seriously to contain the tiger. India and Japan and many like minded Asian countries have to contribute a lot to realize their perception.

Both world wars took place in Europe because European powers were unable to manage European balance of power and pursued for their parochial interests. In Europe, these battles were fought since the Thirty Years War 1618-1648. By 1945, Europe has had 300 years of doing that, and had become exhausted from fighting it out. Apart from the break-up of the Yugoslav federation, there hasn't been an old fashioned, territorial battle on European soil, killing thousands of people, since 1945.[21] But in Asia there is a strong possibility of war even today due to unresolved territorial possessions which are going on between Japan and China, China and South Korea, China and Vietnam, India and China and so on with the baggage of history.

But the basic difference between European and Asian scenario is that European powers fought against each other after Europe had already established its supremacy over the global system but Asian powers are fighting against each other much before Asia has established its dominance over the global system.

Despite this ultimate reality it is an open secret that Asia is gaining and even the sole super power the United States has recognized this reality and stressing more energy and diplomacy to sustain its national interest in Asia-Pacific. Needless to say that India has increased its global profile since last two decades and slated to sustain this process. The Chinese have perceived this assertion as the growing Indian design to be part of encircling China policy of the west led by the United States. The fact remains that Europe is struggling with the economic recession but Asia is doing well on the same front despite many global odds. India has emerged as one of the fastest growing economy of the globe despite many hurdles and slated to sustain the process in foreseeable process.

At this juncture of international politics it is certain that Asia-Pacific is going to play bigger role. But the billion dollar question remains to be unanswered that the prevailing divergences of interests among major Asian powers will create new balance of power or China will be able to establish its own hegemony over Asia-Pacific. The United States has now shifted its focal attention towards Southeast and East Asia and in recent years increased its activities in all corners of Asia. Another point which remains of utmost importance is that emerging Asian powers are seeking its due share in the high table of global governance. It vindicates the events of last one decade at least that Asian powers are more concerned for their own national interests than their due share into global governance. The shifting self-image and national role conceptions of Asia's three major players-China, India and Japan are a good starting point for an analysis of Asia's role in global governance.[22] But this kind of awareness has remained confined only in climate change and yet not expanded for larger issues which has shaped the international system since a long time.

The major problem in Asia-Pacific remains the growing trust-deficit among the major stake holders. India and China has reached far ahead in terms of trade. They had roughly $ 67 billion dollar bilateral trade in the financial year of 2012 and slated to cross $ 100 billion in 2015 but it has not been translated into strategic spheres.

In post-Cold War scenario, China has almost solved its boundary problem with majority of its neighbors. China has 14 neighbors. It has solved the boundary dispute with Myanmar on the basis of McMahon Line in 1960's only but declined to do so with India. It has also resolved outstanding boundary disputes with Russia despite rhetoric. Russia has longest boundary of 4,300 KM with China and a history of bilateral contacts for about 400 years. For much of these 400 years, both countries have had a hostile relationship and unsettled boundary. The situation changed after the downfall of the USSR.

But at India front despite 17 round high voltage dialogue since 2003 till July 2014, no tangible progress has been made to resolve most thorny boundary disputes.

Since a long time China has adopted the policy of *Encircling India* within South Asia. The central objective of this policy is to encircle India within South Asia. The issue of Tibet still rules the roost. China is claiming that entire Arunachal Pradesh is its own territory and termed it as southern Tibet. Nehru inked a wide ranging treaty in 1954 with China and accepted Chinese sovereignty over Tibet. Former Secretary General of the Foreign Affairs Ministry, Sir Girja Shankar Bajpai opposed this deal. He wrote a letter to his friend and "warned that communist China was no different from Russian Communism in its expansionist's aims...." The current thinking in New Delhi was of 'the naturalness of indefinite continuance of indefinite peace and friendship between China and US'. Bajpai feared that 'those on whom the P(rime) M (inister) now relies most for advice completely and vehemently reject any possibility of a change in what appears to be China's present policy of peace with its Asian neighbors."[23] Few years before 1954, Sardar Patel advised Nehru not to believe China. Writing to Nehru on 7th November 1950, Patel warned Nehru that "China is no longer divided. It is united and strong. Recent and bitter history also tells us that communism is no shield against imperialism and that the Communism are as good or as bad imperialists as any other. Chinese ambitions in this respect not only cover the Himalayan slopes on our side but also include parts of Assam.

...Chinese irredentism or imperialism are different from the expansionism or imperialism of the western powers. The former has a cloak of ideology which makes it ten times more dangerous. In the guise of ideological expansion lie concealed radical, national or historical claims."[24]

Nehru had not concealed the Kautilyan realist advice of Patel and persuaded Wilsonian notion of idealism which was bound to fail. Tibet is at the heart of the India-China rivalry for dominance in Asia. When

Tibet was occupied by China in early 1950s it changed the asymmetry between the two sides. China was able to exercise geo-strategic influence over much of south Asia and challenge India's dominance in the region. India recognizes that the loss of Tibet as a buffer zone crippled the security of its northern frontiers forcing it to maintain hundreds and thousands of soldiers along the Himalayan frontier. Until Tibet will not resolve, China will not resolve boundary with India. China is fearful with the increasing pace of dissent against its illegitimate rule in Tibet and probably awaiting for the demise of the Dalai Lama. China perceives that in post-Dalai Lama, lack of accepted leadership will weaken the Tibetan movement. Since 2009 till June 2014, more than 125 self immolations have been taken place seeking independence. China is afraid of this mode of protest because it is not only indicative of sustainability of Tibetan resistance against Chinese occupation but also fearful that this peaceful way of protest will provide more strength to Tibetan cause in the international community.

The growing Indo-US bonhomie has further complicated the situation for China. It will create more irresponsible behavior from Chinese side in foreseeable future to contain growing Indian proximity with the United States.

Tibet is of great national concern as it covers almost one third of entire Indian Territory. Another important asset which Tibet possesses is that it is the origin of eight out of ten inter-country rivers of Asia. In this scenario, China has started to divert the flow of Brahmaputra River just before it is entering into India. China may do the same thing with the other westward river, entering into India and also going into Pakistan as well as rivers which flow across Southeast Asia in eastern sector.

It has been argued that 21st century conflict will be over water. Tibet is extremely important for that purpose and it is the water house of Asia. The prevailing divergences of China with Southeast Asian countries over the issue of South China Sea may propel China to blackmail these countries over flow of water in the rivers originated from Tibet and flowing in these countries.

China has sustained the pace of 8-10 per cent growth rate since last one decade and slated to sustain the tempo. Needless to say that it requires unprecedented amount of energy to cope with the situations. The Chinese have opted hydroelectricity as one of the clean options to fulfill its energy requirements. Huge hydroelectricity projects for energy and water diversion schemes for food sufficiency are strategic measures in China's growth path. Tibet, which serves as the headwaters of many of Asia's largest rivers, including the Yellow, Yangtze, Mekong, Salween, Brahmaputra, Irawaddy and Indus, is of existential importance for China. Without Tibet, China's hydrological supremacy would be overturned from water independence to dependence.[25]

Mao Zedong a long time ago realized the water-resource value of Tibet when he remarked, "The south has a lot of water, the north little.... If possible, it is okay to lend a little water."[26] Beijing's total control over Tibet in effect is the total control of the water resources. "Absolute territorial sovereignty" over the waters gives an added strategic sharpness to China's regional approach and its increasing "hydro-egoism" dictates the riparian relations with countries downstream. The classic lines, "He who holds Tibet dominates the Himalayan piedmont; he who dominates the Himalayan piedmont threatens the Indian subcontinent; and he who threatens the Indian subcontinent may well have all of South-East Asia within his reach, and all of Asia",[27] become relevant. This statement of Mao is not only important for Chinese imperialist design for Tibet but for Southeast Asia and for the hegemony over Asia as well. Mao had an expansionist agenda of Chinese imperialism based on whims and fancy. Mao Zedong had been influenced by historical considerations. In 1930, he "openly declared that the correct boundaries of China would include Burma, Bhutan, Nepal, Taiwan, Korea and Ryukyu Island. These remarks were contained in the original version of the Chinese Revolution and the Communist Party,[28] but were deleted from the later versions of the book with a view to avoid suspicions in the minds of the leaders of these countries".[29] The way China is tempering with the natural flow of water form Tibet originated rivers, taking assertive postures in the disputes of South China Sea and East China Sea vindicates that it has been nursing the ambition to dominate Asia as uni-polar power since last many decades.

> Staple visa is another severe problem. China earlier was issuing staple visa to the people of Arunachal Pradesh and now the same treatment Chinese are doing with the people of Jammu & Kashmir terming it as a disputed territory. In this way the Chinese have taken a U-turn which they had taken during Kargil conflict between India and Pakistan (1999). They advised Pakistan that Kargil is a bilateral dispute and India and Pakistan must resolve it bilaterally. The change in Chinese attitude vindicates the point that China is extremely jealous of deepening India-US relationship and feeling threatened for its interests. That fear of China has dictated its pro-Pakistan policy despite the fact that Islamic terror groups are active in Chinese western province of Xinjiang. There are ample proof that vindicates that non state actors in Pakistan is fomenting these groups and given training ground and shelter in Pakistan. Former Prime Minister of Pakistan, Yousuf Raza Gillani had termed China Pakistan relations 'deeper than Sea, higher than mountain and sweeter than honey'. The growing importance of India in the chess board of Asia has prompted China to accord special status to Pakistan. This has also renewed Chinese presence beside Pakistan in Sri-Lanka, Maldives, Bangladesh, Nepal and Myanmar.
>
> In mid-1980s by a perceptive analyst of Asian affairs made a remark about Sino-Indian relations, Jay Taylor, which remains as relevant now as it was during the Cold War era. He wrote: "Over the long term, India and China... will always tend toward a rival relationship and thus each will seek a security link with a different superpower.... Both India and China want to avoid war and concentrate on development.... Yet the volatile

agents of nationalism and history produce a mysterious chemistry...strength and size carry with them their own rationale for status and influence, and both India and China may well find themselves drawn into future regional conflicts or possibly intervening in neighboring countries because of some instability or action that is perceived as threatening.... The odds are that over the long term there will be more rivalry than cooperation between Hindu and Han.[30]

India and Japan relations have improved in a significant manner after the end of the Cold War. However just after May 1998 Pokhran nuclear blast, Japan imposed plethora of sanctions along with western powers and Australia against India. But within years it has been withdrawn. Japan and China have increased their divergences in recent years over many thorny issues particularly on East China Sea. Despite simple divergences, China and Japan are now competing on dangerous points like ownership of disputed islands in East China Sea. East Asian balance of power politics also played its role. Japan has remained major Asian players since centuries. In 1905, Japan defeated Czarist Russia, which was one of the important super powers of the contemporary international system. Even during both world wars, Japan was a great power and holds this position during cold and post-Cold War era too. The fact remains that Japan is one of the significant investors in China. They are high profile trade partners too. Despite these realties, in post-Cold War scenario, China-Japan relationship has declined. China views Japan as one of the obstacles of its evolution as an international power. Since Japan has defeated China in the past therefore the jingoist Chinese viewed Japan as an enemy. Few years before his death, eminent American scholar, Samual P. Huntington had argued that if United States wanted to sustain its unipolar status then it has to accommodate Japan and India as two important partners. He stressed that Japan will contain China from the east and India from the west.[31] American, Secretary of State, Hillary Clinton had stated that the United States will be happy to see India playing bigger role at the Asian platform. The much debated nuclear deal (2008) is a point in this direction that despite many odds, the United States has managed the deal. Many other areas of cooperation have intensified since then between both countries and with other Asian allies as well as at multilateral level. Japan is an old US allies and both countries have intensified their relationship further and that is the key of growing Japan-India relationship. It is the traditional notion of balance of power. According to the neorealist thinker, Kenneth Waltz 'Because the future is uncertain, states are more concerned about relative gains and how gains will be divided. For this reason cooperation is hard to achieve in international relations. The basic nature of the international relations is therefore essentially conflict.'[32]

The original twist came into Indian foreign policy with the regime of Narasimha Rao (1991-96). He was one of the best pragmatic Indian Prime Ministers in terms of pursuance of foreign policy. He discarded Pandit

Nehru's Wilsonian idealism and adopted Kautilyan realism. He ignited new twist with United States, ASEAN, China, Iran, Israel, Africa and above all launched important '*Look East*' policy to strengthen India's traditional relationship with Southeast and East Asia. Under his dynamic leadership India began to reorient its foreign policy after the Cold War, the idea that much of Asia and the Indian Ocean formed its "extended neighborhood" began to take root. As India's relations with Southeast Asia, Central Asia, the Persian Gulf, and Middle East began to acquire a new dynamism, the old notion of reclaiming a security and political role from Aden to Malacca, so emblematic of Lord Curzon's British India, began to resurface.[33]

It does not mean that other sub regions of Asia are not important for the calculus of India's foreign policy. We have our stakes in newly emerged Central Asia, Middle East is also important for us because more than 6 million of our people are employed there and it is one of the biggest source of our increasing energy resources. India had collaborated with Iran in the development of a new port complex at Chah Bahar on the eastern coast of Iran. It is very close to Pakistani port of Gwador, which is handed over to China by Pakistan in February 2013 for all round development. Chah Bahar could become India's gateway to Afghanistan and Central Asia. There is also another project that involves linking Chah Bahar port to Iranian rail network that is also well connected to Central Asia to Europe. Islamabad and Tehran conflicting interest over Afghanistan has played a pivot role in the formation of the Indo-Iranian nexus.[34] Due to western countries sanctions over Iran, India has reduced its oil and gas import from Iran and it has not taken positively by Iran. But in August 2012, Prime Minister, Dr. Manmohan Singh visited Iran for participation in 16th NAM Summit despite US dissent. In August 2013, newly Iranian President, Roohani has taken over and Indian Vice-President had landed Tehran to be present in swearing in ceremony of the new President. The increasing incidents of Shia's carnage in Pakistan have further emboldened Indo-Iran relations. Interestingly at the same time India has also developed good relations with Saudi Arabia, which is bitter enemy of Iran. Recent high voltage visits have further emboldened their bilateral relations.

But East, North East and Southeast Asia are our extended neighborhood and additionally prosper and stabilized and we have to maximize our interests in post-Cold War scenario when new security architecture is emerging in Asia.

In contrast to all these regions, the greater coherence of ASEAN and the goodwill of countries like Singapore provided the opening for sustained Indian diplomacy in the region. While the steady expansion of economic links provided a new basis for India's cooperation with the region, it was the admission of India as an institutional partner of ASEAN that allowed India to develop an all-encompassing engagement with the region. From the tentative sectoral dialogue partnership to a more affirmative nod to the membership of the East Asia Summit (EAS) process in 2005, India's Look East policy advanced steadily and became one of the organized components of its external relations. Besides a new level of political comfort at the highest levels, ASEAN offered a model for globalization just when India was fighting many demons in its mind about economic reform. This debt of gratitude was freely acknowledged by Prime Minister Manmohan Singh, speaking in 2006, he stated, at the creation of India's Look East policy as India's finance minister and later had the opportunity to elevate it to a higher level.

"I must pay tribute to our East and Southeast Asian neighbors for shaping our own thinking on globalization and the means to deal with it ... in 1992 our Government launched India's "Look East" policy. This was not merely an external economic policy; it was also a strategic shift in India's vision of the world and India's place in the evolving global economy. Most of all it was about reaching out to our civilization Asian neighbours."[35]

While India was eventually admitted to the ARF in 1997, there was an explicit understanding that India would play a low-key role for the moment, and as its economic interaction with the region expanded it would be possible to eventually consider wider political and security relationship. In India's own understanding of the history of its Look East Policy, the first phase was focused exclusively on economic and institutional partnership. It was only in the second phase that began with the turn of the millennium that the security dimensions of the Look East policy came to the fore. As India's External Affairs Minister Yashwant Sinha pointed out in September 2003—

"The Look East policy began to move away from exclusive focus on economic issues in phase one to a broader agenda that involves security cooperation, including joint operations to protect sea lanes and pooling of resources in the war against terror. The military contacts and joint exercises that India launched with ASEAN states on a low-key basis in the early 1990s are now expanding into full-fledged cooperation."[36]

Besides Southeast and East Asia, Middle East, Central Asia and Russia is also extremely significant in the larger calculus of security architecture in the Asia-Pacific. Middle East is the biggest producer and exporter of natural gas and oil for the entire globe. Since India has sustained its massive growth since last two decades therefore consumption of energy is increasing in India. Presently India is number 5th global consumer of energy and slated to 3rd by 2020 after pushing Japan and Russia. Without the free flow of energy India could not ensure the pace of its overall development. Besides energy security perspective, Middle East is also important for India because of gamut of factors. Annually our middle east diaspora's are sending a huge amount as remittances back to home and through this process strengthen Indian economy. Indian diaspora is leading sender of remittances in the globe and our Middle East diaspora contributes enormously in our overall remittances. India has done well taking principled stand in Palestine dispute. India has also taken balanced stand in terms of Saudi Arabia and Iran trust deficit and maintained high profile relations with both. On Syria front, India has taken a principled stance of adherence with the United Nations norms.

India has also enhanced its engagements with the republics of Central Asia. It is the region which contains enormous amount of energy reservoir. The joint development of Chah Bahar natural port by Iran and India in eastern Iran near to Pakistani port of Gwador could be a big facilitator of economic relationship with Central Asia. The Delaram-Zaranj road constructed through western Afghanistan by India is connecting Central Asia directly to the Sea and it will be a Himalayan jump in the engagement process with Central Asia. It has also provided an alternative sea route to Afghanistan because till the creation of this road, Afghanistan was dependent on Karachi port only. This has emboldened Afghanistan's position vis-à-vis Pakistan.

Russia remains an important power to be reckoned with in Asia-Pacific. Without Russia the security architecture of Asia-Pacific will remain volatile. Despite its decayed power status it still remains a strong military power. It has also possessed huge energy resources. India has many convergences with Russia beside stability in Afghanistan. During Cold War era, India and Russia were all weathered friends. This sentiment is still survived but many Russian apprehensions could be erased by India through revised deepening of ties.

Although China and Russia has mended their relationship since the end of the Cold War but they still have some serious apprehensions against each other. China and Russia has 4,300 KM border, on one side of which live fewer than 6.5 million Russians while on the other live 140 million Chinese. Russian Far East, which has nine provinces, is 36 per cent of the Russian national territory. Russian Far East is resourceful and has more than 15,000 miles of sea coast—is one of the world's greatest storehouses of untapped natural resources and represents a valuable and strategically desirable piece of real estate. Yet, holding just 4.4 per cent of Russia's population and contributing a mere 5.6 per cent to the country's GDP, this area has significant security implications for Russia and for the Asia-Pacific community generally.[37] The area is less developed and Chinese side is better developed. The area is also close to East Asia, economic hub of the globe. President Putin in a speech in 2000 warned that if development did not take off the population would be speaking "Japanese, Chinese and Korean". Russia has recently invested hugely in the region.[38] Chinese have felt that Russia is a decaying power and once they will be very weak they could acquire these areas. This Chinese mindset has been apprehended by the Russian therefore Russia is a reluctant economic partner of China. In 2011, Russia and China bilateral trade volume was of $ 83 billion which is expected to touch $ 200 in 2020.[39] Russian strategic thinker, Sergei Karaganov has expressed fears that Russia's eastern regions and even the entire country could "turn into an appendage of China—first as a warehouse of resources and than economically and politically. This will happen without any aggression or unfriendly efforts on China's part, but will happen by default." Moreover he says Russia's "semi Dependency" on China could add "a great deal of international weight" to the PRC," which should concern other countries of the Asia-Pacific community."[40] Keeping this possibility in mind, Russia has expanded its engagement process with major powers of Asia-Pacific.

Moreover, the Russian initiative for a strategic triangle with China and India in the 1990s was aimed at containing the US hyper power. That context has rapidly changed with the relative decline of the US. It is the rise of China in their vicinity that will effect the relative power position of Russia and India in the Asian inter-state hierarchy. As a consequence, India is pushing Moscow to play a bigger role in the Asian strategic landscape and this is leading to greater political coordination between New Delhi and Moscow on regional security issues. For many Indian realists, a stable balance of power in Asia cannot emerge without India and Russia working together to manage China's rise.[41] It is a point of convergences for India and India must seize this opportunity to regain the old saga of Russia-India friendship. India must convince Russia that its deepening bonhomie with the United States is required to achieve larger canvass of its national interests in the backdrop of changing international system. Russia also need to understand that India has its own priorities and must respect diversification of Indian foreign policy. It is an open secret that Russia and India is all set to gain in the emerging security architecture in Asia-Pacific and if they will cooperate with the pre Cold War era spirit they will gain absolutely. India and Russia are oldest and trusted friends. The post-Cold War era has created gamut of convergences between both countries and they need to exploit this situation.

Maritime security is a matter of serious concern for India and other Asian countries as well. The rising incidents of piracy are vindicating it. No country could develop their strategic capability without developing their navy. India has an advantage position within Indian Ocean due to its geo strategic location. Indian Ocean is an important sea route for international trade. Southeast Asian countries are extremely crucial for the safety of the sea lanes of the communication particularly into the Indian Ocean and in the South China Sea.

The new outward orientation of the Indian Navy steadily gathered momentum in the 1990s with wide-ranging contacts bilaterally and multilaterally. India began to expand its joint naval exercises with all the nations of Southeast Asia, stepped up its port calls in the region and received ships from the region at its own ports. The Indian Navy conducted naval exercises for the first time in South China Sea in 2000. While the visit was seen by some as a challenge to China, by entering its strategic waters, the Navy also included simple exercises with the PLA Navy.[42]

At the end of 2004, the Indian Navy was quick to respond, on its own, to the tsunami disaster and later joined the navies of the United States, Japan, and Australia to provide relief in Southeast Asia. The scale of India's tsunami relief operations that involved thirty-two ships in five different operations on the Indian coast, Maldives, Sri Lanka, and Indonesia was impressive. This signaled both the operational readiness of the Indian Navy and its immense potential to contribute to future humanitarian and other contingencies in Southeast Asia.[43] Indian navy has done many joint exercises till date with the navy of many Southeast, East Asian countries including Australian navy, which is next door neighbor of Southeast Asian countries. India is focused more on expanding its own regional profile rather than the creation of a new alliance and thus maintaining autonomy in foreign policy. This was reflected in the Indian Navy's initiative to convene for the first time an Indian Ocean Naval conclave in February 2008.[44] Only littoral navies from South Africa to Australia were invited. That the navies of the United States, China, and Japan were not invited is explained by Indian officials in terms of geography, but there is no mistake in the enduring intent of India to affirm its own independent engagement of the Indian Ocean littoral. China poses the most powerful challenge to Asia's balance of power. By 2013 China has emerged as single largest military expender in Asia with roughly $ 150 billion dolor. But despite China's growing economy and the military power, the United States remains and is likely to remain for a long time, the preeminent military power in Asia. While China's naval build up gives it an increasing capacity for denying areas close to its shores to the United States and its allies but any effort by China to dominate the sea lanes of communication in Asia and Indian Ocean can be countered by the naval forces of the United States, in cooperation with Japan and India. In the backdrop of South China Sea, East China Sea and growing border disputes with India could propel this kind of deepening cooperation among like minded countries. India has already started Malabar naval series of joint exercises with these countries since 2007 and intended to be present in the South China Sea (SCS) despite often made Chinese warnings. ASEAN disputants' countries over SCS keep requesting India to increase its presence in SCS. In December 2012, Indian Navy Chief, Admiral D.K. Joshi stated that if required Indian navy will not hesitate to be in SCS. It was fiercely opposed by China but welcomed by the Philippines. Vietnam has emerged as the fulcrum of India's Look East Policy. Despite low volume of trade, India and Vietnam has excellent level of bilateral strategic relations. Concerned over China's assertiveness in the South China Sea, Vietnam wants India to 'rise quickly' in the region.[45]

Two and half decades are over since the launching of Look East policy. India has achieved a lot in terms of improvement of relationship with our eastern extended neighborhood. The seeming incongruity of bringing India into an avowedly East Asian forum was explained by Singapore's Senior Minister Goh Chok Tong when he revealed some of the thoughts that resulted in this decision in early 2005:

"With India's rise it will be increasingly less tenable to regard South Asia and East Asia as distinct strategic theatres interacting only at the margins. US-China-Japan relations will still be important, but a new grand strategic triangle of US-China-India relations will be superimposed upon it ... Re-conceptualizing East Asia holistically is of strategic imperative ... It would be shortsighted and self-defeating for ASEAN to choose a direction that cuts itself off from a dynamic India."[46]

As the focal point which I insisted since beginning that major divergences among basic stake holders in Asian balance of power is prevailing, this has prevented the emergence of Asia in 21st century. Here lies the convergence of interests between India and Southeast Asia and East Asia because both wanted multiplicity in Asia. These convergences of interests India enjoys with the major powers of Asia as well. The dramatic rise of China, the slow but certain reemergence of India, the reassertion of Japan, and the uncertainties in the policies of a power that has dominated the region for more than half a century. The United States have compelled Southeast Asia to rethink its strategic environment and devise new approaches to managing the emerging challenges to its security. Referring to the emerging multiplicity in Asia, Singapore's Senior Minister Goh Chok Tong said:

"As they grow and take on new roles, it is inevitable that China, India and Japan will all loom larger on each other's radar screens. And since East Asian integration will be loosely multipolar, the jostling between New Delhi, Beijing and Tokyo that will certainly ensue must be squarely confronted and cannot be wished away. ... However, competition need not lead to conflict if it can be managed within an agreed framework. This, for example, was the original, and remains the essential, raison d'être of ASEAN."[47]

Minister Goh, of course, was not merely seeing the regional balance in terms of China, Japan, and India. For him, the question of future US role was even more important. He argued: The US will remain a key, indeed the dominant, player well into the 21st century. American power will provide the overarching strategic unity—

"India's Geopolitics and Southeast Asian Security within which the interactions of Chinese, Indian and Japanese interests with American interests will be an increasingly important factor. An East Asian architecture that does not have the US as one of its pillars would be an unstable structure."[48]

India probably first time since independence has been able to maintain simultaneous good relationship with China, Russia, Japan and the United States. It has manifested the Indian capacity to nurture its major power aspirations and sustainability of autonomy in foreign policy. But here lies some myth. With the increasing pace of United States India's relationship particularly after nuclear treaties (2008) China is behaving as it perceives a threat with the emerging relationship between both oldest and largest democracies.

Despite cooperating on the issues of climate change and various other platforms like BRICS, Trilateral Cooperation etc there are inherent divergences between India and China. In May 2013, the Chinese Prime Minister visited New Delhi. It was his maiden visit after he has taken over in March 2013. But just weeks before his visit, Chinese troops had intruded in Ladakh sector of western borderland and returned after three weeks stay. In second week of July 2013, there was another incident of incursion by the Chinese army in the same sector. In August 2013 the PLA intruded in the eastern province of Arunachal Pradesh. This had happened when Pakistan's newly elected Prime Minister, Nawaz Sharif and Indian defense minister, A.K. Antony were in Beijing. China keeps playing double game with India since last few years. It is in contrast to the Chinese attitude during Kargil (1999) crisis when China advised Pakistan and India to settle this issue on bilateral level. China has adopted a new attitude because of growing Indian bonhomie with the United States and Japan. Growing Indian presence in South China Sea and deepening Indian ties with Vietnam is also a case in point which has propelled Chinese to think that India is making a circle against her with the tacit understanding with the U.S.

In the meanwhile the United States has already announced that it will increase its presence in Asia-Pacific after a small absence due to Iraq and Afghanistan preoccupation. President Obama had visited Myanmar in November 2012 just weeks after his re-election and participated ASEAN Summit also in Cambodia. It was his maiden Myanmar visit after re-election. It was also maiden visit of any US president since decades. President Obama had a whirlwind tour of Southeast Asia in May 2014 as well.

The US has also engaged Australia in a new way and declared that South China Sea dispute must be resolved with the compliance of the international law. However in its latest White Paper, *China's Peaceful Development,* China proclaims it will unswervingly follow the path of peaceful development and actively enhance friendly cooperation with neighbors to promote a harmonious Asia.[49] But in practice it seems that it is not willing to accommodate the interests of major countries of Asia therefore the climate of trust deficit is looming large over Asia and prevented Asia to dominate the global system.

In this prevailing situation how India could maximize its national interests in Asia-Pacific. India needs coherent policy formulations to cope with the new situation. India has to diversify its focal attention towards all directions of Asia-Pacific with particular attention to Southeast and East Asia. India needs to enhance its relationship with all disputants of South China Sea, whom grievances against China are genuine. India has enhanced its presence in South China Sea. The wider ramification of this growing Indian involvement was further emboldened by December 2012 comments of Chief of Navy Staff, Admiral D.K. Joshi, in which he stated that Indian Navy was prepared to intervene to protect Indian interests in South China Sea. Admiral Joshi's statement was greeted by Chinese warnings in which they termed it outside unilateral interference by India and a sense from commentators that the "threat pushed by India to China is the military cooperation between India and Vietnam," and that although India was" an outsider of the South China Sea disputes, however, with its Looking Eastward Strategy, it (India) is now fixating the region."[50] Conversely, while the Indian government tried to smooth Joshi's comments away, South China disputants such as the Philippines welcomed it."[51]

Long back Kautilaya had advocated for asymmetrical policy which requires aligning with the like minded countries to contain a stronger power. ASEAN came into being in 1967 against the hegemonic design of China. Today even after over $ 300 billion bilateral trade with China they have thorny strategic relations. We have to convince the countries of ASEAN and East Asia that India is here to protect their territorial integrity. India and the countries of ASEAN and East Asia aspires a multilateral Asia. India needs to seize the opportunity. An editorial of Jakarta Times commented to this issue as:

"The evolving geo-strategic framework inexorably impels countries in Southeast Asia to accept China and India as major regional powers. In the first case, it is necessary consequence of the former....Beijing has also shown an unequaled zest in its economic diplomacy with the Association of Southeast Asian Nations, ASEAN. Delhi on the other hand has been a late bloomer....ASEAN wants India's presence as much as India needs to be active in the region....ASEAN makes available a strategic framework and regulated forum which India can bluntly interact with economic powers Japan and South Korea along with fellow regional power China. This is an opportunity in which Delhi must not be hesitant. It can not afford to miss the boat again."[52]

From 2011 to 2012, India-China trade was reduced $ 74 to $ 67 billion dollar again with huge Indian trade deficit. In contrast India and ASEAN had $ 57.7 billion trade in 2011 which has jumped to $ 79 billion dollar in 2012, which is unexpected. If road and rail link connectivity infrastructure will be created this bilateral trade has the potential to jump many folds. Former Prime Minister, Manmohan Singh had declared that by March 2016 we will link ASEAN with road and rail network. We must convert this rhetoric into reality. This connectivity has enormous potential and we must maximize our national interest through integrating ASEAN by land reducing our sea born trade. The potential of trade is immense between ASEAN and India if this connectivity infrastructure will be created. It could be replicated into strategic domain due to convergences of interests.

India and Japan and India and South Korea relations has also to play a pivotal role in shaping Indian position in Asia-Pacific. India and Japan relations have increased many folds since last one decade. Despite comparatively low volume of bilateral trade they have excellent strategic relations. Given the emerging security architecture of Asia-Pacific it has immense opportunity to grow rapidly in coming years. In December 2012, Prime Minister, Shinzo Abe's PDP got majority along with its one small coalition partner in Japanese election and got majority also in the July 2013 Senate (Second Chamber) elections. It is first time after many decades when a ruling party has its comfortable majority in both houses of the parliament. In the backdrop of East China Sea dispute this political stability may harden anti China posture of Japan and could propel the process of the repeal of the Article 9th of the Japanese constitution, which debars Japan to opt military means to settle disputes.

South Korea is also an important hub of economic activities in Asia. Beside that due to North Korea problem we have common route of instability (Pakistan) and therefore these convergences of interests needs to be strengthened in foreseeable future. We have to do all possible efforts to strengthen the process.

Australia is a continent itself but it is by all counts an extended Asian country. Due to less population and huge landmass embedded with enormous natural assets it has to play a major role in the security architecture of the Asia-Pacific.

Australia is our neighbor in terms of Indian Ocean littoral state. New architecture of power in Asia-Pacific is emerging and needless to say that Indian Ocean has to play a significant role in the reshaping of this emerging architecture of power. The geopolitics of Indian Ocean is now taking a considerable urgency. More than half of the global trade traverses through the Indian Ocean. Noted author, Robert Kaplan has written a marvelous book "*Monsoon; The Indian Ocean and the Future of American Power*". He advocated a powerful case that the Indian Ocean will be the centre of 'the new Great Game in geopolitics' referring to the strategic competition between India and China in their aspirations for great power status and their quest for energy security.[53] Indian Ocean is the only arena where we have some concrete leverage over China and we need to strengthen it by making alliances in the area with the like minded countries. Australia-India cooperation could be significant for both because of convergence of interests in the Indian Ocean. Despite all round sanctions after May 1998 Pokhran blast, Australia-India has done well since last one decade but they need to do further to consolidate their relationship. Australia has already conceded Indian demand to sell Uranium. During her 2012 trip to New Delhi, Prime Minister, Jullia Gillard had further cemented the ties. Trade between both countries is doing well. But Indian leadership should not take Australia granted. For an example, an Indian Prime Minister has not visited Australia since Rajiv Gandhi in 1986—this is seen by many as an indication of the thinness of the bilateral ties.[54] We need to correct these impressions for earning the faith of our partners.

In May 2014 in the leadership of Shri Narendra Modi, BJP government has taken the charge at the centre. It is the maiden government after 1984 election which has its own majority in the Lok-Sabha (Lower Chamber of the Indian Parliament). The Modi government invited all leaders of the SAARC to witness his swearing in ceremony and each SAARC leaders attended the ceremony. PM Modi had bilateral meetings with all SAARC leaders on the first day of his government. That has shed the perception that India is not respecting the sentiment of its neighbors. It may be early to predict new government policies for larger Asia-Pacific. But the early indications are that this government will start from Vajpayee led NDA first government (1998-2004) and strengthen and upgrade that policy. During Shangri-La strategic dialogue in June 2014, Japanese PM, Shinzo Abe had expressed his all round cooperation with Modi government. The Chinese government mouth piece, the Global Times has also opined mixed signals. The United States is bit apprehensive about Modi government intentions but expressed desire to upgrade the relationship. One thing is ample clear that the Modi governments will one of the rarest governments which will work for the promotion and protection of national interests as opined by Kautilya. On the larger canvass of the Asia-Pacific it is intended to score master stroke to garner maximum benefits form the changing security architecture of the region. PM Modi has visited China five times previously and has been praiseworthy for Chinese developmental model. He will wish to resolve thorny issues particularly border issue with China but bread could not make by one hand only. Chinese foreign minister has visited New Delhi in the second week of June 2014 and met his Indian counterpart and the PM Modi. But he refused to remove staple visa for Arunachal Pradesh inhabitants. PM Modi met Chinese President along with Russian, South African, Brazilian Presidents in BRICS Summit in July 2014 and that was his first global interface after taking the reins of power in May 2014. China has to shed its superior mentality if in real terms Asian century has to be established. In contrast the strategic environment will be turbulent and uni polarity of the United States will be sustainable.

It is an open secret that till all important Asian powers will not cooperate to ensure Asian century, it is not possible. India-China cooperation will be the key of this realization. Both countries have millennia old historical linkage, but they never accepted each other as their friends. After many decades of the spread of Buddhism in China, Han Yu, an anti-Buddhist intellectual in the 9th century (who later became the harbingers of

Confucianism). Put the issue starkly in his 'Memorial on Buddhism' written in 819.

"The Buddha was of a barbarian origin. His language differed from Chinese speech; his cloth of a different cut; his mouth did not pronounce the prescribed words of the Former Kings; his body was not clad in the garments prescribed by the former kings. He did not recognize the relationship between prince and the subject, nor the sentiment of father and son."[55] At the same vein both countries learnt a lot from each other in ancient time. Noted Chinese philosopher, Fahian visited India in 401 BC, took considerable interests in contemporary health system in India. According to him—

"All the poor and destitute in the country...and all who are diseased, go to these houses, and are provided with every kind of help, and doctors examines disease. They get the food and medicine which their cases require, and are made to feel at ease, and when they are better, they go away of themselves."[56]

In ancient India, consumer habits were rapidly influenced by innovations made in China. Kautilaya's Sanskrit treatise on economy and politics, *Arthshastra*, first written in 4th century BC gives a special place to 'silk and silk cloth from China among precious articles and objects of value. There are even references in *Mahabharata,* written thousands years before *Arthshastra* regarding this and even there are similar references in the ancient Laws of Manu.[57]

India and China are bound to gain in absolute terms in case of cooperation and bound to lose in case of conflict. They became weak and indirectly invited colonial powers to invade them because they were not united in first and second millennia. Like climate change, justice based international economic order and like minded common issues they must enhance the arenas of convergences to maximize their national interests.

The international politics of 21st century has given the prominence to Asia. We have to mark our strong presence in the security architecture of Asia-Pacific. We need not to allow any single power to dominate the situation. We need to be proactive and sustain the process of engagement to these countries.

Our diaspora is also there in good number and could be an asset in the promotion of our interests. Our growing aura is all set to increase in foreseeable future in Asia-Pacific. Our growing profile in Asia-Pacific will not only fulfill our national interests but will also provide stability to the security architecture of Asia-Pacific and thus promote global peace and justice. The articles included in this book are intended to highlight all those issues and will be helpful to formulate new policies to address the emerging situation.

NOTES

1. *Human Development Report 2013,* The Rise of the South: Human Progress in a Diverse World, UNDP, 2013, p. IV of the Introduction.
2. Ibid, p.2.
3. *White House*, Washington, 2009
4. *White House,* Washington, 'President Bush Speaks at Tsinghua University, 22 February 2002.
5. *US Department of Treasury,* Washington, 2009.
6. Kuroda, Haruhiko, Speech by Haruhiko, Kuroda, *President of Asian Development Bank*, at the emerging market forum, Oxford, U.K, 2005
7. Walter Lohman, John Fleming & Olivia Enos, *A New View of Asia; 24 Charts that Show What's at Stake for America,* Heritage Foundation, 7, October 2013, p.11.
8. Taiwan-China Trade Reached $ 168.97 billion in 2012, *China Customs,* Beijing, 18 January 2013.
9. 'Thunder out of China', *Economist*, 4 May 2013, p.45.
10. Walter Lohman, John Fleming & Nicholas Hamisevicz, *Key Asian Indicators,* Heritage Foundation, January 2011, p.16
11. *Op. cit*, No.5.
12. Amitav Acharya, Power Shift or Paradigm Shift? China's Rise and Asia's Emerging Security Order, *International Studies Quarterly* (2014) 58, p. 158.
13. Ibid, pp. 158-159.
14. Many Chinese analysts take this to be a major indicator of Chinese restraint. *The Washington Post,* Washington Post, August 23, 2012.
15. Mearsheimer, John J. China's Unpeaceful Rise, *Current History*, 2006, 105 (690), p. 161.
16. Keith Bradsher, Philippine Leader Sounds Alarm on China, *New York Times*, New York, February 5, 2014.
17. Teddy Ng, 'Shinzo Abe Slams Beijing "Provocations" on Island Tour', *South China Morning Post,* Hong Kong, 18 July 2013.
18. Parasnips Unbuttered' *Economist*, 25 May 2013.
19. Rama Lakshmi, 'India, China Remain at Odds Over Alleged Border Incursion', *Washington Post*, Washington, 2 May 2013.
20. *Op. cit*, No.18.
21. Meghnad, Desai, The Resurgence of Asia, *Asian Affairs*, Vol. XLIII, No.1, March 2012, p.6,
22. Kal J. Holsti, 'National Role Conceptions in the study of Foreign Policy', *International Studies Quarterly*, 14(3), September 1970, pp.245-6.
23. Bajpai to Subimal Dutt, 18 October 1954. It has been claimed that Patel's famous letter to Nehru on Tibet was actually drafted by Bajpai. (Personal communication from his son, K.S. Bajpai).
24. Guha, Ramchandra, *India After Gandhi: The History of the World's Largest Democracy*, Macmillan, London, 2007, p. 169.
25. "Independent" in terms of rivers originating in its territory and not being "dependent" on the headwaters from other countries.
26. Nickum, James E. '*The Status of the South to North Water Transfer Plans in China*' [Online web] URL: http://hdr.undp.org/en/reports/global/hdr2006/papers/james_ nickum_china_ water_ transfer.pdf.
27. Ginsburg, George and Michiel Mathos (1964), *Communist China and Tibet: The First Dozen Years*, Martinus Nijhoff.
28. Current Background, U.S. Consulate General, Hong-Kong, n°135.

29. K.P.S. Menon, *China: Past and Present,* Asia Publishing House, Bombay, 1968, 21, Parmanand, p. 163.
30. Jay Taylor, *The Dragon and The Wild Goose: China and India* (New York: Greenwood Press, 1987), pp. 232, 250-51.
31. Samual P. Huntington, *Cultural Conflicts and Restructuring of the World Order,* www.fdi.gov.cn.
32. Kenneth N. Waltz, "Reflections on Theory of International Politics" in Robert O. Keohane (ed.) *Neorealist and Its Critics,* New York, Columbia University Press, 1986, p. 102.
33. C. Raja Mohan "Rediscovering Lord Curzon", in *Crossing the Rubicon: The Shaping of India's New Foreign Policy* (New Delhi: Viking, 2003).
34. Raja, Asif Haroon, 'Hamid Karzai has preferred India over Pakistan', *Pak Tribune*, 27 October 2011.
35. Prime Minister Manmohan Singh's address to Asia Society Corporate Conference, Mumbai, 18 March 2006, available at <http://www.pmindia.nic.in/speeches.htm>..
36. Speech by External Affairs Minister Yashwant Sinha at Harvard University, 29 September 2003, available at <http://www.mea.gov.in/>
37. Lee, Rensselaer, 'The Russian Far East; Opportunities and Challenges for Russia's Window on the Pacific', *Orbis*, Vol.57, No.2, Spring 2013, p.315.
38. Brenton, Sir Tony, Russia and China; An Axis of Insecurity, Vol. 44, No. 2, *Asian Affairs,* July 2013, p. 243.
39. Ibid, *Op. cit.*, No. 16.
40. Karaganor, Sergei, "Russia's Asian Strategy," *Russia in Global Affairs,* July 2, 2011.
41. Chellancy, Brahma, "Vodka Cocktails: The Indo-Russian Relationship," *The Economic Times,* December 19, 2010.
42. Stratfor, "India Challenges China in South China Sea", 26 April 2000, available at http://www.atimes.com/ind-pak/BD27Df01.html.
43. See Vijay Sakhuja, "Indian Naval Diplomacy: Post-Tsunami", Institute for Peace & Conflict Studies, New Delhi, 8 February 2005, available at <http://ipcs.org/Military_articles2.jsp?action=showView&k Value-1652&key Article-1019&status=article&mod =a>.
44. For details, see the official website of the Indian Navy, <indiannavy.nic.in/ion. htm>.
45. Wary of China, "Vietnam looks up to India," *Times of India,* New Delhi, 11 May 2014.
46. "Reconceptualising East Asia", Keynote address by Senior Minister Goh Chok Tong at the official launch of the Institute of South Asian Studies, Singapore, 27 January 2005, available at http://www.isasnus.org/events/addresses/Lhtm.
47. "Constructing East Asia", Speech by Goh Chok Tong, *Asia Society, 15th Asian Corporate Conference,* Bangkok, 9 June 2005, available at <http://www.asiasociety. org/conference05/goh.html>..
48. Ibid.
49. Zhao, Kejin, "China's Internal Debate on Strategic Choices in the Asia-Pacific Region," *Korea Observers,* Vol. 43, No. 2, Summer 2012, p. 306.
50. Hạo Zhu "China Warns India against Oil Exploitations", *Global Times,* December 5, 2012.
51. Bagchi, Indrani, "Manila Hails Navy Chief's Stand on South China Sea," *Times of India,* New Delhi, December 19, 2012.
52. "Is India Ready to be a part of Southeast Asia Again?", Editorial, *Jakarta Post,* June 18, 2007.
53. Kaplan, Robert D, *Monsoon, The Indian Ocean and the Future of American Power,* Randon House, New York, 2010.
54. Former Prime Minister, Manmohan Singh was scheduled to visit Australia for the CHOGM meeting in Perth in late October 2011 but he did not attend due, it was claimed, to his crowded international schedule. Till May 2014 no Indian Prime Minister has visited Australia.

55. Sen, Amartya, *The Argumentative Indian,* Penguin, London, 2005, p.170.
56. Leon, Hurvitz and Tsai Heng-Ting, "The Introduction to Buddhism" in Wm. Theodore de Bary and Irene Bloom (eds) *Sources of Chinese Tradition,* Vol. 1, Columbia University Press, New York, 2nd Edition, 1999, pp.425-26.
57. In his well researched study Buddhism, Diplomacy, and Trade, Tansen Sen shows that the size and continuity of Sino-Indian trade relations are often underestimated. For example, in contrast with the common presumption that the trade between the 11th and 14th centuries. Also, Sen provides evidence to conclude that Buddhism, too, continued to flourish simultaneously in Song dynasty China and in Eastern India in the early part of the second millennium.

1

Sino-Sri Lankan Relations: Foreign Policy Challenges for India

Alok Kumar Gupta

Sri Lanka's socialist march did not ever quite catch up with China's socialist market economy, but since the first Rubber-Rice pact that was signed in 1952 China-Sri Lankan relations have been a source of unity and continue to be on an upward trajectory as of now. The crusade-like Chinese initiative in the immediate neighbourhood of India over the last decade clearly betray their paranoia about India enhancing its ratings as a parallel 'power-centre' in the emerging new Asian balance of power for the twenty-first century. China lies at the centre of the huge Asian landmass with Sri Lanka sitting astride in the Indian Ocean with tremendous strategic importance not only for India but most of the powers of the world to be recon with.

China shares land borders with as many as fifteen Asian countries and maritime boundaries with eight other countries of Asia.[1] China is being governed by a political regime which is considered non-democratic as well as repressive by most other countries of the world and has often been castigated for its human rights records. Therefore, the geo-political situation of China makes it imperative to maintain a very high standard of sharp and polished diplomatic resources to maintain cordial and peaceful relations with all its neighbours and at the same time mobilize its diplomatic resources to further her economic interests and strengthen its military power projection. The fact also remains that while the vacation of Soviet military bases from Cam Rahn Bay and of the American military bases in Subic Bay generated widespread perceptions about a new "power vacuum" in Asia, China alone made most serious efforts towards stepping in as the next

Asian leader.[2] China approached this ambitious objective by adopting twin policy of strengthening its (economic and military) power projection capabilities while simultaneously stressing on its policy of 'seeking peace' with major powers, especially those in its neighbourhood.[3]

China has been quite successful in engaging both the global powers as well as Asian countries, which becomes evident from the expansion of China's bilateral trade with most countries of Asia and the world. Chinese engagement of different region of Asia too has been steady and successful. However, South Asia represents one area where China has been walking extremely thin ice, trying to deal with South Asia's major player, India, through its smaller neighbours. Despite progress on Sino-Indian Confidence Building Measures (CBMs) and talks on border dispute between India and Pakistan the relations between China and India has been full of ups and downs and both countries have been suspicious of each other's intentions. There are of course obvious reasons for the same. China sees India emerging as a rival pole in Asia and has consistently refused to change its original hard-line stand. It regards India as a threat to its growing military and economic clout. It is in this backdrop that the Chinese have started undertaking economic projects in Pak Occupied Kashmir (POK) and almost all the other countries of South Asia. China has been instrumental in developing the ports in Pakistan (Gwadar), Sri Lanka (Hambantota), Myanmar (Sitwe), and Maldives (Submarine base Marao). This is sheer realpolitik by China an avowed believer in the realist paradigm of international politics. The several moves by China in the adjacent South Asian region further establish the claim of Encirclement Theory. The 'String of Pearls' theory is another strategic dimension of Chinese intentions in the Southern Asia.

Growing Importance of Sri Lanka

Over the recent past Sri Lanka has gained increased importance to China's regional strategic calculations thereby becoming one of the new pivots of China's South Asia Policy. This development has been reasonably underscored by the media and the foreign policy observers within India. Indian policy analysts has been referring this as China's soft power rise in South Asia and expressed the same as "creeping expansionism" of China around South Asia. This expansionism of China is in almost all the areas such as economic, military, political, and strategic. Such encroachment into India's traditional sphere of influence and immediate neighbourhood is of great importance and is a sort of coup that is being engineered by China which shall have far reaching implications for India within South Asian region. The most serious of which would be disturbance of balance in the Indian Ocean with growing power projection by China in the region. The growth of bilateral trade of China with the countries in the region is on the rise. China has been extending all kinds of support to Sri Lanka including in the fields such as culture, education and sports. The numerous points of contacts are also developing at an alarming rate. Thus, China seems to have leapfrogged India in its backyard.

China has often been accused of encircling India through hobnobbing with its neighbours and developing military bases in and around the region. Under such circumstances India's strategic interests in the region shall be doomed and it shall be at a great loss if fails to maximize its national interests. It shall have to face serious constraints towards promoting its economic and security interests. Recent development within Sri Lanka has posed a different kind of problem where Indian foreign policy makers are finding it difficult to call their shots because of domestic political compulsions. Foreign policy of India is being held hostage to domestic political conditions; put precisely the centre-state relations. Hence, it makes it imperative to take a stock of developments that have taken place in the recent past in terms of Sino-Sri Lankan relations to better comprehend the enlarging 'string of pearls' and its consequent impact on Indian foreign policy.

China is being projected as another emerging super power in the world. Being in the immediate proximity of India and a power to be recon with within the vicinity of Southern Asia also makes it essential to arrest the fast changing dynamics of China's foreign policy in Sri Lanka. Accordingly, the author explores the points of contacts which have developed during the last few years between China and Sri Lanka. It is an endeavour to find the implications of such developments on India's foreign policy and the kind of challenges that the same shall pose in future.

China's Economic Relations with Sri Lanka

As China's economic power has grown, investing overseas has been a tactic used across the world by China to help bolster the national interest. The rubber-rice barter trade agreement that the two countries of China and Sri Lanka signed in December 1952 to establish diplomatic relations has come a long way by the year 2014. In 1952 premier Zhou visited Sri Lanka for the first time and since then, top level leaders from the two sides have visited each other many times, the latest being Sri Lankan President Mahinda Rajapaksa's sixth visit to Beijing in May 2013.[4] Rajapaksha described China as an important partner, noting that the friendship between the two countries goes back centuries. Responding in equal terms Chinese Premier Li Kequiang said the two sides have developed a healthy and stable relationship and suggested strengthening infrastructure cooperation, implementing major projects on ports, railways and highways, expanding pragmatic cooperation and research on aerospace and marine science, and broadening cooperation in culture, education and tourism.[5]

China played a remarkable role towards bringing the Sri Lankan economy back on track in the aftermath of civil war between separatist Liberation Tigers of Tamil Eelam (LTTE) and the Sri Lankan government in 2009. China provided US$ 1.2 billion assistance in the form of grants, loans and credit, representing 54 percent of the total US$ 2.2 billion committed by foreign countries and multilateral agencies. In the year 2010 the assistance was to the tune of US$ 821 million and in 2011 US$ 784.7 million.[6] Needless to say that China remained involved in almost all the large-scale projects in Sri Lanka.

Sri Lanka is also looking forward for a Free Trade Agreement with China which shall make China, Sri Lanka's biggest trading partner, surpassing India. Bilateral trade between the two countries has also been growing considerably, and it has been US$ 659.94 million in 2005, US$ 805.1 million in 2006, US$ 958 million in 2007, US$ 1.13 billion in 2008 and US$ 3.14 billion in 2011. On the other hand, Sri Lanka's exports to China have increased from a mere US$ 28 million in 2005 to US$ 108 million in 2012.[7] Bilateral trade exceeded $3 billion for 2013 and China is Sri Lanka's second largest source of imports behind India.[8] The statistics alone indicate the inexorable rise of China's financial stake in Sri Lanka. China's financial foreign policy rests on twin strategies of: (i) accumulating foreign currency reserves, and (ii) sending money abroad in the form of FDI, aid, assistance an loans according to US economic advisor Ken Miller in *Foreign Affairs*. Sri Lanka is one of the models for the latter part of this strategy.

The milestone of the bilateral ties that was set with the completion of the Bandarnaike Memorial International Conference Hall in 1973; was once again celebrated when China refurbished the Hall at its own cost for the 2013 Commonwealth Heads of Government Meeting (CHOGM). It also facilitated the meeting of a high-powered Chinese business delegation with its Sri Lankan counterparts, in which deals amounting to over US$1.5 billion were signed.[9] India decided not to participate in the CHOGM-2013 meeting though advanced a different reason than the fact of domestic political bargaining by the government of Tamilnadu. Therefore, at times it smack mishandling of the conduct of foreign policy by India in its immediate neighbourhood, which may be on account of compulsions of domestic politics or misinformation from the grounds in neighbouring countries by our own diplomats.

China's "Going Out Policy"

China has a "going out policy" which encourages overseas investment. Under this policy Sri Lanka has been a favoured investment destination for China. Sri Lanka had the largest foreign direct investment i.e. nearly 24 percent of the inflows from China in 2013.[10] China signed 16 agreements in one go with Sri Lanka in later part of 2012, ranging from visa exemption, marine development to economic and technology cooperation, and promised to expand investment and increase imports from the South Asian country.[11] Other agreements include favourable loans offered by Chinese banks to some major infrastructure projects in Sri Lanka and cooperation on telecommunication and railway system renovation, scientific research, climate change, disaster prevention and relief, animal husbandry, agriculture product processing, bio-energy, and tourism.[12]

The broad spectrum of Sino-Sri Lankan ties is trying to serve the Sri Lankan dream project of transforming Sri Lanka into "Asia's miracle". China remains involved in almost all the large scale projects under construction in Sri Lanka. Some of the biggest projects financed by China include a $ 1.3 billion coal power plant on the north-western shore and a host of other investments in the south including a $1.2 billion port and a $209 million airport, with a pledged $760 million to improve country's road network and highway construction.[13] Hambantota project, which is a showpiece of country's significant and growing cooperation with China, is almost complete.[14]

Hambantota Port: Its Strategic Importance

Hambantota is a peaceful fishing town in the southeastern coast of Sri Lanka located at about 240 kms from Colombo and approximately about 444 kms away from South India. China is instrumental in developing the port of Hambantota in Sri Lanka which is positioned very strategically along the 'oil route' and lies on one of the world's busiest sea routes. This is one of the steps taken by China to hold control over the Indian Ocean slowly and secure its access to its energy supplies. The construction of a modern port in this area is now being carried out with the help of the Chinese Government similar to the one at Gwadar in Pakistan and Sitwe in Myanmar.[15] The ports of Gwadar and Sitwe were of interest to the Chinese as they would play a vital role in the transportation of oil, while avoiding route through the Malacca straits, into the mainland China. Hence the fishing towns were converted into ports by the Chinese. The strategy employed in the case of Sri Lanka seems to be deceptively similar as economic benefits are not the only consideration here. The cost of construction of the port in Hambantota is around $ one million with 85 per cent Chinese funding.[16] This has been thus a dual-use infrastructure to be built in four phases spread over fifteen years.[17] The port also happens to be very close to India, which is a cause for security concern of the nation as noted by the Major-General (Retd.) Dipankar Banerjee of the Institute of Peace and Conflict Studies, New Delhi.[18] The construction of this port will bring China within breathing distance of India's southern coast where sensitive installations including power plants are present.[19] It could also help China in keeping a track of India's nuclear, space and naval establishments in South India and also serve as a listening post.[20] China's economic interests in the construction of this port seem to be sparse.[21] While China claims that the interest in building the port is only to safeguard itself from piracy or blockade by foreign power, it is evident that the interest in the port is a part of its encirclement policy around India. Though China claims that the port envisages building oil and gas terminals, berths and port facilities, the port shall help China towards forward-deployment of its naval and air forces, stage rapid reaction forces, and build facilities for the repair and maintenance of Hambantota; it can also monitor US activity at Diego Garcia.[22] Moreover, the brand new port of Hambantota, historically not a traditional shipping route, is the perfect location to meet the strategic objectives of the maritime silk road (MSR).[23]

Bilateral Trade and Commerce between China and Sri Lanka

Oil and Gas Exploration Rights

China has been offered oil and gas exploration rights in the Gulf of Mannar.[24] Neil de Silva, Sri Lanka's Director General of the Petroleum Resources Development Secretariat (PRDS) observed about his government's decision to offer exploration rights to china: "It is the government's decision, may be to strengthen its relations with China. However, we have to live with regional politics. What we have to do is to manage them to get maximum benefits to the country.[25]

International Airport at Mattala

China agreed to provide concessional funding for several projects, including the second International airport at Mattala. Both the countries signed three framework agreements worth $410 million for the same. As mentioned later in the text that Indian Prime Minister too has proposed to develop ports and air-fields in Sri Lanka which shall add to her economic infrastructure. Therefore, Indian policy makers seem to have taken adequate note of this development. However, the development on this front is yet to be observed as to how India pre-empts Chinese engagement in this area.

Development Assistance

China has helped Sri Lanka by giving technical support as well as financial aid in major infrastructure projects including the Puttalam Coal Power Project. Other major pacts signed include one on economic and technical cooperation, a memorandum of understanding on two-way investment promotion cooperation and an MoU on the film industry.[26] Commerce Ministry of China also signed an annual granting agreement with Sri Lanka worth $ Seven Million and the Chinese Vice Minister has also indicated that future development assistance will be provided by China to raise the living standards of the people and achieve a higher growth in Sri Lanka.[27]

China's Arms Supply to Sri Lanka

Sri Lanka suffered from a protracted civil war within the country. Liberation Tigers of Tamil Elam (LTTE) has posed tremendous challenge to the state and government of Sri Lanka. The construction of the port saw a sudden spurt of activity during the war, indicating indirect aid to the war itself. Ever since the Chinese government grabbed this project, it has been giving all the aid, arms and diplomatic support Sri Lanka needed to defeat the Tigers, with no worry about other nations concerns.[28] Thus, the two and a half decades long ethnic conflict in Sri Lanka has resulted in the modernization of Sri Lanka's armed forces. China has emerged as a major source of military equipment to Sri Lanka, ranging from armoured vehicles, artillery guns and gunboats to aircrafts. Besides, China has supplied a variety of heavy machine guns and assortment of personal weapons.[29] China has become the biggest supplier of arms in 1990s, through nurtured ties with the nation, when India and the Western governments refused military aid to the nation in its war against the LTTE. The supply of arms has only increased since 2007, when US suspended military aid to Sri Lanka on counts of Human Rights violation.[30] In April 2007, Sri Lanka signed a classified $37.5 million deal to buy ammunition and ordinance for its army from the Chinese. Sri Lanka was given six F7 jet fighters by China, free of charge after 10 military aircrafts were destroyed on a daring raid by the Tamil Tigers.[31] Chinese Jian-7 fighter jets, anti-aircraft guns, JY-11 3D air surveillance radars and other weapons supplied by China played a vital role in the Sri Lankan military successes against the LTTE in 2009.[32] In the year 2007, China also encouraged Pakistan to sell weapons to the Sri Lankans as well as train Sri Lankan pilots to fly Chinese fighters.[33] China's encouragement led Pakistan to increase its annual military allowance to Sri Lanka to $100 million.[34] The Sri Lankan Army Chief, Sarath Fonseka, also mentioned that Sri Lanka was forced to turn to China only because India refused to sell offensive weapons to Sri Lanka.[35]

More than 6000 civilians died in Sri Lanka due to the war with the separatist Tamil Tigers[36], and about 50,000 civilians were trapped in a ten square kilometre area[37], which caused a great deal of concern amongst Amnesty International and the Human Rights Watch Organization.[38] Amnesty International stressed on the need for the Security Council to intervene and demanded to provide full access to the humanitarian organizations to check the growing infringement of human rights by using heavy artillery in the so-called 'safe-zones' in the Sri Lankan nation.[39] The Chinese Government lent political support to Sri Lanka thereby blocking the crisis from being put on its agenda in the Security Council or even the situation being discussed. The Chinese objections ensured that no resolution was passed when a debate on the same was conceded and the Council took the minimalist option of releasing a statement of concern.[40] In fact, even Russia helped in blocking a binding motion in the UN Security Council over Sri Lanka.

The Indian Ocean: Strategic Concerns for China and India

The Indian Ocean contains one-third of the world's population, 25 per cent of its landmass, and 40 per cent of the world's oil and gas reserves. It is also the locus of important sea lanes of communication (SLOC)[41] and is important to India from economic, legal, political and military perspectives. The Ocean is also critical for global trade and a half of the world's containerized freight, a third of its bulk cargo and two-thirds of its oil shipments travel through the Indian Ocean.[42] Therefore, the magnitude of strategic interests of India that is involved can only be imagined and is difficult to be measured. The rationale behind the Chinese strategy is quite evident: to encircle India as well as avail the benefit of friendly nation states along the "oil route" as about all the oil that is imported from the middle east is be sea and as mentioned above, all the pearls prove to aid the dragon to bring home the much required oil supplies to meet its energy needs as access to land mass around this ocean is important to bring home the petroleum supplies. Also, the concern of safety in the Straits of Malacca presents an important challenge to the Chinese. Mastering this area will help China in its attempt to become a great power as it would otherwise be handicapped without the supply of its energy.

The Chinese desire to have a control over the seas has been seen from the ancient times. China views the Indian naval presence as its only weakness although India has no desire to match China's military prowess. So, to make its presence visible in this area, China has been trying to build ports around this area in Myanmar, Pakistan and Sri Lanka.[43] China is only trying to encircle India by building these dependency ports in furtherance of their need to establish their presence in the Indian Ocean, as pointed out by Navy Chief Admiral Sureesh Mehta.[44] Gen Zhao Nanqi, Director of the General Logistic Department of the PLA said that Indian Ocean was no longer just the Ocean of the Indians and armed conflicts in this area were also being taken into account.[45] The moves of China need to be carefully watched, to understand the nuances of its policy of encirclement. China has escalated its influence on the Southern Asian area by providing much-needed economic, social, military assistance to the smaller states of this region to try and exercise its superiority in the Indian Ocean. Therefore, engaging Sri Lanka by building ports and developing air-fields in future China is further strengthening its presence in and around the Indian Ocean, which undoubtedly impinges on India's security concerns. There is no doubt that in future Indian Ocean will develop into an area where both these powers would compete with each other for dominance of the sea lanes of communication and it may turn Indian Ocean into a battle field.

Strategic Cooperative Partnership

China and Sri Lanka have signed an agreement to upgrade their relations to a "strategic cooperative partnership" during Rajapaksha's visit in May 2013. The agreement envisaged greater cooperation in law enforcement, security and defence, with Sri Lanka planning to launch a telecommunication satellite at a cost of US$ 320 million in partnership with China's State-owned great Wall Industry Cooperation. Both the countries have signed three other agreements in the fields of education, mass media and culture. They have also signed agreements for cooperating between film industries and in agriculture mechanization.[46]

Sri Lanka has recently opened a Consulate in Chengdu, where Pakistan too has an already active Consulate. Reportedly, Chengdu military region coordinates China's military strategy in South Asia.[47] Several reports have revealed that China is using its soft power expansion to further its military interests and consolidating its dominating presence which shall make China a pre-eminent power in the region. Soft power is thus a means for China to build and consolidate its hard power thereby maximizing its security interests.

Maritime Silk Road (MSR): Heritage to Geo-political Game

During Tang Dynasty of China Maritime Silk Route was a major channel of communication, through which ancient China made contacts with the outside world. Since, then it was often discussed in history of China and the world as an ancient system of inter-state communication and channels of trade and commerce. However, with the recent intentions of revival it has given indications of evolution of a new kind of geo-political strategic game-plan of China in the Indian Ocean and its vicinity.

It envisages connectivity with Southeast Asia, South Asia, West Asia and even Africa by building a network of port cities along the erstwhile silk route as Maritime Silk Road (MSR). This shall link the economic hinterland of China which aspires to improve its geo-strategic position in the world. The recent commitment from Sri Lanka to join the Maritime Silk Road indicates the proximity of the two states' strategic aspirations and is a reflection of the assimilation of national interests.[48]

The MSR is a vital strategic project for China in the Indian Ocean, and will increase up the western coast of India and further west to Iran, a vital exporter of oil to China. With this policy China is trying to defy the 'string of pearls' theory borrowing the metaphor of friendly ties that stands attached to the philosophy of ancient MSR by building a new MSR. However, it is quite obvious that Chinese leadership is trying to impart a new lease of life to China's peripheral policy and diffuse the tension owing to the emerging geo-politics of Indian Ocean. Fact remains the China is ever innovative when it comes to pushing its existence, its philosophy, and its game-plan in the southern Asia. China has made a smart move of inviting India to join the MSR. However, it has posed a serious challenge to India in terms of dilemma of either joining China and works together in the maritime domain or limit China's expansionist policy in the Ocean.

Sino-Sri Lankan Convergence: It's Impact on Sino-India Relations

There is hardly any doubt that the strong presence of China in Sri Lanka either through construction of a strategic port or through the supply of arms and ammunition or greater bilateral trade and commerce would make Sri Lanka heavily dependent upon China. Sri Lankan economic and military stake with China would belittle India's role in Sri Lanka, the nation-island otherwise has been a traditional and natural ally of India. India banks heavily on her smaller neighbours in terms of their support on different multilateral international forum. Growing dependence on China would mean India loosing support of such countries in the international forums in the future. It would also mean India loosing bilateral trade with its neighbours.

Indian Ocean is an important and strategic sea lane of communications. Chinese dominance over Indian Ocean would mean an eclipse on Indian presence over the same.

India as Stakeholder

There is hardly any doubt that China is all set and working hard to assume a leading role in emerging Asia. Probably, those countries which will have strong economic and political partnerships with China would be benefited by the changing economic fortunes of the second largest economy of the world. China and Chinese goods have also entered heavily into Indian market, economy as well as psyche of the people. Therefore, the implications of China's growing soft power influence are likely to be critical considerations for India and a real foreign policy challenge to hold on to its traditional allies, else China will wean them away from India.

Aid and trade have been important instruments of fostering better relations with Third World countries, especially South Asia. From 1956 to 1973, nearly 20 per cent of China's aid was targeted to South Asia, with Pakistan receiving 13.1 per cent, Sri Lanka 3.5 per cent and Nepal 2.9 per cent.[49] During recent years, China has expanded its economic assistance to Sri Lanka many times more as explained above factually.

It is quite obvious that India had cordial and deep rooted relations spreading across all areas from culture, trade, commerce, education, to strategic with Sri Lanka. However, of late it seems India has not only miscalculated its relations with Sri Lanka but has also left the turf wide open because of policy bankruptcy thereby creating a vacuum which has provided enough space for China to intervene and consolidate. It has happened in spite of the fact that ties between Sri Lanka and India is older than that between China and Sri Lanka.

India cannot afford the presence of any non-traditional friend within the vicinity of Indian Ocean and Southern Asia. India is clearly pre-eminent in the security matrix of Sri Lanka, yet China has continued to expand its soft power influence in both these countries. The fact remains that China is not part of South Asia, but through systematic efforts, China has made its presence felt in a big way in India's neighbourhood—in Nepal, in Pakistan, in Myanmar, in Sri Lanka, in Maldives, in Bhutan, in Bangladesh. China is not a littoral state of the Indian Ocean, but it is making its presence felt through expanding and deepening relations with Sri Lanka, Maldives, Myanmar, Mauritius, and Seychelles.

The way China has cultivated India's long-time rival Pakistan, is suggestive enough that China is working hard to checkmate India's influence in its neighbourhood, and hence it must be a matter of great concern for India and its foreign policy makers. V Suryanarayanan has correctly mentioned that Chinese diplomacy is aimed at counter-balancing India's pre-eminent influence in its immediate neighbourhood. India's maritime ambition, thus are being challenged and contested. Almost 55 per cent of India's trade passes through the Strait of Malacca, some countries continue to oppose allowing it to play a prominent role. China has voiced displeasure at the growing Indian naval presence in the region. China also opposed Vietnam granting exploration rights to Indian company

ONGC Videsh in offshore blocks located in disputed waters.[50] Despite the fact that India does not share a contiguous maritime border with South China Sea its maritime interests in the region are well established. The broader interest is to ensure that China's increasingly assertive position over maritime territorial disputes in the South China Sea is not repeated in the Indian Ocean. With Hambantota in Sri Lanka, an expanded Chinese naval presence in the Indian Ocean could result in a role reversal of its position in the South China Sea; whereas China is the coastal state and India the external maritime power in the South China Sea, the tables are turned in the Indian Ocean. This could entail Chinese interventions in disputes over the demarcation of maritime boundaries that India has with its neighbours namely Sri Lanka, Bangladesh, Pakistan and intelligence gathering and exploitation of maritime resources close to India's coastline. Biomass poaching and piracy on sea is recent breed of criminal activities that India requires to address with a heavy hand and strong naval presence in the blue waters. The Asian maritime domain is most likely to emerge as an increasingly active theatre of inter-state rivalries, given concerns of a strategic void created by a more "hands-off" approach by India.

Policy Choice for India

India requires impressing upon the smaller neighbours such as Sri Lanka that they should not allow themselves to become a pawn in the geopolitical game of bigger powers in the region. Smaller countries of the region must know that it is far easier to deal with India than with China. They must understand the dynamics of the on-going Sino-Indian competition in the region and thus their policy must be to avoid any considerable involvement in the geopolitics of the region, else they may have to suffer at the hands of both China as well as India.

"Maritime Asia" has emerged as a new geopolitical frame of reference in recent years as the nations of Asia evolve into major trading and resource-consuming powers with economic growth contingent on sea-borne trade. India is no exception, with 95 per cent of its total external trade by volume and 75 per cent by value now conducted by sea, and with more than 70 per cent of its oil imports transiting the maritime domain.[51] To protect these burgeoning maritime interests, the Indian government requires maintaining a multi-dimensional Navy with extended outreach and sustainability. The Naval modernization will have its own course but the diplomatic community of India must think beyond that and design the geopolitics of the region in a manner that it is able to hold on its traditional sphere of influence without being interventionist. India must cultivate political trust by investing political and economic capital in the neighbourhood.

China on the one hand engaged in encircling India with its power projections and presence in the neighbourhood; on the other hand becoming assertive by frequent intrusions into Indian Territory. India rather than responding befittingly has ordered for raising another mountain division to put its house in order. Such policy responses are rectification measures; however, at the same time India too should enhance its engagement with its neighbour at all levels and in all field economic, political, cultural, cooperation, military exercises, sports, education, tourism and security.

India must also play a constructive maritime role by generating a 'maritime concert' as suggested by Shivshankar Menon by taking the neighbouring states into confidence as the fact remains that China is a growing maritime power as well and is moving at a great speed to architecture a geo-politics for itself in a manner that it is able to safeguard its strategic and economic interests in a sustainable and assertive manner. India must learn the lesson and act before it is too late. Prime Minister Narendra Modi has initiated positively in this direction while calling all SAARC leaders including Sri Lankan President in his swearing in ceremony in May 2014.

NOTES

1. Based on Beijing's territorial claims, China shares its land borders with the following 15 countries: Afghanistan, Bhutan, India, Kazakhstan, Kyrgyzstan, Laos, Mongolia, Macao, Myanmar, Nepal, North Korea, Pakistan, Russia, Tajikistan, Vietnam. And it shares its maritime boundaries with the following 8 countries: Brunei, Indonesia, Japan, Malaysia, Philippines, South Korea, and Vietnam. With some of these countries China shares both maritime and territorial borders. See Singh, Swaran, "China and The Emerging New Balance of Power in Asia", *Asian Strategic Review*, 1997-98, Published by Institute of Defence Studies and Analysis, pp.221-222.
2. Ibid., no.1, p.223.
3. Ibid., no.1, p.223
4. Kumar, Krishna, "Friendship bridge across Asian waters Sino-Sri Lankan relations grow apace with trade gains made over decades", February 26, 2014, www.dailymirror.lk visited on March 6, 2014.
5. Ibid, no.4.
6. Ibid., no.4.
7. Ibid, no.4.
8. Goodman, Jack, "Sri Lanks's Growing Links with China, *The Diplomat*, March 06, 2014.
9. Ibid. no.4.
10. Ibid., no.4
11. Zhu Zhe, "China signs 16 agreements with Sri Lanka", *China Daily*, September 18, 2012.
12. Ibid., no.11.
13. Ibid.,no.11.
14. Sudha Ramachandran, "Sri Lankan waters run deep with China", *Asia Times*, August 13, 2010. Hambantota is more than just a port. On completion, the Hambantota Development Zone will include a liquefied natural gas refinery, aviation fuel storage facilities, three separate docks that will give the port transhipment capacity, dry docks for ship repair and construction, and bunkering and refuelling facilities.
15. Raman, B, "China's interest in naval base: Gwadar or Hambantota or elsewhere?" *Sri Lnaka Guardian*, December 31, 2009, <http:www.srilankaguardian.org/2009/12/chinas-interest-in-naval-base-gwadar-or.html>
16. Ramachandran, Sudha, "China moves into India's backyard", *Asia Times*, March 13, 2007. Retrieved from http://www.atimes.com/atimes/South_Asia/ICD13Df01.html>.

17. Sakuja Vijay, China's Diplomatic and Strategic Balancing Acts in Southern Asia, *Indian Journal of Foreign Affairs*, vol.14, no.3, July-September 2009, p.54.
18. Page, Jeremy, "China helping Sri Lanka in battle against Tamil Tigers", *Tehran Times*, May 10, 2009, Retrieved from <http://www.tehrantimes.com/index_View.asp?code=193629>
19. Kumar, P C Vinoj, "The Dragon's Newest Pearl", *Tehelka*, May 23, 2009, Vol.6, Issue 20, Retrieved from http://www.tehlka.com/story_main41.asp?filename-Ne230509the_dragon.asp>
20. Raman, B., "Gwadar, Hambantota and Sitwe: China's Strategic Triangle", Retrieved from http://www.saag.org/common/uploaded_files/paper2158.html
21. Ibid., no.20.
22. Ibid., no.17, p.55
23. Goodman, Jack, "Sri Lanka's Growing Links with China", *The Diplomat*, March 06, 2014.
24. Ibid., no.17, p.55.
25. Raman, B., "China's Oil Quest across India's Cauvery Basin", *SAAG Paper No.2181*, March 26, 2007. As quote in Sakuja Vijay, Ibid., no.17, p.55.
26. Reddy, B. Muralidhar, "China, Sri Lanka ink deal to develop Hambantota:, *The Hindu*, Colombo, March 5, 2007, Retrieved from http://hinduonnet.com/2007/03/05/stories/200703050628 1200.html
27. Reddy, B. Muralidhar, "Chinese Aid for Sri Lanka", *The Hindu*, Colombo, December 24, 2009, Retrieved from http://beta.thehindu.com/news/international/article70004.ece
28. "China a major player in Sri Lankan War", *Thaindian news*, Retrieved from http://www.thaindian.com/newsportal/world-news/china-a-major—player-in-sri-lanka-war_100187453.html
29. Ibid., no.17, p.54.
30. Ibid., no.18.
31. Ibid., no.18.
32. Chellaney, Brahma, "China fules Sri Lankan War", *The Japan Times*, March 4, 2009, Retrieved from http://search.japantimes.co.jp/cgi-bin/eo20090304bc.html
33. Ibid., no.17.
34. "India upset with China over Sri Lanka Crisis", *The Times of India*, New Delhi, April 26, 2009
35. Cherian, John, "Changing Equations", *The Frontline*, Vol. 26, Issue 12, June 6-19, 2009.
36. Crawshaw, Steve, "An urgent need for UN action in Sri Lanka:, The Huffington Post, May 6, 2009, http://www.huggingtonpost.com/steve-crawshaw/an-urgent-need-for-un-act_b_197840.html
37. Cherian, John, "Changing Equations", *The Frontline*, Vol. 26, Issue 12, June 6-19, 2009.
38. "UN Security Council: Demand immediate access and accountability in Sri Lanka", Retrieved from http://www.amnesty.org/en/for-media/press-release/un-security-council-demand-immediate-access-and-accountibility-sri-lanka
39. Sri Lanka: Security Council Must Act", Retrieved from http://www.amnesty.org.au/news/comments/20961/
40. Blair, David, "Sri Lanka analysis: China emerges as key player in victory over Tamil Tigers", *The Telegraph*, May 18, 2009.
41. "India and the Emerging Geopolitics of the Indian Ocean Region", Retrieved from http://www.apcss.org/core/Conference/CR_ES/030819-21ES.htm
42. Ibid.,no.17, p.54.
43. "China afraid of India's naval presence in the Ocean", Retrieved from http://zeenews.com/news555196html
44. Ibid., no.17, p.54.
45. Yossef Bodansky, "The PRC Surge for the Strain of Malacca and Spratly confronts India

and the US", *Defence & Foreign Affairs Strategic Policy*, Washington DC, September 2005, p.6.

46. Ibid. no.4.
47. V. Surayanarayan, "Explaining China's Growing Influence in Sri Lanka", www.asiastudies.org Retrieved on February 21, 2014.
48. Jack Goodman, "Sri Lanka's Growing Links with China", *The Diplomat*, March 06, 2014.
49. Ibid., no.18.
50. Chietigj Bajpaee, "Reaffirming India's South China Sea Credentials", *The Diplomat*, August 14, 2013.
51. Ibid.,no.25.

2

India's Strengthening Relations with West Asia

Alokka Dutta

West Asia has always been a crucial region for India primarily, though not exclusively, because of the fact that this region alone accounts for over fifty percent of the oil consumed by India. Also, because of her large Muslim population base, India has a direct stake in the peace & prosperity of the region. This is certainly a factor which can allow her a greater voice in the affairs of this region vis-à-vis the other emerging giant of Asia, namely China. The relations between India and West Asia especially the Gulf countries are not the recent phenomenon. They go back to many centuries old. These relations have always been cordial, friendly and mutually beneficial. Since ancient times, India has had economic, cultural and political contacts with this region; This region has not been only strategically important to global powers such as the US and-European countries, but also to India due to its geo-strategic location, adequate availability of energy resources, a home for a considerable number of Indians and big source of remittance for India along with the emerging prospects in the field of education and health sector. Not only this, centuries old interactions between India and the region and its pivotal roles in the Muslim world make the West Asian countries, also politically and diplomatically important to India. Many West Asian countries have always supported India at the international forums. The other equally important factor that should be taken into account is the socio-cultural affinity of Indian Muslims with two holy paces Mecca and Medina located in this region. Every year, more than a lakh Indian-Muslims go there for pilgrimage. They work as the binding force between the regions. They carry the Indian culture and values with them and spread the same in the region. This reinforces common brotherhood between India and West Asia.

It is also true that India has always been supportive of Arab cause, especially Palestinians since India's independence. The great leaders like Mahatma Gandhi and Pandit Jawaharlal Nehru strongly supported the rights of Arabs. They felt that the socio-economic and political problems of West Asian people were not 'different from those of Indians. The both leaders had the same view on the issue of Palestine and other West Asian in the same sense that England belongs to the English or France to the French.[1] India had in fact, supported the cause of Palestine in every UN and other international forums. She extended all possible material and moral support to Palestinian people.

It is however witnessed since the early 90s that India's West Asian policy began to shift from its earlier policy. It is now debated whether India's changing West Asian policy is in favour of India's national interest or not? This could be understood by considering some factors which are vital in explaining India's interest in West Asian countries.

Economic Factors

No doubt political and diplomatic factors based on national interest, are important. But at the same time, economic interest is one the most crucial factors that should be given priority, while formulating foreign policy. Taking this factor in to consideration, India is having a good relation with the West Asian countries since ancient times. The trade relation between the two traced back to the early part of the 20th century. Geographical proximity and economic interdependence are perhaps responsible factors for having greater interaction between, two regions which leads to mutual bene?ts. There have been substantial commitments of investments by way of joint ventures from both sides. Many agreements were signed between India and these countries in order to promote trade and investment in their countries. It is noted that Indian imports from the region were estimated at more than $3 billion, while exports were estimated at less than $ 2 billion in 1991. These values increased to more than $ 8 billion of imports and less than $ 4.5 billion of exports to this region in 2000.[2] It is thus observed that bilateral trade got impetus on account of economic liberalisation taking place in India and the West Asian countries. The total valtie of trade with this region was more than $ 5 billon in l99l than $ 12 billion in 2000. This would be expected go upto $ l30 billion by 2013-14 which was around $100 billion 2009-10.

It we look in terms of country wise, Saudi Arabia is one of the most important trading partners in the Gulf region. It is the 14th largest market for India and accounts for 7 percent of India total exports.[3] On the other hand, India is the fifth largest market for Saudi Arabia contributing about 4.5 percent of its total exports. Thus on the trade front, India has to explore opportunities-to add more items to its export basket. Currently India's export to Saudi Arabia mainly constitutes cereals, man made filament, apparels & clothing, Iron and Steel.[4] The country has to focus more and more on value added industrial products and services. It is moving steadily towards a free market economy with gradual decontrolling of many important sectors of the economy. The service sector that offers potential of greater employment opportunities has been identified as one of the major focal areas. This offers an excellent opportunity to Indian industry to forge partnership with its counterparts in the Kingdom to build strong and vibrant economic relations between the two countries..

UAE is another major trading partner of India in the Gulf region. It is in fact India's biggest market in this region. India's exports to the UAE are diversified and contain a large basket of goods. Thus the significance of the UAE. For India is not only for imports but also for exports. This is so because UAE has emerged as the topmost trading partner in the region. The UAE alone represents 70 per cent of India's exports to the GCC Countries.[5] Exports to the UAE comprise 6 percent of India's global exports. The major items of exports from India are gems and jewellery, textiles, manufactures of metals, machinery and instruments, plastic and linoleum, tea, Basmati rice, drugs, pharmaceuticals and chemicals primary and semi-finished iron and steel. Apart from this, information and news exports are emerging as a new area. On the other hand, India's main imports from the UAE are petroleum crude and products, pearls, precious and semi-precious stones, gold metaliferious ores and scrap, fertilisers and organic and inorganic chemicals.

There are many advantages to have good trading relations with the UAE. As it is the nearest destination and Dubai has emerged as the major trade centre and a gateway to entire Arab world. Almost 95 percent of trade to the GCC and 85 percent to the WANA region transits through Dubai. It is noted that many Indian companies are setting up their centre in Dubai and Sharjah and bidding for many ventures into the world market. Thus we can say that UAE is an important trading partner in this exports.[7]

There is substantial trade to Qatar via Dubai. A number of consumer goods from India are available and popular in Qatar. There are good prospects for diversification and expansion due to the low level of customs duties in Qatar (4%), which is close to the proposed common GCC external tariff of 5 per cent. India's export basket is fairly diversified and includes foodstuffs, spices, tea, coffee, textiles, ready-made-garments, jewellery, light engineering goods, basic chemicals, steel pipes, and consumer electronics. As the Qatari market is competitive and highly quality conscious, There is a room for expanding our exports further in areas where we are globally competitive.

India's imports from Qatar consist largely of urea, ammonia, sulphur, ethylene and polyethylene. India has substantial dealings with the Qatar Fertiliser Company (QAFCO) and the Qatar Petrochemical Company (QAPCO). India has not been a major customer for Qatari crude oil/products. However, it is set to emerge as one of Qatar's most important customers for LNG. With the third largest gas reserves in the world, Qatar is poised to emerge as a significant international supplier of energy for many decades to come. The Government of Qatar has made large investments in the development of its two LNG projects and port at Ras Laifan. With its large, expanding and long term requirements of natural gas, India is naturally keen to take advantage of the existence of a reliable and virtually inexhaustible source of natural gas situated so close to its own consuming centres.' This is the biggest agreement of this type in the world and will significantly raise the economic and commercial profile of India in Qatar, and of Qatar in India. This will also make India the biggest buyer of natural gas from Qatar.

India and Bahrain enjoys a trouble free and close political relationship. They also have a mutually beneficial bilateral economic cooperation. Bahrain is a small country but important one. Both these countries are very close to each other in many respects. India also exports a comparatively large amount of goods and services to Bahrain. Since most of Bahrain's needs are met through imports. There exists a good potential for enhanced exports from India. The Indian private sector could play a more active role in this area; Participation in exhibitions, bilateral business visits and consistency in quality and supply schedules can go a long way in promoting Indian exports. The policy of Bahrain Government joint ventures especially in the small and medium industries.[8] India can take a lead in this field in order to enhance exports to Bahrain.

There are mainly five items of exports from India to Bahrain. These are textile, wood, vegetables, meat and rice. Moreover, there are good prospects for export of Indian products, particularly agricultural products, sanitary fixtures, drugs & pharmaceuticals', plywood, ceramic tiles, power generation and transmission equipment, light engineering goods, leather products, textiles and related products. Information technology is the new emerging field of India's efforts. There are a large number of NRI business communities in Bahrain, which is engaged primarily in trading activity. They have invested in their business establishment in Bahrain. "These establishments include agencies for Titan and IHMT watches, India televisions, etc.

Our relations with Oman are historical There is evidence of people-to-people contacts dating back to the seventh century. In olden days, there was constant sea trade between the two countries. An Indo-Oman Treaty of Friendship, Navigation and Commerce was signed by Sultan Said and the President of India in 1953. It was probably one of the first agreements to be signed between India and any Arab country. The umbrella agreement for cooperation in the hydrocarbon field was at breakthrough in exploiting the potential for economic competition with Gulf States. The economic content was further concretized with the signature of the Agreement on Economic, Trade and Technical Cooperation which aimed at strengthening cooperation in the economic, commercial, industrial, tourist and technical fields. There was also the setting up of a Joint Commission to meet annually to follow up and to review developments.

The recognition of Oman's strategic significance was further highlighted by the demonstration of a new political will and new economic initiatives. India's need for energy sources particularly for the Southern Grid and the possibility of supply of gas through a submarine pipeline heightened the awareness on both sides of the existence of common strategic interests. This has become explicit in Oman's proposal to develop a 'Strategic Trade Alliance'. It is interesting to note that Oman is the only country in the region where India has the surplus balance of trade.[10]

The cooperation between India and Kuwait has increased in the field of science and technology. A number of visits have taken place between the two countries especially between the two apex bodies in the field of science and technology Kuwait Institute of Scientific Research (KISR) and Council of Scientific and Industrial Research (CSIR). A number of Indian Scientists/Researchers are with KISR and other such organizations to develop cooperation for mutual benefits.

The trade relations between India and Iran continued to register growth. The new economics policies followed both by India and Iran provided new opportunities for economic cooperation. This is of course in the field of energy sector oil and gas. The other fields where cooperation is required are in the field of textile machinery, bio-technology, power generation, agro-processing. Apart from this, Iran could play a very important role in providing India and commercial linkages with the central Asian countries. They are emerging as big markets for Indian goods.

India and Iraq have traditionally been very close to each other. Iraq was one of the major sources of India's oil imports and also was good markets for Indian goods. But after the Gulf crisis in 1990-91 and in 2001, its economic activities were badly disturbed. Iraq is fighting its own battle to get rid of foreign powers such as the US and the UK. They have undemocratically invaded Iraq and are still occupying it, taking the pretext of bringing democracy there. As far as the relation with Israel is concerned, it must be taken into consideration of the national interest in mind. Israel can not be more important than these Gulf countries from any point of view. The previous NDA government was misled and adopted the policy which favoured Israel rather than Gulf countries. It is noted that as soon as this current regime came to power, it is realised by the government and there is a correction in its foreign policy towards the Gulf.

We further see that India's economic relations with Yemen has the positive sign after the first meeting of Indo-Yemen joint committee which cooperation such as trade and investment, small scale industry, telecommunication, hydrocarbons, civil aviation, construction, science and technology, health and education, etc.

Relative importance of the Gulf in comparison to Israel. It is noted that there is a flourishing mutually beneficial economic connection with the Gulf region for India. India's crude oil import from the Gulf is worth $17 to $18 billion annually, India's annual trade with Arab countries is about $10 billion. Whereas, Israel's annual trade with India is only about $ 1.2 billion. Thus we can argue that the Gulf countries are vital destination not only for trade and investment but also for energy supply to India.

Energy Factor

The energy factor must be taken into account, while deciding West Asian policy. This is so because the Gulf energy is not only important to the Indian economy but also to the world economy. It is considered to be the integral part of the global economy because of its one third share of world oil production. The Gulf has well over half of the world's proven oil reserves. Most of the supply required to meet growing world demand is expected to come from OPEC especially from the region. It is expected that production would rise to 60 mbd by 2020 from 28 mbd in 1998. Virtually all this increase would come from this region.[11] Thus, the Persian Gulf region remains the largest depository of oil reserves and the major source of hydrocarbons. OPEC estimates are that oil reserves are over one trillion barrels, which can meet the requirement for more than 40 years. This was all due to the new discoveries which added the net 415 billion barrels to the World reserves.

The global proven natural gas reserves are put around 15.9 trillion cubic meters which is 38 per cent increase over the 1988 estimates. Despite all, this can not be ignored the pace of energy consumption which is so high that can upset current supply of energy. It is also obvious that hydrocarbons are non-renewable source of energy. So, their life span is bound to be limited. But this is also true that threat is not so imminent as far as physical reserves are concerned. Definitely, it is going to continue a longer period of time. It is also possible that by that time, there may be more new discovery of oil and gas in this region.

Thus, the Gulf holds an indispensable position in terms of energy stock for most of the countries like India. The region holds 63 percent of total world oil reserves and 34 percent of the world proven natural gas.

Additional advantage to the Gulf. Thus it is now clear that the Gulf is enormously important to India simply because it meets the bulk of our energy needs and having a large number of Indians in the Gulf. India must adopt a policy which can promote mutual understanding the economic cooperation. India has to play proactive role in order to maintain its interest in the region. If India wants to maintain its growth of 7-8 percent in GDP. It is also clear that Gulf is strategically the most important to India mainly due to its close proximity geographically. Hence, importing oil from this region is economically most viable.[12] Thus having a cordial, strong and good relation with West Asian is crucial for India.

According to the Vision Document, the share of oil and gas in the total energy will be 45 percent by the year 2025. India's oil consumption has exceeded

100 million tones of which 33 million tones are indigenous. While remaining 77 million tones comes from other countries. The demand for crude oil and petroleum products is expected to grow to 190 million tones in 2012, and 364 million tones in 2025. On the other hand, it is noted that domestic production has been declining. Indian oil reserves would dry up even if only 30 percent of its demand were met from domestic production. The demand is growing at the rate of 5.77 percent to meet this growing demand. There are five countries that provide bulk of it. These countries are Saudi Arabia, UAE, Kuwait, Iran and Nigeria accounting for more than 75 per cent of oil. This clearly indicates the importance of these countries as far as the case of India's imports is concerned.

It is also observed that Saudi Arabia is the leading country that account for nearly 20 per cent of total imports. The GCC countries such as Saudi Arabia, UAE, Kuwait, Qatar and Bahrain account for more than fifty percent. The Persian Gulf which include Iraq and Iran constitutes around 60 per cent of import.[13] Thus, India is presently importing 70 per cent of hydrocarbon which is expected to grow in future, since the consumption of energy is rapidly increasing in India owing to development taking place in different sectors of the economy. It is evident that there is a dominance of the GCC countries in terms of oil supply to India.

Just like food and defense, energy security challenges is one of the most important concerns for India in the age of globalization and liberalization. So, it has been realized that it now is strategically important for India to have strong economic linkage with the Gulf countries in order to meet energy security challenges. This is so because India still imports more than 60 percent of its oil from the Gulf countries and this percentage is expected to rise further. Presently India ranks sixth in the world in terms of energy consumption. The US, China, Russia, Japan and Germany comes before India in this respect. India is amongst those countries which imports over 70 percent of petroleum requirements from outside the country. Moreover, it is important to note that out of the total petroleum imports, more than 60 percent comes from the Gulf which constitutes six Gulf Cooperation Council countries such as Bahrain, Kuwait, Qatar, Saudi Arabia, United Arab Emirates and two more countries, Iran and Iraq. These countries are crucial countries for oil importer like India and China which has also recently become a net importer of oil. Hence, we can say that Gulf has immense significance for India not only for trade and energy but also for employment opportunities available in this region and remittances sending home.

Employment Factor

The Gulf countries are not only important from trade and investment, oil and natural gas point of view, but they are equally crucial for India in terms of employment to Indians in their respective countries. It is reported that at least 5 million Indians are employed in this region. These expatriate Indians remit more than $10 billion dollars to India every year.[14] Prior to the mid 70s, there were mainly Arabs such as Egyptians, Yemenis, Palestinians, Lebanese and Sudanese in this region. It was noted that the Gulf monarchies grew increasingly worried about the possible political repercussions in the 1970s. Palestinians were viewed as politically subversive, Yemenis were involved in various anti regime activities. As a result, the Gulf countries started to opt of workers from South and South East Asia who were seen as less likely to get involved in host countries politics.

After the oil boom of 1973, the Gulf countries recruited foreign workers from both Arab and Asian countries for construction and industrialization. Indians also benefited from it. These were about 2.5 lakh Indian expatriates in 1975. This number rose to over 1.5 million in 1991. In the year 1999, there were 3 million Indian nationals gainfully employed in the Gulf. The number of Indian workers in the Gulf reached over 3.6 million in 2004. Of this, Saudi Arabia alone had 1.5 millions Indians and UAE had 1 million Indians. Qatar and Bahrain had more than 1,00,000 Indian each. There were about 4.5 lakh Indian expatriates each in Kuwait and Oman.

It is also true that Saudi Arabia and the United Arab Emirates import the maximum number of Indian labour in their respective countries followed by other GCC countries. This is evident that there is a shortage of manpower in these, countries which is supplied by surplus manpower countries like India. The Indian government is now changing its migration policy in order to promote manpower employment in these countries. This is important because the manpower contributes significantly in the development of 'country where they are employed as well the country—wherefrom they come. Hence, we can say that this expatriate Indian labour force is the real asset to India and to the host countries as well. This is sò because both India and host countries are beneficiaries on accounts of the contribution made by these-expatriates.

Moreover, it also noted that all the Gulf States have launched many developmental programmes and schemes for overall "development of their countries. They need highly qualified and trained personnel who can work in their developmental-project. Hence, they will have to rely on skilled expatriate workers. It is 'here suggested that Indian government must act in this direction in order—to enhance the prospect of Indian workers in this region. Since India has vast reservoir of well trained technical manpower in all—disciplines such as Engineering, Medical, Management, Computer Sciences, etc. It is desirable that a large number of Indians may be able to find lucrative job abroad, especially in the Gulf. This can be made possible if we have strong and friendly relations with West Asian countries as we have had in the past.

Remittance Factor

It is proved beyond, doubt that Gulf remittances brought by the Indian expatriates help in the foreign exchange earnings to a great extent. It was fully realized by-the Indian government at the time of the Gulf crisis which took place in 1990.

Before the Gulf war, the annual remittances were more than $2 billion. By 1994-95, it amounted to $ 6.2 billion. At the turn of the century, this amount went up to 12 billion in 2000-2001. By 2003-04, it amounted approximately $ 14 billion a year which was a major asset to the country. In 2005, India's remittances reached $ 21.7 billion that replaced China whose remittances were $ 21.3 billion. Of India's $ 21.7 billion, $ 16 billion came from the Gulf countries.[15] In 2010, the World Bank reported "that India had received $ 55 billion from abroad". It was estimated that during the last 5 years the remittances have been more than double and India continues to retain its position in the World. It is interesting to note that the major chunk of remittance is still coming from the Gulf. Thus the Gulf region is very important for India in this respect. This huge amount definitely strengthens India's balance of payment. Kerala is one of the Indian states whose economy is largely based on the Gulf remittances. There are many other such states like Andhra Pradesh, Tamil Nadu, Punjab, Bihar, etc., where a huge amount of remittances are coming. These remittances' are used for economic development by migrants households in India.

Social and Cultural Factor

Education and health which are in fact the crucial factors for human resource development is identified as a major sector for future cooperation between India and the Gulf countries. Many agreements were signed between the two sides to promote-cooperation in the field of education and arts. Two important languages Arabic and Persian of this region have been taught in India for a long time. In the same way, "Urdu and Hindustani are spoken and understood the people in the Gulf region. Bollywood film stars are very popular in the Gulf for their performance. They frequently visit Dubai, Muscat and many other Gulf cities on their popular demand by people. This all clearly indicates the significance of common culture prevailing in the Gulf and India. Not only this, there are over 60 Indian schools which have been established in the Gulf countries. All schools follow CBSE pattern, except one which is affiliated to the KSB (Kerala State Board)". Indian Ambassador is the patron of all the Indian schools in the country. The control of the Indian schools has under the Board of Directors who is appointed by the Ambassador from among permanent members of the Indian community. The Board coordinates the functioning of management committees of all Indian schools

There are more than 30 Indian schools in the UAE. They are doing well and are catering the needs of Indian children and Emiratis to the Central Board of Secondary Education. They are all well established and are serving the needs of the large Indian community residing in Kuwait and the Kuwaitis alike. It is noted that there are four major Indian schools such as Indian school, Muscat: Indian schools, Al Ghubia Indian school, Wadi Kabir and Indian school, Dar Sait that are located in Muscat (Oman). Recently an Indian school of Seeb an adjacent township has started functioning. The oldest school is Indian school

Muscat initially known as Arya Kelavani Mandal which was founded in 2nd July 1939. Hindu Maliajan Association took the responsibility of managing the school. Thus, the presence of 15 Indian schools in various pans of Oman indicates that Indian community attaches a great deal of importance to education for its coming generation. For higher and technical education, their wards generally come to India.

There is an educational prospects in both sides. Indian IT companies have been actively involved in setting up an IT park in Muscat & Knowledge Oasis in Muscat (KOM). Both the IT colleges have an Indian connection. One is in affiliation with Manipal Academy of Higher Education while other is a joint venture with Birla Institute of Technology Ranchi.[18] Both are doing very well there.

Omani companies also have several Joint ventures m India. Oman Computer Services International develops Computer Software at Bangalore. Shantha Bio-techniques, Hyderabad is one of India's most well known bio-technology company. Nisma Airocon International, Chennai manufactures heat pump air conditioners. The Zubair group has setup a furniture manufacturing unit in Tamilnadu in collaboration with Balaji group of Chennai. Bahwan Cybertec have an IT training company in Chennai and regularly send trainees from Oman to India. These trainees go back to Oman with great satisfaction.

Sultan Qaboos university in Muscat is the only university which is well reputed and most important institution of higher learning in Oman. It Was found that many Omanis have studied in India and they still keep coming in large number to Indian universities and institution of higher education especially in technical subject such as engineering, IT and medicine. Bangalore, Pune, and Chennai are the major cities where they prefer to come for education. It is presently estimated that there are over 1500 Omanis who pursue higher education. It was also found that every year a number of Qmani officials co me to India to acquire training in different fields under the ITEC programme of the government or India. There were about 53 Omani officials will come to India in 2004 for number of training courses in different fields such as IT, audit, pharmaceuticals, Entrepreneurship, language Agriculture and rural development Accounts and Finance, Educational Planning and Administration, etc. This sector in fact needs to be addressed more seriously for mutual benefits. More and more Gulf students should be attracted to pursue their higher education in India.

As far as the socio-cultural factor is concerned, it is witnessed that a large number Indian Muslims go to two holy places (Mecca and Madinah) for pilgrimage every year on the occasion of Eid-Adha. This pilgrimage provides enough opportunities for cultural interaction between Indians and West Asian people. This cultural interaction strengthens our overall relations for our mutual benefit.

Conclusion

Our interest in West Asia is manifold. We can now conclude by saying that there is a need to further strengthen our relations with West Asia, especially the Gulf countries. Now, the time has come to be interdependent so as to get maximum benefit in the process of development taking place in both sides. This is very much possible in the era of globalization and information technology. The economic and diplomatic potential of India is fully realised by the West Asian countries. They have no inhibition to expand their ties with India in any strategic field. Working together would make them in a position to meet the challenges created by globalization. Hence, India needs to pursue a proactive economic policy towards the region. India must act in such as way that it can be instrumental to promote stability in this region which is always beneficial for the region and India's energy security and manpower employment. It would be a wise step to further develop economic, diplomatic and cultural relations with these countries. India must adopt a policy, which can promote to seek Indian manpower in the region more and more so as to earn foreign exchange. An emphasis should also be given to diversify the relations beyond trade, energy and expatriates. This is also true that the influence of China and Pakistan is increasing in West Asia. To compete them, India has to play proactive role in order to maintain its interest in this region. On the one hand, after a long period of time, these countries are hoping to become the shapers of their own destinies, on the other hand, there is resurgence of Taliban posing an imminent threat. Strong governance will be the need of the day, & since that this region practically is the neighbourhood of India, with Pakistan as a failing state, the role of India will become significant in the coming days. Her secular credentials, pro-Palestine stand, empathy towards the Kurdish community, experiences of viable democracy, her effective leadership in playing the role of a mediator & her contribution towards Peacekeeping operations, all place India in an esteemed pedestal in the region Thus we see that India now has a variety of interests in West Asia. These interests will only be best served if we adopt a pragmatic Indian policy based on existing reality.

NOTES

1. A.K. Ramakrishnan "Mahatma Gandhi Rejected Zionism" Released August 15, 2001 The Wisdom Fund, P.O. Box 2723, Arlington, VA 22202 website : http://www.twf.org
2. Bansidhar Pradhan, "Changing Dynamics of India's West Asian Policy" International Studies, vol. 40, no. 1, 2004, p.,4
3. Anisur Rahman, Indo-Saudi Relations : A Need for Coming Closer, Strategic Bulletin, Vol. IV No. 2&3, May-Sep 1999 p., 20
4. Jaideep Singh and Tersest Schaffer, Overview South Asia Monitor, CSIS, vol.9, Issue#2, Thursday 29, 2004 (accessed through Internet)
5. Shivaji Sarkar, "Tapping Alternative Market", Special Gulf News, (accessed through internet) published on 14/8/2004
6. Ibid
7. Govt. of India, Annual Report, 2000-2001, The Gulf, West Asia & North Africa, p., 38

(accessed through Internet)

8. Indian Embassy (Bahrain) Indo-Bahrain Relations (accessed though Internet) http://indianembassy-bah.com
9. Embassy of India (Muscat), Indo-Oman Relations (accessed through Internet) http://www.indemb-oman.org/india-oman-relation.html
10. Muhammad Azhar, Gulf Economies and Indo-Gulf Relations, (Delhi: New Horizon Publishers, 1999)
11. Anisur Rahman, "Gulf a Crucial Factor in India's Energy Requirements for Development" in S.N. Malakar (ed) Book on India's Energy Security and the Gulf, (New Delhi, Academic Excellence 2006) p.,28
12. Ibid
13. Girijest Pant, India's Energy Security: The Gulf Factor, Occasional Paper Series: CWAAS/SIS,JNU,GSP 2002
14. Anisur Rahman, Indian Labour Migration to the Gulf: A Socio-Economic Analysis (New Delhi: Rajat Publications, 2001) p., 34
15. The Times of India, New Delhi, Friday, November 18,2005
16. Ministry of Overseas Indian Affairs, Government of India, Annual Report 2010-11
17. P.C. Jain, Indian in Oman, GSP Occasional paper, Series (CWAAS/SIS/JNU New Delhi)
18. Embassy of India, (Muscat). Into-Oman Relations, (accessed through internet) http://indemb.oman.org/commercial-services-eco relations.html

3

China-Bangladesh Relations: Implications for India

Bibhuti Bhusan Biswas

I

The era of globalization that has replaced the bipolar world of the Cold War days has enhanced the importance of foreign affairs across the globe and the need for less resourceful nations to work ever harder for attaining its foreign policy goals.[1] In the foreign policy of China, first priority been given in peaceful policy towards her neighbours in China's overall diplomatic pattern.[2] China will unswervingly pursue a foreign policy of building good neighbourly relationship and partnership with its neighboring countries and always be their good neighbour, friend and partner. This desire comes from China's traditional culture and is deeply rooted in China's foreign policy. It reflects China's idea of pursuing peaceful development. With China's fast development, international community, especially China's neighbours, attaches more and more importance to China and is concerned about how China will get along with its neighbors and what opportunities China's development will bring to them. China and its neighbouring countries have always been deepening mutual understanding through contact and communication, pursuing development through learning from each other and enhancing harmony through respect for differences, which has promoted development and progress of all parties. China deeply cherishes the hard-earned opportunity of peaceful development and sincerely hopes to join hands with its neighbours to maintain and develop a peaceful and harmonious environment.

The People's Republic of China and Bangladesh establishing diplomatic relations on 4th October 1975, four years after the founding of Bangladesh as a result of a shift in the policy of the then Bangladeshi President Ziaur Rahman.[3] Since then both the countries have engaged in active cooperation in diverse fields, the foundation of which was laid with the signing of a bilateral agreement in 1976. Bangladesh's relations with China is not occurring in a vacuum—it is taking place in an international strategic context, where the interests of foreign powers set the parameters within which it has to maneuver.[4] Since establishing diplomatic relations Bangladesh-China friendship has come a long way, and, despite the radical changes that have occurred during this period in the domestic politics of both the countries as well as in the international arena, the cooperation between them has endured and intensified. China has emerged as a reliable partner to Bangladesh, extending economic, military and diplomatic support, while simultaneously attempting to gain a strategic foothold in South Asia and benefit from Bangladesh's natural resources.[5] Strategically, Bangladesh and China have mutually benefitted from bilateral relations. Bangladesh receives massive military aid, military training, technology and equipments from China. The bilateral relations are likely to continue in the near future, as the Chinese Ambassador Mr. Zhang Xianyi said in October 2009, on the Dhaka-Beijing bilateral relations, 'We're tested friends, tested by time...we are all-weather friends and we trust each other and we've cooperation in every field.'[6]

II

The main aim of China's foreign policy towards Bangladesh is to use its natural resources in their favour.[7] However, there was a surge in China-Bangladesh relationship in the year 2005. This year was celebrated as 'China-Bangladesh friendship Year' to mark the 30th anniversary of diplomatic relations. As per the 13-point Joint Communiqué signed between the two countries during Wen Jibao's April 2005, Bangladesh tour, China would assist Bangladesh in water management, nuclear energy, trade and investment, training of security and defense personnel as well as infrastructural agreement, which has led to the signing of a 10-point joint communiqué in 2010.[8] Besides, the two countries signed the cooperation agreement on the 'Peaceful Usage of Nuclear Energy,' as per which China would assist Bangladesh in the development of nuclear energy for power generation, medicinal and other development uses.[9] In addition, the China-Myanmar-Bangladesh road and rail link received fresh impetus in 2010 with all three countries agreeing to sign an agreement to develop transit facilities. Moreover, Bangladesh has sought China's assistance to develop and use the Chittagong port, as well as a deep sea port at Sonadia Island in Cox's Bazaar in Bangladesh.[10] The tri-nation cooperation in opening up transit facilities will boost trade in both Bangladesh and China. However, the Chinese-backed infrastructure development in Bangladesh, while a boon for economic prosperity in the country, could pose challenges for India in the coming decades.

In the mid-1980's, both the nations extended cooperation to the domain of commerce, culture and education.[11] China currently is the largest regional trading partner of Bangladesh, having surpassed India in terms of trade volume.[12]

Although there is a huge imbalance in this regard, the Chinese government is keen about narrowing it down by absorbing greater amount of imports from Bangladesh, and also by enhancing the level of investments there. In short, there is a genuine willingness to promote the overall economic well-being of Bangladesh, which is a reflection of China's goodwill toward it. As per the statistic from the Ministry of Commerce and economic of the Chines Government, in 2006-2007, while Bangladesh's imports from China were as high as US$ 3.33 billion, its exports to China amounted to just US$ 200 million. In order to bridge this huge trade gap China has not only provided economic aid to Bangladesh but also signed the Asia-Pacific Free Trade Agreement to remove tariff barriers to 84 types of commodities imported from Bangladesh. Bilateral trade amounted to US$ 7 billion in 2010.[13] China has also taken the initiative to develop natural gas resources and nuclear power plants in Bangladesh. The landlocked Yunan province of China has sought to engage in economic cooperation with Bangladesh to rectify its own regional inequalities and gain access to the Bay of Bengal. Bangladesh too, has offered to set up a Special Economic Zone for China. The 'Agreement on Economic and Technical Cooperation' and the 'Framework Agreement' on a concessional loan provided by China to Bangladesh are two other significant treaties signed by the two nations.[14]

The road link connecting China and Bangladesh via Myanmar will reduce the distance between China's Yunnan Province and Bangladesh's Chittagong to 111 km[15], which will further boost economic activities between the two countries. In the long run, this could prove to be vital for Bangladesh as it will aid in addressing several socio-economic issues in the conflict-stricken south-west part of the country. Moreover, recent reports suggest that there is potential to extend the tri-nation road link to the Kunming highway in China, which it being built to connect the Yunnan Province to Bangkok in Thailand.[16] The wider network of road links will provide an avenue for Bangladesh to connect to the rest of South East Asia in the future. This highway would give Bangladesh an entry into the Mekong sub-region, which already includes China, accelerate trade and facilitate people-to-people contact. China, on the other hand, will benefit from developing the Chittagong port and constructing a deep sea port at Sonadia Island in Bangladesh, giving it direct access to the Bay of Bengal. This will serve to reduce China's dependence on the Malacca Straits.

III

The Defence Co-operation Agreement was signed between Bangladesh and China during the visit of Bangladesh Prime Minister, Begum Khaleda Zia's visit to China from December 23 to 27, 2002, which covers military training and defence production.[17] The Agreement signed with China was to meet present day need of Bangladesh's defence forces. This new agreement was signed to help institutionalize the existing accords in defence sector and also to rationalize the existing piecemeal agreements to enhance cooperation in training, maintenance and some areas in production. The major significance of the Defence Cooperation

Agreement is that it is the first such agreement ever signed by Bangladesh in its history. Defence Cooperation Agreements are normally signed when: Countries perceive enhanced threat perceptions; Countries are amenable to be used in a region for balance of power politics; and Countries fear retaliation in response to their territories being used for proxy war and terrorism by third counties against another country.

In 2006, in a report submitted to the United Nations by China, for its exports and imports of major conventional arms revealed Dhaka is emerging as a major buyer of weapons made in China. China sold 65 large caliber artillery systems, 16 combat aircraft and 114 missile and related equipment to Bangladesh in 2005. Besides this, some 200 small arms like pistols and sub-machine guns have also been imported along with regular 82-mm mortars.[18] In 2008, Bangladesh set up an anti-ship missile launch pad near the Chittagong Port with assistance from China. The maiden missile test was performed on May 12, 2008 with active participation of Chinese experts. It successfully test-fired anti-ship missile C-802A with a strike range of 120 km from the frigate BNS Osman near Kutubdia Island in the Bay of Bengal. BNS Osman which was commissioned in 1989, is a 1500-ton Chinese built Jianghu class Frigate, and the C-802A missile is a modified version of Chinese Ying Ji-802 with weight reduced from 815 kg to 715 kg in order to increase the strike range from 42 km to 120 km.[19]

Bangladesh government has placed order with China's Wuchan Shipyard for supplying two sophisticated warships, one of which shall be handed over to Bangladesh by this year. The warship sized 64 meter in length with the capacity of 648 tons has highest speed of 28 nautical miles. The manufacturers of these warships are paying attention to the special requisition of the Bangladesh Navy keeping various types of most sophistical weapons and equipment. China earlier supplied similar warships to Pakistan. With the placement of order for supplying warships, Bangladesh has entered new vista of defense cooperation with China.[20]

Bangladesh government has also decided to procure a number of sophisticated helicopters, aircrafts and warships for the domestic security as well as sufficient efficiency of safeguarding country's interest. Besides, Bangladesh Navy has also decided to add Corvet and Off-the Shelve frigate in near future. It has already procured two more warships named 'Bijoy' and 'Dhoshwari'. Shoulder launched surface-to-air missile system has been added in these warships. It has purchased two helicopters for another warship named 'Bangabandhu'. Besides, Bangladesh Navy has earlier purchased 21 units of high-speed boats. Additionally manufacturing of two units of maritime patrol aircrafts, five units of patrol crafts and one oil tanker is undergoing now.[21]

The current government in Bangladesh has made an elaborate plan for significantly strengthening its defense facilities by procuring huge number of military hardware as well as sophisticated equipment and weapons with the target of transforming Bangladesh Army, Bangladesh Air Force and Bangladesh Navy into sufficiently advanced on facing any internal or external security threats. Special emphasis is being given to strengthening Bangladesh Navy for safeguarding huge natural resources in the Bay of Bengal. It is believed by economic and petroleum experts that by 2030, Bangladesh's economy will grow hugely thus placing the country to the economic status of developed nations, if the petroleum resources within the Bay of Bengal will be properly explored.[22]

IV

In the energy sector China's role has been significant, and there is much scope for its further expansion. For instance, Chinese technical assistance in gas exploration and transportation would be of tremendous value. China values Bangladesh for its immense natural gas reserves where Bangladesh's geographical proximity to Myanmar makes these reserves accessible to China through pipelines. China and Bangladesh encourage and support their own enterprises to carry out two-way investment and mutually beneficial cooperation, and provide facilitation for enterprises of both sides in project contracting and labor service cooperation. The Bangladesh side welcomes the active involvement of Chinese enterprises in the energy sectors in Bangladesh. The Chinese side would encourage and support capable and reputable Chinese enterprises to explore and carry out investment cooperation in energy sector in Bangladesh, and to provide possible facilitation and financing support for the mutually agreed cooperation projects. China National Petroleum Corporation signed a Memorandum of Understanding on Cooperation in Oil and Gas Sector with Bangladesh Oil, Gas & Mineral Corporation and Bangladesh Petroleum Corporation. Dhaka has granted China exploration rights for developing its natural gas fields at Barakpuria, which hold an estimated reserve of 390 million tonnes over an area of 6.69 square kilometers. China has channeled massive investment towards the development of these gas fields that are some of the world's largest reserves of best quality bituminous coal, which is ash free and with little sulphur content.[23]

V

India and China are keen on maintaining peace and stability in their respective neighbourhoods. Among the South Asian states, Bangladesh is an important player in Beijing's political-military calculus and provides China with added leverage to check Indian forces. This is evident from the regular political exchanges and enhanced military cooperation between the two countries. Bangladesh maintains a very close relationship with China for its economic and military needs. Over the years, the two sides have signed a plethora of bilateral agreements that range from economic engagements, soft loans, social contacts, cultural exchanges, academic interactions, infrastructure development and military sales at friendship prices. Top-level state visits, both by the ruling party and the opposition leaders to China have increased markedly and in the coming days both Beijing and Dhaka is like to continue the same parameter in terms of their relationship.

Presently in Bangladesh domestic turmoil is hindering functions of the government. However, Prime Minister Sheikh Hasina, despite her strong friendship with India, has continued with the look East policy of her predecessor Begum Khalida Zia and strengthened the links with China. During her visit to China, an agreement was signed with a Chinese company for oil / gas exploration in Bangladesh. She also sought Chinese help for the upgradation of Chittagong into a modern deep sea port. Her Government has sought to calm Indian concerns by reassuring India that India will also be allowed to use the Chittagong port modernized with Chinese help.

Sheikh Hasina also discussed with the Chinese plans for linking Yunnan with Bangladesh through Myanmar by a modern road. If the Chinese company finds oil or gas in Bangladesh it is only a question of time before the Chinese production facilities in Bangladesh are connected with those in the Arakan area of Myanmar, so that oil and gas from Bangladesh can flow direct to Yunnan through the pipeline connecting Arakan with Yunnan now being constructed. There has also been talk of a Chinese-aided railway line from Yunnan to Bangladesh via Myanmar.[24] Whereas, New Delhi is trying to get transit through Bangladesh to connect her North-East states for socio-economic developments despite many odd. New Delhi should cultivate long lasting relationship with Bangladesh without any reservation for any political regime in Dhaka. Both the country should work together without any mistrust, which will benefit both sides equally.

During the visit of Chinese Vice President Xi Jinping to Dhaka on June 13 and 14, 2010, Mr. Xi "proposed to give assistance to Bangladesh for building a deep seaport in Chittagong and installing the country's first space satellite." Briefing reporters on the outcome of the talks, Foreign Minister Dipu Moni said the Chinese side assured more investment in Bangladesh, and promised to reduce the bilateral trade imbalance by allowing more Bangladeshi products to have duty-free access to the Chinese market. She added that the Chinese agreed to help Bangladesh in ensuring food security and in combating militancy and terrorism.[25] China is taking advantages of New Delhi's passive attitude towards her neighbours to promote their policy of go out. India would have taken positive initiative to get access of Chittagong port very initially, but India failed to promote her interest in Bangladesh despite several options before India.

While the primary aspect of the relationship between China and Bangladesh is economic, it is unlikely to remain so in the future, given China's strategic interests in the South Asian region. In this context, the role of Bangladesh, as well as other smaller countries such as Nepal and Bhutan, which share their borders with north and eastern India could be crucial in shaping the regional order of South Asia. More importantly, China's growing sphere of influence in its western region could pose security challenges for India, especially the sensitive north-east region. The next few years therefore, are crucial for India, as it must tread carefully while formulating its policy towards Bangladesh.

Unfortunately, however, Indo-Bangladesh relations since the post-Mujib era until recently have often been marked by discord rather than co-operation.

However, it is true that some positive uptrend has been seen in Indo-Bangladesh relations during recent time. Both sides took advantage of improved political relations to discuss long-standing irritants such as demarcating borderland, combating cross-border terrorism, greater access for Bangladeshi goods in India and improved road-rail connectivity. India has tried to deal with a major grievance of Bangladesh by allowing unilateral concessions. Over the years, India and Bangladesh have signed several treaties and agreements with respect to trade and investment. However the cooperation between the two countries has been periodically slow and has sometimes even failed to produce the desired outcome, resulting in growing mistrust among Bangladeshis towards India's policies; this mistrust has also been largely fueled by the Islamist forces in Bangladesh. This could be one of the main reasons why the two prominent parties i.e. Awami League, which is widely considered to be India-friendly, and the main opposition party, Bangladesh Nationalist Party, are keen to pursue a long-term economic relationship with China.

Nevertheless, it is also true that Bangladesh cannot completely block India, and both countries will need to work towards resolving its existing issues, especially those related to water and border killings. In addition, India will need to consider providing transit facilities to Nepal and Bhutan to use the Chittagong and Mongla ports in Bangladesh, which will enhance development of the smaller countries surrounding India. Moreover, economic progress has the potential to positively impact the north-east region of India and contain the insurgencies that have plagued the region for decades.

Indeed, India needs to shed its 'big brother' attitude towards neighbouring states while moving away from a form of coercive diplomacy. In this context, perhaps the Gujral Doctrine needs to be reflected on which emphasised that "with its neighbours like Bangladesh, Bhutan, Maldives, Nepal and Sri Lanka, India does not ask for reciprocity, but gives and accommodates what it can in good faith and trust."[26] It will be interesting to see how the cooperation between China and Bangladesh consolidates over the next few years.

Awami League has returned into power second term in just concluded elections. It is maiden in the case of Bangladesh since 1991 when it resumes democracy as a mode of governance. Since her first term PM Hasina has been cooperating with India on gamut of issues. Bangladesh is not only important for bilateral one but for the deepening relations with Myanmar, which is the key of land entry of India into ASEAN also it is utmost important. It is also important for containing insurgency in our Northeast and for the sustainable development of this far flung region of the country. New government is already in New Delhi (Modi Government) as well. It is known for its nationalist overtones and Bangladeshi migrants were one of the issues in some of the Indian states during just concluding (2014 general) elections. Now dust of elections are over therefore the government must work to fulfill larger canvass of national interests. Engaging Bangladesh will serve this purpose well therefore the new government must carry forward the relationship and make Bangladesh an important regional partner. We could develop gamut of regional platforms as well to enhance our bilateral and multilateral cooperation.

While India should be wary about China's expanding influence with the neighboring countries in general and in Bangladesh in particular, it should also act decisively on policy issues to ensure that the new cooperation forged between China and Bangladesh remains purely on economic terms.

NOTES

1. Nalini Kant Jha, *Domestic Imperatives in India's Foreign Policy* (New Delhi: South Asian Publishers, 2002), pp. 1-10.
2. John W. Garver & Fei-Ling Wang, "China's Anti-encirclement Struggle," *Asian Security*, Vol. 6, No. 3, 2010, pp. 238-261.
3. Kyoko Inoue, "Sub-Regional Relations in the Eastern South Asia: With Special Focus on Bangladesh and Bhutan," Joint Research Program Series No. 132, *IDE, JETRO*, 2004, pp. 15-16.
4. Ruksana Kibria, "The Political Dimension of Bangladesh-China Bilateral Relations," Department of International Relations, University of Dhaka, 2011, p.1.
5. Urvashi Aneja, "China-Bangladesh Relations: An Emerging Strategic Partnership?," *IPCS*, Special Report 33, November 2006, p.3.
6. http://www.bdsdf.org/forum/index.php?showtopic=1920&st=225 [Accessed on 16 September, 2013].
7. Jagannath P. Panda, "Dragon Looks South: Current Drives in China's South Asian Neighbourhood Policy," in Srikanth Kondapalli and Emi Mifune, eds, *China and Its Neighbours* (New Delhi: Pentagon Press, 2010), p.191.
8. Ibid.
9. Piyali Dutta, "India-Bangladesh Relations: Issues, Problems and Recent Development," *Institute of Peace and Conflict Studies*, Special Report no. 97, September 2010, New Delhi, p.10.
10. Iftekhar Ahmed Chowdhury, "Bangladesh-China: An Emerging Equation in Asian Diplomatic Calculations," *Institute of South Asian Studies*, working paper no. 105, 31 March 2010, Singapore, pp. 9-10 and also see Ibid.
11. China and Bangladesh, the Ministry of Foreign Affairs of the People's Republic of China, 25 August 2003. See http://www.mfa.gov.cn/eng/wjb/zzjg/yzs/gjlb/2681/t15842.htm [Accessed on 16 September 2013].
12. http://www.eastasiaforum.org/2011/08/29/the-strategic-implications-of-the-economic-rise-of-china-and-india/ [Accessed on 16 September 2013].
13. Anisul Huq, a leading exporter said: 'The size of China's domestic market for apparels is huge and Bangladesh has unused capacity to supply many categories of garments at competitive prices,' *New Age*, 17 March 2010.
14. Kazi Chesham and Mohammad Mahabubur, "Sino-Bangla Relations and Bangladesh's Look East Policy," *The Daily Star* (Dhaka), 23 May 2005.
15. Ibid.
16. Indeed, Bangladesh had agreed to build a strip of road within Myanmar. The proposal was that China could fund yet another portion connecting it to the Myanmar road system linked to China, which would mean Bangladesh and China would be connected by road, "PM for Direct Road, Rail Links with China," *The Daily Star*, 21 March 2010.

17. Subash Kapila, "Bangladesh-China Defence Cooperation Agreement's Strategic Implications: An Analysis," *South Asia Analysis Group*, Paper No. 582, 14 January 2003.
18. Richard A. Bitzinger, "Asia's Defence Industries: Challenges and Policy Options," *RSIS Commentary*, 15 September 2010 at http://www.rsis.edu.sg/publications/Perspective/RSIS1152010.pdf [Accessed on 16 September 2013].
19. http://www.defence.pk/forums/bangladesh-defence/214660-china-bangladesh-relation.html#ixzz2HNGqhSZo [Accessed on 16 September 2013].
20. http://www.asian-defence.com/2012/10/bangladesh-buying-warship-from-china.html [Accessed on 16 September 2013].
21. "Bangladesh Buying Warship from China," *News Desk* (Dhaka), Vol. 7 Issue 43, 07 November 2012.
22. Ibid.
23. Tarique Niazi, "China's March on South Asia," *Association for Asian Research*, 6 March 2005. http://www.asianresearch.org/articles/2613.html [Accessed on 16 September 2013].
24. "Dhaka-Beijing joint statement outlines closer cooperation," *Daily Star*, 20 March 2010. This article is also the source of other data cited from the joint statement.
25. B. Raman, "Chinese Interest in Hambantota, Chittagong Ports- An Update," *Chennai Centre for China Studies*, C3S Paper No.516, dated June 16, 2010.
26. "Aspects of India's Foreign Policy," *Speech by I.K. Gujral at the Bandaranaike Center for International Studies in Colombo*, Sri Lanka, 20 January 20, 1997, available at http://www.stimson.org/southasia/?sn=sa20020116302 [Accessed on 16 September 2013].

4

Indo-Japan Deepening Relationship in the Context of New Security Architecture of Asia-Pacific

Chandra Mohan Upadhaya

Indo-Japan relations have grown phenomenally since last 15 years. In May 1998 India denoted nuclear devices and welcomed by series of sanctions by all important western countries. Japan and Australia were also included in this list and imposed gamut of sanctions on India. Today in the second decade of 21st century the security architecture of Asia-Pacific is changing very rapidly. Indo-Japan relations are cementing in post-Pokhran scenario. Two millennia ago the seminal Indian strategic thinker, Kautilya stated that foreign policy is only convergences of national interests and other kinds of convergences hardly matters. India and Japan sharing many things but due to divergences of ideology they were almost hostile to each other despite normal business. In 21st century Japan is also confronting against many contemporary problems. Many of these problems are common between both countries. This paper is intended to dwell upon these issues in its larger context. The paper will have four parts; Historical Backgrounds, Cold War Scenario, post-Cold War Scenario and finally Conclusion.

Historical Backgrounds

A unique paradox has defined India-Japan ties. On the one hand is the absence of any major dispute; on the other, the richness in relations has not been fully exploited for many years due to gamut of factors. Looking back in time, the post-Second World War period saw both countries share intellectual discussion and a common vision of Pan Asianism. Japan also held a special place in being a prominent support base for members of the Indian revolutionary freedom struggle. Thereafter, the saga of India-Japan relations was that of benign neglect for much of the Cold War period.

Rich cultural, literary and religious linkages coalesce to provide a positive bedrock to India-Japan relations. Historically, India-Japan relations have existed for more than a thousand years. It is said that Japan first came into contact with India during the reign of Emperor Kimmei (539-571 A.D.).[1]

Buddhism was the first common link between both sides, although it did not really find its way directly between the two countries. Korea was instrumental in introducing Japan to the Buddhist philosophy. Buddhism became the state religion of Japan under the rule of Prince Umayado (593-622 A.D.).[2]

The Buddhists promoted art, culture and philanthropy, thereby gradually spreading the roots of the religion to many parts of the country, even as it branched out into several cults and sects of their own like *Tendai* and *Shingou.*[3] The influence was deep and widespread. According to Haijima Nakamura, "Without Indian influence, Japanese culture would not be what it is today."[4]

These Japanese links with Buddhism in India continue even today with a number of Japanese visitors travelling to cities like Bodh Gaya. The Japanese initiative (along with Singapore) behind the revival of the Nalanda University in Bihar, India as a prominent seat of learning also has its roots and connections with Buddhism. Back in history, Nalanda was a Buddhist seat of learning from the fifth or sixth century CE to 1197 CE and continued to receive support and patronage from a number of Buddhist emperors.

The second vital connection between both sides was a result of the common feeling of Pan-Asianism. During the period of the Indian Renaissance (1881-1905), India was keenly looking at building a spirit of Asian oneness. The trend towards Asian-ness identifying with and aligning with the rest continued as intellectuals like Swami Vivekananda travelled to many parts of the region. Swami Vivekananda visited Japan in 1893 and was impressed by Japanese nationalism.[5]

Despite Japan's aloofness with the rest of the world, the connectivity between India and Japan remained with the fast-growing Japanese spinning industry, which found India as a source of raw cotton. India also became a destination for finished Japanese goods. Perhaps the most significant bilateral contact was that of Indian industrialist J. N. Tata who visited Japan in 1893 and set up an office there. The initiation of trade ties led to the establishment of a Japanese consulate office in Bombay and consulate general office in Calcutta. An Indo-Japanese Trade convention was also signed in 1894 which marked the beginning of "opening of regular ocean transport" between the two sides.[6]

Japanese calls for an Asian identity incorporating countries like Persia, India, China and Japan emerged during the Russo-Japanese war in 1904-1905.

Following its victory in the war with Russia in 1905, Japan came to be perceived as a role model on combating colonialism, even as its own negative imperial dominance was watered down. In India, there was an obvious and vocal admiration of the Japanese success. In her address to the Indian National Congress in 1917, Annie Besant spoke about the Japanese victory. Indian leaders like Gandhi, Nehru, Gopal Krishna Gokhale and Bal Gangadhar Tilak were all unanimous in their jubilation over Japanese victory.

The Japanese responded positively to the Indian enthusiasm. Speaker of the Japanese House of Peers said:

> "It was the sacred duty of Japan as the leading Asiatic state to stretch a helping hand ... to India, who is capable of civilization, and free them from European yoke."[7]

The Congress party decided to follow the *swadeshi* system of boycotting foreign goods, Japanese goods however were excluded from the banned category. In fact, a prominent Indian newspaper *Kesari* clearly called on people to choose Japanese goods over all other foreign manufactured ones.[8]

Any study of India-Japan relations during this period would thus be incomplete without a brief discussion of how prominent Indian revolutionaries like Rash Bihari Bose and Subhash Chandra Bose developed intimate links with Japan. R.B. Bose who came to be known as the "Bose of Nakamuraya" not only took political asylum in Japan, married a native woman, but also spent his entire life in the country as a Japanese citizen (from 1924) till his death in January 1945.[9]

The noted Japanese historian, nationalist and ardent supporter of Indian independence, Shumei Okawa, wrote a book entitled *The Current Status and the Origin of the People's Movement in India* in 1916, in which he warned the Japanese people that by trusting the British they were making a grave mistake and endangering themselves to incurring the wrath of 300 million Indians.[10] There was tremendous public sympathy and contempt for the British government which ordered the deportation of Bose and a few other nationalists from Japan. Japanese groups like the *Genyosha* and *Kokuryukai* began to connect with spirit behind the Indian freedom struggle (despite having ideological differences over the means) as part of their larger aim to work towards the liberation of Asia.[11]

R.B. Bose's legacy of revolutionary streak in seeking independence for India as connecting with the Japanese was in many ways carried forward by another legendry Bose—Subhash Chandra Bose, who was fast emerging on the horizon of the Indian freedom struggle. S.C. Bose came to Tokyo in 1943 via Germany and met R.B. Bose. He had made it clear that he would not mind working with British enemy states—Japan and Germany in his struggle for independence.

Subhash Chandra Bose met Prime Minister Tojo who seemed to be impressed with Bose's intelligence. According to some, the INA had been "encouraged" by the Japanese in the hope that it would lead to a Japanese invasion of India.[12] Bose formed a Japanese-approved and recognized independent "Provisional Government of (Azad Hind) Free India" based in Thailand. In 1943, Bose attended the Greater East Asia Conference in Tokyo. Japan also captured the Andaman and Nicobar Islands and handed them over to Bose's provisional government as a mark of recognition to it.

The Indian National Army then, under the leadership of S. C. Bose decided to enter India with the Japanese Army. Following some initial discomfort over the inclusion of Indian soldiers in its assault on Indian borders, the Japanese conceded. The INA attacked and took over the British post at Mowdok in India. The Japanese had started to feel the heat of the British counter-offensive. The INA reached and captured Kohima (Assam) and their counterpart Japanese forces tried in vain to gain control over Imphal. The combined Indian and Japanese forces finally buckled under British attack and had to retreat in 1944-1945.

On the cultural and literary front, the legendary friendship between Okakura Tenshin and Indian poet Rabindranath Tagore during this period is well known, which cemented ties and even today remains an inspiration for both countries. Okakura first visited Kolkata in 1902 with the aim of inviting Swami Vivekananda for the Parliament of Eastern Religions to be held in Japan. He also utilized this visit to study Indian architecture and arts as well as also assist India in its struggle for freedom through inspiring young Indians to aim for complete independence.[13] Tagore also visited Japan three times and became a key cultural ambassador of India in Japan.

Japan's wartime Prime Minister Tojo referred to India in his speech to the Japanese Diet in 1942 after the defeat of Singapore:

> "This is the best opportunity for India to rid itself of the despotic policy of oppression by the British and participate in building the Greater East Asia Co-prosperity Sphere. The Japanese Empire hopes to restore India to its original status, whereby the nation belongs to Indians, and we will provide all help to the patriotic efforts of the Indian people. It would be really unfortunate if India does not return to its history and traditions; awaken to her mission."[14]

Japan's militarisation and imperialist lash-out in the 1930s, relations between India and Japan began to deteriorate. Japan's advancement into China—the Manchurian Incident, its actions in Korea (1910-1911) eroded the positivity which defined and underlined bilateral relations between both sides. Nehru was critical of Japan and openly critiqued Tokyo for its Westernisation, expansionism and imperialistic tendencies. He noted, "Japan not only followed Europe in industrial methods, but also in imperialistic aggression."[15] Nehru was tilted towards China therefore he could not understand the warmth gestures of the Japanese. He avoided Japan even after independence.

When India gained independence, India took on the yoke of anti-colonialism and anti-imperialism. Nehru organised a conference on Asian relations in March 1947. The Bandung Conference was held in 1955. This was Nehru's "honeymoon" period with China.

However, this enthusiasm did not translate into an upswing in relations as the Cold War also cast its shadow on India-Japan ties. The chill in relations was evident since Japan became an ally of the United States, while India chose to espouse the path of non-alignment, but with a definitive tilt towards the Soviet Union.

The Cold War Era

The end of the cold war has witnessed a new realization of Indian realism based on foreign policy. The launching of "Look East Policy" in 1992 was an important step in this direction as far as Asian balance of power is concerned. In the aftermath of its "Look-East Policy", India economic links with the ASEAN Countries in general and Japan in particular have seen a constant improvement. In 2010-2011, the amount of trade was US$ 57 billion. India and the ASEAN have agreed to work towards meeting an ambitious trade target of US$ 70 billion by 2012. Economic relations with South East Asian countries have emerged as a major pillar of the relationship. With the implementation of India-ASEAN Free Trade Agreement in Goods, trade with ASEAN has grown by 37% to a level of almost $ 80 billion by the end of 2012. In 2011-12, India-Japan bilateral trade was $ 17.7 billion. Bilateral trade reached US$ 16 billion between January-November 2012 and slated to increase rapidly due to inherent nature of growing bonhomie.[16]

We are aware about the fact that divergence of opinions were expressed since the end of the cold war that Asia will be an important player in 21st century world. With end of the cold war new lines were brought by the formulators of foreign policy that both World and Asian system must be multi-polar. This is one of the most significant divergences of interests between India and China, which believes World, must be multi-lateral but Asian balance of power must be uni-polar super headed by China. Japan also thinks similar to Indian line therefore since the end of the cold war, bilateral relationship between India and Japan has been deepening. It is due to growing convergences between both countries. There are diverse shared concern of both countries like the G-4 campaign for enlargement of United Nations Security Council, cooperation to guard against China's hegemonic role in Asia, joint strategies to handle maritime and space security issues, etc. This is vindicated with the frequent high voltage meetings between the leaders of both countries.[17] In comparison with relations with China such bilateral visits are extremely productive. For example, during Prime Minister, Koijumi's visits to India in 2005, an eight fold initiative was launched between both countries. It included the following points:[18]

- Enhanced dialogue and exchanges, including high-level strategic dialogue
- Comprehensive economic engagement
- Enhanced security dialogue and cooperation
- Science and technology initiative
- Cultural and academic initiatives

- Cooperation in ushering a new Asian era
- Cooperation in the UN, specifically for Security Council Reform
- Cooperation in responding to global challenges and opportunities

Particularly India-Japan relationship has grown rapidly since last one decade. Due to inherent geo-political, economic and strategic dimensions this bilateral relationship is all set to reformulate new Asian balance of power based on multiplicity. No concept in the realm of international politics has been discussed more often than balance of power. It has been defined in so many ways, despite diversity of description it has remain an ambiguous idea. Used objectivity or descriptively, the term indicates the relative distribution of power among states into equal or unequal shares. Traditionally, it refers to a state of affairs in which no one state predominates over others. Prescriptively, it refers to a policy of promoting a power equilibrium on the assumption that unbalanced power is dangerous. Prudent states that are at a disadvantage in the balance of power will [or at least should] form an alliance against a potentially hegemonic state or take other measures to enhance their ability to restrain a possible aggressor. Also, one state may opt for a self conscious balancing role, changing sides as necessary to preserve equilibrium. A balance of power policy requires that a state moderate its independent quest for power, since too much power to one state may bring out self-defeating reactions of fear and hostility from other states.[19] China, Japan, India and Vietnam are indulged in the balance of power within Asia and other countries didn't want China's supremacy therefore their bonhomie is deepening in an excellent manner since last one decade and all set to grow in the foreseeable future. In the year 2012, China has exposed that it could use force to take Islands of East China Sea under Japanese rule since many decades. In many areas of China including Hong Kong protests against Japan had been organized which demanded capture of Japan ruled Islands in East China Sea. Including United States, India had also insisted amicable resolution of disputes and adherence with international law by all concerned parties. Because of border disputes, India is also apprehensive about Chinese steps therefore it has strengthened its bilateral relationship with Japan in a massive manner. These events vindicate that balance of power theory is working well in Asian theater and all set to sustain the process due to Chinese reluctance to accommodate the aspirations of other countries.

The new security architecture within Asia is emerging. In this process many traditional players have to lose some power, while some new players are supposed to acquire new acumen in the chessboard of this emerging power game. Long back during the Peloponnesian War, Thucydides (c. 471-400 BC), the great Athenian historian, regarded in the west as the founder of international relations theory, identified the root cause of the war between Sparta and Athens as their struggle for power. He argued, "what made war inevitable was the growth of Athenian power and the fear which this caused in Sparta. In the first stage of the war, Sparta, the predominant power, decided to wage war against Athens ; while in the second stage, Athens, the rising power, was determined to conquer Sparta.[20]

Of course, time and context has changed but the real struggle of power still holds the same dimension.

The new balance of power in Asia is all set to reshape existing security architecture. However the theory of balance of power according to its proponents has come into being with the theory of Prisoner's Dilemma. Balance of power has been one of the most debated concepts of the international relations. The balance of power is a kind of compromise among states that find its order preferable to absolute chaos, even though it is a system that favors the stronger and more prosperous states at the expenses of the weaker. Great powers play the dominant role in balance of power system because of their preponderant military force and their control of key technologies.[21] The cold war era just after the end of the Second World War is a classic example of balance of power between the United States and the Soviet Union. In the post cold war era even the prevalence of the anarchic international environment has created a fear psychosis. Military build-ups and its competition by rival powers have left every harbinger of the international system insecure therefore all countries are trapped in a dilemma. This kind of phenomenon is called the Security Dilemma.[22]

Pandit Jawaharlal Nehru was one of the founders of Non-Alignment Movement just after the end of the Second World War and he insisted that there is a fundamental difference between Asia and Europe. Europe had the legacy of conflict and in contrast Asia had a little legacy of conflict and better spirit of cooperation. According to him

> "There are many ways of distinguishing between what may be called the approach of Asia and the approach of Europe.... Europe has a legacy of conflicts of power, and of problems which come from the possession of power...The European approach is a legacy of the past conflicts of Europe. I do not mean to say that we in Asia are in any way superior, ethically or morally, to the people of Europe. In some ways I imagine we are worse. There is, however, a legacy of conflicts in Europe.... There is no basic legacy of conflict (in Asia).That is a very great advantage for Asia, and it would be folly in the extreme for the countries of Asia, for India, to be dragged in the wake of the conflicts in Europe."[23]

Right from Keshore Madhubani to many pundits of international relations is saying that Asia is emerging but the billion dollar question is why Asian powers are not cooperating and thus negating utopian idea of cooperation among Asian countries better than the European countries dreamt by the Wilsonian practitioner of foreign policy, Nehru. It is the lust of balance of power and historical baggage both are propelling factor of increasing cold war within Asia and thus negating the utopian ideas of Nehru of Asian cooperation. China, India, Japan, South Korea, Indonesia, Iran and Vietnam are some of the important Asian powers. The changing power configuration in Asia has turned Nehru's hypothesis and Asia seems to follow European model of conflict, however the post second world war Europe has emerged as a beacon of cooperation and has won Nobel Prize for peace (2011-12) and must be emulated by other regional groupings. Major Asian countries are not cooperating because there is a divergence of interests among them. China wanted its unipolar dominance over Asia but wanted multi-polarity at the global level. India, Japan, South Korea, Indonesia, Iran and Vietnam wanted both Asia and the globe multi-lateral. Long back Kautilaya, one of the earliest global seminal strategic thinkers had stated that convergences of interests are the basic determinates of foreign policy. There are convergences of interests between India and Japan. This bilateral relationship could be one of the most deepening relationships of 21st century Asia. It is also an open secret that they had average relationship during the cold war. Even after cold war during 1998 Pokhran bomb blast, it took the world by surprise. Many countries including Japan reacted sharply to the tests. It suspended all political exchanges and even economic assistance was frozen for nearly three years. However, a turnaround in the damaged ties was achieved in August 2000, when the then Japanese Prime Minister Yoshiro Mori paid a five-day visit to India. Mori and the then Indian Prime Minister Atal Behari Vajpayee called for a "global partnership." From then on, the relations have witnessed steady progress. During the visit of the Indian Prime Minister Manmohan Singh to Tokyo in 2006 during the tenure of Shinzo Abe, the two Prime Ministers decided to go for a "strategic partnership."

Japan imposed sanctions on India during atomic explosion in 1998. But lot of water has already crossed over the Ganges since then. China-Japan divergences are increasing since last many years. In July 2012, Japan recalled it envoy from Beijing over the disputed territory in the East China Sea.[24] It is another coincidence that in July 2012 only, China refused to issue Visa to an athlete belonging to Arunachal Pradesh, which China perceives it own territory.[25] Despite 17 rounds of high voltage bilateral dialogue till July 2014 there is not an iota of progress over thorny boundary dispute between India and China. Other divergences like water flow from Tibet, trade deficit and many other issues are also sustaining the trust deficit. These prevailing situations have brought India and Japan closer. Chinese officials are worried that the growing relationship between India and Japan are its main rivals in recent years, is meant to contain and counter Beijing. According to two leading foreign policy experts from China Institute of International Studies "India's border dispute with China have yet to be resolved, therefore it views a stronger relationship with Japan as a way to counter balance China's growing influence in the Asia-Pacific region."[26] As China's dispute with Japan escalates over Islands in East China Sea, China seems worried that India will throw its weight in favor of Tokyo. Chinese experts believe that India and Japan share much strategic common ground on China. First time probably in contemporary history, Chinese experts have accepted that India is working on the reciprocation of Chinese policy of encircling India within South Asia and therefore deepening its relationships with all estrange neighbor of China.[27]

It is also a fact that after the end of the cold war India has emerged as a stable economic hub and Japan being one of the biggest global investors has stake with the increasing profile of India at the global level.

India-Japan relations have undergone a significant and qualitative shift in recent years. The government and the people of Japan were appreciative of India's sympathetic response to the earthquake and tsunami that struck the country in March, 2011, and the ensuing nuclear crisis. India sent variety of relief materials. The Japanese Prime Minister, Mr. Yoshihiko Noda, came to India on a State visit on 27-28 December, 2011, for the Annual Summit between the two countries. A Joint Statement titled 'Vision for the Enhancement of India-Japan Strategic and Global Partnership upon entering the year of the 60th Anniversary of the Establishment of Diplomatic Relations was signed by the two Prime Ministers during the Annual Summit. During the visit, the Japanese side renewed its commitment to flagship infrastructure projects like the Delhi-Mumbai Industrial Corridor Project and the Dedicated Freight Corridor West Project, and expressed support for the new Chennai- Bengaluru Industrial Corridor Project.

The External Affairs Minister visited Tokyo for the 5th Strategic Dialogue, which was held on 29 October, 2011. Indian Defence Minister visited Japan from 1-3 November, 2011, for the annual Defence Ministers' meeting. The year 2011 also saw visits by Indian Minister for Parliamentary Affairs, S&T and Earth Sciences (January-February 2011), Minister of Commerce and Industry (February 2011), and Minister of State for Planning, Science & Technology and Earth Sciences (October 2011) to Japan. The Lok Sabha Speaker also visited Japan from 2-6 October, 2011, along with a Parliamentary delegation. In 2011, bilateral trade between the two countries reached $ 17.7 billion.[28] It is expected that this figure will increase further as a result of the India-Japan Comprehensive Economic Partnership Agreement (CEPA), which came into force on 1 August, 2011. For the 8th consecutive year India in 2011 continued to be the largest recipient of Japanese ODA. During the New Delhi visit of the Japanese Prime Minister Noda in December 2011, the Japanese side renewed its commitment to the implementation of flagship infrastructure projects, namely, the Delhi-Mumbai Industrial Corridor project and the Dedicated Freight Corridor West Project and expressed support for the new Chennai-Bengaluru Industrial Corridor project.

United States as a Factor

President George W. Bush ruled 8 years between 2001 to 2008, he had intended to provide a new place to India in Asia, however the foundation was laid down in the last days of President Clinton, when Indian Prime Minister, Atal Behari Vajpayee outlined that United States and India are *natural allies* during his 2000 Washington visit. During President Bush era this relationship was further expanded and put China in a situation which is known as 'Prisoner's Dilemma' in international politics. China was of course one of the factors of President Bush outreach to India. It was clearly articulated by Robert Blackbwill, US Ambassador to India for first two year of President Bush rule.

"President George W. Bush based his transformation of United States-India relations on the core strategic principle of democratic India as a key factor in balancing the rise of Chinese power. To be clear, this was not based on the concept of containing China. As you know, there is no better way to clear a room of Indian strategists than to advocate containing China. Rather, it is centered on the idea that the United States and India in the decades ahead both had enormous equities in promoting responsible international policies on the part of China and that deep United States-India bilateral cooperation in that respect was in the vital national interests of both countries. It was with this strategic paradigm in mind that the Bush Administration treated India with at least as much importance as China."[29]

China looms large in India's mind. The baggage of 1962 still hounds Indian psyche. In the meanwhile India-United States bonhomie remained a sustainable affair since last one decade. China is very sensitive to a growing US-India relationship. China is fearful that this ongoing closeness is bound to weak her position and intended to establish a new balance of power in Asia which must be based on multi-polarity.

Japan-United States bonhomie is one of the oldest in Asia since the end of the Second World War due to prevailing situation during cold war. The post cold war Asian architecture of power has further consolidated U.S-Japan relationship. In recent years, China has been assertive and negating the international law abided rights of neighboring countries particularly in South China Sea and East China Sea and considered both waters as their own lakes. Japan is not weak like other Chinese contested neighbors over water and has challenged China. Interestingly the United States has extended its support to Japan and reaffirmed that International Law must be followed. It has further put strain in the bilateral relationship of Japan and China and in contrast strengthens United States-Japan relationship. This situation is converging with Indian interests therefore since last once decades India-Japan bilateral relationship has emerged as an important determining bilateral relationship in Asia.

This has cornered China at certain extent which forced Chinese policy formulators to admit the importance of cooperation while understanding other sensitivities. It is vindicated by the editorial of June 2009 of 'Global Times' mouth piece of the Chinese government.

"India has long held contradictory views on China. Another big Asian country, India is frustrated that China's rise has captured much of the world's attention. Proud of its 'advanced political system', India feels superior to China. However, it faces a disappointing domestic situation which is unstable compared with China's. India likes to brag about its sustainable development, but worries that it is being left behind by China. China is seen in India as both a potential threat and a competitor to surpass. But India can't actually compete with China in a number of areas, like international influence, overall national power and economic scale. India has apparently not realized this. Indian politicians these days seem to think their country would be doing China a huge favor simply by not joining the 'ring around China' established by the United States and Japan. India's growing power would have a significant impact on the balance in this equation, which has led India to think that fear and gratitude for its restraint will cause China to defer to it on territorial disputes. But this is wishful thinking, as China won't make any compromises in its border dispute with India. And while China wishes to coexist peacefully with India, this desire isn't born out of fear."[30]

China's concerns about expanding Indo-US defense cooperation acquired an extra edge as it saw Tokyo joining Washington in the security outreach to New Delhi. Japan has been the last among the great powers of the world to sense India's rising power potential. However, during the final years of the premiership of Junichiro Koizumi and the brief tenure of Shinzo Abe, Japan has moved rapidly to define a new approach to India.[31] Unlike much of East Asia, India carries no baggage about Japan's history or a grudge against its nationalism. The implementation of the Indo-US nuclear agreement and likely change in Japan's policy on sensitive exports to India could open the doors for a very rewarding high technology partnership between Tokyo and New Delhi. India and Japan have also agreed to expand their current defense cooperation which is focused on securing the sea-lanes in the Indian Ocean, immensely vital for Japanese access to energy and raw materials.[32] Since the United States still remains the biggest balancer of Asia therefore deepening of United States-India relationship has pushed for a better Japan-India relationship. We are aware about the Chinese reservations of the admission of India on East Asian platforms. India did admit on these platforms despite Chinese protest and it has emboldened Japan therefore this relationship is bound to deepen in foreseeable future. Prevailing Sino-Japan trust deficit over gamut of issues has raised ample opportunity for deepening India-Japan relationship. Prime Minister Abe is an old Indian friend. In his previous term also he had vowed for better relations but due to fall of government he could not done much. But after December 2012 Diet election he has secured majority in the Senate also in July 2013 and it has happened in Japan since decades. Russia has also felt the heat of resurgent China particularly in its far east, which is sparsely populated but heaven for natural resources with huge landmass. Chinese have eyed on this far flung Russian region due to its geographical proximity. Despite Kurile Islands dispute between Russia and Japan, warmness has been noticed between estranged allies recently in the aftermath of aggressive Chinese postures against Japan and Russia. In case of East China Sea dispute between China and Japan has deepened. China has meanwhile refused to obey 1982 Laws of the Sea and other relevant international laws. This has propelled the ongoing tension between both rivals and it has charged the atmosphere in East Asia. Needless to say that increasing Russian role in the Asia-Pacific is intended to contain China and of course that is a point where convergences of interests compels India, Vietnam, ASEAN, Australia and the United States to extend their all round support to this initiative.[33]

Since the end of the cold war coincided by the launching of Look East Asia policy, India has given unprecedented importance to Asian balance of power within the contours of its foreign policy. It was emphasized as the core of post cold war Indian foreign policy. It was articulated by Prime Minister, Atal Behari Vajpayee during his 2002 visit of Singapore.

'Look East' policy was not limited to Southeast Asia. Vajpayee declared that geography and politics make India an important part of the Asia-Pacific community and that "it does not require formal membership of any regional organization for its recognition or sustenance".[34]

In recent years India has shed down it Nehruvian shyness and has expressed deep interest in the affairs of all issues of Asia-Pacific. It could be said the India has now initiated third phase of *Look East Policy* [LEP] with special focus of security issues beside other issues of importance. The third phase of the LEP was marked by India's public claim of its engagement in affairs in East Asia and Asia-Pacific at large. The move began by the speech of Indian Defence Minister A.K. Antony in the first ASEAN Defence Ministers' Meetings Plus (ADMM) in October 2010 in Hanoi. Never before had an Indian official publicly supported and committed to secure the freedom and safety of navigation in Asia-Pacific region. It was the bold step which was need of the hour in the changing contours of architecture of balance of power in Asia-Pacific. Including friendly countries of the region, United States is also intended that India must enhance its presence in the region. It was vindicated by the speech of Defense Minister, A.K. Antony:

"The security of sea lanes of communication is vital in today's world. It is in the common interest of nations to keep sea lanes open, secure and free for navigation, trade and energy supplies. Piracy remains a serious challenge for the world community, as we have witnessed in the Gulf of Aden and adjoining areas. The Indian Navy is actively engaged in providing anti-piracy patrolling and escort operations in the Gulf of Aden for over two years now. India is committed to working together with other countries in the efforts to address piracy. The security of sea lanes is important for the Asia-Pacific region, which is now one of the most important drivers of global economic growth. Through the Regional Cooperation Agreement on Combating Piracy and Armed Robbery against Ship in Asia (ReCAAP) and the Malacca Straits mechanisms, we are partnering with other countries in the region to improve the safety of navigation in the region. Cooperative approaches on maritime security would offer benefits for the region as a whole."[35]

Japan is an important power of East Asia. Growing uncertainty between Sino-Japan relationships has given a new twist to Japan-India deepening relationship. India and Japan has been part of many bilateral and multilateral military exercise with like minded countries since last one decade. Defense cooperation and non security threat cooperation like disaster management is also going on. Both countries have maintained high level summits since last many years and trade is also gradually catching up. In the Second half of 2012, China has claimed over the East China Sea Islands which is under Japanese control for last many decades. China is willing to transform its new wield aura to dominate its neighbors which has bitterly resisted by Japan in particular and rest in general. India has not only supported Japan in these disputes but called upon international community to ensure the compliance of the norm of international law of navigation and other rights. China has adopted the globalization process in 1978 almost 13 years ahead of India therefore Japanese companies have invested in China in a massive scale. The conflict over Islands between Japan and other major divergences between China and Japan have sowed the seed of trust deficit between Japan and China. This situation has compelled Japan to rethink over the relocation of their investment in India. Already Japan has increased the pace of investment in India but in the prevailing situation it is bound to further accelerate the pace in India. India also needs to facilitate the investment through immediate clearance. Needless to say that it will be positive for the growth of the Indian economy in a sustainable manner. United States better relationship between Japan and India has further emboldened the scope of this triangular relationship,as three large economics and militaries in Asia are poised to influence the Asian order in foreseeable future.[36] In November 2012, Prime Minster, Dr. Manmohan Singh had scheduled to visit Tokyo for bilateral talks but it got postponed due to sudden announcement of election for the Japanese parliament. Despite that Japanese Prime Minister telephoned Dr. Manmohan Singh and stated that our relationship will be deepening further and that shows the warmness between both countries. Dr. Singh visited Tokyo in the middle of 2013. It also vindicates the point that Japan-India relationship is one of the most important defining Asian and global relationship of 21st century.

In December 2012 former Prime Minister, Shinzo Abe party has returned into power after gaining almost two third majority in the Diet and declared Abe as the new Prime Minister. Since Second World War, Japan is struggling for political stability. In July 2013 Senate elections also PDP and its allies got majority. Frequent change of government has weakened Japan's standing on certain key foreign policy issues. Prime Minister, Abe is known for his strong nationalist views. Asked how he could maintain his staunch stance on the East China Sea islands, called Senkaku in Japanese and Diaoyu in Chinese, while protecting Japan's substantial business interests in China, Abe blamed Beijing for any deterioration in business ties.

"It was wrong for China, as a country responsible to the international community, to achieve a political goal by allowing damages to Japanese-affiliated companies and Japanese nationals that have made contributions to Chinese economy," Abe said. "I want to clearly state that."[37] 9th amendment of the Japanese constitution debars Japan to take military way; it was incorporated after the Second World War devastations. But in the changing context Prime Minister, Abe is intended to repeal this amendment and if done will put another pressure on China due to high technological edge of the Japanese and their glorious military legacy.

In his previous tenure, Prime Minister Abe was known for his inclination for India. In the fast changing geopolitics of East Asia and Chinese assertive initiatives will further cement India-Japan bilateral relationship. Just after his election PM Abe has visited many important ASEAN countries. He has given utmost importance to Vietnam which has been solid container of China since decades. Overall ASEAN came into being against China in 1967 and even today when their bilateral trade has gone over $ 300 billion, trust deficit is still prevailing. ASEAN countries wish that Japan and India should come together and must take principle line of the compliance of the international law to resolve thorny issues including South China Sea.

PM Abe was the chief guest of the 2014 republic day and in December 2013 Japanese king visited India. Although trade and investment has remained low between both of the countries but at the strategic level both are availing excellent relationship. Given the prevailing trust deficit between China and Japan, India-Japan relations are bound to grow and trade and investment will grow simultaneously.

Concluding Remarks

It has been argued by the pundits of globalization that it has reduced the tensions between the countries through trade. China and Japan has huge bilateral trade. But it seems that the soft power of the globalization is not working well. Japanese Prime Minister Shinzo Abe caused a stir in Davos, Switzerland, when he noted in January 2014 that Britain and Germany went to world war in 1914 even though they had close economic ties much as China and Japan have now.[38]

China has immense rivalry over South China Sea with ASEAN countries and over East China Sea with Japan. With the growing economic might China wanted to convert it into military might. Japan being a centuries old powerful country is hell bent to oppose it. India and Japan have convergences of interests in the contemporary global order as well in Asia-Pacific order which is likely to sustain in foreseeable future also. As security analyst Raja Mohan stated "For nearly four decades, Japan-China have had closer relations with each other than India. As they clash today, both attach considerable value to their relationship with India, which has the potential to alter larger Asian context. Rising China's interest is essentially a negative one, to keep the relationship with India tranquil as its confronts Japan in the east. Tokyo's interest is positive, as it seeks to build a strong strategic partnership with Delhi to balance on increasingly assertive Beijing."[39]

Given the Kautilyan notion that there are no permanent friends or foes in foreign policy and only convergences of interests is pushing factor in foreign policy, India-Japan relations are bound to reach new heights in foreseeable future because of the growing convergences of interests. Deepening Indo-Japan relations has the immense potential not to keep Asia multi polar only but intended to propel Indian significance in the larger canvass of the Asia-Pacific.

In May 2014, NDA government has taken over in New Delhi in the leadership of Modi. Modi had visited Japan during his tenure as the Chief Minister of Gujarat. He has personnel connectivity with PM Abe. PM Abe has expressed his desire to welcome Modi in Tokyo during his May 2014 Shangri-La security summit in Singapore. Given the prevailing trust deficit between Japan and China, there is all possibility of proximate bilateral relations with India and Japan. Since both countries are important stakeholder of Asian balance of power therefore their deepening bonhomie is all set to attract more allies of convergences of interests in foreseeable future. This relationship is all bound to go forward and will determine the shape of Asian security architecture.

NOTES

1. David Brewster, "The India-Japan Security Relationship: An Enduring Security Partnership?", *Asian Security*, Vol. 6, No. 2 (2010), pp. 95–120; Bill Emmott, *Rivals: How the Power Struggle between China, India and Japan Will Shape Our Next Decade* (London: Allen Lane, 2008);.
2. Kalidas Nag, "Greater India", *Greater India Society Bulletin*, No. 1, November 1926, p. 32.
3. Ibid, pp. 33-34.
4. Haijima Nakamura, *Japan and Indian Asia* (Calcutta, 1961), p. 1.
5. Birendra Prasad, *Indian Nationalism and Asia, 1900–1947* (Delhi: B.R. Publishing Corporation, 1979), p. 31.
6. T.R. Sareen, "India and Japan in Historical Perspective", *Lecture Series on Japan,* Issue No. 4 (New Delhi: The Japan Foundation), January 2007, pp. 10-11.
7. Ibid, p.15.
8. *Op cit,* No. 5, pp. 44-45.
9. Takeshi Nakajima, *Bose of Nakamuraya: An Indian Revolutionary in Japan,* Translated from Japanese by Prem Motwani (New York: Promilla and Co. Publishers, Bibliophile South Asia, 2005).
10. Ibid, p. 124.
11. Ibid, p. 117.
12. R.B. Smith, "The Tokyo Conference and the Greater East Asia Perspective, 1943", in Chad J. Mitcham (Ed.), *Changing Visions of East Asia 1943–93: Transformations and Continuities* (London: Routledge, 2007), p. 24.
13. Kazuo Azuma, "Meeting of Okakura Tenshin and Rabindranath Tagore as a Great Opportunity", from *Path from India, Path from Japan: Lecture Series on Japan-India Relations,* Compiled by Sengaku Maeda (New Delhi: Northern Book Centre, 2008), pp. 127-140.
14. *Op cit,* No. 9, p. 256.
15. Jawaharlal Nehru, *Glimpses of World History* (Delhi: Oxford University Press, 1989 [1933–1934]), p. 457, as cited in Christopher Jaffrelot, "India's Look East Policy: An Asianist Strategy in Perspective", *India Review*, Vol.2, No. 2, April 2003, p. 39.
16. *Annual Report, 2012-2013,* Ministry of External Affairs, Government of India, New Delhi, 2013, Pp-9-12.
17. While two Indian Presidents visited Japan viz., Rajendra Prasad in 1958, and R. Venkataraman in 1990, Only Japanese Emperor visited India in December 2013. However Japanese Prince visited India twice in 1960 and 1992. Nine Japanese Prime Ministers visited India viz. Kishi in 1957, Ikeda in 1961, Nakasone in 1984, Kaifu in 1990, Miyazawa in 1992, Mori in 2000, Koijumi in 2005, Abe in 2005 and Hatoyama in 2009, while only eight such reciprocal visits were from India viz. Nehru in 1957, Indira Gandhi in 1969,

Rajiv Gandhi in 1985, P.V. Narasimha Rao in 1992, A.B. Vajpayee in 2001, Manmohan Singh in 2006, 2008, 2010 and 2013. MEA Report on India-Japan Relations at http://meaindia.nic.in/meaxpsite/foriegnrelation/japan.pdf.

18. *Ministry of External Affairs Annual Report* 2005-06, Government of India, New Delhi, 2006, p. 34.
19. Grifiths, Martin & Terry O Callaghan, *Key Concepts in International Relations*, Routledge, London, 2004, p. 2.
20. Qing Simei, *From Allies to Enemies: Vision of Identity, and U.S-China Diplomacy, 1945-1960*, Harvard University Press, Cambridge, 2007, p. 297.
21. Griffiths, Martin & Terry O Callaghan, *Key Concepts in International Relations*, Routledge, London, 2004, p. 13.
22. Herz, John, H, Idealist Internationalism and Security Dilemma, *World Politics*, Vol. 2, 1950, pp. 157-158.
23. Jawaharlal Nehru, *India's Foreign Policy: Selected Speeches*, Sept. 1946-April 1961 (New Delhi: Publications Division, Government of India, 1961), pp. 22-23.
24. Japan Recalls China envoy over territory dispute, *The Hindu*, New Delhi, July 16, 2012.
25. Dasgupta, Saibal, MEA fumes as sports min team ignores China sunb, *The Times of India*, New Delhi, 15 July 2012.
26. Dasgupta, Saibal, China sees growing India-Japan ties as move to counter it, *Times of India*, New Delhi, September 20, 2012.
27. Ibid.
28. *Ministry of External Affairs Annual Report*, Government of India, 2011-12, New Delhi, p. 28.
29. "Transcript: Senior Ex-Diplomat on India-United States Relations", *Financial Times Online*, 6 May 2009, available at <http://www.ft.com/cms/s/0/1ec735fe-3a12-11de-8a2d-00144feabdc0.html> .
30. "India's unwise military moves", editorial in *Global Times*, 11 June 2009, available at <http://opinion. globaltimes.cn/editor-picks/2009-06/436167.html>.
31. James Lamont, "United States agrees weapons sales to India", Financial Times, 20 July 2009, available at <,http://www.ft.com/cms/s/0/663e6e04-7507-11de-9ed5-00144feabdc0.html.
32. Gurpreet S. Khurana, "Security of Sea Lines: Prospects for India-Japan Cooperation", *Strategic Analysis*, Vol.31, No.1, January 2007.
33. Dr. Indrani Talukdar, A 'Reset' in Russia and Japan Relationship? Indian Council of World Affairs, 3 March, 2014, p.1.
34. Atal Behari Vajpayee, "India's Perspectives on ASEAN and the Asia-Pacific Region", 21st Singapore Lecture, Institute of Southeast Asian Studies, 9 April 2002, available at http://www.iseas.edu.sg/ vajpayee.pdf.
35. India calls for cooperative approach to ensure security of sea lanes, *Asian Military Review*, October 12, 2010.http://www.asianmilitaryreview.com/News/index.php?hNewsId=1359.
36. Chenllancy, Brahma, *Asian Juggernaut: The Rise of China, India and Japan*, Harper Collins, New Delhi, 2006.
37. China's island dispute moves 'wrong': New Japan PM, *The Daily Star*, Dhaka, January 11, 2013.
38. KEITH BRADSHER, Philippine Leader Sounds Alarm on China, *New York Times*, New York, February 5, 2014.
39. C. Raja Mohan, Retooling for a new Asia, *The Indian Express*, New Delhi, January 23, 2014.

5

Role of Russia in Emerging Asia-Pacific

Deepak Yadav

The Asia-Pacific region has been identified as the world's new center of gravity. The emerging new architecture revolving around Asian powers has given rise to questions about Russia's role in the region, given that the Eurasian giant has an Asian presence in the Far East. The mutual threat perceptions between Russia and other Asian nations have altered over the course of Twenty years since the collapse of communism. Russia is now recognized as a non-threatening great power with global significance. The Asia-Pacific has always been a region of great importance for super powers throughout Cold War and after due to its unique geo-political and geo-economic importance. Both USA and USSR was engaged in a great ideological battle to get hold on this region and this is still continuing even after end of Cold War. Russia has a long and varied history as a serious strategic player in Asia. It is only recently that it has been completely written off by the end of the Cold War and its attendant beliefs in the end of geopolitics. The mutual threat perceptions between Russia and other Asian nations have certainly altered over the course of 20 years since the collapse of communism, and Russia is now widely recognized as a non threatening great power with global significance. However, regional analysts are still skeptical over the degree to which Russia's vested interests lie in Asia, and whether these interests are compatible with those of other regional players.

Russia is distinctly interested in Asia-Pacific affairs because more than two-thirds of its territory is situated in this region. Development of the rich natural resources of Siberia and the Far East will be of exceptional importance for the future progress of Russia and the many states of the Asia-Pacific. The population of these areas is small compared to the total population of Russia. This makes it even more important to ensure transparency, predictability, stability, and security along the vast perimeter of Russia's eastern boundaries. On the whole, inter-state relations in the Asia-Pacific region and the trajectories of their evolution are favorable and meet the fundamental interests of Russia. The developments in the Asia-Pacific deeply affect the political and economic climate worldwide. During recent decades, the economic center of the world has been moving gradually toward the Asia-Pacific, and the international relations in the region are becoming more and more important in global affairs.

Russia consistently supports the establishment of a just and democratic world order based on strict observance of the international legal norms, goals, and principles of the UN Charter and on comprehensive security, sovereign equality, and mutual respect for the legitimate interests of all states. The fact that the vast majority of the Asia-Pacific states share this approach seems to explain why peace and stability prevail in the region. Since the Cold War ended, the political situation in the Asia-Pacific has been relatively stable and predictable. Many Asia-Pacific states have mutual territorial claims, and sometimes these contradictory claims can lead to drastic and even dangerous conflicts. However, these states have practical experience in solving such problems, which helps to avoid military action, material damage, and loss of human life. The agreements on the mutually acceptable demarcation of a huge part of the border between China, on the one hand, and Russia, Kazakhstan, Kyrgyzstan, and Tajikistan, on the other hand, are a good example of this problem-solving skill. India and China also have good prospects for settling their border claims.

Although the Southeast Asian countries and China have not agreed on the ownership of the Spratly and Paracel Islands, they have elaborated a Code of Conduct in the South China Sea and are looking forward to arrangements for joint exploitation of the areas in dispute. Russia welcomes the commitment of the countries participating in developing the Code of Conduct because it is an important step in resolving the territorial dispute. Rather than resuming their confrontation over two islands near the east coast of Kalimantan, Malaysia and Indonesia opted to settle their dispute through the International Court of Justice.[1] From time to time, the dispute over the Senkaku Islands ignites, but in words rather than military actions. Today, when inter-state relations in Asia have a five relatively low conflict potential, it is unlikely that territorial disputes could generate a serious challenge to regional security and stability.

The growing interest of Russian military-industrial and energy companies in Southeast Asia will give Russia cause to become increasingly interested in the security and stability of vital water corridors in the waters of East Asia. Despite protests from Beijing, Russia is intensifying its connections with Vietnam, arranging for joint oil and gas exploration and signing military contracts, including the sale of six submarines in 2009. Thailand, Indonesia, Laos and Malaysia are among other potential targets for Russia's armament deals. Most of those countries are America's partners in the "hub and spokes" cooperative security system and their close relations with Russia will only prove beneficial for the U.S., as Moscow would be more inclined to engage in conflict resolution that might erupt between China and them. Another area of joint interest is North Korea and nuclear non-proliferation. As stated in the Russian Foreign Policy Concept, political stability in Asia is crucial to Russia foreign policy priorities, especially on the question of non-proliferation. The readiness to participate in Korean talks and enforce a peaceful resolution is even more evident when placed in the context of Moscow's ambition to build a Trans-Korean railroad and a direct pipeline from the Russian Far East to the Korean market.[2]

The USSR was feared until the late 1980s for its bold force projection into the South Pacific and Indian Ocean. Some, such as Richard Herr, openly worried that the U.S. and Australian policy of "strategic denial" vis-à-vis the USSR in the South Pacific had failed, and that regional governments had better acquaint themselves with this new reality. Canberra and Washington even worried that, in a nuclear war with the Soviet Union, the Naval Communications "North West Cape" facility would be a tempting first target—either by a nuclear strike or Special Forces raid—to prevent an American retaliation from the nuclear submarines which the base commanded. In fact, the Soviets, according to one among their ranks, carried out some of their training in the deserts of Kazakhstan to mimic the arid conditions of the Australian desert in the event of a future raid. Since the 1990s, many have perceived Russia as a feeble giant with clay feet. This soundly demonstrates the current dismissive consensus around Russia's role in Asia. This default position made sense when Russia was indeed riddled by chronic internal ills, violent conflicts, economic misery, separatism, a public health collapse, and the largest peace-time depopulation in recorded history. But it no longer makes sense today.

Russia-China Strategic Co-operation and the Geopolitics of Asia-Pacific

Russia being the largest country and China being the most populous country on the planet, both collectively are undoubtedly the two major powers of the international system. Russia being the successor of erstwhile Soviet Union wishes to regain the role once Soviet Union enjoyed whereas China being a communist country is also showing signs of new ambitions based on her history, population and military power and also her emergence as an important international economic actor. Relations between Moscow and Beijing have gone full circle in the past half century, from alliance to containment and now to strategic partnership.

To understand the ebbs and flows in Moscow's China policy it is necessary to look into the Soviet history. History which is characterized as chronicle of the past provides the solid base for building up future relationships. In International

Relations, there is no permanent 'friend or foe', today's bitter enemy can become tomorrow's staunchest ally. It is interest which runs supreme, and Russia and China are not exceptions to it. Despite being communist countries both Soviet Union and China counted each other as enemy number one and targeted each other with their nuclear weapons. But today Russia and China no longer consider each other as enemy and both countries have developed "very deep" relations in the strategic field.

China has the largest population in the world, while Russia is the largest nation in terms of territory. Both are permanent members of the United Nations Security Council. Obviously, the significance of Sino-Russian relations extends far beyond the interests of the two nations. It also affects the stability of Asia and the world at large.

Soviet-China relations before disintegration of USSR were characterized by a number of ups and downs. In February 1950 just four months after establishment of the PRC the two countries signed the treaty of Friendship, Alliance and Mutual Cooperation. The first half of the 1950s was the honeymoon period. However, by the late 1950s differences in national interest and ideology emerged leading to serious disputes in early 1960s which developed in to acute conflict and border clashes in 1969. Hence in the late 1960s and 1970s the USSR regarded China as one of its main rivals and stationed approximately one million troops and one third of its SS-20 intermediate-range ballistic missile along the Sino-Soviet border, threatening to make a 'surgical' first strike on China', nuclear bases. Under serious threat, China had to prepare for a military intrusion from north. However, in 1980s two countries came to realization that these were not in the interests of either side and they made effort to alleviate the situation. These efforts resulted in the normalization of the relations during a state visit to Beijing by the then Soviet President Mikhail Gorbachev in May 1989. (Qimao, 1999, pp. 206-207)[3]. In the words of Gorbachev, 'New Thinking' stood for—

> "We need normal international conditions for our internal progress. But we want a world free of war, without arms races, nuclear weapons and violence, not only because this is an optimal condition for our internal development.". (Gorbachev, 1987: 10-12).[4]

On 15 September 1992, President Yeltsin signed the "Order of Russian Federation's Relations with China" and reaffirmed that—

(a) there is only one China;
(b) the PRC government is the sole legal representative of China;
(c) Taiwan is the part of China; and
(d) Russia will never establish official relation with Taiwan.[5]

Both Russia and China are opposed to US hegemonic policies and favour a multi-polar world order with different power centres. In April 1997 Chinese president Zemin paid another visit to Moscow on April 23 and the two countries issued a joint statement on the multipolarisation of the world and establishment of new international order. The statement rejected hegemony and power politics, and stated that 'Cold War' mentality must also be abandoned and bloc politics opposed. They called for preservation of the Anti Ballistic Missile (ABM) Treaty of 1972 between Soviet Union and USA and they supported lifting the UN Security Council sanctions against Saddam Hussain regime in Iraq.

On 24 November 1998, when Jiang Zemin paid another crucial visit to Russia, the Russian side reaffirmed its "four nos" position. The basic thrust of which was—no support for any conception of 'Taiwan's independence; no acceptance of the position of 'two Chinas' or 'one China and one Taiwan'; no support for Taiwan's participation in the UNO or other international organizations in which only sovereign states participated; and no sales of weapon to Taiwan. [6]

NATO bombing on Yugoslavia from March end to mid June 1999 without getting any authorization from the UN Security Council sent shock waves in both Russia and China and tended to bring together the two in joint opposition of NATO action. NATO's intervention on 'humanitarian ground' was an ominous development. Being multi-ethnic and multi-religious states, both Russia and China have their own separatist movements, Russia in Chechnya and China in Taiwan, Tibet and Xinjiang province. Being a Slav country, Yugoslavia was traditionally friend of Russia and attack on it, aroused Russian sentiments in the form of massive protests in Moscow.[7]

Both Russia and China have greater common ground to chalk out their strategy to deal with outside world compare to the issues on which they are at odds. Russo-Chinese link is built on a number of shared concerns which includes:

- The struggle against US led unipolar hegemonism;
- Unilateral humanitarian interventionism by passing UN;
- Islamic extremism and secessionism;
- Opposition to NATO enlargement and inter-reference in the internal matters;
- Opposition to NMD(National Missile Defence) and TMD(Theatre Missile Defence);
- Opposition to US withdrawal from ABM Treaty of 1972;
- Restructuring of UN;
- Opposition to US led NATO forces to stay longer in the Central Asian region;
- Near mutual acceptance of Russia's hegemony as a guarantor of order in Eurasia;
- Strengthening the SCO; and
- Working together in the multilateral forums like WTO etc.

The declaration of 'New World Order in 21st Century' confirms that relations between two 'headed eagle' and 'dragon' have reached on its height. Both countries have gone very far and deep in their defence translations and no longer count each other as enemies. Their defence personnel, scientists, students are getting training in each other's establishments. Russia is building up nuclear reactors in China and has offered partnership in the state in the state owned space agency GLONASS which itself indicates the comfort level in their ever flourishing bilateral relations.

One of the prime reasons for developing close ties between Moscow and Beijing in the US factor, the common cause of concern for the both countries. US's continuous military and economic support to Taiwan and its huge military presence poses grave threat to the Chinese sovereignty. USA has also agreed to deploy TMD technology to Taiwan, which may virtually neutralize Chinese missile capabilities and would disturb the strategic balance in the region.

Russia is consistently under immense pressure from western human rights groups and media on the issue of human rights violations in the Chechnya war. These groups had virtually shut their eyes on Moscow Theatre tragedy and Beslan School crisis in which hundreds of Russian people lost their lives. It shows as if these human rights groups and media people are acting at the behest of their respective governments to settle their political goals with Moscow. When the issue of human rights violations by US forces comes from Iraq or Afghanistan, these groups keep their mouth shut.

To neutralize these double standards on terrorism, both Russia and China call for implementation of UN charter and International Laws globally without any fear or favour. The most frequent violator of international laws, Israel always go unpunished due to overt and covert support from the USA but a single incidence of Tianmen Square in China made her virtually untouchable in the international politics.

Initially there was some opposition within the Russian establishment to the entry of the US troops in Central Asia, an area of traditional Russian influence. However, subsequently, Moscow decided to allow air corridors, the use of its bases for the search and secure operations as well as sharing of intelligence regarding the terrorist networks operating in Afghanistan. Uzbekistan offered its airspace and bases to the US troops ahead of other CARs, whereas Moscow preferred to maintain the façade of coordinated stand of all the CIS states. Kyrgyzstan claimed that the granting of Manas air base was coordinated in advance with its partners in the CIS Collective Security Treaty.

Manas airbase of Kyrgyzstan is just 200 miles away from Chinese territory from where US troops can keep their eye on Chinese troop movements. Presence of US troops in such a close to Chinese border made security expert in Beijing uncomfortable. Beside military bases in Pakistan and Kyrgyzstan, US acquired military bases in Baghram and Kandahar in Afghanistan and bases of Khanabad in Uzbekistan.

Development of closer ties between Russia and US, especially after coming of Obama regime is causing concerns in Beijing. Before Obama regime, Bush administration worked closely with Russia especially after September 2001 terrorist attack.

After the September 11, 2001 attacks on New York and Washington and subsequent military action taken by US and NATO against Al-Qaeda and Talibans have radically altered the geopolitical situation in Central Asian Region. Russia and Central Asian republics acquired a prominence place in the US military strategy in Afghanistan military bases in Baghram and Kandahar in Afghanistan and the bases of Khanabad in Uzbekistan. It is believed that these facilities helped US military to quickly establish air superiority thought Central Asia and even to the Middle East. It is believed that in offering bases to the USA, the Central Asian States sought security against the threat of terrorist attacks as well as gain maneuvering space vis-à-vis Russia and China. CARs hoped to gain financially from the US presence.

The impact of post-September 11 developments on China has been the mixed one. China gained in so far as combating international terrorism became the number one task of the US policy. Prior to it economically and militarily growing China was increasingly being projected as emerging strategic rival of sole super power. China reluctantly, joined the international community in supporting the US war against terror but with certain conditions. China wanted UNSC to play central role in the war against terrorism as a guarantee against the US unilaterism. In fact China insisted that struggle against terrorism also includes the 'East Turkistan' terrorist forces or the Uighur separatist movement in Xinjiang province.[8]

There is no doubt that the prospects of a prolonged US military presence in Central Asian region are not welcome to either Russia or China. Post September 11 developments in the region are seem as a set back to SCO, because SCO was created to forge Russia-China partnership in the Central Asia for jointly maintaining peace, stability and economic cooperation in the region and keep a check on the Western influence in the region.

Russian and Chinese interests also converge on the issue of eastward expansion of NATO. First time ever NATO crossed the border of a non-NATO remember country i.e. Afghanistan in the name of fight against terrorism. Both Russia and China opposed the bombing on Belgrade, the capital of Yugoslavia in 1999. Also the US B-2 bombers dropped bomb on Chinese embassy in Belgrade causing many casualties. These incidences proved beyond doubt that US led NATO forces are crossing their granted mandate in the name of fight against terrorism and in the name of humanitarian intervention. Russia and China have their own set of problems in Chechnya and Xinjiang respectively.

At the time when NATO bombing was on, the 50th anniversary celebrations of the founding of NATO took place in Washington in which all the former Soviet republics with exception of Russia participated. What aroused the further Russian and Chinese concern and even the concern in countries like India was the enunciation of new strategies doctrine of NATO that permitted use of force by it in regions beyond the areas of its traditional responsibility comprising the territories of its member states. So, now NATO forces could be used anywhere.

Against such unilateral hegemonism of the US and NATO. Russia-China wants a multipolar world with many power centres. The declaration between Yeltsin and Jiang Zemin in 1997 openly talked about establishment of multipolar world based on principles of Panchsheel. Both call for respect of State sovereignty, equality of states eschewing of pursuit of hegemony, non-interference in internal affairs of other states, an equitable and just economic order and the strengthening of UN. Both Russia and China also seeks to work closely with NAM and champion the cause of third world.

The major bone of contention in the smooth relation was border dispute which is now resolved. China has not only settled in border dispute with Russia but also with the Central Asian Republics in a peaceful manner. With the border dispute gone there is no any serious issues left between Russia and China to doubt each other's intention.

Peaceful solution of Korean Peninsula problem is also in the priority list of Russia and China. The proposed NMD system of the USA is expressly aimed at providing defence against the 'rogue' states like Iran, Iraq and North Korea etc. The launch of Pyongyong's rocket over Japan in 1998 provided justification to US for such apprehensions. Russia and China therefore, have sought to minimize the perception of North-Korean threat. They favour a rapprochement between North and South Korea and one between US and North Korea.

To counter the eastward expansion of NATO and with drawl of US from ABM Treaty of 1972, President Putin made an overture to European Union and NATO to reach some compromise solution. He called upon to EU and NATO to join forces with Moscow and set up a joint anti-missile shield during his visit to Rome on 5th June, 2000. He said that such a system will avoid creating problems linked to an imbalance in the equilibrium of forces and ensures 100 percent security to European countries.[9]

As far as economic ties between Russia and China are concerned, it lag behind political, diplomatic, strategic and military ties. It is apparent that the two countries are also to create economic interdependence. The economies of the two countries are mutually complementary. Russia is the major producer and supplier of energy while China is energy hungry and its needs are growing. Russia's main exports apart from defence equipments include fertilizer, steel, timber and machinery, while its main imports are consumer goods and food items.

There are some major pre-requisites for further growth in the scale and diversifications of Russo-Chinese economic collaboration. These are implementing joint programmes in the fuel and energy sector; stepping up cooperation in the field of investment; involving Russian companies in the strategy of accelerated development of China's western region; expanding cooperation between the two countries' border region and cooperation in the manufacturing sector and joint mastering of high technologies.

By strengthening trade with China, Russia will try to reduce its shortage of light industrial goods and electronics, create an economic infrastructure using cheap Chinese labour in the less developed areas of Russian Far East. Russia will also be able to reduce the financial crunch of its arms manufacturing units by selling weapons to China which includes more than $2 billion every year. Russia can also benefit by sending part of its well educated labour force to China to help create high technology industries and reduce the chronic unemployment among highly educated youths.[10]

On the other hand China will get benefitted by sending a certain amount of its unskilled labour force to Russia to work in the unstaffed industries. The excess of labour force available in China is about 200 million. This arrangement will reduce some burden of unemployment among Chinese people. In addition, China will have a chance to participate in the economic opening of oil fields resources in Russian Far East and Siberia.[11]

Conclusion

Given the contours of the Sino-Russian strategic partnership and its likely durability, what should be the U.S. response? Perceiving this partnership as a full-fledged alliance, directed across the board against U.S. interests, is a mistake. The common rhetoric is easy to sustain, but what will happen if the United States negotiates with Russia in earnest on an antiballistic missile compromise? Would Chinese opposition to changes in the regime really block a bilateral deal? Are China's interests really engaged in NATO enlargement?

Sino-Russian cooperation will not markedly change questions on issues such as Taiwan or NATO enlargement. These issues remain bilateral or regional; the outside partner has little standing. Moreover, issues such as these remain subject to a dynamic outside the control of the distant partner. Russia will act in its own interests in Europe, and China in Asia. For example,

China remains comfortable with a framework in Korea that excludes Russia and Japan. Russia's European interests could well lead it much closer to Europe and the European Union in the years ahead. Chinese analysts can not confidently exclude the European turn they feared in the early 1990s. Chinese economic interests place the United States, Japan, and a wide variety of Asian countries far ahead of Russia.

Although Sino-Russian economic ties have expanded, they have not reached the levels outside the arms trade that many in Moscow expected or hoped. Sino-Russian cooperation at the UN could make future peacekeeping operations more difficult to negotiate (e.g., Macedonia) or make vetoes more likely as both countries now hold leverage over this body. Although current U.S.-Russian differences are serious, U.S.-Russian strategic talks on missile defense could yield a satisfactory outcome for Moscow that would complicate the situation in Beijing. Moreover, serious challenges have not yet arisen in Central Asia, though the next decade will bring changes of leadership, regional instability, and other problems there. If sustained Chinese migration pressure appears in the Russian Far East, the current strategic partnership will be difficult to maintain. Washington still controls many levers of influence, and the most ambitious bilateral expressions of solidarity and cooperation have yet to be tested.

The most important near-term consequence of Sino-Russian partnership is a negative one: the Russian contribution to Chinese military modernization. For the foreseeable future, China will have an enduring need for Russian military technology and systems, while Russia will have a variety of reasons to sell. Official statements from senior Russian defense officials indicate that they believe Russia has a long lead on China in key military capabilities and thus that current sales do not create a military threat to Russia itself. Russia's own economic problems and the ideological motivations of some in the Russian foreign policy community create incentives for sales, not restraint. These sales—and the broader defense and technology cooperation that is linked to them—could in time alter regional military balances in areas of vital U.S. interest in East and Southeast Asia or the Taiwan Strait. China does not need to match the military of the United States and its allies to affect this alteration. It need only develop capabilities that substantially raise the cost of U.S. intervention in the region.

Russia and the United States have gamut of divergences but many convergences. The situation of Iraq and Afghanistan may bring both closer. Although China-Russia relations have gone up in recent years by all counts but still trust deficit is prevailing due to inherent divergences particularly on strategic issues. Russian Far East is under threat due to Chinese immigration. The escalating trust deficit between China and Japan in East Asia is very close from this region. This region has abundance of natural resources. In addition this area has huge sea coast therefore Japan has also intensified its relations with Russia in recent years particularly after December 2012 when PM, Shinzo Abe has taken over. The United States has obvious interest to keep Asia-Pacific multi-polar and that is also Russian national interests. Despite many divergences this particular pressing need could be facilitator of better Russia-United States bonhomie and needless to say that it could be detrimental for China. Long back the Chinese have forgotten the advice of Deng, who advised not to assert militarily and sustain economic growth. The Chinese assertiveness in South China and East China Sea has alarmed the regional countries too and Russia is not aloof from this impending danger. In recent years Russia has reformulate its Asia-Pacific policies to cope with the emerging situation and make alliances with like minded countries in the region. Russia is all set to advocate multiplicity in Asia-Pacific which China is bound to oppose therefore in foreseeable future trust deficit is bound to propel between both countries.

NOTES

1. Rouben Azizian and Boris Reznik (2006), *Russia, America, and Security in the Asia-Pacific,* Asia-Pacific Center for Securities Studies, Honolulu, pp. 23-33.
2. Anton Barbashin, "A Pacific Vision for Russia and USA," *The Diplomat,* December 6, 2013.
3. Qimao, Chen (1999), "Sino-Russian Relationship after the Break Up of the Soviet Union" in Chaufrin Gennady (eds.), *Russia and Asia: Emerging Security Agenda,* New York: SIPRA, OUP.
4. Gorbachev, Mikhail (1987), *Perestroika: New Thinking for our Country and the World,* London: Collins. pp. 123-128.
5. Chufrin, G. (1999), *Russia and Asia: The emerging Security Agenda,* New York: Sipri Oxford University Press, pp. 292-296.
6. Jingjie, L. (2000), "Pillars of the Sino-Russian Partnership", *Orbis,* 44(4): 527-539.
7. Saiget, Robert J. (2000), *China, Russia beef up cooperation on Ethnic Separatism, Taiwan, Terrorism,* Hong Kong: AFP.PP.102-110.
8. Moltz, Clay (1995), "Regional Tensions in Russo-China Rapprochement", *Asian Survey,* 35(36): pp.23-54.
9. Menon, Rajan and Charles E. Ziegler (2002), "The Balance of Power and US Foreign Policy Interest in the Russian Far East" in Thorton J and Ziegler E.C. (eds.), *Russia's Far East a region at risk,* London; University of a Washington Press, pp.17-23
10. Shaumian, T.L. (2003), "Geopolitical Changes in Central Asia and Positions of Russia, China and India" *China Report,* 38(3): 361-363.
11. Mikhail Alexseev, "'The Chinese Are Coming': Public Opinion and Threat Perception in the Russian Far East," *Program on New Approaches to Russian Security: Policy Memo 184* (Washington, D.C.: Council on Foreign Relations, January 2001).

6

Reinforcing India-ASEAN Connectivity

Ganganath Jha

India attaches importance to its connectivity with ASEAN and this matter is on the top of its agenda of cooperation. The connectivity is bound to contribute to people-to-people ties and strengthen strategic, cultural and economic relations. Although geographically, ASEAN region was linked with India, but this factor was not given due consideration in post-independence era. When we compare ourselves with China in Southeast Asia, we find that China has built roads and bridges even in those areas which were inaccessible in the past. The Chinese connectivity from Kunming to Yangon, Vientiane, Hanoi and Bangkok have improved their economic and strategic profile in the area. They have build an infrastructure to nurture commercial interests in the region and they are destined to play an important role in regional economic and strategic matters. On the other hand, India which possessed an effective trading infrastructure in the region during the Colonial period, found them inaccessible in the post-independence era. The Stilwell Road, traversing through Kolkata, to Kunming via Assam and Mandalay, was broken during the Second World War and it was not repaired due to several reasons. China came under communist system and it was then interested in exporting revolution. The strategic developments in the Northeast region of India were also not favourable to think about business and trade via that region. The insurgents in Assam, Nagaland, Mizoram and Manipur and on the other hand, in Myanmar's Chin and Kachin areas were too disturbing. The emergence of East Pakistan, (Bangladesh), created barriers in the path of smooth passages in that region. When Myanmar came under military rule in 1962, India felt strategic setbacks and connectivity became disturbed. Above all, when India was militarily defeated by China in 1962, it changed the perspectives and mindset of the nation.

The idea of Afro-Asian solidarity was diluted and anti-China propaganda became prominent. Subsequently the creation of Bangladesh in 1971 and the projection of some Americans that like Pakistan India too will disintegrate turned India inward looking. The formidable creation of Pindi-Beijing-Yangon axis fomented seeds of secessionist violence on India's northeast and Western regions and thus security matters alone attracted the attention of our decision makers.

There were other developments also which obstructed our relations with eastern neighbours. The Cold War politics of the two super powers drove India to support the Soviet outlook and ASEAN supported the Americans. India opposed the US containment drives in Southeast Asia and supported Vietnam's struggle against the Americans. On the other hand, the ASEAN countries supported the US by providing the bases and manpower to crush communist movements in the region. The political differences, the ideological nuances, the economic and security priorities between India and ASEAN were vastly different and neither India nor ASEAN were interested in business matters amongst them. India had become almost isolated in the ASEAN region because of ideological considerations. ASEAN believed in market economy and India in controlled economy. ASEAN pursued privatization policies and India supported nationalization. However when the Soviet system failed and disintegrated in 1991, new world order started taking shape. Certain norms for democracy, human rights, environment and free trade were to be evolved to suit the interests of the Western World. Thus there were prescriptions and suggestions how to pursue democratic values, how to define human rights, how to award patent rights and how to conduct free trade at the global level. The prescriptions generally were meant for the countries in the third world and this phenomenon alerted them to form new combinations and groupings to cope with the challenges.

Hence ASEAN began to think seriously of India and other countries in the neighbourhood and the kind words of ASEAN leaders towards India started coming out in the media and the government circles. This generated positive response in India, which too was keen to review its domestic and foreign policies to cope with the challenges of the emerging new world order. It began to talk about Look East policy to nurture fraternal ties with Southeast Asia and remove all hindrances in the path of closer relations. Prime Minister of India, P.V. Narasimha Rao (1991-95) undertook the task of economic restructuring and reforms to bring about suitable conditions for economic and strategic cooperation with the outside world. When Singapore proposed that India should be offered the dialogue partnership of ASEAN, India readily agreed. India did not hesitate to be associated as a sectoral partner in 1992. Thus the formal relations of India with ASEAN started at the institutional level. The partnership proved successful, and this level of relationship was upgraded to the status of Dialogue Partnership in 1995. Thus India became a full fledged member of ASEAN Regional Forum (ARF) which is a forum to discuss security matters. Although sectoral partnership was confined to cooperate in trade, investment, tourism, science and technology sectors only, but dialogue partnership enabled India to take part in broader security and economic matters.

In realistic terms, ASEAN would always like to promote business relations with India and other South Asian countries. Indian diplomats are trained in protocol matters and they are generally more interested in extra-business matters. The mission to do only business is beyond their comprehension. The contemporary trends indicate that candidates selected into foreign service belong to engineering, medical or social science stream and the percentage of economists in IFS are low. Most of them do not have the knowledge of the language of the country where they are posted. They are generally transferred from the Embassy by the time they get certain level of understanding of that country. Moreover there are plum posting in some ASEAN countries and diplomats do lobby support to get them to enrich themselves. In order to promote multi-faceted relations, dedicated and specialized experts are needed and that is possible only with the structural reforms in IFS system of recruitments and training. The business sense of our diplomats is to be fine-tuned to cope with the challenges in the ASEAN region. However, we find that Indian government is determined to pursue the policy of togetherness and partnership with ASEAN and Indian business houses and their research Wings—FICCI, ASSOCHAM and others—provide necessary feedback to promote trade and investment relations. We have proved successful in ASEAN due to their insights and our trade figures are going to touch $ 70 billion in 2012. We have already signed Free Trade Agreement (FTA) with ASEAN and expressed faith in the "ASEAN Way". We are fully acquainted that ASEAN is striving to community building as per the Bali concord II and it will be in order here to explain the meaning and contents of that charter. The objective of ASEAN community declared in 2003 is to promote greater political, economic and socio-cultural cooperation amongst the member states through the ASEAN Security Community (ASC), the ASEAN Economic Community (AEC), and the ASEAN Socio-cultural community (ASCC).[1] Noem M. Morada has explained that the ASC is envisioned to elevate further political and security cooperation to live at peace with one another and with the world at large in a just, democratic and harmonious environment. Its norms and principles emphasize (a) reliance on peaceful processes in the settlement of intra-regional differences; (b) subscription to the principle of comprehensive security rather than to a defence pact, military alliance or a joint foreign policy; (c) promotion of regional solidarity and cooperation; and (d) abiding by the UN Charter and other principles of international law and uphold ASEAN's principles of non-interference, consensus based decision making, national and regional resilience, respect for national sovereignty, the renunciation of the threat or the use of force, and peaceful settlement of differences and disputes.[2]

The second aspect of ASEAN Community—the AEC—is aimed at the creation of a stable, prosperous and highly competitive ASEAN economic region where there is a free flow of capital, goods, investments, and services that would lead to equitable economic development and significant reduction of poverty and socio-economic disparities in the region by 2020. It also envisions ASEAN as a single market and production base, where there is a deeper and broader level of economic integration of its members, and the benefits of integration contributes to the narrowing of the development gap between the more developed and less developed ASEAN countries.[3] In order to achieve AEC, the Association has identified 11 priority sectors of cooperation, which include: (a) agro-based products, (b) automotive, (c) electronics, (d) fisheries, (e) rubber based products, (f) textiles and apparel, (g) wood-based products, (h) air-travel, (i) information and communication technology, (j) health care, and (k) tourism. Road maps for each of the priority sectors in the form of framework agreements and protocols are desired to serve as the basis of economic integration.[4]

Thirdly, the ASCC is aimed at realizing a community of caring societies in ASEAN where members cooperate in social development to improve the standard of living of disadvantaged groups and people living in rural areas. It seeks to ensure the protection of workers in the process of regional economic integration through training, science and technology development, job creation and social protection.

The proposal of ASEAN community affirmed commitments to existing economic cooperation frameworks, regional plans of action and initiatives for ASEAN integration (IAI) and outlined plans for the creation of an ASEAN Economic Community entailing the harmonization of customs procedures and technical regulations, the removal of non-tariff trade barriers and the establishment of a network of free-trade-zones, and the progressive withdrawal of capital controls and the strengthening of intellectual property rights.

Connectivity Agenda

In pursuance of establishing ASEAN community, several initiatives have been taken. One of them is the Master Plan on ASEAN connectivity. This plan was adopted by the ASEAN leaders at the 17th ASEAN summit in Vietnam in October 2010. This highlights the key strategies and actions within the three pillars of physical, institutional and people-to-people level. All the countries of ASEAN are to be connected through an effective network of roadways, railways and airways by 2015.[5] Taking into consideration the evolution of economic corridors in the region, the connectivity with South Asia, Central Asia and West Asia to ASEAN can be possible by roadways and railways via China on one side and India on the other. China which is an aspiring super power, has built several roads traversing through Tibet, Pakistan, Nepal, Myanmar and Laos with China and it is striving to connect neighbouring Central Asian republics like Kazakhstan, Tajikistan and Mongolia with China. When China became a member of World Trade Organization (WTO) in 2001, it focussed its attention to fulfil its obligations. It was given five years to build and complete domestic connectivity and China succeed in that endeavour. This facilitated China to increase GDP to surpass Japan within five years.[6] Nishimura, Executive Director, Economic Research Institute of ASEAN & East Asia (ERIA), has observed that AEC is a two trillion dollar economy in 2009 which is double the size of Chinese starting point in 2001. If ASEAN will complete connectivity by 2015, ASEAN GDP will also double in the span of 10 years to reach that level.[7]

Thus the Master Plan on connectivity to link up different parts of ASEAN and to bring all the people of ASEAN closer to one another has been accelerated. Several economic corridors have been planned in ASEAN and surrounding countries and now the efforts are made to make them more interconnected and efficient. Ong Keng Yong of Singapore has observed that "Southeast Asia may be bypassed if the region is not economically competitive and not well connected to the other important economic nodes around the world. Therefore ASEAN strives to be open, outward looking and connected to other countries and regions. ASEAN is committed to adding value to its relationship with its dialogue partners and those partners having an interest in the region."[8] Thus ASEAN has evolved ASEAN Connectivity Coordination Committee (ACCC) and its terms of reference were finalized in Ho Chi Minh City in December 2010. In addition to ACCC representative, each ASEAN country is expected to nominate a national coordinator to oversee the implementation of specific plans and projects in the respective ASEAN countries. The ASEAN secretariat has decided to establish an ASEAN connectivity unit to monitor the implementation of the Master Plan.

China is enthusiastically supporting connectivity projects with Southeast Asia and it is appreciated. ASEAN Foreign Minister's Connectivity Road trip has already taken place to compliment China when the foreign ministers travelled along Route 3A of North-South Economic corridor from Chieng Rai (Thailand) to Kunming (China) through Laos from 23 to 25 January 2011. This was followed by the meeting discussing future details of connectivity between the two. Another country which has substantially contributed in building roads and bridges in the ASEAN region is Australia, which helped in the construction of Lao-Thai friendship road over Mekong River, is Australia. However, the contribution of the United States in building an effective infrastructure for connectivity in the ASEAN region is most important. It has build not only roads but numerous ports and airports in Thailand, Vietnam and the Philippines under the programmes of SEATO. Now Asian Development Bank, IMF and World Bank are willing to fund construction of corridors and connectivity, which will effectively interconnect the entire world. This will ultimately help in the fulfilment of UN Development goals at the global level.

India's Roadmap

India is keen to reinforce its connectivity at the domestic level, but has not proved as successful as the situation demands. Of course there are some roads, ports and airports of international standards but an effective network of connectivity is yet to emerge especially in Hindi heartland and seven states of the Northeast. We know that in order to increase GDP and ties with the neighbourhood, connectivity is a facilitator, but we are not ignorant of the bureaucratic loopholes. Yet we are trying to reinforce our connectivity with ASEAN to keep pace with developments in the region.

India does share 1600 Kilometre long land border with Myanmar and maritime border with Myanmar, Thailand and Indonesia. There are various proposals to build roads through the land border and work is in progress to complete them. Firstly India constructed a 2 lane asphalt road from Kale (Kalemyo) to Tamu of 144 Kilometre which was opened to traffic in February 2001. This has been connected to Moreh in Manipur by a bailey bridge over Mahuya creek and the road from Tamu to Moreh is also called Indo-Myanmar Friendship road. Secondly India is building a road to link Mizoram with Mandalaya through Rih-Tiddim and Rih-Falam roads. The construction of Rih-Tiddim for 80 Kilometre stretch is to be completed by 2013 and thereafter Rih-Falam road for 151 Kilometre is to be undertaken and the progress of the work is satisfactory. Thirdly, the most important is Kaladan Multi Modal Transport project for which the agreements were signed between the governments of India and Myanmar in April 2008. Kaladan River starting from Chin state traverses through Mizoram and from there it runs up to Sittwe to Bay of Bengal. The dredging of the Kaladan River for 158 Kilometre has nearly been completed to make it navigable. The land locked region of Mizoram in north-eastern India is to be provided a network of river and road transport. On the other hand, Kaladan project will also connect the eastern Indian seaport of Kolkata with Sittwe in Myanmar through inland waterway. In May 2011, Indian government was given clearance over 196.75 hectares of forest land for the construction of a road from National highway 54 to the Indo-Myanmar border, where the road will then continue through Myanmar's Chin state. The project is endeavoured to enable Sittwe port accommodate larger vessels of up to 6000 tons and will increase shipping volume as well as constructing two jetties to facilitate extensive loading and storage facilities that will significantly expand Sittwe's current size and capacity.[9]

Despite constraints and limitations, India is determined to connect ASEAN with railways and roadways and make it possible to travel from New Delhi to Hanoi and Singapore. The project for Delhi-Hanoi Railway was launched after first India-ASEAN summit in Cambodia in 2002. This programme was supported in 2003 as a cooperative venture under Mekong-Ganga Cooperation and India reiterated support for open skies and open roads at India-ASEAN summit at Bali in 2003. The trilateral highway project between India, Myanmar and Thailand under MGC initiative began in 2005. This highway of 1,360 Kilometer will connect Moreh in India with Maesot in Thailand through Pagan in Myanmar. Another proposal is Dawai (Thailand) Chennai (India) corridor project. Besides ASEAN is interested in the construction of India-Myanmar-Thailand-Laos-Cambodia Highway and link it with the proposed Mekong-India Economic corridor. Proposed by ERIA, this economic corridor is to link Cambodia, Laos, Vietnam and Myanmar to the South-eastern region of India and aimed at the creation of multi-country infrastructure, freight corridor and a centre of industrial activity. India is happy to support this project as it is going to empower and enable intraregional production chains giving a boost to regional economic integration and economic activity.[10] India has offered open sky facility to ASEAN in 2003 and ASEAN countries have signed agreements for a direct flight to New Delhi, Chennai, Kolkata and Mumbai. The ASEAN leaders are satisfied with Indian response and ASEAN foreign ministers are going to undertake a connectivity road trip from Tamu to Guwahati to celebrate 20 years of dialogue partnership with India in December 2012.

Free Trade

India offered the facility of free-trade to ASEAN in 2002. Framework agreement on comprensive Economic Agreement was signed at India-ASEAN summit at Bali on 8 October 2003.[11] Article 2 discussed measures for economic cooperation and stated that in order to establish an India-ASEAN Regional Trade and Investment Area (RTIA) which includes a free-trade-area (FTA) in goods, services and investment and to strengthen and enhance economic cooperation, they resolved to undertake the following:

(a) Progressive elimination of tariffs and non-tariff barriers in substantially all trade in goods;
(b) Progressive liberalisation of trade in services with substantial sectoral coverage;
(c) Establishment of a liberal and competitive investment regime that facilitates and promotes investment within the India-ASEAN RTIA;
(d) Provision of special and differential treatment to the New ASEAN Member States;

Article 2 further elaborated:

(a) Provision of flexibility to the Parties in the India-ASEAN RTIA negotiations to address their sensitive areas in the goods, services and investment sectors with such flexibilities to be negotiated and mutually agreed based on the principle of reciprocity and mutual Benefits;
(b) Establishment of effective trade and investment facilitation measures, including, but not limited to, simplification of customs procedures and development of mutual recognition arrangements;
(c) Expansion of economic cooperation in areas as may be mutually agreed between the Parties that will complement the deepening of trade and investment links between the Parties and formulation of action plans and programmes in order to implement the agreed sectors/areas of co-operation; and
(d) Establishment of appropriate mechanisms for the purposes of effective implementation of this Agreement.[12]

The RTIA laid the solid foundations for FTA and objectives of the agreement were to: (i) Strengthen and enhance economic, trade and investment co-operation between the Parties; (ii) Progressively liberalise and promote trade in goods and services as well as create a transparent, liberal and facilitative investment regime; (iii) Explore new areas and develop appropriate measures for closer economic co-operation between the Parties; and (iv) Facilitate the more effective economic integration of the new ASEAN Member States and bridge the development gap among the Parties.[13]

The framework agreement (RTIA) also provided agreement on trade in goods towards progressive tariff reduction on 105 agreed items. Tariff reduction for ASEAN-6, namely Brunei, Indonesia, Malaysia, Philippines, Singapore and Thailand were planned to be completed by 2007 and for the CLMV by 2012. The Idea of a FTA with a ten-year time frame was mooted by India during the first summit. However the idea of FTA had certain issues of negative listing, rules of origin and the level of tariff reduction on agricultural commodities, which delayed the implementation of the agreement for nearly nine years.

A framework agreement for the creation of FTA with Thailand under early harvest programme was signed in 2003, under which 84 items could be imported from Thailand at 50 percent of the normal rate of duty prevailing in India. Similar agreements were signed with Singapore. India took active interests in Thailand's initiative for Asian Bond Fund and provided $ 1 billion as a modest contribution to consolidate India's partnership with the ASEAN. The framework agreement for comprehensive economic cooperation is indeed a landmark document through which India provided "fast-Track" tariff concessions to ASEAN partners. The proposal was to achieve US$ 30 billion target for India-ASEAN trade by 2007 which stood merely at $ 10 billion in 2003. India also offered to run daily flights to major Indian cities including New Delhi, Kolkata, Mumbai and Chennai. The proposal to hold Car Rally had also been made on the eve of India-ASEAN summit which was flagged off from Guwahati in the following year. This Car Rally was to emphasize the geographic connectivity of India with Southeast Asia through a land route.

The third India-ASEAN summit was held in Vientiane in 2004. The participants signed a partnership pact for Peace, Progress and Shared Prosperity containing a long-term vision for boosting trade, investment, tourism, culture, sports and people to people contacts. It also included Action Plan touching upon the entire gamut of political and security cooperation, including food, human resources, energy, finance science and technology, IT, communication technology, health and agriculture. Prime Minister Manmohan Singh on the eve of the summit said that a "long-term partnership agreement with ASEAN would provide a new dimension to our relations. He said that new India is on the horizon and the future lies in working together with our neighbours in the East, with whom we have profound civilization ties". At the same time, he spoke about linking India with East Asia and ASEAN for the community building.

India's trade relations with ASEAN are expanding. From US$ 2.4 billion in 1991-92, it reached US$ 23 billion by 2005-6.It is understood that as and when FTA will be implemented in letter and spirits, the volume of trade will exceed the targets. The Chinese have already signed FTA with the ASEAN and with this they have established a combined market of 1.7 billion people, regional GDP of $ 2 trillion and international trade worth $ 1.2 trillion. China's trade with ASEAN is worth about $ 104 billion. They have certain advantages over India in the ASEAN region, but it is suggested that if FTA with India becomes operational, it would also be a market of 1.5 billion people and regional GDP of $ 1.5 trillion. India and China are also exploring the feasibility of an India-China bilateral FTA on the pattern of ASEAN.

If the agreement is signed, it may complement India-ASEAN tree-trade proposals. At the same time, it will brighten the prospects for better economic and security understanding and confidence building.

India's major export items to the ASEAN market are gems and jewellery, machinery and instruments, dyes, semi-finished iron and steel, oil meals, drugs, pharmaceutical and fine chemicals, non-ferrous metals, plastic and linoleum products, manufacture of metals, man-made yarn fab & made ups, meat and preparations, cotton yarn, fabrics and madeups. India's major items imported from ASEAN are electronic goods, vegetable oils, organic chemicals, wood and wood products, coal, coke and briquettes, non-electrical machinery, transport equipment, metal ferrous ores & metal ferrous ores & metal scrap, artificial resins, plastic materials, printed books, pulses, electrical machinery, and non-ferrous metals, etc. India's trade with ASEAN countries is hovering around 7-9 percent of its total trade every year.[14]

Bilaterally, the trade between India and Singapore have been increasing. From $ 6.6 billion in 2004-05 it has reached $ 8.7 billion in 2005-06. India's trade figures with Thailand have increased from $ 1.22 billion in 2000-01 to $ 2.2 billion in 2004-05. As far as Indonesia is concerned, the trade figures increased from $ 3.9 billion in 2004-05 to $ 4.3 billion in 2005-06. Similarly trading figures with Malaysia have increased and it is one of the top ten investors in India. Again the trade between CLMV countries and India are increasing substantially. However, it is investment relations which have to be attended with utmost care. The environment has been disturbed especially after the suspension of Tata-Singapore Airline project and that of special economic zone at Nandigram, Haldia, where Indonesia's Salim group has had lot of stakes. Despite obstacles, avenues are explored to strengthen investment relations. Malaysia and Singapore are major investors in India. Malaysia has made substantial investments in expanding capacities in selected infrastructural areas such as logistics, highways, and ICTs in India. On the other hand, Singapore has made investments in health care, real estate and tourism. Their technology park in Bengalore has created a positive environment for investments in India.

There are several areas of collaboration between India and ASEAN countries which can prove mutually beneficial. For example, energy, edible oil, pharmaceuticals, IT and BT are prospective areas of joint ventures. It is commonly understood that Indian Origin entrepreneurs owns the largest palm oil refinery in Malaysia, the largest carbon-black manufacturing units in Thailand and a large number of textile factories in Indonesia.[15] One the other hand, Tata, Reliance, Birla and Ranbaxi are noted Indian companies which have potential to invest in the ASEAN region. Indian companies are especially in the ASEAN region. Indian companies are ready to invest in auto-components sector in Thailand, for motor vehicles and energy sector in Indonesia and Vietnam, and for Information and Communications Technology (ICT) in the Philippines.

In food processing, forest products and cooking oil, there are abundance of scope for collaboration with Indonesia, Malaysia and Myanmar. Malaysia and Indonesia are major palm producers and Thailand has much expertise in food processing industry-particularly in deep sea fishing and other marine related activities. The information technology (IT) is an area when India has advantages and Singapore's Info-Comm Development Authority has signed an MOU with NIIT. Entertainment and multi-media especially films and TV programmes of India are popular in the ASEAN region. The collaboration in those areas could be fruitful to both sides. Both India and ASEAN can be benefited if there are investments in drugs, pharmaceuticals and human resource development.

The initiatives to promote economic relations are in progress. Amita Batra has noted that "The ASEAN-India FTA that became effective from January 2010 has a tariff reduction/elimination schedule covering about 80 per cent of traded goods between the two regions. The gradual tariff reduction schedule beginning from January 2010 is to be fully implemented by the end of 2013 and 2016 in respect of the two "normal tracks". For special products, the applied MFN rates are to be reduced in a phased manner. A negative list with 489 items that are excluded from the list of tariff concessions has also been indicated."[16]

When FTA became operational, the trade volume increased and to quote Ambassador of the Republic of Indonesia, Andi M. Ghalib "in terms of the achievement of ASEAN Community in 2015, India supports economic integration of ASEAN countries and it also hopes that the Agreement on Economic Partnership between ASEAN and India will be realized by the end of 2011. The partnership is crucial to bring the trade and economic cooperation between ASEAN and India into a higher level. There are vast opportunities that may rise with the establishment of ASEAN Economic Community in 2015 coupled with India's high economic growth in the region. ASEAN and India's population count for one third of the world's population projected to be the "main drive" for the world's economy in the next few years."[17] He further stated that "The projected US$ 50 billion worth of trade in 2010 between ASEAN and India first announced in 2007 during the 6th ASEAN and India Summit has been achieved in 2010, wherein India's export to ASEAN amounted to US$ 22.52 billion and its import was US$ 27.81 billion or an increase by 22 per cent. In view of the above, both

ASEAN and India are quite optimistic that the trade between them would hit US$ 70 billion in 2012—in line with the implementation of ASEAN and India Trade in Goods Agreement. There is high hope that the two parties would be able to complete the negotiation for the FTA on Services and Investment by the end of this year. FTA in Goods with ASEAN was operationalised from January 2010. Once fully implemented, the FTA will help create a market of nearly 1.8 billion people and combined GDP of US$ 2.8 trillion. The ASEAN-India FTA would also be the cornerstone of the growing and prospering partnership in the region."[18]

Regarding bilateral trade with Indonesia, the Ambassador stated the following: "Noting that the bilateral trade volume between Indonesia and India had increased nearly threefold since the establishment of the Strategic Partnership between the two countries, the two leaders agreed to set the new target for bilateral trade volume of US$ 25 billion by 2015. During the last state visit in India, 14 (fourteen) MoUs and Agreements signed on G-to-G as well as 18 (eighteen) MoUs signed on B-to-B. Post the state visit, these 18 (eighteen) business deals worth US$ 15 billion, covering Indian investment in natural resources, infrastructure, and services in Indonesia. Bilateral trade between our two great nations has grown significantly in the last few years. In 2005, there was the target of achieving a bilateral trade volume of US$ 10 billion by 2010. This target was attained in 2008, two years earlier than scheduled. Trade volume of Indonesia and India in 2010 has reached US$ 13.2 billion. The realization of India's investment in Indonesia has also increased, from US$ 11.6 million in 2007 to US$ 28.5 million in 2010. This as a consequence, makes Indonesia as the second largest trade partner of India in ASEAN."[19]

Foreign Direct Investment (FDI) from the ASEAN region are trickling in slowly in limited areas and they are mainly for infra-structure building, hotels and tourism services, heavy industries, chemicals, fertilizers and food processing. Total Indian FDI in the ASEAN region by 2004 were merely $ 225 million and that of ASEAN in India stood at $ 2 billion.[20] Amita Batra has commented that "as for financial integration, India has attained the status of an attractive investment destination and has made large strides in capital account liberalizations. Despite this, India absorbs less than one percent of the global FDI flows while China corners almost eight per cent."[21] Indian investments in various industries include mining, automotives and machinery, clothing, agricultural and chemical and ASEAN investments in India are low and considered less than two per cent of its global investments.

To conclude, it can be stated that India has given importance to connectivity at various levels and the agenda of MGC, BIMSTEC and India-ASEAN summit are suggesting ways and means to effectively link all Indian cities with the 10 ASEAN states. We find that the balance sheet of economic relations are satisfactory. Although negotiations over FTA was long, but now its implementation will facilitate India's economic integration with ASEAN. The implementation of FTA can be facilitated with connectivity. India's success in ASEAN will facilitate it to attain the objectives of a rising power. India has a vision to emerge as a developed nation by 2020 and this objective will be fulfilled if our relations with eastern neighbours are strengthened. India has been projected as one wing of ASEAN jumbo jet and Japan, Korea and China as another wing. India is striving to act as an effective wing of the ASEAN in the same way as Plus Three. With more than 500 million middle class population vast territory and immense natural resources and expertise, it can substantially contribute to rise of Asia but that requires networking, confidence building and cooperative environment, which is slowly and steadily taking shape.

NOTES

1. ASEAN Secretariat, Towards an ASEAN Community, Public Information Series, Jakarta, 2003, p.5
2. Noel M. Morada, "ASEAN at 40: Prospects for community Building in Southeast Asia", *Asia-Pacific Review*, Vol.15, No.1, 2008, p. 40.
3. ASEAN Secretariat, n.1, pp. 5-6.
4. Morada, n.2, p.41
5. Ong Keng Yong, Director, Institute of Policy Studies, Singapore, The lecture on India-ASEAN Strategic Dialogue at ICWA, New Delhi, 3 March 2011.
6. Hitedoshi Nishimura's lecture in Delhi Dialogue, March 2001, in S.T. Devare & Vibhashu Shekhar, Ed., *Delhi Dialogue III*, Manohar Publishers 2012, p.87.
7. Ibid, p.87.
8. Yong, n.5.
9. Burma Centre, "Section III: India-Burma Relations, Key Features and concern", India-Burma Relations-Trends and Developments (1990-2011), New Delhi 2011, p.78.
10. C.P. Joshi, India's Minister of Road Transport and Highways, *Delhi Dialogue III*, New Delhi, 2012, pp.73-74.
11. Framework Agreement on comprehensive economic cooperation Between the Republic of India and the ASEAN. Department of Commerce, Government of India, http:// commerce.in/trade/international ta framework asean.asp
12. See the text of the treaty, ibid.
13. Ibid.
14. Swapan K Bhattacharya, "India's Economic Relations with the ASEAN, *World Focus*, New Delhi, 2006, PP.28-32.
15. Faisal Yahya, "India and Southeast Asia Revisited", *Contemporary Southeast Asia*, Singapore, 2003, pp.79-103.
16. Amita Batra, India-ASEAN FTA: Towards comprehensive Economic Partnership", in Jha Ganganath and Shekhar, ed., Rising India in Changing Asia-Pacific, New Delhi, Pentagon, 2012, p.147.
17. Andi M. Ghalib, Ambassador of the Republic of Indonesia, "ASEAN and India: A Perspective from Indonesia", New Delhi, IPCS, May 2011, pp.2-3.
18. Ibid.
19. Ibid.
20. Vibhanshu Shekhar, "India-ASEAN Relations: An overview", New Delhi, IPCS, pp.4-7.
21. Amita Batra, n.16, p.152.

7

India's Drifting North Korea Policy: An Overview and the Road Ahead

Geetha Govindasamy

Introduction

With the death of Kim Jong Il on 17 December 2011, Kim Jong Un emerged as the youngest leader of a reclusive, nuclear—armed North Korea. Given Pyongyang's development of illicit proliferation activities, North Korea is one of India's most complex foreign policy challenges. Even though India is 5072.86 km away from North Korea, the emergence of an unpredictable leadership in a precarious environment has multiple implications for Indian security and interests.[1] The chapter argues that New Delhi has neglected North Korea and that it is time to bring back Pyongyang in focus in Indian foreign policy priorities. Given the uncertain situation that is emerging and more importantly, India's interests in the East Asian region, the chapter will analyse New Delhi's potential role in resolving security issues on the Korean Peninsula, a stance which is endorsed by the United States as well as Japan and South Korea. By examining the impact of the North Korean weapons proliferation policy on India, the chapter also develops scenarios for improved New Delhi-Pyongyang relationship in the future.

Overview of North Korea's Proliferation Activities

India is, by and large a spectator where North Korean issues are concerned. However, prior to discussing New Delhi's strategic interests and role in the East Asian region, it is important to appreciate that India-North Korea relations should not be viewed in isolation but within the context of Pyongyang's international proliferation activities. Like past leaderships, Kim Jong Un firmly believes nuclear and missile development is essential to thwart any attempts of invasion or a regime change, namely by the United States. North Korea's proliferation developments are worrying for many reasons. On 10 January 2003, it was the first country ever to withdraw from the 1968 Non Proliferation Treaty, leaving it free of adhering to international safeguard measures of the International Atomic Energy Agency (IAEA). This is dangerous as the North has already diverted plutonium from civilian use for weapons use and has an active enrichment uranium programme for weapons purposes. Further, it tested nuclear weapons in 2006, 2009 and the latest on February 2013. At the time of writing, rumours of a fourth test was circulating within the South Korean media. The North has hundreds of short- and medium-range ballistic missiles and is in the midst of developing intercontinental ballistic missiles.[2] It is a well known fact that Pyongyang has assisted some countries in their nuclear weapons programme, especially in politically unstable regions such as the Middle East and South Asia. Apart from such activities, it is also an exporter of ballistic missiles systems and technology to rogue states. The Kim regime sells chemical weapons and the main buyers are Syria and Iran.[3] Some observers are certain that Pyongyang also maintains biological weapons capabilities.[4]

Presumably to shore up the standing of the inexperienced leader—Kim Jong Un, the government in Pyongyang discharged a rocket which disintegrated moments after it was launched on 12 April 2012.[5] A month later, Pyongyang resumed the construction of a light water reactor, designed to provide North Korea the option of extracting plutonium to boost its nuclear weapons program.[6] In December of the same year, the isolated country successfully launched a long-range rocket into orbit. After unsuccessful attempts, in February 2013, Pyongyang initiated its third and successful nuclear test. However, it is believed that Pyongyang lacks capabilities needed to miniaturize a nuclear warhead to mount on a long-range missile. Having said that, according to Joel S Wit and Jenny Town, North Korea's illicit activities are dangerous for a variety of reasons.[7] One of the reasons the United States is protected is because North Korean long range missiles are incapable of carrying heavy nuclear warheads. However, Pyongyang might attack Japan and South Korea by putting nuclear warheads on shorter-range missiles. Not surprisingly, the potential for inflicting major damage in Tokyo and Seoul are enormous. Wit and Town further assert the threat of a war is possible in the region. They argue that North Korea is suffering from international sanctions and is hungry for hard cash. There is no guarantee that the international community may be able to stop North Korea from becoming a major exporter of nuclear and missile technology, especially to rogue states. Equally, the consequences would be grave if the international community attacks an unpredictable North Korea that possesses such technology. Additionally, if preventive attacks are made, there is always the risk of a miscalculation or intelligence failure on both sides. This could trigger a war which will destabilize the East Asian region. One of the direct consequence of an impending war is the possibility of Japan and South

Korea nuclearizing as a result of China's inability to stop North Korean proliferation activities. To sum it up, the more weapons arsenal North Korea possesses, the more unstable the East Asian region is going to be due to unpredictable reactions and responses from North Korea and its immediate neighbours. Such unpredictability from North Korea does not bode well for Indian domestic security and economic interests in East Asia.

Threats to Indian Domestic Security

Threats to Indian security should be viewed within the context of the relations between rogue states seeking powerful weapons and an impoverished North Korea. For various reasons, India's neighbours—Myanmar and Pakistan have a history of dubious interactions with North Korea.

In the past, India's insecurities increased due to Burma's close ties with North Korea. In 2010,evidence provided by Burmese defectors like Sai Thein Win demonstrated that Burma had an embryonic nuclear weapons programme. Though information is sketchy at best, two reports on Myanmar's nuclear capabilities, published in 2010, by the Democratic Voice of Burma and the Washington-based Institute for Science and International Security further alluded to direct links between Myanmar and North Korea.[8] North Korea is said to have assisted Burma's nuclear weapons program by providing free technology and selling weapons related parts. More importantly, in May 2012, during a meeting with President Lee Myung Bak, President Thein Sein candidly admitted that in the past, Myanmar had purchased military goods from North Korea for its weapons development programme. On one hand, recent developments give the impression that India should not be too concerned since president Thein Sein has already agreed to provide information about Burmese nuclear activities, end military ties with North Korea, as well as grant access to the Atomic Energy Agency (IAEA) inspectors to investigate any irregularities of his country's nuclear development. On the other hand, in July 2013, the US blacklisted Lieutenant-General Thein Htay, a senior Burmese army officer for purchasing military goods from North Korea in contravention of United Nations United Nations Security Council Resolution 1874, which prohibits the procurement of military goods from Pyongyang.[9] This implies that President Thein Sein is uncertain of the true status of Myanmar's nuclear activities, has little influence over the army and its activities despite recent elections and the opening up of Burma.[10] If this is the case, Thein Sein's offer of nuclear transparency might very well create a conflict between the Burmese executive and the military. So what does all of this mean for India?

There have been cases where ships and planes loaded with North Korean weapons still either transit or have Burma as their final destination. However, thus far they have successfully been diverted or blocked by multination agencies.[11] Given the country's geo-strategic location, of particular concern to India is that further civil conflicts in Burma would threaten India's border security. There is a risk of non-state actors/rogue military officers getting their hands on North Korean conventional equipment to aid/overcome counter-insurgency campaigns near the country's borders. If violence spills across the India-Myanmar border, New Delhi is bound to see a rise in the flows of refugees (besides Rohingya Muslims) on the north eastern part of the country. Burma's unconfirmed nuclear development as well as military goods purchased from North Korea is an undefined calculus of risk which poses a threat to Indian security management of its borders.

Even if Burma's nuclear development and recent transparency offer is not an immediate threat to India, the nuclear and missile cooperation between Pakistan and North Korea that began in the early 1970s certainly is a matter of serious concern.[12] In the last few decades, India's territorial sovereignty and integrity has been threatened by covertly and overtly support by neighbouring states. For instance, in the 1980s, the Indian government was convinced that Pakistan supported the 'Khalistan' independence movement by supplying Khalistani militants with North Korean weapons.[13] More detrimental was the fact that Pakistan's Ghauri and Ghaznavi series of missiles were similar to that of North Korea's No Dong I and Taepo Dong 1 missiles respectively.[14] In return for North Korean missile related goods, Pakistan is also suspected to have provided Pyongyang with crucial technology relating to the gas centrifuge uranium enrichment which allowed the Koreans to transfer from a plutonium-based nuclear programme to a uranium-based one.[15] In sum, trading of missile and nuclear technology between North Korea and Pakistan assists Pyongyang to develop its nuclear capabilities and provide the rogue state with hard cash. Simultaneously, it advances Pakistan's own nuclear ambitions. Even if there is no connection between these states, India is wary as instability and uncertainty within Pakistan could revive weapons and nuclear proliferation connection between Pyongyang and Islamabad which would impact India's security. Moreover, if one assumes that the alliance between Pyongyang and Islamabad has not ended and that this connection actually aids in developing weapons programme, given the strategic location of Pakistan, the security of Pakistani nuclear arsenal is questionable due to possible terrorist attacks or even weapons falling into the hands of non-state actors, especially those who are anti-India. India already has countless evidence to prove that Pakistan is a hotspot for various non-state terrorist forces, some of them inimical to India. New Delhi has no choice but to be cautious and enhance its own ballistic and nuclear programmes to prepare for any threats and instabilities. But more importantly, India needs to find a way to break the Pyongyang-Islamabad connexion.[16] One way of doing this is by strengthening ties with North Korea.

Indian Response to North Korea

How is India responding effectively to the challenges emanating from North Korea's proliferation activities? North Korea has hardly figured in Indian foreign policy calculus. Thus far, even though bilateral relations have been growing, New Delhi's approach to Pyongyang has been mostly apathetic. North Korean affairs remain as a discursive platform for Indian commentators rather than initiating concrete government policy.

For instance, the appointment of suitable Indian ambassadors abroad is critical as nominations reflect importance attributed to bilateral relations. The 2012 appointment of Shri Ajay K. Sharma, a stenographers' cadre officer who has no experience in any economic, political or cultural bilateral dealings, as envoy to North Korea illustrates how insignificant North Korea is in New Delhi's Look East Policy. Moreover, it implies Indian policymakers' lack of perceptiveness of where or how North Korea as a nuclear hotspot in an important geopolitical location should be incorporated into India's foreign policy. In addition, bilateral ties could be jeopardized due to an inexperienced diplomat who might not be able to offer expert guidance and frank counsel on North Korean affairs as well as reshaping the mission to serve Indian interests within the context of East Asian geopolitical security considerations. Lastly, the reluctance of Indian Foreign Service officers of being posted to Pyongyang sends out an adverse message that North Korea has become unimportant in Indian strategic calculations, especially to officials in Pyongyang.

Likewise, on the political front, New Delhi's lack of leverage in issues pertaining to North Korea also needs to be addressed. Indian policymakers have continuously advocated that North Korea should dismantle its nuclear programme. However, India's role and commitment in formulating genuine multilateral disarmament initiatives against North Korea's nuclear program is vague. New Delhi has been reticence in participating in any US-driven agenda to bolster sanctions against Pyongyang. Though it has an observer status, India opted out of signing the 2003 Proliferation Security Initiative (PSI) designed to actively interdict ships belonging to rogue states that could be ferrying suspected nuclear parts or designs.[17] Equally, there has been no enthusiasm for actively contributing to implementing the 2009 UN Security Council's Resolution 1874 regarding North Korea. Multilaterally, India has no standing. It is not a member of the Six Party Talks, involving United States, China, Russia, Japan and the two Koreas, a forum to negotiate the dismantlement of North Korea's nuclear program in exchange for aid. Because of India's past lacklustre policy towards the Korean peninsula, at least in terms of security considerations, the major powers, namely China, have effectively side-lined India's potential complimentary role in negotiating peace on the Korean Peninsula together with major powers. Nevertheless, recent developments seem to favour a more robust but indirect Indian involvement in securing a peaceful Korean peninsula.[18]

There are several reasons as to why India's potential complimentary role in East Asian security matters. First, the US, Japan, China, Russia and South Korea have failed to stop North Korea's game of nuclear brinkmanship. The Six Party Talks stalled in late 2008 as Pyongyang refused to dismantle its nuclear program.

Failure in engaging North Korea multilaterally means India, as a neutral party, has the potential to mediate peace.

Second, with liberalisation and economic growth, Indian companies are actively investing in Japan and Korea. Any instability in the Korean peninsula will disrupt trade between New Delhi and its North Asian trade partners. The converging of interests has resulted in both South Korea and Japan actively seeking India's support in discussing approaches to North Korea in the near future. Working to promote common interests, South Korea and India are now sharing intelligence of proliferation activities by North Korea and Pakistan.[19] Similarly, Tokyo and Delhi cooperate on issues relating to regional security such as nuclear disarmament and non-proliferation.[20] For India, support from regional allies makes it easier to take on a more prominent role in maintaining regional security as well as looking after its interests in advancing the Look East Policy not only economically but also strategically.

Third, China is concerned with the extent to which the Americans are going to be influential in the Asia-Pacific region. For now China seems to be frustrated with North Korea, particularly after its third recent nuclear test in 2013. Supporting tighter UN sanctions and closing accounts of North Korea's Foreign Trade Bank in China shows that President Xi Jinping is taking a tougher stance towards Pyongyang.[21] Nevertheless, to protect its own security and influence in the region, Beijing will continue being Pyongyang's biggest ally and benefactor. In addition, the US pivot towards Asia since 2011 has forced China to emphasize its relations with Laos, Cambodia, Myanmar and North Korea to counter-balance United States (US) preoccupation with Asia.[22] For these reasons, it is not surprising that the US wants India to counterbalance China in regional issues. The US is pushing New Delhi to be more involved in Asia-Pacific political as well as security cooperation.[23] Surely, this provides India the unique opportunity to be part of this multilateral agenda by expanding bilateral relations with North Korea.

Developments in India-North Korea Relations

India's relations with North Korea have been uneventful in the last forty years. It established relations with North Korea in 1973, resulting in both countries maintaining embassies in Pyongyang as well as New Delhi. Bilateral trade indicates that India is one of Pyongyang's major trading partners with annual trade amounting to roughly \$500-million. In spite of this, North Korean activities relating to assisting, selling and trading missile weapons and technology with Pakistan, Myanmar and China have hindered bilateral relations. India is always quick to condemn any North Korean nuclear tests for fear of adverse impact on regional security. In 1999, relations worsened when India impounded the North Korean vessel *MV Ku Wol San* which was anchored in Gujarat's Kandla port. The vessel contained missile components, blueprints and manuals and was believed to be heading to Karachi, confirming the Pakistan-North Korea proliferation axis.[24]

Nonetheless, North Korean internal socio-economic situation has provided a platform for India to penetrate the hermit kingdom. Facing famine and food shortages for the past few decades and its economic zones in Nampo, the Kaesong Industrial Complex and the Mount Kumgang tourism project not yielding much needed revenue has forced North Korea to attempt to draw outside investment. The year 2011 saw North Korea inviting the Indian ambassador in Pyongyang to tour several economic areas between Pyongyang and Nampo. In the same year, a North Korean delegation visited India to learn about how to establish special economic zones. Though these visits failed to produce any meaningful results in bolstering economic bilateral relations, it does give credence to the fact that Pyongyang is looking for foreign investors in improving its economy.

Near-perfect isolation, a lack of investment and natural disasters has resulted in the government in Pyongyang requesting and accepting humanitarian aid from international contributors. Like so many other donors, when floods hit North Korea in 2011, India provided $ 1 million in emergency food assistance to Pyongyang through the United Nations World Food Program.[25] Apart from that, many North Koreans receive training annually in India in diverse fields, including IT and science and technology. Interestingly, the number of North Koreans receiving scientific and computer training in India is on the rise.[26] These developments bode well for a positive future in enhancing India's role in mitigating North Korean brinkmanship in particular and being involved in North East Asian security in general.

Possible Indian Involvement in the Korean Peninsula

Given that India has diplomatic relations with both Koreas, it is up to policymakers to seek opportunities to fashion substantive relations on the Korean peninsula. For a start, Indian policymakers could play a major role by publically lending support to both Koreas in getting involved in policies that aid the process of initiating a regional peace structure on the Korean Peninsula. Indian involvement should not include intervention but advance the process of engagement between the Koreas while retaining its own political manoeuvrability. This is crucial as India stands to gain economically if reunification does takes place on the Korean peninsula. Indian technology and capital combined with the North's relatively cheap manpower and resources could provide access to huge inter-Korean projects in a unified Korea.

Since her inauguration as South Korea's President in 2012, Park Geun Hyehas adopted a strategy of 'trustpolitik' that underpins her recognition that a long-term diplomatic vehicle for building trust with North Korea offers the best prospect of mitigating the possibility of conflict on the Korean Peninsula. Madam Park is actively seeking support for a multilateral framework through the establishment of a Northeast Asia Peace and Cooperation Initiative, an extension of the 'trust politik' policy which "envisions a long-term trust-building process among regional countries including North Korea, which starts from non political concerns and progresses to security cooperation".[27] According to Park Ihn-hwi, a professor at Korea University in Seoul, any country or organisation that has a stake in Northeast Asian issues has the institutional right to participate in the initiative.[28] Therefore, it is not surprising that bilateral relations seem to be progressing well as during Madam Park's visit to New Delhi in January 2014, India and South Korea agreed to share classified information about the nuclear activities of North Korea and Pakistan.[29] As a rising Asian power, India should strive to be more involved in the Northeast Asia Peace and Cooperation Initiative which currently only involves the US, South Korea, China, Russia, Japan and Mongolia. Understanding that to improve Inter-Korean relations, South Korea needs international coordination and backing, New Delhi's support and participation would certainly be welcomed by Madam Park. By being part of the Northeast Asia Peace and Cooperation Initiative, India can play a larger role in regular high-level meetings and policies that deal with regional issues relating to terrorism, nuclear proliferation, environment as well as humanitarian and disaster relief.

Nonetheless, India's participation in the above initiative will only be valued if its relations with North Korea is further strengthened. Given how unlikely North Korea is to denuclearize, at least in the immediate future, an alternative strategy emphasizing on encouraging and promoting internal reforms in North Korea may be key to slowing down its weapons program. Hence, India's interest is best served by assisting North Korea move towards reforming its economy. The obvious strategy would be to trade with and invest in North Korea while continuing to work towards denuclearization. Recently North Korea announced the opening of 14 special economic zones. In order to support large scale projects in these economic zones North Korea is in dire need of foreign investments. These investment do not only include capital but also the building of physical as well as institutional infrastructures. As long as countries investing in these economic zones are not aiming to instigate a regime change, Kim Jong Un is likely to welcome direct investments that provide the North with technology and market oriented business practices.[30] As Paola Subacchi rightly points out,

> The expansion of special economic zones—supported by increased private investment, especially from firms that are not South Korean or Chinese—would significantly improve the odds that North Korea's regime eases its repressive rule and embraces a program of economic reform, as China did more than three decades ago. The task of defusing the threat to regional peace and stability that North Korea poses should be one that is shared across Asia.[31]

Since South Korean investments are tied to political relations and the issue of unification and investments from China are associated with Beijing's own development strategies, there are no immediate incentives for North Korea to reform.[32] However private investments from other than South Korea and China would be easily accepted and this would encourage North Korea's opening up and engagement with the outside world. Given that an Indian was one of the six foreign experts invited to Pyongyang, North Korea, in October 2013, to discuss the establishment of special economic zones (SEZs) during an international conference, shows that New Delhi already has an advantage in pursuing investment opportunities in the hermit kingdom.[33] As mentioned before, the North Korean SEZs would require infrastructure investments which relate to land development, energy, water and waste management as well as telecommunications. While these requirements would not immediately reform North Korea, they will at least allow the isolated country to engage with the outside world. Citing China's transition to a market economy as an example, Bradley O Babson postulates SEZs permit

> confidence-building in being able to conduct business in new, more internationally acceptable ways and provides a testing ground for policies that could be applied more widely in the future. SEZs have played this role in other countries transitioning to market economies, notably China.[34]

India's national security interests demand the emergence of an economically strong North Korea. North Korea is rich in natural resources but industrially still under-developed. India can help by beefing up North Korea's intermediate levels of technologies by building up its industrial base. India could assist both by governmental aid and Indian private investments in fields such as agro-tech and forestry based industries, communications development and IT education. Moreover, it is a well-known fact that North Korea depends heavily on primary products, which means it desperately needs to develop its manufacturing sector. Without investments from the outside world, it will lack the necessary machinery, equipment, and technology to develop its manufacture sector. While it remains to be seen the extent to which North Korea will develop its SEZs, if countries like India are willing to take the risk and invest in North Korea, it would be able to build linkages with the local economy, facilitate modern management practices as well provide employment for the locals. Kevin Sheppard notes that foreign investors in North Korea other than China and South Korea, have wider range of contacts with ordinary North Korean authorities, business persons, and labourers.[35] This kind of personal relations with Pyongyang could cement and strengthen India's ability to be a potent player on the Korean peninsula.

Concluding Remarks

The continuing unpredictable threat from North Korea means that India must make significant investments in its foreign policy. One of the key weaknesses of Indian foreign policy is that it does not address North Korean proliferation activities appropriately. It is imperative that Indian policymakers recognize North Korea's strategic objectives and the threat they pose to national interests and institute policies that would encourage closer relations with the Korean peninsula.

Therefore, a reorientation of India's foreign policy that forges a space for New Delhi to play a positive role in enhancing regional and global stability is desperately needed.

Unlike the near inimical triangular relations between Japan, China and both Koreas due to past history, India has no historical baggage in the East Asian region. India already has established diplomatic relations with both Koreas, unlike compared to the US and Japan. Though both are major players in inter-Korean issues, Washington and Tokyo do not have diplomatic relations with Pyongyang. Hence, New Delhi can act as an honest broker in the region and act independently if needed according to its own strategic calculations. A deepened and strengthened dialogue with India surely would be viewed as a positive contribution by Pyongyang which has had a constructive relationship with New Delhi thus far. I would argue that the North Koreans would welcome India's involvement since they do not feel threatened by Indians. On the contrary, it is likely they would want a more robust involvement of India in the Korean peninsula, in spite of the geographical distance, probably to diversify the involvement of investors. Given that the Six Party Talks have been suspended since 2009 and sanctions have failed to initiate any positive responses from Pyongyang, it is time a non-aligned player like India shares the responsibilities in ensuring peace not only on the Korean peninsula but also in the Asia-Pacific region. This allows New Delhi to make its presence felt across the whole policy spectrum, thus becoming—albeit inadvertently—a regional power, outside its immediate neighbourhood.

Gradually, the Indian influence in Korean affairs would eventually provide complementary political and economic voice to that of other major regional players, which would allow New Delhi to protect its security and national interests. In order to achieve this, New Delhi has to seriously restructure its North Korea policy.

NOTES

1. "Distance from North Korea to India", http://www.distancefromto.net/distance-from/North+Korea/to/India, 12 August 2013.
2. Mark Fitzpatrick, "North Korean Proliferation Challenges: The Role of The European Union", Non-Proliferation Papers, EU Non-Proliferation Consortium, No. 18, June 2012.
3. Changsop Pyon of Radio Free Asia's Korean Service interviewed Bruce Bechtol, Professor of International Relations at Angelo State University in Texas, United States. The transcript can be accessed at Radio Free Asia, http://www.rfa.org/english/news/korea/interview-10032013130040.html.
4. "Arms Control and Proliferation Profile: North Korea", http://www.armscontrol.org/factsheets/northkoreaprofile
5. Choe Sang-Hun and Rick Gladstone, "North Korean Rocket Fails Moments After Liftoff", *The New York Times,* 12 April 2012, http://www.nytimes.com/2012/04/13/world/asia/north-korea-launches-rocket-defying-world-warnings.html?pagewanted=all.
6. Choe Sang-Hun, "North Korea Said to Resume Work on Nuclear Reactor", *The New York Times,* 17 May 2012, http://www.nytimes.com/2012/05/18/world/asia/north-korea-resumes-work-on-nuclear-reactor-group-says.html?ref=world.

7. Joel S Wit and Jenny Town, "7 Reasons to Worry About North Korea's Weapons", *The Atlantic*, 16 April 2013, http://www.theatlantic.com/international/archive/2013/04/7-reasons-to-worry-about-north-koreas-weapons/275020/.
8. David Santoro "Thein Sein faces nuclear challenge," *Asia Times Online*, 8 August 2013,http://www.atimes.com/atimes/Southeast_Asia/SEA-02-080813.html.
9. Nan Tin Htwe, "Uncertainty over Thein Htay sanction", *Myanmar Times*, 8 July 2013, http://www.mmtimes.com/index.php/national-news/7405-uncertainty-over-thein-htay-sanction.html.
10. Mathew Cottee, "Burma's Nuclear Program: Who's in Charge?", *The National Interest*, 24 September 2013, http://nationalinterest.org/commentary/burmas-nuclear-program-whos-charge-9120?page=1.
11. North Korea's Illegal Weapons Pipeline Flows On, *Wall Street Journal*, 6 November 2013, http://online.wsj.com/news/articles/SB10001424127887323830404578144981537771060.
12. A.K. Sachdev, "North Korea's Missile Programme: A Matter of Concern", http://www.idsa-india.org/an-dec-00-7.html.
13. Indrani Bagchi, "Kim Jong-il's death: India fears revival of North Korea-Pak nuclear bonding", *The Times of India*, http://articles.timesofindia.indiatimes.com/2011-12-20/india/30537516_1_hatf-kim-jong-il-missile
14. A.K. Sachdev, "North Korea's Missile Programme: A Matter of Concern", http://www.idsa-india.org/an-dec-00-7.html.
15. "Pakistani Hands emerge in North Korea's nuclear threat to US. Should India be worried?", *India Today*, 29 March 2013, http://indiatoday.intoday.in/story/pak-hand-emerges-in-north-koreas-nuclear-threat-to-us.-should-india-be-worried/1/259886.html.
16. "Pakistani Hands emerge in North Korea's nuclear threat to US. Should India be worried?", *India Today*, 29 March 2013, http://indiatoday.intoday.in/story/pak-hand-emerges-in-north-koreas-nuclear-threat-to-us.-should-india-be-worried/1/259886.html.
17. Sreeram Chaulia, "Wary India frisks North Korean freighter," 21 August 2009, http://www.worldsecuritynetwork.com/India/Chaulia-Sreeram/Wary-India-frisks-North-Korean-freighter.
18. Ibid.
19. Kim Tae-gyu, "South Korea, India to share nuke intel on North Korea", Pakistan, *Korea Times*, 3 July 2013, http://www.koreatimes.co.kr/www/news/nation/2013/07/116_138578.html.
20. Jeffrey W. Hornung, "Japan and India's Growing Embrace", *The Diplomat*, 12 January 2013, http://thediplomat.com/2013/01/12/japan-and-indias-growing-embrace/?all=true.
21. Matthew Pennington, "China frustration with North Korea offers hope for US", *Associated Press*, 6 June 2013, http://news.yahoo.com/china-frustration-nkorea-offers-hope-us-070734955.html
22. Jeffrey Cho, "China-North Korea relations under Xi Jinping", *East Asia Forum*, 11 January 2013, http://www.eastasiaforum.org/2013/01/11/china-north-korea-relations-under-xi-jinping/
23. James Lamont, Anjli Raval, Michiyo Nakamoto, "US pushes India to take bigger Asian role", *Financial Times*, 25 October 2010, http://www.ft.com/cms/s/0/cbbdbc42-e056-11df-99a3-00144feabdc0.html#axzz2gl2s5Yhu.
24. V. Sudarshan, "This Ship Is Loaded", 23 October 2006, http://www.outlookindia.com/article.aspx?232925.
25. Palash R. Ghosh, "Why Does India Have Relations With North Korea?, Why Does India Have Relations With North Korea?", 30 December 2011, http://www.ibtimes.com/why-does-india-have-relations-north-korea-213592.
26. Palash R. Ghosh "Why Does India Have Relations With North Korea?", http://

www.ibtimes.com/why-does-india-have-relations-north-korea-213592, 30 December 2011.

27. "Park to Unveil Vision for Peace, Cooperation in Northeast Asia", *Korea Herald*, 5 May 2013, http://m.koreaherald.com/view.php?ud=20130505000158.
28. Park Ihn-hwi, "Northeast Asia and the Trust-building Process: Neighbouring States' Policy Coordination", *International Journal of Korean Unification Studies*, Vol. 22, No. 2, 2013, pp 1-17.
29. Tridivesh Singh Maini, "Park's Indian visit builds upon long-standing foundations", *Global Times*, 11 February 2014, http://www.globaltimes.cn/DesktopModules/DnnForge%20-%20NewsArticles/Print.aspx?tabid=99&tabmoduleid=94&articleId=841825&moduleId=405&PortalID=0.
30. Lee Jong Hwa, "Is North Korea Open for Business", *Project Syndicate*, 16 Jan 2014, http://www.project-syndicate.org/commentary/lee-jong-wha-advocates-a-chinese-style-period-of-economic-reform-and-liberalization-in-north-korea#Twzp6BG0zKF6Vww1.99; Paola Subacchi, "The Business of Korean Reconciliation", *Project Syndicate*, 6 January 2014, http://www.project-syndicate.org/commentary/paola-subacchi-reports-on-the-opportunities-and-challenges-posed-by-the-kaesong-industrial-complex.
31. Paola Subacchi, "The Business of Korean Reconciliation", *Project Syndicate*, 6 January 2014, http://www.project-syndicate.org/commentary/paola-subacchi-reports-on-the-opportunities-and-challenges-posed-by-the-kaesong-industrial-complex.
32. Kevin Sheppard, "Buying in to the Hermit Kingdom: FDI in the DPRK", *Korea Economic Institute Academic Paper Series*, Vol. 5, No. 11, 2010.
33. "Canadian, other Foreign Experts in North Korea for Rare International Conference", *The Associated Press*, 16 October 2013, http://www.ctvnews.ca/business/canadian-other-foreign-experts-in-north-korea-for-rare-international-conference-1.1499008#ixzz2vS6yqrKH
34. Bradley O. Babson, "North Korea's Push for Special Enterprise Zones: Fantasy or Opportunity", *38 North*, 12 December 2013, http://38north.org/2013/12/bbabson121213/
35. Kevin Sheppard, "Buying in to the Hermit Kingdom: FDI in the DPRK", Korea Economic Institute Academic Paper Series, Vol. 5, No. 11, 2010.

8

India, China and Tibet in Early 20th Century: An Imbroglio

Koushiki Dasgupta

Historians have long debated on the relevance of history in policy making. The designs of foreign policy are often influenced by the teachings of history. However, it depends on the policy makers how they use history.[1] In the disputes of India-China relations; however, history has a direct bearing on policy. In order to understand the roots of the problems between Sino Indian relations, the question of Tibet had never been displaced by historical records like other issues. From late 19th to early 20th century Tibet emerged as the strategic point of entry between India China relations. The principal legacy of this period has been carried out even in this century. However, in this study a basic outline has been drawn to understand the background of Anglo Chinese interactions over the question of Tibet—confined exclusively to India, China and Mongolia.

From the ascendency of British Empire in India, Anglo Tibetan relations reflected a great many themes. At the first stage the economic and political ambitions of the British Indian government basically their interest to gain access to the trans Himalaya and Tibetan refusal to its entry set the background for further developments. The most crucial part of this interplay was Chinese relationship with Tibet because of the official view that Tibet was part of the Chinese empire. It is generally agreed that from 7th to 9th centuries A.D Tibet was a powerful country and during the Tang dynasty rule in China, Tibet claimed to have an equal treatment with China, however, from 17th century onwards China's attitude to Tibet began to get conditioned by the broader aspects of central Asian policy as well as Britain's bid for a share of the central Asian trade developed new connections. In the year 1873, the urgency of adopting an active Tibetan policy was felt by the British government[2] in India on commercial and strategic grounds. Reverend Graham Sandberg, an eminent Tibetologist pointed out,

> '...they are (Tibetans) peace loving, and their confidence could easily be won. The development of the natural resources of the country-rich as it is in gold and wool and borax-under British auspicious and assistance would forge a clasp to the bond in the shape of self interest'.[3]

Britain at that point of time was too much interested to open up trade routes like Burma-Yunnan, Kashmir-Chinese-Turkestan, and India-Tibet-Sichuan. While exploring one of the routes one British official was killed and Britain forced China to sign the Chefoo Convention of 1876. However, the question was that the Chinese government would never welcome a British visit to Tibet because the Chinese influence in Tibet might have been disturbed and there was no guaranty that the Tibetan would accept a British mission on virtue of Anglo Chinese agreement. Tibetans were resentful that they were excluded from the convention. Interestingly the Chefoo Convention of 1876 incorporated a special article on the right of a British mission to Tibet; however, the fate of this much expected mission went into oblivion when China offered to recognize British control over Burma in lieu of cancelling the proposed British mission to Tibet. The British government was eager to have a settlement on the Burma question...a long dispute between China and India, and Lord Duffrin readily accepted the Chinese proposal. Ultimately the Anglo Chinese convention of 1886 put a check on supposed Tibetan connection with British India. A year after Tibet decided to set up a check post at Lingtu, 18 miles south of their frontiers with Sikkim. This incident led to a border skirmish between Tibet and British India leading to another Anglo Chinese Convention of 1893, Here China was compelled to accept British rights in Silkkim, allow British to open a market at Yadong-southern Tibet while allowing extra territoriality to the British in Tibet. But such facilities were not offered to Tibetan traders in Sikkim.

However, it cannot be denied that both China and Tibet opted for a Tibetan seclusion from British India. However the policy of Tibetan seclusion is keen to its history and culture. Travelers, scientists, geographical explorers, from different countries apart from the politician tried to open Lhasa in several occasions whenever they were exploring central Asia. One must note that, even though China accepted the policy of Tibetan seclusion from rest of the world especially from British India, she herself never gave up the desires of having control over Tibet. At different occasions whenever Tibet went to a conflict with her neighbors, either with Sikkim or with Nepal, the British government asked China to bring their Tibetan feudatories into line. China, indeed was desperate to get their control over Tibet accepted internationally, admitted t a point that her influence over Tibet is very nominal and the actual decisions were taken by the Lamas only.

After China's defeat in the Sino-Japanese war over Korea in 1895, her reputation in Tibet began to decline. Chinese settlement over Sikkim without the reference of Lhasa increased Tibetan suspicion as well as British resentment. The British Indian government was in a dilemma of communicating Tibet because it was impossible to communicate with Lhasa either through Peaking or through any other party. For this reason the British Indian government decided to interfere into Tibetan affair directly. In their words,

> 'We regard the so-called suzerainty of china over Tibet as constitutional fiction. China is always ready to break down the barrier of ignorance and obstruction and to open Tibet to civilizing influence of trade; but her pious wishes are defeated by the short sighted stupidity of the Lamas.'[4]

Anew chapter was opened with the advent of Lord Curzon in India. In the mean time Chinese authority over Tibet was proved to be a shadow and Britain had less need of her support against a possible confrontation with Russia and China's drawbacks had already been proved by Japan. To break the deadlock direct communications with Lhasa became a necessity. In the words of Lord Curzon, 'we seem, in fact, in respect of your policy towards Tibet, to be moving in a vicious circle. If we apply to Tibet, we either receive no reply, or are referred to the Chinese resident. If we apply to the later, he excuses his failure by his inability to put any pressure on Tibet'.[5] It was a situation when Nepal and Bhutan were trading with Tibet without any problem, but in case of the Indian merchants the visit to Tibet was through Nepal. Such a condition affected imperial dignity as well as imperial interest. China enjoyed almost a monopoly over the Tibetan market and the Tibetan population were no or less depended on their suzerain for their needs because they produced no manufactures. China naturally was not ready to share these with Britain. If British intimacy with Tibet could have made possible, articles could be supplied from India much more cheaply than China. Tibetans consume tea more; in that case better quality of tea could be supplied from Darjeeling at a cheaper price than the brick tea of China. To make it a reality, direct communication with Tibet was important by simply ignoring or bypassing China.

There was another concern too. The apprehension of Russia's southward expansion in central Asia was becoming a threat for the security of British Indian empire. Curzon declared, 'Chinese suzerainty over Tibet is a fiction, a political affectation'. He was true too some extent because after the consolidation of the power of thirteenth Dalai Lama, China was found to be inactive in Tibetan affairs and if China no longer controls Tibet, there would be a political vacuum soon. In that case Russia might have been interested to use Tibet as a buffer, even though Curzon realized Russia's inability to pose a direct military threat to India. The economic aspects were significant too in this case,

> To have a direct communication with Tibet, the search for a suitable emissary began and several names came into the list. Prior to that Curzon proposed London for a tripartite meeting between India-China and Tibet. However, the British government in London was a bit anxious of a probable face to face interaction with Tibet, rather they preferred the policy of engineering a Nepalese incursion into Tibet, so that Tibet could be forced

to come to terms and some of the border questions could be resolved without misusing British money and manpower. Curzon refused to this proposal and it was due to his over ambitious mentality that the London government at last permitted for a restricted delegation to Tibet, strictly on the basis of trade and frontier issues.

'China and Tibet should be given emphatic assurances that the missing was of an exclusively commercial character that we repudiated all designs of a political nature in Tibet, that we had no desire to declare a protectorate or permanently to occupy any portion of the country...'[6]

However, rumors and speculations about a secret Tibetan visit to Russia and an alleged Sino-Russian Treaty of 1902 made Curzon furious. This treaty was supposed to sanction Chinese territorial integrity in lieu of Russian influence over Tibet, Mongolia and Xinjiang. Even if there was not a treaty, Curzon continuously stressed on the secret game what China and Russia was playing with Britain. The Chinese were alarmed at this aggressive turn in British policy. China denied any secret agreement with Russia in which Russia was assured of a free action in Tibet. China declared that, it had nothing to gain by handing Tibet to Russia since Chinese government was a friend of Russia and Britain equally, it would not help one at the expense of the other. Even the London government was not certain of the agreement between Russia and China.[7] Irrespective of London's view, Curzon strongly focused on the supposed understanding...a game, which he was to frustrate at any cost.

As soon as the efforts of a proposed conference went in vein, there left no other option before the British government in London but to approve a small military expedition to Tibet reluctantly under Francis Younghusband in 1904. Colonel Younghusband was chosen to investigate if there was any Russian perfidy in Tibet. The Home government agreed to the mission proceeding as far as Kampa Dzong, a small station a few miles across the Tibet Sikkim border. The Tibetans refused to negotiate and asked the mission to go back. then the mission advanced towards Gyantse through Chumbi valley. The Tibetans resisted, troops sent and Younghusband Mission turned into a military expedition. This mission was resulted in the Anglo Tibetan Convention of 1904 which was virtually imposed on Tibet by the British.Its provisions were,

1. Two trade marts were opened at Gartok and Gyantse.
2. The Tibetans abolished all dues on trade to and from India.
3. An indemnity of half a million pound was to be paid by the Tibetan government in its seventy five installments. The Chumby Valley was to remain under British occupation until the payment was complete.
4. Without British consent no Tibetan territory to be ceded, leased to any foreign power, no concession for roads, mines etc.[8]

The Lhasa Convention was signed in 1904.In the final document there was no Chinese signature. The British accepted Chinese suzerainty but without an official Chinese seal.

The convention obliged Tibet not to allow any foreign representative entry to Tibet. But the question was about the status of Tibet. Could Tibet under Chinese suzerainty was independent to make treaty with any other state? If this convention too some extent sanctioned independent status to Tibet by making treaty with her, the Anglo Chinese convention of 1906 followed by the Anglo Russian Convention of 1907 ended all such aspirations. The new British liberal government of 1905 gave priority on Anglo-Chinese relations over Anglo Tibet relations. Although the Chinese poison over Tibet was not changed, the new British government now set off to improve the relation. The Anglo Chinese convention restored China's control over Tibet, without specifying the nature of control. However, the Anglo Russian convention accepted Chinese control over Tibet, and pledged not to deal with Tibet without the consent of China. The Chinese demands were accepted and the Adhesion Agreement of Peaking was signed in 1906. China agreed to pay the Tibetan indemnity of the 1904 convention, Britain accepted Chinese suzerainty over Tibet. It can be said that both China and Tibet achieved their goals...Tibet became a part of China and Britain received the sole rights of enjoying privileges over Tibet. In late 1906,Zhang Yintang called on a tripartite conference in Simla where the Tibetans were terms as delegate and both the British and Chinese were termed as plenipotentiary. However, Tibet refused to accept the Anglo Chinese convention of 1906 and repudiated it at Simla. Even though another Anglo Chinese trade Regulation came in 1908 Though made between Britain and China, this treaty accepted one Tibetan delegate and Tibet did not object and it although one provision was there that a diplomatic sanction of the 1904 Anglo Tibetan convention into this treaty. It was the first international agreement where Britain managed to get both China and Tibet to accept the agreement.

As an imperial power in Asia Britain was anxious about its relation with China and other states falling under Chinese sphere of influence because of their commercial interest in china. They were too much sympathetic to determine china's status over Tibet. As soon as Britain realized Tibet's strategic position to China and the moment china realized the intentions behind British sympathy, the relationship took new a new turn. On face of the growing Chinese control over Tibet after 1908, Dalai Lama fled to India in 1910. The Chinese then inflicted into Nepal, Sikkim, Bhutan and the tribal areas of north of Assam. The Chinese attempts of converting Tibet basically into a province of China alarmed Britain and gradually Anglo Chinese relations went into a change. Now the deposed Dalai Lama looked for help from British India against China. The reassertion of Chinese authority in Tibet in 1910, and its attempts to collect taxes alarmed the British because they apprehended that China would now try to make its presence felt in the Indo Tibetan border from Gartok in the west and Rima in the east. In the early years British administrative control was limited to the Brahmaputra Valley in the east, they could not access the densely forested hilly tracts of north eastern frontiers of India. The tribal's lived there. In order to avoid a direct conflict with these people specially at a time when British commercial interests were expanding into the east, the government decided to draw a line in 1873 (the inner line), that could not be crossed without a permit. It was an administrative boundary, however, one international boundary line was drawn in 1874 as east as far east as the Baroi river. Inspite of that the British time to time tried to expand beyond the outer line...no clear cut boundary line was there in 19th century. Both China and Tibet knew it. The gradual unauthorized expansion of the British into the north east beyond outer line made China alarmed, particularly after the Younghusband Mission and Lord Curzon's forward policy leading to a probability of making Tibet a protectorate. China did not sit idle and took her own forward policy close to India's north east frontier and set the motion for a chain of developments leading to the Simla Conference. Dorothy Woodman wrote,' Until the arrival of the Younghusband Mission in 1904 suggested a potential rival in Tibet, China had never shown any interest in the areas between the Outer Line and the Himalayan ranges.[9]

The policies taken by both the British Indian government and China made the north eastern tribals simply a pawn into the hands of these great imperial powers. The fall of the Manchu dynasty in China as well as the decline of Chinese control over Tibet, inspired the British to take a new policy of holding Tibet into the tutelage of the British government. Apparently they were talking for the independence of Tibet but her status as a sovereign state of China was yet to be changed. The British had to define its policy towards China and Tibet without violating the Anglo Russian Convention. The British appeared as an honest broker between China and Tibet and asked for a tripartite conference between Britain, China and Tibet. Britain was suspicious of a Tibetan link with Russia and they were to make a settlement of the boundary problems. In 1912 Britain send the new Chinese government an ultimatum that Britain would accept Chinese suzerainty over Tibet, if China withdraws all her claims on Tibet as a part of China. There would be nonofficial Chinese troops in Tibet. If these conditions were met then Britain would recognize the new Chinese government. Until these were met The Indo Tibetan border would be closed for all Chinese. China was left with no option but to accept the British proposal in enfeebled condition after the revolution of 1911.The conference started in 1913 in Simla between the Chinese, Tibetan and British representatives. Indian Foreign Secretary Henry McMahon appeared from the British side and it was very clear for the first day that who was actually conducting the conference. China had serious object in providing Tibet an equal status that of making her a treaty making authority. Britain secretly or openly encouraged Tibet for a bargaining on maximum possible autonomy from China and greened British protection against all future Chinese aggression to Tibet. If the British had to make Tibet an independent state, dependent completely on British Indian government, then the issues involving Tibetan Chinese relations and Sino Tibetan borders were to be taken into consideration. Side by side the definition of an India Tibet border was necessary for rule outing out future Chinese activities in the north eastern frontier. The

Simla conference divided Tibet into two zones, inner Tibet and outer Tibet. It set the India-Tibet frontier east of Bhutan along the crest of Himalayas, what came to be known as the McMahon Line. The British obtained the right to station a resident in Lhasa and exclusive trading rights in Tibet. Tibet achieved nothing except signing a treaty by her own. China refused to sign the principal agreement on the status and boundaries of Tibet on the ground that Tibet was subordinate to China and it had not the power to make treaties. The Chinese being neither consulted nor informed on Anglo Tibetan trade and the definition of the frontier. Although these agreements required Russian approval because it was a breach of the Anglo Russian Convention of 1907,but in 1917 the new communist government in Russia repudiated all international agreements of the Tsars. On the withdrawal of the Chinese, a declaration was issued that the convention was to be binding to the governments of Britain and Tibet and so long as the Chinese government withheld its signature, it would be debarred from the enjoyment of privileges accrued from it, However, just one month after the convention, Britain entered into the First World War and it had to concentrate into the European fronts.

The early British encroachments on Tibet were appeared to be a symbol of British imperial policy in Chinese consciousness. But after the Younghusband Mission Tibet appeared as a back door to China and Tibet's strategic position was raveled. In late 19th and early 20th century the international relation between Britain, China and Russia shaped the status of Tibet as a buffer state in inner Asia. Before the coming of the western colonial powers in Asia Tibet had to depend on the Mongols or on the Chinese for military protection. But after the emergence of European colonial powers in Asia the previous balance of power changed. For decades the interplay of British diplomacy and its fragile polices on Chinese control over Tibet proved the strength of British strategies far greater than a week divided China. How far the British were interested for the autonomy Tibet remained a question because they tried to protect the non coercive regime in Tibet for a secure frontier. However, in 1949 a stable communist government became ready to take over Tibet. And independent India became agreed to dismantle all her rights over Tibet. However, none of the new states i.e. the independent Indian government and the communist government of China inherited a defined frontier and the alignments of this frontiers had never been properly surveyed or delaminated. India inherited a sensitive boundary. Prime Minister Jawaharlal Nehru could not have been unaware of the fact that by not ratifying the tripartite agreement of 1914 and the McMahon Line, China readily forth a claim to Indian border territory, now claimed by New Delhi, but pointed out as Tibetan on Chinese maps, On 20th November, 1950, Nehru declared, ... 'our maps show that the McMahon line is our boundary and that is our boundary—map or no map. The fact remains and we stand by that boundary, and we will not allow anybody to come across that boundary.'[10] The disputed border issues between India and China gradually became a serious burden for the new independent state. The game what the British had left unfinished was now once again resumed with more vigor.

The McMahon Line was an imaginary one and it was never marked physically by other sides. What was a problem earlier now aggravated into a dispute between India and China.

China claims that McMahon Line is a disputed one therefore any border settlement on the basis of this line is not possible but China has resolved its boundary with Myanmar in 1960's only on the basis of this line only. As far as just over 4,000 KM Line of Actual Control (LAC) between India and China is concerned right from Ladakh to Arunachal Pradesh it runs with Tibet border. Main land China is far flung area from India-Tibet border. Due to Nehruvian idealism, we have lost our leverage over Tibet but still we have enough cards to play and maximize our interests. Tibet is the core issue between both countries. Perhaps China is awaiting the demise of Dalai Lama and than it will be ready to resolve the border dispute. In the meanwhile India must act as a strong country and in retaliation of stippled visa to Arunachal Pradesh people by China, we must also issue the same for the Tibet people because it is also disputed till date. Since 2009 more than 130 Tibetans have self immolated and after Vietnam crisis in 1970's perhaps it is the first time in the global history when people are burning themselves to dissent against the coercive regime. Human right is being eliminated in the case of Tibet in a brazen manner. It is high time for the global civil-society to raise this issue till its logical resolution.

NOTES

1. A good discussion on the relation between history and policy making could be found in Ernest R May, *Lesions of the Past; The Use and Misuse of History in American Foreign Policy*, New York, 1975.
2. A deputation from the Royal Society of Arts (consisting of Dr. Campbell, T.T. Cooper, Dr J. Hooker and B.H. Hodgson) drew the attention of the Secretary of State for India on the questions of trade with Tibet and talked about a mission to Tibet. For details see, T.T Cooper, *Travels of a Pioneer of Commerce*, London, 1871, B.H. Hodgson, *Essays on the Language Literature, and Religion of Nepal and Tibet*, London, 1874.
3. G. Sandberg, *An Exploration of Tibet*, Calcutta, 1904, pp.13-14.
4. Hamiton Papers, Curzon to Hamilton/PS/7/151, No, 182,8th January, 1903.
5. Papers relating to Tibet, Paper 1920 of 1904, Vol. 67, No. 26, Curzon to Hamilton, 30 March, 1899.
6. Curzon to Hamilton/PS/7/151, No.182, 8th January, 1903.
7. Foreign Office, 800/120, Satow to Lansdown, 11 September, 1902.
8. C.U. Aitchison, *Treaties, Engagements and Sanads*, Calcutta, 1929, Vol 14, p. 25.
9. Vide Parshottam Mehra, *The Younghusband Expedition: An Interpretation*, New Delhi, 1968, p. 120.
10. *White Papers on Indian States*, Delhi, Manager of Publications, Government of India.

9

India and China in West Asia: Energy Geopolitics and Strategic Objectives

Krishan Gopal

Geopolitics as an approach to the study of international relations stresses the importance of locational factors in influencing relations among nations. Thus, geopolitics emphasizes geographic factors as important determinants of government policy and major determinants of the relative power position of states. The importance of various geographic factor changes with developments in many areas, including the passage of time advances in technology, the need for access to raw materials, and changes in national and international political goals and judgments as to legitimate means of pursuing international objectives. The issue of access to energy resources involves strategic interests.[1]

Energy Scenario in India and China

Both India's and China's interest in the West Asia in first and foremost energy driven. The energy sector in India decides the direction of economic growth, as there is a direct correlation between the two. Faster economic growth in India continues to accelerate the demand for energy products. Therefore, India is one of the fastest growing energy markets in the world, with the demand continuing to outstrip the supply. The main drivers of energy consumption in India are electricity generation, industrial operations, transportation and urban and rural household uses. In government, there is a growing awareness that, if a high rate of economic growth is to be sustained, the power supply would have to grow by about 9 per cent per annum.[2] It is expected that, if India's economic growth reaches 7 per cent per annum, energy needs are expected to rise by 10 per cent annually.[3]

India's continued reliance on coal as a leading energy source is mainly influenced by cost factors besides imported oil resources. From the Indian perspective, fuels that are dependent on fluctuating international oil prices pose problems of uncertainty and foreign exchange exposure.[4] The price of Indian coal is fairly stable as it is not subject to the uncertainties of the exchange markets.[5] There is also a strong belief that the backbone of the electricity generation programme must be based on domestic sources of fuel.[6] Although India's primary energy source coal is abundantly available, there is a shortage and stagnation in the country's crude oil production. With the lack of exploration projects to exploit the domestic oil reserves, India is forced to rely on external sources to address its future energy needs. As a result, the country is resorting to large-scale oil imports, thereby causing a steep rise in its oil import bill.

China is the—world's second largest oil importer after the United States. The rapid growth in crude oil imports has significantly altered China's position in the world oil market. China now accounts for 6 per cent of global oil consumption compared to 3.5 per cent in 1988, whilst its share of world production only amounts to 3.9 per cent. China's economic development and its aspirations to diplomatic superpower status depend heavily on its Persian Gulf oil. However, China's potential exposure to economic dependence and to the political turbulence of the Persian Gulf touches a very raw nerve in its strategic thinking.[7]

Energy Politics

Despite talk of India and China staking up forces to set up some kind of a buyers and consumers cartel, competition rather than rivalry better describes the relationship between the two countries in the global energy sector. India is of the opinion that joint bids in third countries will bring down the price. But it is not about money. It is geopolitics. That is why for the Central Asian states and Iran in the Gulf, China is an important neighbor, an economic power and veto-wielding member of United Nation Security Council (UNSC). Besides, given China's long-term strategic thinking Beijing has quietly been building stakes in these countries. China has promised to veto sanctions against Iran in the ongoing nuclear crisis, besides selling technology for their missiles.

The Kingdom of Saudi Arabia, the largest supplier of oil to China and India, is building new refineries and increasing exports with the aim of strengthening political and economic ties with Asia's growing economic giants. These petro political partnerships are key to Saudi Arabia's efforts to contain Iran's political influence and military growth, especially its nuclear programme. Through oil diplomacy, Saudi Arabia hopes to sap Iran of important regional partners, a diplomatic coup the United States and other Western nations have so far filed to achieve. Despite Saudi Arabia's considerable economic clout, geopolitical constraints, and the economic incentives facing China and India present considerable obstacles to this ambitious foreign policy goal.

Saudi Arabia, the only country that produces more oil than Iran, is determined to eliminate Iran's geo-political trump card.[8] Saudi Foreign Minister Prince Saud al-Faisal has assured China that the Kingdom will met China's energy needs if it stops importing oil from Iran, and has attempted to convince Beijing that a nuclear-armed Iran will foment instability throughout the Middle East. Both Saudi Arabia's increase in oil exports to India and the security aspects of the Riyadh Declaration, which highlight Saudi Arabia and India's shared interest in combating Iranian-backed violent Islamic extremism, are similarly meant to persuade to New Delhi to scale back its trade with Iran and support Saudi Arabia's foreign policy goals.[9]

The Arab spring has presented India with an opportunity for greater engagement with the region. Coming as it does on the heels of India's 'look west' policy the country is helping with institutions and knowledge-building in nascent democracies like Egypt. The GCC countries too are looking to non-western economies to invest their surplus funds, especially now, given their recent disenchantment with the United States role in the region. India, therefore, becomes a natural choice for playing a leading role. Defence ties between India and the GCC countries are also set to increase. Ties between India and Saudi Arabia assume special significance in this context. The official visit of PM Manmohan Singh to Riyadh in 2010 and the Riyadh declaration signed in 2010 and February, 2014 visit of Saudi Prince Salman bin Abdulaziz Al Saud—crown price, deputy prime minister and defence minister of Saudi Arabia elevated the bilateral engagement to 'strategic partnership', covering security, economic, defence and political areas.[10] India-Saudi Arabia ties are no longer seen through the prism of India-Pakistan relations. Next, India's ties with Iran has not deterred the deepening of Indo-Saudi ties.[11]

Indian policymakers choose to believe that over the long-term China will inevitably develop highly aggressive tendencies, pushing ahead vigorously with the development of tactical, strategic, and theater nuclear weapons. But a good case can be made that China's challenge to India is wrongly perceived. India is far more threatened by being left behind economically than by military and political pressure. It is economic competition with China in regional and global markets that will determine the winners and losers in the 21st century. In turn, China will have acknowledge India's desire to be viewed as the pre-eminent regional power in South Asia to a greater degree than it has to date.[12] Curiously, although India is usually described as the world's largest democracy and China the largest authoritarian, communist regime, these ideological and institutional differences seem to matter very little in determining how they shape their policies towards one another.[13]

China's access to oil and gas from Gulf, greatly constraining its geo-strategic options. Not least, China's emergence as a major and growing oil importers has raised the potential cost of policies that serves to destabilize the Gulf. Chinese policy in the region has get to catch up with this reality. Like the US, China now has a vital interest in abroad range of issues such as ensuring security of the Strait of Hormuz, averting a dangerous regional arms race, and helping bring some modicum of stability to Iraq shared by all major oil consuming countries.

Energy Security Strategies

As of now, India generates around 50 per cent of its electricity from coal-fired power plants, around 32 per cent from oil and the rest from natural gas, hydroelectric and nuclear resources. Since the capacity addition through thermal, hydroelectric and nuclear resources is unable to keep pace with the rapidly increasing demand for electricity, India has decided to make natural gas the fuel of choice for future electric power generation projects. Indeed, the country's consumption of natural gas has risen faster than any other fuel in recent years. Since the bulk of the country's energy supply originates from the West Asia, any future conflicts and/or political realignments in the region may exacerbate the problems of India's energy security. However, unlike the oil trade, which is regulated by the cartel rules of the Organisation of Petroleum Exporting Countries (OPEC), trade in natural gas is unregulated. Hence, there is room for considerable flexibility in fixing natural gas prices through long-term contracts.

To ensure that its energy strategy revolves around its long-term objectives, India has considered various options to import natural gas either through pipelines or as LNG. The leading pipeline proposals, mostly trans-border in nature, include the importation of natural gas through pipelines from Iran, Oman, Qatar, Turkmenistan, Bangladesh and Burma. Among these projects, the Indo-Iran gas pipeline is under serious consideration by India as other proposals are considered uneconomic and/or politically impossible.

The Indo-Iran Pipeline Project

The proposal for an Indo-Iran trans-Pakistan pipeline project was first mooted in 1989 by then Deputy Foreign Minister of Iran Ali Shams Ardekani. At the time, the official Indian response was largely negative as the country had poor relations with both Iran and Pakistan. However, after considering the feasibility of the pipeline project for 4 years, especially its ability to deliver supplies over the long term, India finally signed a Memorandum of Understanding with Iran 1993.

There are three option available for the Indo-Iran gas pipeline project; that is, overland, deep sea and shallow sea. For India, more important than the economic cost and technical complexity of this project is the safety and security of its supply. Initially, India entertained the trans-Pakistan route as its preferred option for the Indo-Iran pipeline project. However, at the time Pakistan cited a lack of confidence between itself and India as the main reason to not to enter into the project.[14]

As a result of Pakistan's failure to take a firm political decision in favour of the overland pipeline project, India decided to look for alternative energy route. With Pakistan's reluctance to provide transit for the Indo-Iran gas pipeline project, Iran was also looking at the possibilities of building the pipeline in deep waters, thereby avoiding Pakistani territory. When India and Iran started exploring the deep-sea option, Pakistan realized that its stakes in the pipeline project were under threat. It realized, the deep-sea option for a Indo-Iran pipeline would deprive Pakistan of both transit revenues and the opportunity to purchase gas from the pipeline at subsidized rate. As a result, the Pakistan government announced that it would permit an Indo-Iran pipeline to pass through Pakistani territory.

A number of factors compelled the Pakistan government to review its views on the trans-Pakistan route for the Indo-Iran pipeline project. The first is its desire to exploit the country's geo-strategic location as an advantageous transit country for this and future pipeline projects originating in the West Asia and Central Asia, it is unlikely to exploit its geo-strategic position in the region unless the end destinations of the pipelines are India or China. With China showing little interest in trans-Pakistan pipeline projects, the country is pinning its hope on the Indo-Iran pipeline project.[15]

Pakistan also realized that the Indo-Iran pipeline project would have enormous benefits for its economy. Such a pipeline could accrue to Pakistan an income of US$ 14 billion in savings.[16] Although the transit fee would not wholly redress Pakistan's acute foreign debt crisis, it would partly alleviate this problem. Finally, Pakistan, like India, suffers from a growing oil-pool deficit. Pakistan's power generation is heavily dependent on fuel oil, and it is a net oil importer with an oil import bill of over US$ 1 billion per annum.[17]

The strategic shift to include Pakistan in the Indo-Iran pipeline project has the capability to gorge a new relationship between Indian and Pakistan. The trans-Pakistan pipeline has immense potential to create a conducive atmosphere and add new meaning to the bilateral relationship. Such a relationship would also facilitate India's long-term commercial interests in Central Asia. The beneficial effects of trans-Pakistan pipeline project would also spill over into areas such as commodity trade, science and technology, and human resource development in both India and Pakistan.

Political Strategy of Development of Chahbahar and Gwadar Ports

In order to address its need to secure energy routes, and to counter the growing Chinese influence in the Arabian Sea, Persian Gulf, and the Indian Ocean, India brought Iran into an economic and strategic alliance. India spent huge amount on the Iranian Port of Chahbahar. Iran is already working on Chahbahar port in Sistan-Baluchistan, which will be easily accessible for Indian imports and exports through road and rail links to Afghanistan and Central Asia. The development of Gwadar in Pakistan by China, and Chahbahar by India, resulted not only in open rivalry and competition between the two countries in the region, but also raised contention for the economic and natural resources of Central Asia.

Chahbahar's geo-strategic location plays an important role in connecting India to Afghanistan and Central Asia both militarily and economically. India sees Central Asia, Iran, and Afghanistan situated at the crossroads of overland trading routes as a potential consumer market for India products. Similarly, Iran wants to get India's cost effective source of high technology inputs.[18] India's ultimate objective is to by pass Pakistan, and also cooperate with Iran on a highway system that leads from Chahbahar port into Afghanistan and Central Asia.

On the other hand, active Chinese cooperation in the Port of Gwadar, since it is the only port, which can serve the best interests of both China and Pakistan in the region. The Port will, therefore, enable China to keep a strict watch on India's growing influence in the Indian Ocean, the Arabian Sea, and Persian Gulf. Hence, the possibility of any future economic and military collaboration between India and the US in the region can be effectively dealt with. Another geographical advantage of the port is that it will reduce the distance for energy imports from Persian Gulf to China. Gwadar also holds a geo-strategic significance for China because of its proximity with the sea lane between the West Asia and China. It is vital for oil trade. As a gateway to the Indian Ocean, Gwadar will provide Beijing with a listening base from where the Chinese may exert surveillance on hyper-strategic sea links. The military activities of the Indian and American navies in the region can also be closely watched. Gwadar port will also provide a strong base for Chinese ships and submarines. Since Gwadar Port can fulfill its political, security and commercial objectives vis-a-vis India, China has spent a huge amount on its construction.

More significantly, Gwadar Port provides both Pakistan and China to strengthen its security vis-a-vis India. The port win also help both China and Pakistan to promote trade with Gulf states possessing 63 per cent of world's oil reserves.[19]

China has acknowledge the strategic significance of Gwadar no less than that of the Karakoram Highway.[20] This will further strengthen the relations between China and Pakistan. China is also interested to turn Gwadar into an energy-transport hub by building an oil pipeline from Gwadar into China's Province of Xinjiang. The proposed pipeline will carry crude oil from Arab and African states. Gwadar's strategic advantage to China is due to its close proximity with the Strait of Hormuz. The presence of the US forces in the region poses not only a threat to Chinese navy but, also to its commercial interest. Gwadar provides China with a strong base where it can monitor US naval activity in the Persian Gulf, India in the Arabian Sea, and the future of Indo-US maritime cooperation in the Indian Ocean. China has already set up electronic posts at Gwadar for monitoring maritime traffic through the Strait of Hormuz and the Arabian Sea.

Chahbahar is a part of the Indian grand design to apparently develop transportation infrastructure. It is however viewed with suspicion to sabotage Pakistan's future strategy of expanding its influence in Central Asia and beyond. Chahbahar provides India with any easy access to Afghanistan and Central Asia through Indian Ocean. India's ultimate desire is to connect Chahbahar with Central Asian countries through roads and a network of railway system to bypass Pakistan, and to reduce the dependency of Central Asian countries on the Pakistani port of Gwadar. Iran is already enjoying close socio-cultural and economic relations with the Central Asian countries. Iran is working on several projects in Tajikistan including the Anzob tunnel, and constructed a bridge over the Amu Darya that connects Chahbahar with Khojent route. In addition, the construction of 218 km long Zaranj-Delaram highway that now links Afghanistan to the Iranian port of Chahbahar also connects Herat and Kabul via Mazar-e-Sharif in the north and Kandhar in the south-thereby providing easier access to Afghanistan and possibly even further, to Central Asia via Iran.[21] Because of the fact that Central Asian countries are land-locked, they depend on Iranian ports, especially, on Chahbahar for trade and commercial relations with the rest of the world. Moreover, Afghanistan is more friendly and close to India than Pakistan. In this regard, with its eco-strategic positioning in Iran, India gets a pivot opportunity to have an access to warm waters through this region. The creating of North-South Corridor is the best prospect for Iran to expand its transit corridor to India. The idea of North-South Corridor has multiple purposes and is, therefore, seen an opening to bypass East-West Silk Road Project.[22]

Thus, India gains more security, political, economic and strategic advantages depth from Iran, Afghanistan and Central Asia as compared to China. Iran is more stable than Pakistan. It has better relations with Afghanistan and the Central Asian states. Bordering Azerbaijan and Turkmenistan, Iran has a natural geographical advantage by providing access to Sea for the Central Asian States. However, intensifying competition between India and China in Arabian Sea and Central Asia, the growing US concerns about China's offensive capabilities, made the global and regional security environment more complex and sensitive.

NOTES

1. Shiv Kumar Verma, "Energy Geopoliics and Iran, Pakistan-India Gas Pipeline," *Energy Policy*, 35, 2007, 3280-3301
2. Ashok Mubayi, "Indian Energy Market Moves into a new Generation," *Power Economics*, Vol. 4, No. 2, February 2000, 18.
3. "India Needs Long-term Projections for Energy Needs," *The Economic Times*, Vol. 6, 8 Match 2001.
4. Mubayi, *op. cit.*, no.2.
5. *Ibid.*
6. *Ibid.*
7. M.G. Salameh, "Quest for Middle East Oil: The US *versus* the Asia-Pacific Region," *Energy Policy*, 31, 2003, 1085-1091.
8. Aaron Mattis "Oil Sheik-Down: Saudi Arabia Struggle to Contain Iran," *Harvard International Review*, Spring, 2010: 10-11.

9. *Ibid.*
10. Aditi Bhaduri, "Self Interest should Guide India's Arab Policy," *The Hindustan Times* (New Delhi), 4 March, 2014.
11. *Ibid.*
12. Verma, *op. cit.*, no. 1.
13. G.M. Weinbaum, The limits of Realpolitik in the security: Environment of South Asia. In: Balance of Power in South Asia. The Emirates Center for Styrategic Studies and Research. Abu Dhabi; 2000 citied in Verma *op. cit.*, no. 1.
14. Farah Naaz, "Indo-Iranian relations: Vital factors in the 1990s," *Strategic Analysis,* Vol, XXV, No, May, 2001: 227-41.
15. S.G. Pandian, "Energy Trade as a confidence Building measure between India and Pakistan: A study of the Indo-Iran trans-Pakistan pipeline project," *Contemporary South Asia,* 14:3: Sept. 2005: 307-20.
16. Khaleeq Kiani, "Slim prospects of trans-Pakistan gas pipeline," *Dawn, 12 April, 2001,* as cited in Pandian, *op. cit.*, no.15.
17. Hassan Vahidy & Fereidum Fesharaki, "Pakistan's gas discoveries eliminate import need," *Oil & Gas Journal,* 28 January, 2002 24-34 as cited in Pandian *op. cit.*, no.15.
18. Juli A. MacDonald, "Rethinking India and Pakistan's Regional Intend," *The National Bureau of Asian Research Analysis,* 14:4: 2009: 5-26.
19. Rajeev Ranja Chaturvedy, *Interpreting China Grand Strategy at Gwadar*, Institute of Peace and Conflict Studies, 14 February, 2006.
20. *Dawn,* July 4, 2006.
21. *Tehran Times (Tehran)*, November 28, 2011.
22. Mohammad Arifeen, "Chahbahar Port: Its Importance for India," *The News International (Rawalpindi)*, November, 22, 2011.

10

America's Asia-Pacific Engagement: The Implications of a Novae Eastward Overarch

Manan Dwivedi

Background

Asia-Pacific resonates as a region which brings in cherished memories of cultural imageries, sea kissed beaches along with the verisimilitude of religion and diversified identities which tend to amalgamate the region and offers strategically significant lure to extra regional nation state actors to reorder their priorities which are also driven by geo economic interests. The love of literary souls will engender sea and lagoonish imageries of the literary classic 'Papillion'[1] along with the myth and lore of the phenomenon of, "Archaic Globalization"[2] with the visage of Tupia in the locale of Tahiti who hankers after cloth being traded out of the bark of an South East Asian tree in commercial hubs in South East Asia.

The nations during those years hobnobbed with West Asia and the Indian subcontinent through the maritime ways which now have become contested territories in the strategic firmament of the region. The history of the region might not make for interesting reading but the theme of Cultural beatitude remains a pointer of enough characteristic regional significance. The tale of the Navajo tribes in the region being misutilised as fodder military carriers through the United States and the Allied Pacific forces against the Imperialistic Japanese during the hey day of World War II. Also, as an attendant factoid the people in the region have also witnessed the rural and cityscapes of Vietnam, Cambodia, Indonesia, Papa New Guinea, etc. being utilised by Great Powers as an instrumentality of power and its aggrandisement, where-in, the people and the polity responded to tied conditions of an Occidental dominance of the then exigencies of the Cold War era international system.

Asia-Pacific to the rest of the World is known largely as a kind of large collection of Archipelagic islands and cloudy national boundaries which is inhabited by populations to be civilized and modernized which witnessed the Great East Asian Crisis in the late 90's leading to a regional economic downturn. The backyard of the economic and economic juggernauts of Japan, People's Republic of China and South Korea is also another sobriquet and a false subordinated identity which is embalmed on their existential question. In a World dominated by the international Supercop and the Pivot, United States of America, the regional nations have had to contend with the much debated extra regional great power intervention in the light of new contestants in the region of the order of India and China. The Chinese claim to the Spratly and Parcels ion the South China Sea and the diplomatic confrontations with the nations of the order of Vietnam and Philippines also emerge has the recent bones of contentions in the regional matrix of relationships with an inherent impact upon the area's regional Balance of Power equation.

The United States and the Regional Matrix

The United States of America is a great power par excellence. The nation has an unintended intention to be nomenclatured as a "Benign Hegemon".[3] It can also be construed as "Renewed Leadership" in the light of the post-Economic Decline developments in United States where-in, the notion of engaging with a non-eurocentric international polity seems to be the core of the American Foreign Policy think. Thus, the salience of the New American Century seems to be brought to bold relief in the international firmament in the World of 2013. National Security Advisor to President Obama, Tom Donilon, has commented in the Asia Society on March 11, 2013, that,

The nation has always been divided between the twin Schools of "Internationalism/Interventionism" and "Isolationalism". The American propensity to enhance the 20th century Monroe Doctrine initiating with the intervention in the Spanish War, Philippines, Korea, both the great wars, Vietnam, the Iraq wars, Afghanistan, Somalia, Haiti and Bosnia have led to a rising distaste for the American frontier spirit and its espousal of the cause of liberal Democracy internationally. The other strain laments the economic and strategic and domestic overarch of the American empire as it has been trenchantly criticised since the US debacle in the muggy marshlands of Vietnam and Indo-China.

Secretary of State Hillary Clinton has stressed the American intent in the new post September 11 context after the initiation of the Global War on Terror. The Secretary informed the international community that, "With our Southeast Asian allies, Thailand and the Philippines, the United States is working closely on an expanding range of political, economic, environmental, and security-related issues including the Creative Partnership Agreement with Thailand, which brings together Thai and American universities and businesses and the nation state of Philippines, will host the 2+2 Strategic Dialogue."[4] This what the American Secretary of State stated in Honolulu, Hawaii in October 2010 much in tandem with the notion of "Forward Deployed Diplomacy".[5] Now, the GWOT[6] in Philippines is not the only fulcrum around which the US-Pilipino relationship revolves as the interaction goes beyond the terror spectacle and a great deal of extra-bilateralism is reflected the various treaties and concluded negotiations.

The international politics scholars have termed the new tilt as a 'Paradigm Shift" though the objectives and the contours remain the same as before and the similar earlier pretensions abound. It is understood that, "'Forward-Deployed' diplomacy first emphasizes the need for the US to take the initiative to shift the diplomatic front forward rather than the strategic contraction in Asia that occurred during the Bush administration."[7] The tenet also broadly refers to a new approach in American Diplomacy which posits that, "The large US diplomatic system is too conventional and inflexible. Now, US diplomats have realized that they need to transition from traditional diplomatic bureaucracies into flexible rapid response teams, so that people in Asian-Pacific countries can directly experience US foreign policy."[8] Thus, the approach does not constrain itself to the practice commonly followed by United States to deploy armed forces on multifarious borders. It is much beyond that and follows an equally important soft power and negotiating and "presence" strategy with a human touch to counter the militaristic onslaught of an emerging China. In a post-Economic Depression World of United States, the international magnate can no longer afford the economic burden of inflated military budgets after withdrawals from the nation states of Iraq and Afghanistan.

United States of America has initiated a novae Diplomatic initiative for the East Asian nations which is termed as TPP or the Trans Pacific Partnership which in a way competes with the much more East Asian narrative of RCEP or the Regional Comprehensive Engagement for the Pacific where-in, the TPP ought to be a supportive instrumentality for the much more Asian RCEP. The ASEAN portal reports about the regional concern about the recent conduction of Nuclear tests by North Korea which is a matter of concern for the Big six group of nations which have deputed to delve inside the matter of Nuclear Proliferation by the North Korean nation.[9] It is here where the US role has been questioned as it leads up to the contradiction in the American policy think that when it comes to containing a Nuclear Iran or a fake threat in Iraq, then the United States establishment provides boots on ground but the North Korean Nuclear intransigence is dealt with a murmur and a verbal condemnation only. This bespeaks of a double edged policy on the part of the United States vis-a-vis the policy towards a Nuclear armed North Korea.

RCEP serves as a rejoinder to the TPP. There happens to be a more than palpable differentiation between the twin economic arrangements. Beginda

Pakpahan contends that, "The TPP calls for deeper integration than RCEP, promoting trade in goods, services and investment, as well as tackling other issues (for example, IPRs). RCEP will be a partial WTO-plus arrangement, which focuses on trade in goods, several types of services and investment."[10] The author further contends that, " The win arrangements of the order of TPP and RCEP may clash due to the nature of relationship between the US and China, as both intend to spawn their own definition of economic cooperation in the Southeast and East Asian regions in order to further their national interests in the region."[11] Thus, the covert competition witnessed in the relationship betwixt US and China might influence the future portents of the regional economic superstructure. Thus, the Chinese and American clawing strategy inside the shoals of East Asia might bifurcate the regional economic Regime of the dat in the region at large which will have a long termish deleterious impact upon the general sense of economic collectivity in the region.

Still, the regional leaders are flagging off the RCEP more than the externality of TPP as for a few nations belonging to the ASEAN the notion of an America led economic Regime remains an uncomfortable idea to contend with.[12] The Wall Street Journal reports that, "avoid a "noodle bowl" of overlapping deals—even as countries within the region pursue bilateral and trilateral trade deals. If successful, the trading bloc would cover a combined economic output of $20 trillion, or almost one-third of the global economy." [13] Still, happens to be a concern amongst the ASEAN nations that the bilateral and Trilateral frameworks and the FTA's envisaged in the regional framework might not be able to compare favorably with the US supported TPP with its wider Global and quasi Global overarch. Now, PRC too has begin commenting favorably about the RCEP in view of its perceived rivalry with the American Trans Pacific partnership. Interestingly, the Trans Pacific partnership does not include China but has the nation states of the order of Australia and New Zealand as its partners and members in the much more global Economic Regime. Does India emerge as a gainer in the competition between TPP and RCEP? That is a million dollar question.

As the RCEP includes India friendly states and TPP is supported by United States, the Indian nation state can plough along on both the boats as at the end of the day India is always involved in the bilateral and multilateral arrangements in Asia-Pacific. That would be what an E.H. Carr, Kautilya and Neibuhr would suggest India to do. Still, a more saner approach with a mature bent of mind can be in the offing. The Thai Secretary General of Asean, Surin Pitsuwan, reflected this statesmanlike vision at RCEP's launch by saying, "The effort is to try and isolate the two issues (political tussles and economic deals). Economic integration will have to go forward."[14] One more regional prescription can be the striving by the partner AEAN nations to pragmatically understand the extra-territorial ramifications of the twin arrangements and concentrate upon an apolitical and more of an economically oriented Regimen for the East Asian region.

The East Asian Summit: Where does the US Stand in the Fray?

The **East Asia Summit** (EAS) is a forum held annually by leaders of, initially, 16 countries in the East Asian region. Membership expanded to 18 countries including the United States and Russia at the Sixth EAS in 2011. The United States of America since ages has played the effective role of a balancer in the East Asian region and now the age arrives for a true liberal American President to shelve Real Politique behind in the pre-september 11 days and communicate the American assertion for a balanced and stable approach to the regional disputes. President Obama has suggested the eschewing of rhetoric and the adherence to a more mature approach to the South China Sea claims and counter claims in the recently concluded East Asian Summit right in the middle of the advent of the Asian century.[15] Thus, US needs to vindicate its stand vis-a-vis the bad experience and experiments in the nation state of Vietnam which it has largely done with the human centric and sustainable interface with the nation state of Vietnam since the time of resumption of a diplomatic relationship with the same state years ago in the 20th century.

President Obama used his re-election momentum to take on critics and courageously go where no sitting US president had tread before, literally. After visiting Thailand, home of the oldest US alliance in Asia, he made historic visits to Myanmar and Cambodia in his first post election jaunt abroad. President Obama stressed during his historic visit that, "It was time for a US leader to come and encourage political and economic reform."[16] In a related development, during President Obama's visit, "the government of Myanmar released at least 51 political prisoners during the president's visit, assuaging some anger about an amnesty of more than 500 prisoners a few days before that included no prisoners of conscience."[17] Thus, the American agenda apparently stresses on a rapprochement with the Triumvirate of leaders in Myanmar which augurs well for political economic reforms in a nation which was under the scanner of the international Human Rights organizations and the INGO's since a long time during the tenure of Aang San Su Kyi's while she was the first political prisoner of conscience and a was under military detention by the Mynamerese Military junta.

The EAS is just one regional grouping and some members down play its significance, the former Australian Prime Minister John Howard has stated that the EAS was secondary as a regional summit to Asia-Pacific Economic Cooperation (APEC) which has on his view a premier. [18] This effort to relegate the East Asian Summit to the backburner happens to be a manifestation of the predicament of a regional divide as different nations such as China, US and Australia have contending interests in the region at large.

As part of the full and active engagement of United States in the Asia-Pacific region, the East Asia Summit renders an institutional opportunity for the United States to thrust its weight around and a long handle with which to provide a pseudo security Umbrella for the East Asian nations in the long wind to contain the "Han". There is no longer any perceived indifference in the South East Asia after the not so welcomed engagement with the nation state of Veitnam.[19]

An European Union like regional cooperative approach does not exist in the rubric of the North Eastern nation states. There rae a few palpable factors ranging from regional attributes to historicity which have acted as a spanner in the works of a new Multilateral Regime in the regional landscape. These factors include: persistent nationalism and mutual mistrust caused by colonial history and war, territorial disputes, ideological confrontation throughout the Cold War period, US engagement in the region based on a bilateral "hub-and-spoke" system, and the lack of political will in facilitating multilateral cooperation. Political and security matters are still perceived as contentious rather than cooperative in the regional matrices.[20] The presence of Obama at the currently held East Asian Summit has led to the notion of easing out of American wars and nimbly shifting the American Pivot to South East Asia and beyond in the moorish seascapes of Papillon. The American President did refer to the East Asian security affairs but once for a witnessed sea change the stress was on the financial and economic implications of the change in the relationship with East Asia.[21] Along with the intertwined multilateralism of the region with the implicated American interests, the North Korean Regime under Kim Jong Un, too, remains a pointer in the direction of the American efforts of engagement with recalcitrant state actors too.

The American concern in the North Korea remains foremost with the South China sea contestations where-in the regional rivalries between the micro state actors such as Vietnam and Philippines tend to obfuscate the smooth strategic environment in the sea which is a major route through which the international martiome and commercial traffic passes through. The Chinese and American interests here-in clash with the smaller South East nations being sill in the favor of an American Defense and Nuclear Umbrella. The Nuclear ambitions of a Dictatorial Regime in the neighborhood also plays foul of the peace, stability, stolidity and tranquility of the region. The Asian century has the Nuclear North Korea as a significant thorn in the flesh of the Western interests and also the general peaceable nature and context of a sun kissed and wind swept region which is also a major tourist attraction for the rest of the Globe.

Also, the containment Doctrine which reeks of Cold War speak finds its ramification in the Nuclear ambitions of North Korea and the general overreach of United States in the region. In the aftermath of the American plea to reduce tensions in the region and do away with confrontationist rhetoric, the North Korean underground Nuclear tests in the February, 2013 too deserve a mention.

The Korean scenario makes for a tumultuous and interesting reading and strategic observation. It can be amply highlighted that the Autocratic nature of the Regime in Korea makes for an engaging study of personality cult of Dictators in the North Korean Republic. North Korea's confrontational relationship with

United States since the bloodshed and vitriol of the Korean war and political crisis in the 50's along with the Cold war wrangling led to the communist Korea, i.e. the Pyongyang attaining an adversarial relationship with the United States and the NATO block of countries forms an interesting historical narrative.

The stress of the American foreign policy mandarins on the contemporary context of the Asian pivot and Forward Deployed Diplomacy is only a precursor to the economic and strategic containment doctrine which US adheres to in relation with North Korea. The strategic consequences and the attendant fallouts of the series of Nuclear tests conducted by North Korea with the recent one being conducted in February, 2013 is another recent signpost which has raised hackles with the Obama Administration. Also, the moving out of the Korean Republic from the Non Proliferation Treaty will be another theme worthy of academic interest. Another issue specific concern happens to be the exigencies of the Non proliferation movement and the demands of Disarmament by the Western nations. The creation of the six nation group with the Chinese and the American presence can too be delved inside. All in all, the US approach towards North Korea in the light of its "impending intervention" approach towards other crisis centres such as Libya, Mali, etc are also significant discussion themes.

Also, the notion of an Eastward containment is affected by the poignant rendering of incidents of North Korean repression in the context of a personage named as Lee who used to reside in DPRK. He initiated a business of importing automobile parts from the People's Republic of China through the bribing of North Korean border guards. Lee used to invite the clandestine imports through boats across the Yalu river and hide the monetary proceeds beyond the eyes of the authorities underneath his Kitchen floor.[22] He still aggress that he regrets the decision to defect and migrate to Seoul where—in, he still ceases his narration of his great escape when someone begins to mention about Kim Jong Un. Such is the fear which the Americans smell and respond to when a new DPRK denizen sends them a (Save Our Souls) missive.[23]

Also in the light of the recent visit of the American Secretary of State, John Kerry, India and the Asian context can take a turn for a better and a revisited relationship. As the twin democracies of the order of India and United States have embarked on a novae road to a multilateral and a multifaceted relationship, the Kerry interlude also re strengthens the relationship with India in the neo Asian Pacific context. Though bottlenecks in the relationship remain as is made evident by the following diatribe against the Indian business interests by the US interests, "policies by the Government of India to favour domestic producers over US exporters," are "inconsistent with India's international obligations, set a bad precedent, and undermine the culture of innovation that Indian Prime Minister Dr. Manmohan Singh himself has been promoting."[24] Still, long ranging deals on green energy, climate change negotiations, trade in Howitzers and C-130 J special operations from Aerospace major, Lockheed Martin etc are some of the recent tete a tetes which have been grasped between the twin democracies which have a definitive impact upon the Asia-Pacific. In the context of TPP and RCEP, the Indian strengthening will have a counter response from the PRC's establishment. Also, the nations such as Japan and South Korea will look anew towards the American security and strategic Umbrella which the South East Nations always looked with hope and aplomb. Thus, the Indian coming in the US fulcrum through a co equal relationship in the ambit of the 4th Strategic dialogue between both the nations comes with opening new expectations in the region.

Vice President Joe Biden too visited India and he made more than a symbolic impact on the relationship amidst the twin nation states. Most of it was a reiteration of the American take on the strategic dialogue.[25] US Vice President Joseph Biden did not galvanise any significant breakthrough, but provided a valuable opportunity to renew the high-level political contact between the two countries at a time when there is some concern in India that the Obama administration is not paying adequate attention to the bilateral relationship.[26] Los Angeles Times too reported that the objective of the visit is to kick start an old and enfeebled relationship in a comprehensive manner meaning the biometrics of the handshake will extend all across the relational spectrum.[27]

The few deliverables in the visit were pointed out by the analysts as the civil liability legislation remain a major thaw in the relationship.[28] Also, the American nuclear synergy and the talk about an American nuclear Umbrella for Asia will face the same bottlenecks keeping in view the still forcefully pressurising world view of the United States. The Biden visit is a part and parcel of the American inclination to firm up a neglected tie in the larger Asian context as part of the notion of forward Deployed Diplomacy as is the case with the numerous Asia-Pacific nations. Kishore Madhubani too bespeaks of the misfortune of the Asian nations which let the West leap ahead of the rest of Asia after the kick start which the Asians had initiated for themselves.[29] Still, history speaks of US as being still the weakened but a Global leader in more senses than one even in an non Asian context.

Conclusion

Now with the commissioning of the first Aircraft Carrier of an advancing and expansive Chinese Navy and the intertwined notion of the virtual confrontation with the Japanese over the Senkaku Islands,[30] the security and strategic conditionalities might be warped for a stable and equipoise scenario in the region all taking place under the rubric of an American overarch. The national overarch of the regional patriotic implications too tend to mar the politico-strategic landscape of the region. Still, the implications of an American Mt. Sinai approach is not much embroiled in an Occidental-Oriental antagonism in the quintessential Clash of Civilization mould but it is harking back to the crude Hobbesian construct of Realism with veiled references to Bryan Jennings references to ***a Universal's Civiltas.***

The American interest lies in the post American Decline mould of a striving to resurrect its seat of international influence but now it is a policy which is more firmly saddled within an economic move with the cooption of newer actors in the Asian stage too as the Westphalian stage is all set to enter a new order ordained by State centric agents in Asia-Pacific. What remains a million dollar question and an IR holy grail is the notion that to what extent can the American surge in the waters of East Asia be actively and purposefully moderated by a Novae American internationalism but very much in consonance with the entangling alliances of the day.

NOTES

1. Papillon is a Book by Haenry Charreire which tells the story of a fugitive from French Colony of French Guiana where the natural and pristine beauty of the West Pacific with its marshlands, beaches and the sylvan tropics is narrated in its all resplendence. There is also a Hollywood movie by the same name released in 1973.
2. Martell, Luke (2010), "The Sociology of Globalization," *Policy Press*, p. 45. See also Rossi, Ino (2008). *Frontiers of Globalization Research: Theoretical and Methodological Approaches*. Springer Science + Business Media, pp. 33-36.
3. J. John Ikenberry; "America Unrivalled: The Future of Balance of Power," 2002.
4. Hillary Rodham Clinton in a Speech Delivered in Honululu, Hawai in October 28, 2010, "America's Engagement in Asia-Pacific Speech", URL: www.state.gov (Online: Web), Accessed on 15th February, 2013.
5. "US Playing the Long Game in East Asia", *Global Times*, November 16, 2010.
6. GWOT: The term can be expanded as the Global War on Terror which was part of the President Bush's "With us or Against Us" paradigm which was a clarion call and the 21st century American Strategy to counter Al-Qaeda and its affiliates in the aftermath of the WTC bombings.
7. "US Playing the Long Game in East Asia", *Global Times*, November 16, 2010.
8. Ibid.
9. "Statement by the Chairman of ASEAN on Underground Nuclear Tests by the Democratic People's Republic of Korea", URL: www.asran.org (Online: Web), Accessed on 15 February, 2013.
10. Beginda Pakpahan, "Will RCEP compete with TPP?" URL: http://www.eastasiaforum.org/2012/11/28/will-rcep-compete-with-the-tpp/ (Online: Web), Accessed on 17 February, 2013.
11. Ibid.
12. Enda Curran, "ASEAN Leaders push Regional Trade Pacts", *Wall Street Journal*, November 19, 2012.
13. Ibid.
14. "The RCEP and TPP Struggle: India Advantageous", URL: http://legalpronews.findlaw.com/article/00nLdeYa0W8FP?q=Surin+Pitsuwan (Online: Web), Accessed on 19 February, 2013.
15. "Obama Urges Restraint in Tense Regional Disputes", URL: http://www.reuters.com/article/2012/11/20/us-asia-summit-idUSBRE8AJ08520121120 (Online: Web), Accessed on 19 February, 2013.
16. Ernest Z. Bowner, "The ASEAN and East Asia Summits: US Walks Softly While China Welds a Big Stick", "URL: http://csis.org/files/publication/121121_SoutheastAsia_Vol_3_Issue_22.pdf, (Online: Web), Accessed on 19 February, 2013.
17. Ibid.

18. "Graeme Dobell, "APEC Leads Asia Summit, PM Says", Transcript of American Broadcasting Corporation, 14th December, 2005 from the American Program 'AM' which is broadcast on local American Radio.
19. Lee Shin Wa, Korea University, "The East Asia Summit and the Difficulty of Establishing a Security Regime in North East Asia", Council on Foreign Relations Report, 2012.
20. Ibid.
21. "Obama Addresses Pressing Issues at East Asia Summit", URL: http://atlanticsentinel.com/2012/11/obama-addresses-pressing-issues-at-east-asia-summit/ (Online : Web),
22. *The Economist*, March 19, 2013.
23. Ibid.
24. Amrutha Gayathri, "John Kerry's India Visit to Focus on Indo-US Nuclear Deal Hiccups and Others", URL : http://www.ibtimes.com/john-kerrys-india-visit-focus-us-india-civil-nuclear-deal-hiccups-trade-imbalances-defense-deals (Online: Web)
25. C. Uday Bhaskar, "Joseph Biden Visit: Can India Live up to US Expectations". *The Economist*, July 29, 2013.
26. Ibid.
27. Mark Magnier, "Joe Biden's India Trip a Bid to Strengthen Ties," *Los Angeles Times*, July 22, 2013.
28. Ibid.
29. Kishore Madhubani, "Can Asians Think? Understanding the Divide Between East and West" (Steerforth, 2001) Also see, Fareed Zakaria, "The Post American World," Penguin Books, 2008.
30. See *The Economist*, March 19, 2013.

11

India and Xinjiang: A Study of Historico-Cultural Linkages

Mahesh Ranjan Debata

Introduction

India's historical and cultural linkages with China's Xinjiang region through people-to-people contacts are more than 2,500 years old. The foundation stone of this linkage was laid by land trade that witnessed regular contacts between traders/merchants from India, mostly Ladakh and Kashmir, and southern and south-eastern regions of Xinjiang through the Silk Route. The historical and cultural aspects of this partnership were buttressed by a new phase of civilizational linkage with the introduction, spread and prevalence of Buddhism in the region. For a long time, till the advent of Islam in the region, Buddhism remained the most important religious faith among the people of Xinjiang. Buddhist gospels on India's rich cultural heritage and spiritual thought percolated into the hearts and minds of the people of the entire region, further led to cultural efflorescence of Xinjiang, as well as the adjacent regions such as Central Asia. However, the century-old relationship between both the regions ceased to exist after China came under Communist rule in 1949, and further got totally cut off after the Sino-India war in October 1962. The end of Cold War in the early 1990s following the disintegration of former Soviet Union has heralded the dawn of a new era. With the emergence of five independent republics of Central Asia, the strategically located Xinjiang has brought new hopes for India since both Central Asia and Xinjiang regions have been historically and culturally important for India. Amidst talk for revival for the Silk Route, there began the hope to revive the age old ties between Xinjiang and India. For India, this will be a boon in disguise, as India now perceives Xinjiang as a potential landbridge to Central Asia from where it aims at getting the much required energy resources in the near future. Interestingly, cultural content of this relationship, which was once shaped up by trade contacts, is now perceived as a fulcrum to nourish economic cooperation between the two regions. Against this background, this paper discusses the present and future of India-Xinjiang relationship in the light of the historical-cultural contacts between the two regions since ancient times.

Cultural Linkages between India and Xinjiang

The ancient Silk Route helped in integrating the rich cultural heritage of India and Xinjiang and promoted the exchange of idea and intellect, and most importantly, trade and commerce. Almost half of the fabled Silk Route, which winded along between Xian to the east bank of the Mediterranean, was located in Xinjiang, where the ancient Western and Oriental cultures met and flourished. During the Han rule, links with India got a major boost, particularly when Han General Zhang Qian sent his assistant to India to find ways and means for promotion of bilateral trade between the two regions.[1]

Buddhism: Fulcrum of Cultural Linkage

Buddhism, one of the foremost precursors of Indian culture, was the single most important factor that had influenced the relationship between India and Xinjiang. Kumarajiva (344 AD-413 AD), one of the four great sutra translators in China, contributed to the growing cultural link between Xinjiang and India through his preaching on Buddhism. His father, Kumarayana, who was from a noble family in India, went to Kuqa and married the king's sister, Princess Jiva. Jiva renounced family life and travelled to India along with her seven year old son, Kumarajiva and studied under renowned Buddhist masters. At a tender age of seven, Kumarajiva had memorised many sutras and texts, and his name, fame and glory spread throughout five kingdoms of India. At the age of twelve, he travelled with his mother to the oasis city of Turpan in Xinjiang, but the king of Kuqa went personally to Turpan and brought him back to Kuqa. He translated 74 texts in 384 fascicles from Sanskrit into Chinese, which greatly contributed to the propagation of the Dharma in China.[2] Famous Chinese travellers, Fahien and Hieun Tsang, who visited India, had made all out efforts to promote Buddhism along the Silk Road.

By the 7th century AD, all the kingdoms in the Tarim Basin region embraced Buddhism. Sanskrit became the main religious lingua franca. Kashgar, Yarkand and Khotan in the western part of Xinjiang, Tumsuk, Aksu, Kumtura and Kizil in the north, Loulan, Karasahr and Dunhuang in the east, and Miran and Cherchen in the south became important learning centres of Buddhist philosophy and thought. The Kumtura Thousand-Buddha Caves lying 30 kms to the southwest of the Kuqa Prefecture not only symbolizes Buddhism, but also glorifies its noble principles. For all Buddhist people across the globe, it has become an important pilgrimage centre. The Buddhist texts were translated from Sanskrit into local dialect such as Tocharian. By 658 AD, Kuqa became the main hub of Hinayana Buddhism. Fahien and Hieun Tsang confirmed that most of the kingdoms in Kashgar, Kizil, Karashahr and Kuqa followed the Hinayana form of Buddhism, whereas Mahayana form of Buddhism flourished in Khotan and Yarkand. The discovery of Buddhist images, murals, frescoes, some symbols of lotus, mandala, swastika etc. and inscriptions in Sanskrit, Brahmi and Kharostri scripts and artefacts depicting Indian traditions in Kuqa, Kizilgaha, Kumtura, Khotan, Kashgar, Dunhuang, Yotkan, Dandan Uiliq, Niya, Loulan, Turpan etc. bears the testimony of Indian cultural influence.[3]

An ivory plaque collected by Swedish explorer, Sven Hedin from Khotan region of Xinjiang (now kept in the Ethnographic Museum, Stockholm, Sweden) is believed to be more than a thousand years old. It presents a very intricate composition in the form of a *Yantra* or *Mandala*. According to it, Tantric Buddhism, which was originated in India, was popular in Khotan region in the 9th-10th century AD. Other sources confirm that the Khotan region was an important centre of Tantric Buddhism during the early medieval period.[4]

Kashmir Connection

This is but obvious that there is also a Kashmir connection to the whole issue of India and Xinjiang relationship, because this region has a 350-km long border with Indian state of Jammu and Kashmir. As discussed earlier, Kumarayana, the great Kashmiri scholar visited Xinjiang to preach Buddhism and his son Kumarajiva later became the symbol of spreading Buddhism across the entire region. Traders travelled between India and Xinjiang on Himalayan caravan routes over Karakoram Pass between Kashgar in Xinjiang and the Gilgit and Hunza valleys (presently in Pakistan). Later in 18th century, King Gulab Singh (1792 AD-1857 AD), the Dogra ruler of Jammu, pushed his kingdom's boundaries into Xinjiang. Gulab Singh and his military commander General Zorawar Singh looked beyond the frontiers of Ladakh and took measures to safeguard trade routes from raiders and plunderers, besides ensuring the steady flow of trade from Xinjiang into Ladakh and Kashmir, particularly the lucrative shawl wool trade. Gulab Singh's son and successor Ranbir Singh (1830 AD -1857 AD) went one step ahead. He abolished all transit duties on merchandise passing to and from Xinjiang through Kashmir and Ladakh so that the existing trade would get a major boost. The Srinagar-Leh-Yarkand route became the most important thoroughfare between India and Xinjiang during the Dogra rule in Kashmir. The Karakash Valley served as an important caravan route for the north-south trade between Yarkand (China) and Leh over the Karakoram Pass in Leh district of Jammu and Kashmir.

British Era: Political Issues and Trade Contacts

Further, the British authorities in India began to pay great attention to Xinjiang, especially for political reasons and strategic factors. They wanted to gain a foothold in Xinjiang so that any move by the Tsarist Russian ruler to expand beyond his empire could be staved off. At that point of time, under the Tsarist expansion policy, Russia took control of the khanates in Central Asia, especially Kokand, Khiva, Fergana, Samarkand and Bukhara. The British Indian authorities apprehended any further expansion of Tsarist empire towards India either through Afghanistan or through Xinjiang. As a precautionary measure, the British rulers in India first tried to get a foothold in Afghanistan, but failed miserably. Then to establish its presence in Xinjiang, British authorities looked at Xinjiang, where they found a favourable ally in Yakub Beg, a Kokandi general, who ruled over Xinjiang from 1867 AD to 1877 AD. Yakub's dislike for the Chinese prompted him to build harmonious relations with the British Indian authorities, which augured well for the overall relationship between the two regions, especially trade. In 1874 AD, the British authorities signed an agreement with Yakub in order to obtain freedom to trade with low duties in the region. Yakub was instrumental in promoting bilateral trade between his kingdom in Kashgar and India. He blocked all Chinese imports into Xinjiang. Yakub purchased a huge cache of arms and ammunitions worth millions of rupees from British to counter Qing offensive. During this period, Indo-Xinjiang trade was carried on the horseback and mules over the high mountain ranges dividing Ladakh and Xinjiang.[5] However, the ouster of Yakub Beg by Qing rulers and the subsequent increase in bilateral overland trade between Xinjiang and Russia affected India's trade with Xinjiang. Russia remained a dominant force in Xinjiang from 1920 to 1949.

In 1885 AD, a mission headed by Ney Elias, an official of the Foreign Department of the Government of India, arrived in Kashgar to negotiate a trade agreement. From 1890 AD, the Government of India appointed an official resident to be stationed at Kashgar. Colonel Francis Younghusband was the first British official resident in Kashgar, and was replaced by George Macartney in 1891 AD who stayed there until his retirement at the end of the World War.

British consulate in Kashgar is the only diplomatic organization of British Empire in early 20th century in Xinjiang. It handled business activities and other diplomatic activities in Tianshan regions on behalf of British Empire and its colonies such as India. When Tsarist government first set up consulate in 1881 in Kashgar, British Empire was unwilling to be lagged behind, so it also set up a consulate here to contend and collude with the Tsarist Russia influence. Earlier, English requested the Qing government that a consulate and special minister be set up in Xinjiang, because businessmen from India had done business in Kashgar for a long time.[6]

Further, the period from 1890 to 1908 saw an increase in export of coral ornaments to Xinjiang from India. During the rule by Chinese warlords in

Xinjiang in the Republican era, India's trade with Xinjiang continued unabated. The period from 1917 to 1931, India exported goods worth 30 million rupees that constituted cotton goods and silks, dyed skins, indigo, spices and tea to Xinjiang through Kashmir and Ladakh. Merchandise worth 33 million rupees was imported from Xinjiang into Ladakh and Kashmir of which *charas*, Russian gold and paper currencies, gold dust, raw silk, carpets and felts were the main import items. The India-Xinjiang bilateral trade through Kashmir and Ladakh was worth seven million rupees during the year 1920-21.[7] From late 1930s onwards, internal disorders in Xinjiang arisen out of the creation of East Turkestan Republic (1933-34) and subsequent opening of Russian overland trade with Xinjiang dealt a fatal blow to Indo-Xinjiang trade which finally ceased to flow in the year 1949 following the Communist takeover of Xinjiang. In a nutshell, the British period witnessed overwhelming trade and transaction between India and Xinjiang, which rekindled the historical and cultural linkages.

Post-Independence Period

India achieved independence from the British yoke in 1947 and China became an independent republic two years later in 1949. This marked the end of direct India-Xinjiang connection and the beginning of India-China relationship. Following the Communist takeover of China in 1949, China eyed India with suspicion over Indian support to Turkic Uyghur Muslims, the majority ethnic group in Xinjiang, the reasons being (i) the age-old linkage between the people of India and Xinjiang, and most importantly, (ii) sympathetic view from Indian establishment as India had a sizable number of Muslims. The Chinese fear was corroborated by Soviet factor and the relationship between India and the USSR in the post-independence period. The Soviet Union, which had been eyeing to gain foothold in Xinjiang since Tsarist rule in 18th-19th centuries, were able to establish consulates in Xinjiang from 1920 onwards. Even though Russia did not support Uyghurs initially, but provided whole-hearted support to Uyghurs to establish an East Turkestan Republic in 1940s. This marked the beginning of enmity and animosity between China and Russia that persisted throughout the Cold War period till the disintegration of former Soviet Union.

Since Uyghurs have been demanding a separate homeland of "East Turkestan" out of China, the Chinese suspicion on India grew further. In 1950, two top Uyghur leaders, Mohammad Amin Bughra and Isa Yusuf Alptekin, left Xinjiang with 200 families for the Indian State of Kashmir to secure asylum in India. Since both Bughra and Alptekin were spearheading the Uyghur movement in Xinjiang, the Communist leadership in China suspected Indian patronage to these two Uyghur leaders. However, this was proved wrong after Bughra and Alptekin left for Turkey in 1950 without getting any patronage or help from India. Even today, the Uyghur separatists do not curry India's favour or sympathy for their cause – a separate Islamic republic exclusively for Uyghurs. India, having its own problems of separatism and terrorism in the State of Jammu and Kashmir, deplores any kind of separatist and terrorist violence not only in Kashmir or Xinjiang, but also anywhere across the globe.

1962 Sino-India Dispute and Other Issues

With the closure of Indian Consulate General in Kashgar and sealing of Xinjiang's borders in 1949, traditional links between India and Xinjiang were cut off. And since then there was not even any indication on India-Xinjiang connection. Even the symbolic British-India Consulate in Kashgar was made a hotel. The war between India and China in October 1962 finally sealed the fate of a once vibrant India-Xinjiang cultural linkage. Later on, what added insult to injury was the thorny issue of Aksai Chin, which continues to haunt the relationship between the regions even today. Aksai Chin was ceded to British India by Tibet through a treaty in the early 1900s. But since China does not recognize Tibet's independence from China at that point of time, it does not recognize the treaty. The Aksai Chin region, which was controlled by Pakistan illegally, was gifted to China on 3 March 1963, immediately after the Sino-India war (October 1962), and now it forms part of Khotan County of Xinjiang. India still claims the territory of Aksai Chin as its own. Recently, China had put forward the "east-west swap" proposal,[8] which was outrightly rejected by India, Under this proposal, China would abandon its claim on Indian State of Arunachal Pradesh, recognizing Indian sovereignty over that area, in exchange for India giving up its claim on Aksai Chin, recognizing Chinese sovereignty over that area.

Six Decades of Sino-India Relations

Whatever the differences India and China have in the last six decades, both the regions share at least two similar views now: (i) trade and economic partnership, and (ii) fight against separatism, religious extremism and terrorism. In this era of globalisation, when economic development has become the main buzzword, India and China, have emerged as two important global actors. Since economic development has been able to resolve many contentious issues around the world, both the countries believe, this will resolve all extraordinary issues between the two. The Sino-India trade in 2011 has touched 75 billion US dollars and will reach the 100 billion US dollar target by 2015. The economic boom in Xinjiang and the proximity of Xinjiang to resource-rich Central Asia have prompted India to adopt a proactive approach towards Xinjiang. With Xinjiang prospering by leaps and bounds under the Chinese Central government's Great Western Development Programme, a new and dynamic region in their neighbourhood would be available to Indian entrepreneurs for their trade and business activities. The Great Western Development Programme focuses on the development of the entire western part of the country of which the north-western region of Xinjiang forms an important part. The programme lays stress on the all-out development of the region for which trade and economic cooperation with the neighbouring regions/countries is very much essential. Now, Xinjiang has effective border trade with three Central Asian republics such as Kazakhstan, Tajikistan and Kyrgyzstan, Mongolia and even Pakistan. Both India and China are now considering the opening of Xinjiang-Kashmir trade route on the line of Nathu La border point in Sikkim in July 2006. Border trade with Ladakh and Kashmir will not only revive the ancient cross-border trade between the two regions, but also help renewing people-to-people contact as part of the historical and cultural relationship both the regions had nourished earlier. In order to strengthen business relations with India, four trade delegations from Kashgar had arrived in India in recent years and were welcomed by India's business community. Two important issues need to be highlighted here, as they could become a ray of hope for the revival of India-Xinjiang contracts: (i) regional economic integration of Kashgar; and (ii) Silk Road economic belt.

Economic Integration of Kashgar

The year 2004 has been a watermark as far as the issues related to India and Xinjiang are concerned. Firstly, in June 2004, the authorities in Xinjiang promoted a nationwide campaign to achieve economic integration of Kashgar,[9] a town known for its historic role in matters of China's trade through the ancient Silk Route, with eight countries in Central and South Asia including India. The main thrust of Kashgar's economic integration with Central and South Asia to ensure security, stability and prosperity of the volatile region of Xinjiang. In 2009, Kashgar was made a Special Economic Zone (SEZ) on the model of Shenzen and Guangdong. Shenzhen and Hong Kong signed an agreement to invest 3.7 billion US dollars in Kashgar in 2011 and offered 15 million US dollars to help the local enterprises to expand and to provide employment to 30,000 people. The Chinese Central government has decided to provide financial subsidies to the Kashgar SEZ from 2011 to 2015, exempt qualified business enterprises from income-tax, subsidize fixed-asset investment and offer government loans to qualified companies at discounted rates. The government also intends to give discounts to qualified farm product-processing enterprises and other labour intensive companies by reducing their power consumption and transportation fees. The investments in major infrastructure-facilities construction projects in the two zones, including the construction of the China-Kyrgyzstan-Uzbekistan railway and the China-Pakistan railway have increased.[10] For India, the proposal for Kashgar's economic integration with the outside world, assumes greater significance since India had maintained a trade mission in Kashgar from 1890 uptill 1949.

Secondly, a six-member delegation led by the Governor of Xinjiang, Ismail Tiliwaldi, visited India in October 2004, as a follow-up action to the economic integration of Kashgar, in order to revive old ties and promote bilateral interaction with India. Both the sides made proposals for India-Xinjiang land link, air route (Delhi-Kashgar via Urumqi), laying a natural gas pipeline from Xinjiang to India through Ladakh and bilateral cooperation in four fields—agriculture and food processing, traditional medicine and herbs, energy and oil production and tourism. Both sides believed that the road link could transform the two economies. The delegation reiterated how trade contact was the mainstay of cultural cooperation. With a reliable land link through Pakistan to Central Asia still a distant dream, linking Ladakh, which is in eastern Jammu and Kashmir and borders Tibet, to Xinjiang and then reaching out to Central Asia, will not only tap the resources of the region, but also result in greater cooperation in diverse fields. For India, the pipeline proposal with Xinjiang will open new connectivity between India and Central Asia. Since the much-vaunted Turkmenistan-Afghanistan-Pakistan-India (TAPI) and Iran-Afghanistan-India (IAI) pipelines to bring energy resources from Central Asia and Iran respectively, have not been realised so far even after 22 years of discussion and deliberation,[11] due to lack of political will, lack of coordination among the member nations, and most importantly, an apprehension about turbulent situation in Afghanistan and Pakistan, a natural gas pipeline from Xinjiang could be a feasible proposition.

The delegation highlighted the issue of the "evil forces"—separatism, religious extremism and international terrorism. China's north-western region of Xinjiang, which has a border with India's Jammu and Kashmir State, has been facing the challenge of separatism. Since its independence in 1949, this region of China has been a theatre of violent separatism. And the post-Cold War situation in the region has been grim and gruesome. The situation in Xinjiang in the last six years has been very violent, the recent being an attack in Urumqi on 22 May 2014 that killed 35 people and injured more than 100 others.[12] These violent activities not only tormented the restive northwestern region, but also its reverberation was felt in the Chinese capital Beijing. On 28 October 2013, a Sports Utility Vehicle (SUV) knocked down pedestrians and burst into flames near Beijing's Tiananmen Square, killing two tourists and injuring over 40 people. This incident assumes importance because (i) the incident occurred in one of the most heavily guarded areas of Beijing. Although there were major bomb blasts in Beijing in the 1990s that the Chinese government attributed to Muslim separatist groups, this was the first major suicide attack on Beijing in recent years; (ii) the attack took place just weeks before the third plenum of Chinese Communist Party (CCP), which means the attackers had to contend with increased state security. If additional attacks were successfully carried out, they could prove extremely embarrassing for the CCP; and (iii) Beijing apprehends an international connection to this attack, probably believing any Al-Qaeda group as its mastermind. This is being corroborated by one report by *Inspire Magazine*, an English-language publication by Al-Qaeda's Yemen branch, which sought to inspire Muslims in English-speaking countries to carry out lone wolf or small cell attacks against the countries in which they live. The magazine contains stories glorifying Jihad as well as ready-made instructions to carry out attacks. The second edition of the magazine encourages prospective terrorists to turn a pick-up truck into a human lawn mower by placing large steel blades on the vehicles for a large scale attack.[13]

Similarly, the Indian State of Jammu and Kashmir has been a mute spectator to mindless jihadi terrorism sponsored from across the border resulting in an irreparable loss of human lives and public property. Since 1948, Pakistan has been waging a virtual proxy-war against India, which has gained momentum from 1980s onwards. India's concern for growth of religious extremism and terrorism in Xinjiang was much more when several news reports on Uyghur terrorists of East Turkestan Islamic Movement (ETIM) being trained by Al-Qaeda and Taliban in Afghanistan were published. Even in 1999, more than a dozen Uyghur terrorists, who fought on behalf of the Pak sponsored invasion in Kargil sector of India, were caught by Indian security personnel.[14] In this context, exchange of experience and intelligence information between the two as they come closer, in tackling the common menace of terrorism, would be mutually beneficial. Any common perception about terrorism which could emerge between India and Xinjiang out of such exchanges may even influence the Chinese views on the happenings in Kashmir. Though, Pakistan has been an all-weather friend of China, so far China has maintained silence on the Kashmir issue and wants this issue to be resolved bilaterally.

Xinjiang Governor's Visit to India in November 2011

After a gap of six years, the regional government of Xinjiang is keen to revive the frontier trade with India that once flourished along the Silk Route. Xinjiang government's Development and Reform Committee (DRC) seemed to have acknowledged India's claims to Pakistan occupied Kashmir (PoK) ahead of Xinjiang Governor Nur Bekri's visit to India in November 2011, and described Kashgar as bordering India, not Pakistan, and finally making the case for increasing frontier trade with India. There were particular advantages in developing frontier trade with India, said the DRC.[15] It welcomed Indian companies to invest in Kashgar, which possesses great growth potential in bilateral trade. The DRC said it would also favour the opening of international flights from Kashgar to India, and would encourage foreign airlines to open direct flights. Officials from Xinjiang's Political and Legal Committee, that accompanied Nur Bekri during his India visit, said that they would like to work more with India on counterterrorism. Bekri's visit to India at the invitation of the Government of India, under the India-China Distinguished Visitors' Programme, was the outcome of a cultural programme being organised in Kashgar in 2011 and India Ambassador to China S. Jaishankar's visit to Urumqi in October 2011. The Indian ambassador met officials from Xinjiang-based energy companies TBEA and Goldwind, which are interested to invest in India. Trade between India and Xinjiang has soared in 2011, increasing 92.4 per cent year-on-year between January and September 2011, reaching 47 million US dollar, the highest in the past five years.[16]

Nur Bekri, Governor of Xinjiang Uygur Autonomous Region of China, while addressing a Business Session organised by the Confederation of Indian Industry (CII) in New Delhi on 2 November 2011, called for building trade and investment relationship between India and Xinjiang. Bekri said that with extensive economic reforms of last three decades, Xinjiang has developed greatly and now offers huge business and investment opportunities in sectors like oil and natural gas, mining, agriculture, tourism, Information and Technology, pharmaceutical and biotechnology. Besides, Bekri highlighted strengthening of cultural exchanges between India and Xinjiang to build people to people relationship. Nur Bekri, leading an official delegation of 19 officials and leading business people from Xinjiang, held official talks with the Minister for Commerce and Industry of India, Anand Sharma, high profile officials of India's Ministry of External Affairs, besides business leaders, academia and media. He informed that TBEA, a leading global electric service provider of Xinjiang, has signed an agreement for investment of 100 million US dollars in Gujarat.[17]

Speaking ahead of the start of the Shanghai Cooperation Organisation (SCO) summit meeting in Beijing on 30 May 2012, Shi Dagang, Vice Chairman of Xinjiang's provincial government, expressed his government's desire to boost land trade with India. He stated, "we have no land port with India so our trade with India has to be routed through Pakistan, through places like Rawalpindi. It only takes 50 minutes by air from New Delhi to Kashgar, while the land distance is only 1,200 kms. I believe that with our relationship deepening this trade link will be further utilised."[18]

Silk Road Economic Cooperation

In September 2013, Chinese President Xi Jinping, during the 13th Summit of the Shanghai Cooperation Organization Member States held in Bishkek, proposed establishing a Silk Road Economic Belt. Silk Road economic belt aims at all round development of the entire belt that would boost trade, transit and traffic connectivity, besides augmenting people-to-people contacts. One scholar sums up the features of this initiative: (i) This initiative will bring about unity among nations and a commitment to cooperation, by means of greater connectivity and complementarity among East Asia, Central Asia, South Asia, Southeast Asia and West Asia, thus bringing pan-Asian and Eurasian regional cooperation to a new level; (ii) the initiative will boost infrastructure development and structural innovation in order to improve business environment of the region, besides facilitating an orderly and unimpeded flow of production factors and their efficient distribution, accelerating development of landlocked countries and remote and inaccessible pockets, lowering costs and barriers of trade and investment, and driving greater reform and opening up by regional countries; and (iii) this will strengthen people-to-people contact irrespective of nationhood, regions, classes and religions, which further consolidates the foundation of friendship among people and contribute positively to peace and development in Asia.[19] For India, the importance of the Silk Road economic belt stems from a number of factors such as historical, cultural and economic. And this could be a stepping stone to the revival of age old ties between India and the regions along the Route, such as Xinjiang and Central Asia.

Conclusion

To conclude, the revival of India-Xinjiang traditional link that hovers around the historico-cultural tag depends solely on the governments of India and the People's Republic of China. Both the countries are responsible world powers with economic prowess and military might. Xinjiang is important for both these two mighty neighbours. While on one hand, it is China's gateway to the resource rich Central Asia region, on the other, it could be India's landbridge to Central Asia. The development in Xinjiang, whether positive or negative, will have impact on both India and China. Since India and China are moving in the right direction in the recent period, with bilateral trade projected to touch 100 billion US dollars in coming couple of years, and meaningful engagement at political and diplomatic levels, there is a glimmer of hope for a relationship based on mutual trust and understanding. The last few initiatives such as economic integration of Kashgar, visit by two Xinjiang's provincial governors to India in 2004 and 2011, Silk Road Economic cooperation have been interesting and positive signs for both India and Xinjiang. The visits by Xinjiang Governors clearly show that the Chinese leadership are keen to revive the age old India-Xinjiang linkage. Even Indian embassy in China has been participating regularly in Euro Expo in Urumqi for the last few years. In the recent times, the leadership of both the countries has shown desire to strengthen their cooperation. The new Indian government under the leadership of Narendra Modi that came to power in May 2014 has expressed its desire to extend hands of friendship to China in order to resolve all outstanding issues between the two neighbours. As a corresponding gesture, the Chinese leadership had sent its Foreign Minister to India in the first week of June 2014 to facilitate new vistas of cooperation among the two neighbours. Besides, the political community, the business leaders, mediapersons and academicians of both the countries now hope for a better India-China partnership. What is worth noting here is the vehement condemnation of a violent attack in Urumqi on 22 May 2014 by the spokesperson of India's Ministry of External Affairs (MEA). According to the spokesperson, "We strongly condemn the terrorist attack which took place earlier today at Urumqi, China. India opposes terrorism in all its forms and manifestations. We extend condolences to the families of the victims."[20] This is perhaps for the first time, the MEA issued a statement condemning any violent attack in Xinjiang. This is definitely a positive signal for the age-old India-Xinjiang cultural linkage.

NOTES

1. "Historic Silk Road", http://www.China.org.cn/english/MATERIAL/139504.htm
2. For more details, see the conference proceedings of International Seminar and Exhibition on "Kumarajiva: Philosopher and Seer", Indira Gandhi National Centre for the Arts, New Delhi, 3-5 February 2011.
3. "Buddhism and its Spread along the Silk Road", Silk Road Foundation, http://www.silk-road.com/artl/buddhism.shtml
4. For more details, see Mahesh Ranjan Debata, "India and Xinjiang", *World Focus*, vol. xxxi,

no. 11-12, Annual Number, November-December 2010, pp. 528-531.

5. The main items from India exported to Xinjiang were opium, cotton, piece-goods, spices, Indian tea, sugar and indigo, and the imports from Xinjiang included *charas*, tea, silk, wool, felt, carpets, gold and silver, precious stones, horses and mules. Ladakh was connected with the Silk Route at Yarkand by a caravan route running across the Karakoram pass. Bulk of Indian trade with the oasis towns of Yarkand, Kashgar and Khotan was carried through Kashmir and Ladakh. Xinjiang exported gold and silver, *charas*, shawl wool, carpets and felts, tea, Chinese tea-cups, leather-ware, coarse cotton cloths, raw silk and ponies to Ladakh and Kashmir. Under a barter system, the traders from Yarkand used to bring these goods to Ladakh where they exchanged the same with their Indian counterparts. They even moved further to Kashmir, Punjab and Himachal Pradesh to expand their flourishing trade. Similarly, Indian traders went beyond Ladakh towards Yarkand to purchase goods at relatively low prices. Indian traders brought cotton clothes, brocades, Kashmir shawls, indigo, spices, dyed goat skins, opium, preserved fruits, coral, indigenous medicines, sugar and books to Leh. For details, see K. Warikoo, "India's Gateway to Central Asia: Trans-Himalayan Trade and cultural Movements through Kashmir and Ladakh, 1846-1947", in K. Warikoo (ed) *Himalayan Frontiers of India: Historical, Geopolitical and Strategic Perspectives*, London & New York: Routledge, 2009, pp. 1-13.
6. "British Consulate", http://www.kashi.gov.cn/english/Context/History40.htm
7. Warikoo, op. cit.
8. The East-West swap was first proposed unofficially by Zhou Enlai in 1960 when he talked of 'reciprocal acceptance of present realities in both sectors.' In 1980, the proposal was revived in an interview to an Indian defence journal by Deng Xiaoping. He suggested the package deal of China accepting the McMohan Line in the east in return for India recognising the status quo in the west. For details, see Bharat Bhushan, "Sino-Indian Relationship beyond Tibet", *The Daily Times*, 5 July 2003.
9. D.S. Rajan, "Making Kashgar a Centre for Central and South Asia Economic Grouping", Paper No. 1190, 15 December 2004, www.southasiaanalysis.org/papers12/paper1190.html
10. For details, see Bhavna Singh, "China's Modernization Rush: Kashgar at Crossroads", No. 3556, 16 January 2012, http://www.ipcs.org/article/China/Chinas-modernization-rush-kashgar-at-crossroads-3556.html
11. For more details, see Mahesh Ranjan Debata, "Turkmenistan-Afghanistan-Pakistan-India (TAPI): Pipeline or Pipedream", in K. Warikoo (ed.) *Central Asia and South Asia: Energy Cooperation and Transport Linkages*, New Delhi: Pentagon, 2011, pp. 178-192.
12. There have been numerous attacks in the last few years, may be more than 100. The major attacks were—on 4 August 2008, just four days before the Beijing Olympics 2008, a terror strike in Kashgar left 16 policemen dead and 16 others injured. On 5 July 2009, an ethnic riot in Urumqi killed 197 people and injured over 1,600 people. In August 2009, attacks with syringes in Urumqi led to injury of 531 people. On 18 July 2011, 20 protesters were killed in Khotan. Between 31 July to 1 August 2011, two attacks by alleged terrorists left 13 people dead in Kashgar, while security forces gunned down eight suspected Uyghur separatists. On 28 February 2012, rioters armed with knives killed 10 people in Yecheng town in Kashgar, while police shot two of the attackers dead. On 29 June 2012, six Uyghur men tried to hijack a plane that had taken off from Khotan and are thwarted by passengers and crew. Two of the men were killed in the struggle, and 24 crew members and passengers were injured. On 23 April 2013, gunfights in Bachu County killed 15 police and community workers and six terrorists dead. On 26 June 2013, knife-wielding Uyghurs attacked police stations and other important Chinese installations in Lukqun township of Turpan killing 35 people. An attack on a railway station in Urumqi on 30 April 2014 killed three persons and injured over 70 people. For details see, "Victims of Syringe Attacks in Urumqi Rises to

531", 4 September 2009, online: http://english.cctv.com/20090904/110223.shtml (6 September 2009); "11 more Terrorist Suspects Captured after Xinjiang Deadly Attack", www.xinhua.net 29 April 2013. On the latest attack on 22 May 2014, see http://www.bbc.com/news/world-asia-China-27502652

13. Zachary Keck, "Al-Qaeda in Xinjiang Autonomous Region? Was the attack on Monday in Tiananmen Square inspired by al-Qaeda?", *The Diplomat*, 30 October 2013.
14. For more details, see Mahesh Ranjan Debata, "International Response to Uyghur Separatism in Xinjiang", *Himalayan and Central Asian Studies*, vol. 14, no. 4, October-December 2010, pp. 55-78.
15. Ananth Krishnan, "Xinjiang Keen on Reviving Historic Trade Ties with India", *The Hindu*, 2 November 2011.
16. Ibid.
17. "Build Economic Relationship: Xinjiang Governor", 4 November 2011, http://indiacurrentaffairs.org/build-economic-relationship-xinjiang-governor/
18. Ananth Krishnan, "Xinjiang Eyes Direct Land Trade with India, Afghanistan", *The Hindu*, 5 June 2012.
19. Wei Wei, "Silk Route: The way to prosperity for India, China and the Entire Asia", 14 April 2014, http://economictimes.indiatimes.com/opinion/comments-analysis/silk-route-the-way-to-prosperity-for-india-China-and-the-entire-asia/articleshow/33712755.cms
20. "Official Spokesperson's response to a media query on the terrorist attack at Urumqi, China", 22 May 2014, http://www.mea.gov.in/media-briefings.htm?dtl/23345/Official+Spokes persons+response+to+a+media+query+on+the+terrorist+attack+at+Urumqi+China

12

Challenges to Peace Building in Afghanistan

Ms. Mithila Bagai

Introduction

Presidential and provincial elections on April 5, 2014 in Afghanistan marked the first historic democratic transition in the country. Afghans braved the continuing violence unleashed by Taliban and turned out in large numbers to cast their vote. More than 7 million out of the 12 million eligible voters reposed their faith in the democratic system.

Political history of Afghanistan has been punctuated with three Perils or 3P's. And these are polygamic rivalries, power struggle among regional and superpowers which together led to the poor institutions in the country.[1] Though polygamic rivalries have given way to factionalism post Soviet's invasion in 1979 but the other two factors are still reigning. Afghanistan popularly being the 'Land of routes' has been exploited for its geo strategic location. In 19th century Russia and Britain converted Afghanistan into a buffer state. Former wanted to preserve and expand its imperial empire while the latter wanted to protect its newly acquired colonies.

Pakistan has also sought leverage in Afghanistan's internal affairs. Large numbers of Pushtuns inhabit both sides of the border of Afghanistan and Pakistan. And the latter fear that if Afghans become independent and assertive it might lead to secessionism of Pashtunistan, taking away large size of Pakistan's land.

Polygamic Rivalries and factionalism among political parties at the helm in concomitance with power struggle among regional and super powers caused the weakening of political institutions. This has impacted the growth and prosperity, making it one of the worst countries on the Human Development Index.

Recent international intervention of USA in 2001 have improved the social and economic indices of the country but the negative legacies of proxy wars, civil wars and authoritarian regimes are yet to be healed.

Before I talk about the challenges, let us have a brief overview of the Bonn agreement shaped by international community for reconstructing Afghanistan.

Bonn Agreement

Officially known as the Agreement on Provisional Arrangements in Afghanistan Pending the Re-establishment of Permanent Governing Institutions, Bonn Agreement was an initial attempt to recreate the State in Afghanistan. Afghanistan was characterized by 23 years old of ongoing military conflict since the Soviet's invasion in 1979. As the Soviets left, Afghanistan was now at the mercy of various resistance groups scrambling for power. Massoud and Abdul Rashid Dostum were ready to usurp power after fall of Najibullah's government. And Hekmatyar's forces remained in South to launch attack on other resistance groups to seize power. But they were aware that no single ethnic group can sustain power for long, therefore, Afghanistan needs a broad based coalition government. Peshawar Agreement was signed on 24 April 1992 to discuss the power sharing arrangement in the presence of Pakistan Prime Minister Nawaz Sharif. Interim government was to be set up in two stages. In one stage, a two month long transitional government headed by leader of small Pashtun Mujahideen group, Sebghatullah Mujadedi, was to be formed. And in second stage, a longer term interim transitional government to be headed by Rabbani. Mujadedi reluctantly stepped down and Rabbani defied the agreement after coming to power. This caused street to street fighting and various resistance groups scrambled for power. Pakistan during this period funded and trained Taliban and on 26 September, 1996 Taliban occupied Kabul. Notorious for its 9/11 incident, US invaded Afghanistan sending Talibans to mountains to hide. After the commencement of military action on 7 October, 2001 a power vacuum was created and the opposition led by Rabbani barged in to fill the vacuum. But they were made to undergo the Petersburg talks held in Bonn which started on 27 November 2001, under the chairmanship of UN Secretary General's Special Representative for Afghanistan, Lakhdar Brahimi. 1964 Constitution was made applicable till the new constitution comes into place. An interim government comprising 28 members of which two were women took over the authority from 22 December, 2001 till 21 June 2002. Within one month of the establishment, Emergency *Loya Jirga* was convened to chart out the future course of action. This system was based on the traditional open meetings for free debate within local Afghan communities, a system, which at the national level had been a fundamental institution since 1747.[3] Combined with the a strong role for local elders, this system had always moderated the central power of the state by ensuring that there was an organic connection with a network of local leaders and their communities or *Quam* networks. Although, Pushtun groups have dominated the *Loya Jirgah* at times, it was the only institution that would and could give a local mandate to the interim administration.[4] Election of Transitional Authority was established which was to take over from 22 June, 2002. And a Constitutional *Loya Jirga* will be called after 18 months of Transitional Authority to draft a new constitution and organize free and fair elections.

But Bonn agreement was exclusionary. Taliban was excluded from the talks. This is in total contrast to the characteristic of peace making where the actors fighting out in the war can be brought to the negotiating table to break the Mutually Hurting Stalemate (MHS). And therefore, the agreement was bound to fail. And it did. Taliban's exclusion led to the resurgence of violence. Between 2005 and 2006, suicide bombings increased by more than 400 per cent. In January 2014, Taliban blew up the Kabul restaurant popular with foreigners and affluent Afghans, killing Americans, Britons, UN staff and others.[5]

Emergency *Loya Jirga*, though provided political forum for deciding the future of country, was dominated by country's factional leaders, particularly Islamists, as intimidation, vote buying, and political appointments marred the confidence of Afghans.

Framing of the constitution was not without foreign powers meddling. The initial draft delivered by constitutional commission was approved by United States and UN and minor changes was made by small, predominantly reformist bloc within the cabinet, led by Karzai and including several Western educated returnee ministers.[6]

The early organization of simultaneous elections of presidential and parliamentary has been criticized. Though the presidential elections were late by four months but it can have been further delayed so that enough time would have been provided for the disarmament and strengthening of political institutions.[7]

Light footprint[8] by Joint Electoral Management Body (JEMB) led to limited presence of skilled UN international staff and more of unskilled Afghan electoral staff. This led to 'Afghanisation' in which the personnel were hired in large numbers at a short time frame. Cases of electoral fraud like multiple registration cards, tampering of ballot boxes, vote buying and intimidation were also found.

Bonn Agreement provisioned a foreign security force to be deployed before the new Afghan security and armed forces are fully constituted and functioning.

At the request of Bonn signatories, Security Council authorized International Security Assistance Force (ISAF), a non-UN led international security force. Though the presence stabilized the capital and reduced the risk factional violence, crime and terrorism but this security was not shared by the rest of the country. Calls for expansion of ISAF went unheeded until August 2003. ISAF troop contributing countries were cautious of sending troops into potentially insecure areas but sizeable deployments from UK, Canada, Germany and others have enlarged since 2002. But since ISAF was ill-equipped, it was also unwilling to intervene to quell factional violence.

With many potholes in the Bonn agreement, Afghanistan was sure to face many hurdles. With US's forces departing by late 2014, Afghanistan needs to overcome myriad challenges to retain the trust and confidence of Afghanis in the democratic system of the country.

Post-Bonn Challenges in Afghanistan

Afghanistan was once a predominantly rural country, with 20 percent living in cities and 80 percent in the countryside. However, long term warfare, mobilisation of rural male populations and a large refugee exodus has undermined the traditions of village life and rural production, as well as destroying local infrastructure including rural roads, bridges and irrigation networks. With the return of refugees, especially from Iran, there is a need to rebuild a widely based agricultural system with suitable infrastructural input over the next several years.[9]

The challenges which Post-Bonn Afghanistan faces are:

(a) Corruption

Karzai admits,

"There is corruption in the whole system, whether it's the ministries the NGOs, the donor's implementation of projects, in all spheres of the Afghan recovery"[10]

> Afghanistan ranks 174 out of 176 countries according to the Transparency International 2012 Corruption Perceptions Index.[11] The major corruption scandal which rocked Afghanistan was the 2010-2013 Kabul Bank financial scandal involving Mahmood Karzai and others close to Hamid Karzai. They were accused of spending bank's US$1 billion for their own personal lavish life style living and for lending money under the table to family and friends. As of October 2012, the government has recovered $180 million of the $980million fraudulent loans.[12]

The scandal heavily dented the image of Karzai and also the trust of Afghans who were looking for rebuilding of the country.

Afghan National Police and Afghan National Army are considered as a source of fear rather than security. Incompetence and corruption have also plagued the police services. Low level corruption is rampant. The authorities even have to bribe each other to get the administrative work done. Karzai, to mute opposition, against the corrupt official would shift them but would not punish them. And this has generated lot of ill will against his government.

Congressional Research Service Report 2013 mentions that—

Government processing of official documents (e.g., passports, drivers' licenses), in which processing services routinely require bribes in exchange for action. Other forms of corruption include Afghan security officials' selling U.S./internationally provided vehicles, fuel, and equipment to supplement their salaries. In other cases, local police or border officials may siphon off customs revenues or demand extra payments to help guard the U.S. or other militaries' equipment shipments. Other examples include security commanders placing "ghost employees" on official payrolls in order to pocket their salaries. Corruption is fed, in part, by the fact that government workers receive very low salaries (about $200 per month, as compared to the pay of typical contractors in Afghanistan that might pay as much as $6,500 per month).[13]

(b) Patrimonialism

If the 1990's era was free of cronyism in the form of dynastic politics, Karzai brought back the culture of 'it's all in the family.' He supported his allies and relatives with government jobs, money and aid, fuelling their coffers and they in turn, unabashedly, build and flaunted large houses amidst the dire social and economic condition of society.

Thomas Barfield accused Karzai of not being interested in institution building. And rather focussing on tapping the country's resources for his personal well being.

Despite the large sums that the international community was investing in "institution building," Karzai's model of government was patrimonial, in which the government administration and its assets were an extension of the ruler. In such a system, personal relationships determined everything from who would amass personal wealth to who would be thrown in jail. Karzai did not use the assets of the state to centralize power so much as he used them to create a patronage network of personal clients bound to him.[14]

Karzai in response to the accusation of promoting patrons said "You have to carry the past in a way that will not hurt what you are building for the future—have a reasonable sense of inclusivity in order to protect the progress you want to achieve tomorrow. And we have done it."[15] Karzai might have "done" for building the future but his policy of cronyism has surely undone the hopes and aspirations of millions of Afghans who have pinned great trust on him for bringing a democratic system of governance.

(c) Taliban Resurgence—Mission Unaccomplished

Low violence and huge voter turnout of 70 per cent[16] marked the first direct elections of President in 2005. It was termed as the "mission accomplished". Though, occupation of Afghanistan did send Taliban's bags packing back to mountains but this added to the complacency in foreign troops. They did not concentrate on eliminating Taliban.

Thomas Barfield have mockingly commented—

> It was as if a patient stopped taking an antibiotic when the immediate symptoms had ended, disregarding his physician's warning that a full course was required to eliminate the infection.

What could have been achieved in 2004 became difficult to eliminate in 2009. Upped by the success of Presidential elections, Washington reduced the budgeted aid request by 38 per cent (from $4.3 billion in fiscal 2005 to $3.1 billion in fiscal 2006) and also announced in 2005 to reduce the troops by 3000 in the coming year, although it will be replaced by NATO forces.[17] They also did not bring to book Pakistan for aiding Taliban. And the mistake was committed.

Taliban's capacity rose. Afghanistan marred by lack of basic minimum necessities of safe drinking water, sanitation, housing, security, transportation and proper food, resorted to Taliban. Taliban also changed their ideology from being an orthodox and conservative imposer of Shari'ah law to being a nationalist with the aim of freeing Afghanistan once again from Western infidels. In this they received the support from Southern Afghanistan which remained mostly untouched by the developmental efforts. And with this Taliban were able to spread its tentacles in this part of Afghanistan.

Security started deteriorating more on the borders of Pakistan where the suicide bombers appeared for the first time.[18] On 29 May, 2006 a riot erupted due to the fatal traffic accident involving US troops and locals in Kabul. Although the riot was brought under the control but it showed the unpopularity of Karzai regime and distrustfulness towards the foreign occupiers. Later in the summer, the British and Canadian troops deployed in Helmand and Qandahar encountered an unexpected fiercest attack by Taliban. Though the troops defeated it but could not eliminate them. Trouble also surfaced in eastern Afghanistan which experienced cross border attacks from Pakistan's autonomous tribal territories, where al Qaeda and Taliban forces were becoming dominant.[19]

Suicide bombings increased manifold. Between 2005 and 2006, suicide bombings increased by more than 400 percent (from 27 to 139), the use of improvised explosive devises more than doubled (from 783 to 1,677), and armed attacks nearly tripled (from 1,558 to 4,542).[20] Non Pushtuns did not join the war of Taliban against Western infidels.

(d) Opium Production

Karzai's authority is unheard outside the Kabul and in rural areas. Basic conditions remained alienated from Afghans. Foreign assistance is also insufficient. The agriculture is in bad shape. The only option to earn their living is opium. And since this was supported by Taliban, Afghans had sympathy for their objective.

Darvesh Gopal writes in 'Challenges to Nation Building Process in Afghanistan':

> Available Data suggests that poverty had become endemic... Due to poor infrastructure, harsh winters, and lack of other markets, most farmers had

returned to poppy cultivation, leading to the return of Afghanistan into the opium market through 2002.[21]

Production-wise, World Drug Report 2013 ranks Afghanistan as the lead producer and cultivator of opium globally (74 per cent of global illicit opium production in 2012).[22] Poppy cultivation increased nationwide by 18 percent between 2011 and 2012, with a similar increase in Helmand Province, the biggest opium-producing region, despite an aggressive campaign to eradicate the crop and promote alternative jobs.[23] Opium trade has provided $155million of tax to Taliban in the areas they control. A farmer rakes up $120 per hectare and in a good year up to $10,000 per hectare on raw opium.[24] Drug trade works with complicity of warlords; Taliban and security officers have increased the drug addicts in the region and also spread the menace of HIV/AIDS. This is burgeoning problem which the world is really taking interest to curb it. The eradication measures taken to eliminate poppy has led to killing of 102 Afghan police officers, soldiers and civilians by farmers and Taliban and injuring of another 127 people.

Karzai in his interview has admitted growing production of poppy but has also emphasized that poppy constitutes 30 per cent of our economy and to eradicate it, there is a need of holistic measures of improving social and economic condition of Afghans rather than telling them just not to do it.

Karzai said:

> We have very good agriculture. But you can't tell me, 'Well, grow pomegranates, grow grapes, grow cucumbers or watermelons, and I'm not going to buy it from you.' If the international community wants to help us get rid of narcotics, they must help us all around, buying our products.[25]

(e) Dependence on Foreign Assistance

This challenge has become utmost important given the drawdown of American troops in 2014 and the donor fatigue shared by many donor countries. Though Karzai has frequently asked America to withdraw its troops from Afghanistan in order to earn reward from his political allies and not to project himself as a puppet of Western regime, but he knows that his police force is ill-equipped to deal with civilians problems and contain the rising insurgency in the region.

Even historically, revenue has remained a problem. Afghanistan has been dependent on foreign aid to fuel its administration and its economy. Zahir, Daoud and Nader to name a few have lined up to US and other neighbouring countries for funds. It was because of funding that Soviets were able to increase their presence predominantly in the run up to their invasion in the Afghan land. The rulers have failed in pursuing a fiscal policy to strengthen the financial base which has made the survival dependent on others which make donors run Afghanistan as a proxy country.

Afghanistan is in a rebuilding phase and it needs investment for agriculture, troop build up and infrastructure. Though many countries have poured to finance the demand but it has largely ended as a phantom aid. Firstly, total international aid pledged from 2002-13 stood at $62 billion and the international aid spend from 2002-2009 is 43 per cent of the pledged amount, that is, $26.7 billion. The occupying country United States pledged $38 billion from 2002-2013 but could disburse $10.9 billion aid in Afghanistan.[26] Secondly, with less aid and on this, ineffective means of implementing aid assistance have exacerbated the economic situation. The foreign donors are in charge of delivering services which keep the locals away from jobs. So the aid meant for Afghans basically get channelled back to their donor countries in the form of salaries of foreign workers. The Agency Coordinating Body for Afghan Relief estimated that in 2008, of the $15 billion in reconstruction assistance given to Afghanistan since 2001, "a staggering 40 percent has returned to donor countries in corporate profits and consultant salaries."[27]

Thirdly, corruption, undoubtedly, remained a significant factor for pocketing the left over aid.

(f) Economic and Social Condition

Insufficient foreign aid has affected the social and economic developmental efforts. Infrastructure, schools, hospitals, roads, police services, food and nutrition continue to remain in pitiable state for most of Afghans. Business community face serious problems of lack electricity, legal redressal mechanisms, insufficient access to land and capital, high levels of corruption and taxes and poorly trained force. Although women visibility has comparatively increased in Parliament and work force but they continue living a life of fear and hopelessness. Since 2007, some 145 schools are closed in Kandahar and in Southern Afghanistan affecting more 70,000 students including girls and boys. Nationally also, Taliban have threatened and torched schools leaving 2,00,000 children out of schools.[28]

The developmental gap between rural and urban areas has increased. In Kabul, modern buildings have come up alongside private TV channels, shopping malls and Chinese Thai and Italian restaurants. Many young, urban Afghans have embraced international fashion, music, and movies from Europe and Asia.

But outside Kabul in rural areas, basic facilities are still not available. 36 million people continue to live below poverty line.[29] Social Security is still a distant dream for them.

A Lost Decade for Afghanistan?

After 13 years of war and foreign occupation in Afghanistan, is it a lost decade for Afghanistan with no improvements being made in their conditions? The answer is NO.

Kamrany says—

> It is clear that Afghanistan is making a comeback; all they needed was some support along the way.[30]

12 years have made significant improvements with much more to be achieved.

(a) **Security**: Afghan National Forces position has been improved. Security forces including Afghan National Army and Afghan National Police stands at around 3,00,000 from several thousands in 2001.[31] They have been professionally trained and educated and are also send abroad in India, Turkey, the United Arab Emirate, Europe and United States where they get further training. Women have also been included at all levels and they are training other women.

(b) **Education**: In 2002, 8,00,000 students were enrolled in primary schools now there are 8.2 million of whom 40 per cent are girls. Higher education at international level has also emerged.[32]

(c) **Infrastructure build-up:** International aid financed the collapsed structure. Bridges, highways, local roads and irrigation system have been constructed.
Central bank has come up and new afghan currency has allowed international and domestic banks to work. The World Bank has estimated Afghan GDP growth from under $2.5bn in 2001 to over $17bn in 2011.[33]

(d) **Media:** This was entirely banned by Taliban but 6 mobile phone carriers, 75 television channels, over 175 radio stations and hundreds of print publications have come up.[34]

A reporter from *The Guardian*, Nushin Arbabzadah, on her visit to Afghanistan highlighted significant changes that have unknowingly creeped in the lifestyle of Afghanis.

Use of mobile phones has become common and some own two or even three. This is in contrast to 1980s where few owned landline and mobile phones were just non-existent. On her drive from Kabul to Panjsher, she writes,

> "The shops and stalls were bursting with goods, from foodstuffs to drinks to mobile top-up cards to soaps, shampoo bottles and DVDs".

She had to stay long hours in traffic and had difficulty in finding parking space for the simple reason of the large numbers of cars on roads. Resurfaced roads and highways, refurbished schools and new health clinics were commonly found. Returned refugees have opened their businesses, joined NGOs as translators or working as guards in international offices. The picture which Nushin has painted of Afghanistan, gives a ray of hope for Afghanistan and for international community as well.

What Next, Post-NATO Withdrawal?

'In Afghanistan, we do what we can. In Iraq we do what we must.'[35]

The words of Adm. Mike Mullen, chairman of Joint Chiefs of Staff reflect the complacent and obstinate policy being adopted by United States for Afghanistan. But this was not mere rhetoric. USA has spent only 28.8 per cent of total aid pledged by the end of 2009.[36] And the half heartedness is evident in the poor social statistics of Afghanistan.

The problem with Afghanistan is its political and institutional fragility.[37] Accompanied with foreign interference, which has violated the sovereignty and integrity of the country.[38] Third is the deficit of aid and assistance for implementation of modernisation programmes. And lastly, the geo strategic position has made Afghanistan a 'Land of Routes' making it vulnerable to invasion and foreign meddling.

The question is that it's just few months to go for NATO troop's withdrawal and for Afghanistan to slip into oblivion. Urgent measures need to be taken for the consolidation of Afghanistan.

What Needs to be Done?

Political Solution

Amin Saikal has said that the only real solution to the problem in Afghanistan is the political one.[39] And I agree. Whether it was Geneva accords or the Bonn agreement, the affected parties or the losers in the war were not included and the real issue was sidelined. The exit of US troops is nearing and the question is what needs to be done next to hold the country together in terms of security, economy and polity.

Though criticisms have mounted over the issue of holding negotiations with Taliban but this is a pragmatic one. US may have divided Taliban into moderate and extremists, but US have also exhausted its other options. US have spent militarily, economically and politically but violence seems unabated. So the proposal and decision of having negotiations with Taliban is all a left over option. Exclusion of an opposing party in 2001 is a mistake which US has committed at a great cost. And over it, US after toppling Taliban regime confined its military to urban areas and did not work up its way to eliminate Taliban. Since the resources are exhausted, the option is to open public talks with Taliban who are waiting for US to leave and execute its plan of action. Political talks can be held of not only with Taliban but with all opposing parties which will represent the interests of all sections. Media in Afghanistan, though at nascent stage, is also strengthening its roots. Civil Society, if not pervasive, is able to take up relevant issues and is working towards it. Afghans would not like the reversal of progress made post-2001. It also constitutes significant young population. Afghanistan cannot remain isolated from globalisation for long. Hard core repressive policies of Taliban will not be accepted by Afghanis for long. Taliban have also been seen to switching sides in terms of ideology. When in 1991, Taliban's aim was to remove a godless, communist Soviet Union's puppet regime. And after prolonged fighting, Taliban was able to win over them. We also need to accept the reality that Taliban have been educated in Pakistani madrassas. And the country, in its modern period, has not had the pervasive education system. So Taliban imposed what they learnt and believed in. And the Afghanis were forced to accept it.

The international condition has drastically changed. And to evade an issue from condemnation and eulogy of international society is difficult. Therefore, talking in straight terms with Taliban and laying equal emphasis on other opposing parties will help in concluding a balanced and comprehensive talk. Talking to a defeated party is beyond the policy of US. But US, if not publicly then at least privately, accept that a war has no victors but only losers. And US's image of the supporter and promoter of human rights have been affected with the causalities in Afghanistan running into millions. Therefore, talks is the only option left and a renewed military attack or approach is just out of the question with the international economic crisis looming over and other pressing problems to be dealt to. Afghanistan does not belong to Hamid Karzai solely. So exit of US troops cannot hand over the reins of power singularly to a Pushtun man who entered Afghanistan on a motorcycle to take over charge as President and is now looting the resources of country the latest being in Kabul Bank Scandal. This is further eroding the trust of Afghanis and infuriating the opposing parties who is tasting dust in the hinterland whereas Karzai and his allies in support of US and his military is enjoying the political power and financial resources of the country. Talking to opposing parties including Taliban will put confidence and end their alienation. This can only help Afghanistan from slipping into turmoil and turbulence.

Banking on International Community

USA has a lot of homework to do before she packs its bag from Afghanistan. Foreign interference has been the predominant irritant in Afghanistan. The crisis has been exacerbated due to continuous intrusion and interference into its territory, polity and economy. The rationality and cooperation amongst international community will help in rebuilding the country in a long and sincere way. The positive engagement of the international community will help in resolving their conflict and building peace. The neighbouring countries need to realise that an unstable Afghanistan is a mess not only for Afghanistan but the crisis will also spill to their borders. And the US here needs to play a positive and hegemonic role to bring the countries flanking Afghanistan to the table.

First, USA needs to change its policy and approach towards Iran. USA has considered Iran to be a part of 'Axis of evil' and tagged it a notorious nuclear power. It has also imposed sanctions on Iran for its nuclear policy. Though Iran had extended its good hand to share a positive relation with USA but the latter has not reciprocated positively. Instead, it is working on building a negative image of Iran and pitting countries against her. USA needs to stop this for sake of Afghanistan. Afghanistan will be what international community makes of it. The onus of a peaceful and stable Afghanistan lies as much on international community as on Afghanis. Iran has responded positively in containing Afghanistan problem. It faces a mammoth problem of influx of refugees spreading crime, using resources of locals and also adding to the problem of Iranian authorities. Secondly, the drug problem also needs a well deserved effort. These twin problems are haunting Iran and she needs a considerable solution. USA, to save its face, can enter into talks with Iran and if not enter, at least, implicitly support the efforts taken by Iran in diffusing the crisis.

Pakistan comes next. Pashtunistan is the problem Pakistan is not able to get over it. And Pakistan fears that if Afghanistan is able to come out of the impending crisis, the Pushtuns will demand its own land 'The Pashtun land'. This is one of the way through which Pakistan continues making her military relevant to its public. Afghanistan may not face any fragmentation in its State. Though Afghanistan is composed of diverse ethnicities but the Afghanis are also loyal to the Afghan land. It has faced more than three decades of long war but the Afghanistan has not shown any signs of fragmentation. Only the fears have prospered among scholars and writers over the fragmentation of country. The neighbouring countries, too, support their own ethnicities as they did post-Soviet withdrawal in 1991 but their aim is to protect their ethnicities from the discrimination and also persecution from the dominant section but never with the aim of secession. The neighbouring countries, too, did not want the troubled seceded part to be taken over by them. So the question of splitting and secession does not arise. And Pakistan and other neighbouring countries need to take comfort in this fact. There have been ethnic wars but prominent was post-1991 when the flanking countries were fearful of the threat to their ethnic community in Afghanistan. If the international community sits together and pledge not to intervene, foster and fuel the ethnic ignite, much problem of Afghanistan can be solved. Pakistan can concentrate on its own domestic terrorism rather than making its military internationally relevant.

Moscow, too, cannot be left out. Extremism in Afghanistan will be spilled over to neighbouring countries. Penetration of militants into Central Asia and Chechnya is a greatest worry for Moscow. Permission to allow transit of NATO aid through Russia affirms their apprehension. Russia does not want Taliban to become party in the rebuilding process as for their repressive and hard core policies. China, too, is concerned about fundamentalism, given its restive Xinjiang province. China is also investing in the trade and economic matters in Afghanistan. Ayanak copper mines, the second largest untapped resource, have the investment of China which will be the biggest infrastructure project in the country. Positive engagement of the big players is the need of hour. India, though separated by Pakistan, need to keep positively engaging in Afghanistan by building roads, power lines, schools, colleges and hospitals. The largest project undertaken by India is building of road in southern Nimroz area that provides a link for landlocked Afghanistan to port of Chahabar. This road serves to reduce dependence of Afghanistan on Pakistan for its transport links. India cannot and should not counter Pakistan militarily but continue to engage and involve positively.

Saudi Arabia was one among the three countries to establish diplomatic relations with Mullah Omar government. Taliban's Deobandi theological ideology is close to Saudi's Wahabism. Saudi Arabia in cooperation with Pakistan has helped to shape the policy for Afghanistan. Since 2001, Saudi Arabia has been cautious in its dealing with the country but Taliban would prefer the Arabic country to be included in the reconciliation process. Saudi Arabia too can contribute immensely in the reconciliation process. The support of Tajikistan, Turkmenistan and Uzbekistan is too required in the rebuilding process.

And lastly, South Asian Association of Regional Countries SAARC, if it till now has been tagged as irrelevant and defunct, can now come to the mainstream and establish its importance. Afghanistan is a SAARC member. And SAARC can be a platform to bring the neighbouring countries of Afghanistan to the table to discuss and engage in conflict resolution process. Its importance can't be undermined.

Conclusion

Peace building and stability in Afghanistan has been absent despite gamut of efforts since last 3 decades. After 2001 'Operation Enduring Freedom' relative peace and stability has been established. Millions of Afghan refuges have returned their homes after decades and started their life again. People have witnessed the benefits of stability therefore they are willing to establish durable peace. Huge turnout in the first/second phase of Presidential election in April/June 2014 despite threat from the Taliban is vindicating this assertion. There are multiple outsiders actors which could influence peace either way. President Karzai often alleged Pakistan that it is part of the problem not the part of the solution. Pakistan must understand that a stable and peaceful Afghanistan is the lone guarantee of its own stability and peace. Since last one decade more people have been killed in Pakistan than Afghanistan. India must sustain its contribution in the reconstruction process because it is the only way to strengthen peace and stability in a war torn country. International community must understand that it is the golden opportunity for peace. They should not abandon Afghanistan as they had done in 1990. Part of NATO forces need to be there to consolidate peace and stability. Beside this they need to contribute more on reconstruction of infrastructure which could be facilitator of capacity building. Peace and stability in Afghanistan is not only propel development in South and South West Asia but it will contribute positively in the world peace too.

NOTES

1. Nabi Misadq (2006), *Afghanistan: Political frailty and external interference.* Oxon: Routledge. Also See Amin Saikal (2004), *Modern Afghanistan: A History of Struggle and Survival.* New York: I.B. Tauris & Co. Ltd. 2. Louis Dupree. 1973. *Afghanistan.* New Jersey: Princeton University.
2. D. Gopal (2008), "Challenges to Nation Building Process in Afghanistan", *Journal of Polity and Society*, vol. 2, no.1, pp. 70-86
3. Ibid.
4. Ibid.
5. Ben Farmer and Zubair Babarkheyl, "Briton among dead in Kabul suicide attack", *The Telegraph*, 17 January 2014 at http://www.telegraph.co.uk/news/worldnews/asia/afghanistan/10580546/Briton-among-dead-in-Kabul-suicide-attack.html
6. Charles T. Call (ed.) (2009), *Building States to Build Peace.* Colorado, USA: Lynne Rienner Publishers.
7. C. Bennet, S. Wakefield and A. Wilder (November 2003), *Afghan Elections: The Great Gamble.* Kabul: Afghanistan Research and Evaluation Centre
8. Light Footprint: Strong presence of Afghan staff and less presence of international staff.
9. D. Gopal (2008), "Challenges to Nation Building Process in Afghanistan", *Journal of Polity and Society*, vol. 2, no.1, pp. 70-86.
10. "Karzai: Corruption in the whole System", *CNN Money*, 9 October, 2006 at http://money.cnn.com/magazines/fortune/fortune_archive/2006/10/16/8390258/index.html
11. http://en.wikipedia.org/wiki/Corruption_in_Afghanistan Also refer, "How they robbed Kabul Bank", *US Policy in a Big World*, 12 June 2012 at http://www.uspolicyinabigworld.com/2012/06/12/how-they-robbed-kabul-bank/
12. Ibid.
13. K. Katzman, "Afghanistan: Politics, Elections and Government Performance" Congressional Research Service, 2013 at http://www.fas.org/sgp/crs/row/RS21922.pdf
14. T. Barfield (2012), *Princeton Shorts: War for Afghanistan: A brief History from Afghanistan: A Cultural and Political History.* Princeton: Princeton University Press.
15. K. Katzman, "Afghanistan: Politics, Elections and Government Performance," Congressional Research Service, 2013 at http://www.fas.org/sgp/crs/row/RS21922.pdf
16. K. Katzman, "Afghanistan: Politics, Elections and Government Performance," Congressional Research Service, 2013 at http://www.fas.org/sgp/crs/row/RS21922.pdf
17. "Afghan Election Workers Begin Vote Count", *CBS News*, 20 August, 2009 at http://www.cbsnews.com/news/afghan-election-workers-begin-vote-count/
18. T. Barfield (2012), *Princeton Shorts: War for Afghanistan: A brief History from Afghanistan: A Cultural and Political History.* Princeton: Princeton University Press.
19. Ibid.
20. Ibid.
21. D. Gopal (2008), "Challenges to Nation Building Process in Afghanistan", *Journal of Polity and Society*, vol. 2, no.1, pp. 70-86
22. S.G. Jones (2008), "The Rise of Afghanistan's Insurgency: State Failure and Jihad", *International Security*, vol. 32, no. 4, pp. 7-40.
23. World Drug Report 2013, United Nations Office on Drugs and Crime http://www.unodc.org/unodc/secured/wdr/wdr2013/World_Drug_Report_2013.pdf
24. A.J. Rubin, "Opium Cultivation Rose this year in Afghanistan, U.N. Survey Shows", *The New York Times*. (20 November, 2012) at http://www.nytimes.com/2012/11/21/world/asia/afghan-opium-cultivation-rose-in-2012-un-says.html?_r=0
25. Ibid

26. "Karzai: Corruption in the whole System", *CNN Money*, 9 October, 2006 at http://money.cnn.com/magazines/fortune/fortune_archive/2006/10/16/8390258/index.html
27. Lydia Poole, "Afghanistan: Tracking Major Resource Flows 2002-2010", January 2011. http://www.globalhumanitarianassistance.org/wp-content/uploads/2011/02/gha-Afghanistan-2011-major-resource-flows.pdf
28. Matt Waldman, "Falling Short: Aid Effectiveness in Afghanistan", *ACBAR Advocacy Series*, March 2008 at http://www.oxfam.org/sites/www.oxfam.org/files/ACBAR_aid_effectiveness_paper_0803.pdf
29. N. Ghufran (2007), "Afghanistan in 2006: The Complications of Post Conflict Transition", *Asian Survey*, vol. 47. No.1, pp. 87-98.
30. Afghanistan Independent Human Rights Commission Report. November/December 2011. http://www.aihrc.org.af/en/press-release/514/situation-of-economic-and-social-rights.html
31. T.S. Kamrany. "Afghanistan 2002-12: A Decade of Progress and Hope", *Middle East Institute* at http://www.mei.edu/content/afghanistan-2002-2012-decade-progress-and-hope
32. Ibid.
33. Ibid.
34. Ibid. Also Refer N. Arbabzadah. "There is progress in Afghanistan—even if Afghans won't admit it", *The Guardian*, August 6, 2011 at http://www.theguardian.com/commentisfree/2011/aug/06/progress-in-afghanistan
35. Robert Burns, "Mullen: Afghanistan isn't top priority", *USA Today*, 12 November 2007 at http://usatoday30.usatoday.com/news/washington/2007-12-11-3963072919_x.htm
36. Lydia Poole, "Afghanistan: Tracking Major Resource Flows 2002-10", January 2011. http://www.globalhumanitarianassistance.org/wp-content/uploads/2011/02/gha-Afghanistan-2011-major-resource-flows.pdf
37. Nabi Misdaq. 2006. *Afghanistan: Political frailty and external interference.* Oxon: Routledge.
38. Ibid.
39. Amin Saikal, "The Only Real Solution for Afghanistan is a political one", *The Sydney Morning Herald*, October 19, 2010 at http://www.smh.com.au/federal-politics/political-opinion/the-only-real-solution-for-afghanistan-is-a-political-one-20101018-16qso.html

13

Parliamentary Initiatives Towards India in Emerging Asia-Pacific

S. Prabhakar

Introduction—Significance of Parliament and Constitutional Provisions

Today, India has earned the glory of being the largest working parliamentary democracy in the world. Parliament of India is the highest legislative body representing the people in implementing the provisions of Constitution and its goals. The founding fathers of the Constitution of India opted for a parliamentary form of Government in which Parliament is the supreme legislative body and the Executive is accountable to Parliament which exercises control over the formulation and implementation of both domestic and foreign policies. This is made evident in Clause (3) of Article 75 of the Constitution which proclaims that "the Council of Ministers shall be collectively responsible to the House of the People." Parliament wields enormous power in the governance of the country. The actions of government can be questioned and scrutinized by Parliament in its functioning.

There are several provisions in the Constitution which exclusively deal with the foreign affairs and the empowerment of Parliament by Indian Constitution (Article 246) to legislate on all aspects of foreign affairs and the exclusive authority of Parliament to legislate for implementation of international treaties, agreements and conventions, and decisions arrived at any international conferences. (Article 253) India's foreign policy has always been evolved keeping in view the national interests at the core. The basic objectives of our foreign policy are to safeguard our independence, sovereignty and territorial integrity, and at the same time promote best interests of the country.

Parliament has been equipped with many constitutional provisions to address the issues concerning India's role in emerging Asia-Pacific region. I would be highlighting Parliament's role through its initiatives, which includes the initiatives of the Ministry of External Affairs and the Parliamentary Committee system on important powers in Asia-Pacific like China, Japan and Australia. As is well know, Parliament provides to its Members and to the Government to utilize provisions or devices that are made available by Parliament to build and consolidate India's political, economic, trade, commercial, cultural and consular relations with other nations through bilateral, regional and international consultations. By bringing up more and more issues before Parliament concerning the role of Asia-Pacific, we can certain revitalize Parliament's contribution to democracy.

Over the years, Indian Parliament had played its role in taking up the issues concerning Asia-Pacific region. The debates that had taken place in Lok Sabha bear testimony to this. Though we can say that the discussions and debates concerning Asia-Pacific are few and far, unhesitatingly one can conclude that taking it up with the Government by the Members of Parliament itself shows that there is a concern in the public mind about the perception with which the issues and concerns related to the countries of focus in this paper are tackled by Government and at the same time, public and Members of Parliament too would like to know as to what is the status that is prevailing in Asia-Pacific region. Parliament's procedure, debates and extra-Parliamentary activities, however, indicate that Parliament has a definite role in tackling the issues concerning Asia-Pacific region which has a bearing on our country though foreign policy comes under the purview of the executive.

Parliament's main function is to legislate. One can say that since 1977, the era of coalition politics has started. In the coalition era, Parliament is not able to contribute adequately in the sphere of legislation. Government has to take all its coalition partners with it if it wants to implement any scheme or programme. In the process, it faces many hurdles. Hence, avenues for revitalizing Parliament's contribution to democracy and nation building are far and wide. Parliament wields enormous power in the governance of the country. The actions of government can be questioned and scrutinized by Parliament in its functioning.

Parliament has also the power to set up by legislation new machinery and Governmental institutions for the making of foreign policy. In addition, Members of Parliament participating in international delegations including those sent to the UN can share the responsibility for detailed policy making, though perhaps only marginally. Individual Members of Parliament specializing in foreign affairs, whether belonging to the ruling party or the opposition, can influence the making of foreign policy by drawing attention to defects or inadequacies in the policies pursued or proposed by the Government, even when no formal resolution is passed one way or the other.

It may be note that Parliamentary resolutions—either supporting or opposing the policy suggested by the Government or by suggesting or forcing upon the Government new policies, whether of a broad or of a specific nature—are expected to affect vitally the broad orientation, detailed formulation, and implementation of foreign policy.

We propose to examine the major powers in Asia-Pacific Region like, China, Japan and Australia, how India through its parliamentary Initiatives addressed its concerns in Asia-Pacific region, while dealing with these countries, Debates in the 15th Lok Sabha, the role of Ministry of External Affairs, Annual Report of the Ministry of External Affairs for 2012-13, Standing Committee of External Affairs, Consultative Committee for the Ministry of External Affairs, Roadmap for Action, and Conclusion.

Indian Parliament and China, Japan and Australia in Asia-Pacific Region

Indian Parliament had played its role in taking up the issues concerning Asia-Pacific region, particularly major powers like China, Japan and Australia. The debates that had taken place in Lok Sabha bear testimony to this. Though we can say that the discussions and debates concerning these countries is few and far between, unhesitatingly one can conclude that taking it up with the Government by the Members of Parliament itself shows that there is a concern in the public mind about the perception with which the Government is tackling the issues concerning these countries, particularly China and to know as to what is the status in regard to various issues, about which more light would be thrown as we go about in the paper.

From time to time, Parliament had displayed keen interest in India's relationship with China, Japan and Australia. Apart from constitutional provisions, a number of opportunities exist for Members of Parliament to discuss the role of the Government in tailoring foreign policy of the country. Parliament exercises budgetary control by debating the demands for grants of Ministries of External Affairs, which have become the principal opportunity for the said Ministry to report and discuss Government's view on the international situation concerning these countries in Asia-Pacific region.

Though the primary parliamentary weapons for the Members of Parliament are basically Questions, both Starred and Unstarred, to know as to what is happening in countries like China, Japan and Australia, we can also find interests in Lok Sabha Members utilising other devices available to them, namely, debates on Motion of Thanks on the President's Address, General Budget, Demands for Grants of the Ministry of External Affairs, discussion in the Department-Related Standing Committee on External Affairs, discussion on Statement made by the Minister of External Affairs on Foreign Policy of the country, Discussion under

Rule 193 on recent visits to foreign countries by PM, Special Mentions, or his recent visit abroad, etc.

As the Executive, that is, the Government, is accountable to Parliament as per Clause (3) of Article 75 of the Indian Constitution, we can add the happenings concerning the countries of focus in this paper like China, Japan and Australia, in the realm of Government, and say that these too are initiatives of Parliament as ultimately they are answerable to Parliament.

Debates in the 15th Lok Sabha

In the 15th Lok Sabha, till 12th February, 2014, questions (both Starred—oral and Unstarred—written) concerning China, Japan and Australia in its entirety were asked. These questions sought wide range of information from the Ministries, primarily from External Affairs, and from other Ministries like Commerce & Industry, Railways, Finance, Defence, Coal, Textiles, Shipping, Health & Family Welfare, Petroleum & Natural Gas, Agriculture, Consumer Affairs, Public Distribution & Food, Human Resources Development, Road Transport and Highways, Steel, Chemicals and Fertilizers, Heavy Industries, Urban Development, Water Resources, Atomic Energy, Environment and Forests, Culture, Indian Overseas Affairs, Youth Affairs, Power, Tourism.

In regard to China, 185 questions[1] related to National Security Advisor's visit to China, Trade with China, MoUs with China, Stapled Visa by China, Imports from China, illegal imports from China, China activities in Nepal, Trade relations with China, Mysterious Unidentified Flying Object (UFO) over Indo-China Border, Foreign Minister's Visit to China, Indo-China Joint Exercise, Chinakuri Power Station, Duplicate Banarasi Sarees from China, Presence of China in Sri Lanka, Construction of Reservoirs by China, China in Arunachal, India China Friendship Year, China-Pak relations, Trade deficit with China, Control over an island of East China Sea, Indian traders in China, Nepal's proximity with China, Import of apples from china, Resolution of issues with China, India China meeting, Indo-China border talks, China as observer in SAARC, Gujarat CM's visit to China, Kashmiri people visiting China, Demolishing wall in Arunachal Pradesh, dependency on imports from China, infiltration by China into Indian borders, wrong map of India by China, Joint mechanism on boundary with China, security implications of import from China, Telecoms deal with China, cheap imports from China, imports of steel from China, import of biological products from China, China's objection on Highway, China new J&K's line, China Pak nuclear deal, Indian President's visit to China, china's rail service to Nepal, MoU with China for NH projects, Indo-China land issue, Indo-China Secretary level talks, exemption of import duties by China, barriers on Indian imports by China, farmers delegation to China, Indians arrested by China, Seizure of fake drugs from China under 'Made in India' label, etc. were raised by the Members of Parliament (Lok Sabha) in order to know as to what is the authentic information and the latest action that is taking place between India and China from different perspectives.

In regard to Japan, till 21st February, 2014, 62 questions[2] ranging from India-Japan energy dialogue, vaccination campaign against Japanese Encephalitis, Visa pact with Japan, visit by Japanese officials, Japanese assistance in urban transportation, trade agreement with Japan, Joint Venture between India and Japan, Food products imported from Japan, cooperation between India and Japan, Free Trade Agreements (FTA) with Japan. Indian relief workers in Japan, Joint Naval exercise with Japan, outbreak of Japanese Encephalitis, Civil Nuclear agreement with Japan, assistance from Japan for DFC, Indo-Japanese Exchange Programme, loan from Japan, CEPA with Japan, Agreement with Japanese bank, Japanese assistance for Heritage monuments, CECA with Japan, Assistance from Japan for forestry projects, Financial assistance from OECF Japan, Japanese nod for pharma products, cases of Dengue, Malaria, Chikungunya and Japanese Encephalitis, tie up between Indian firms and Japanese steel giants, Indo-Japan security dialogue, Trade delegation from Japan, etc. were asked from the Government.

Likewise in regard to Australia, till 21st February, 2014, 35 questions[3] ranging from Closure of Vocational Colleges in Australia, MoU with Australia, Australian PM's visit to India, Indian investments in Australia, imposition of additional taxes by Australia, killing of Indians in Australia, assistance to Australia, supply of uranium from Australia, India-Australia trade, settlement between ONGC and Clough engineering Ltd., Australia, atrocities on Indians in Australia, exploration in Gujarat by Australian oil exploration company, Australian sports outreach programme in India, FTA with Australia, Indo-Australian cooperation in power sector, Australian's migration policy, Indo-Australian agreement for investments in energy sector, Parliamentary delegation to Australia, Civil Nuclear Agreement with Australia, visit of Australian Foreign Minister to India, Indian students cheated by Australian institutes, road shows in Australia and New Zealand, etc. were posed by Members of Parliament in Lok Sabha to the Government with a view to knowing the latest and authentic information.

Apart from questions, there are many other provisions available to the Members of Parliament of Lok Sabha like Submissions, Motion of Thanks on the President's Address, Budget (General), Demands for Grants under the Ministry of External Affairs, and other Ministries, Special Mentions, Matter under Rule 377, Calling Attention, Short Duration Discussion under Rule 193, etc. to raise issues concerning China, Japan and Australia.

While initiating the debate on the Motion of thanks on the President's Address in 2012, Dr. Girija Vyas of Congress highlighted that China is constructing dam on Brahmaputra river and that Government of India should make efforts to constitute a Joint Inspection Committee to address this matter. She suggested that India, China, and Bangladesh should sign a tripartite international water treaty on the Brahmaputra.[4]

Speaker, Lok Sabha has congratulated, on behalf of Lok Sabha[5], Indian Cricket Team for winning the International Cricket Council (ICC) under-19 World Cup by beating Australia in the final of Town Ville, Australia on 26th August, 2012.

President in his Address[6] in February, 2013 to the joint sitting of the two Houses of Parliament stated, "My Government intends to work with the new Chinese leadership to reinforce the positive direction of our relationship. Our multi-faceted relationship with Japan, which is also a major partner in our infrastructure development efforts, is making good process.

Minister of External Affairs, on behalf of Government of India and people of India, informed the august House that as an immediate step, India is airlifting 25,000 blankets to Japan and India is ready to send search and rescue teams and relief material and that we stand ready to help in the relief, rehabilitation and reconstruction phase. [7] While stating that his Government is deeply committed to promoting the interests and welfare of overseas Indians, he stated that his Government had signed Social Security Agreements with Japan.[8]

A Special Mention[9] was raised by Shri Yogi Adityanath of Bharatiya Janata Party on the need to stop encroachment of Indian borders by China. A Special Mention[10] was raised by Shri Shailendra Kumar of Samajwadi Party regard attacks on Indian students in Australia. Another Special Mention[11] was raised by Shri P.T. Thomas of Indian National Congress on the need to take steps to prevent attacks on Indian students in Australia.

On the discussion[12] on Prime Minister's recent visit to foreign countries, Yashwant Sinha of BJP initiated the discussion and stated that national consensus has always been the guiding factor in our foreign policy and highlighted the position taken by India on the issue of climate change in international fora. While responding, Prime Minister remarked, "Shri Yashwant Sinha brought up the issue of climate change as if we have changed goal-posts. There is nothing of that sort. There was a meeting in Italy along with the G-8 meeting of major economies of the world. India was invited to that meeting where 17 other countries were present. I should, however, mention that the Major Economic Forum Declaration adopted at L'Aquila is not a declaration of Climate Change policy by India, nor is it a bilateral declaration between India and another country or a group of countries. It is a declaration that represents a shared view among 17 developed and developing countries, the latter category including China, South Africa, Brazil, Indonesia, and Mexico."[13]

He also stated that India has been consistently voicing in all world fora that global warming is taking place and that its adverse consequences will impact most heavily on developing countries like India. Further dwelling deep on the issue, he has drawn the attention to the seriousness of global warming and said that it does not automatically translate into a compulsion on the part of India or other developing countries, represented in the Major Economics Forum, to accept emission reduction obligations. He stressed that, "our position and the Chinese position are nearly identical, and we have been coordinating our position with that country on this important issue."[14] He also informed the House that 37 developing countries, including India, China, Brazil, South Africa, and Indonesia have tabled a submission at the multilateral negotiations asking the developed countries to accept reduction targets of at least 40 per cent by 2020 with 1990 as the baseline.[15]

When the above discussion[16] continued on 30th July, 2009, Shailendra Kumar of SP remarked, "according to an estimate, the population of India will exceed the population of China and it will have 1.6 billion people by the year 2050. There will be an acute shortage of food grains by the year 2025 and we will engage in war for water with neighbouring countries."[17] Hence, there is an urgent need to take this projection seriously.

When participating in the discussion Basu Deb Acharia of CPI(M) expressed apprehension to the effect that the US will have the right to check whether India is using any purchased weapon for the purpose for which it was intended. This could mean a weapon system bought by India to bolster defence; say, for instance, against China or if India wants to use it against Pakistan, they will not be able to use it against Pakistan.[18] Responding to this Pranab Mukherjee, the then Finance Minister remarked that "do not treat the sovereignty of 112 to 115 crore people as so cheap that it can be mortgaged, that it can be bartered in any way. I would not have minded if some casual remarks would have been made. Where is the fundamental change of the foreign policy?

During the discussion on Indo-China relations with special reference to recent occurrences[19], 20 Members participated in the debate. Almost all Members raised the issue of incursions along the border; and particularly when Dr. Murli Manohar Joshi of BJP who initiated the discussion on this issue has brought to the notice of the august House that more than 200 incursions took place along the border, while replying to the debate, the then Minister of External Affairs, S.M. Krishna responded, "there is a mechanism which we have created that it gets sorted out there itself. Because it is not a demarcated boundary line and it is only a line of control, their perceptions and our perceptions can certainly differ. As a result of that, we have brought in a mechanism where we try to settle these issues at the local level, at the boundary level, and at the field level itself."[20]

Specifically about incursions along the border, he has informed the august House, "Our Armed Forces are regularly patrolling all areas along the border with China." About infrastructure development along the border between India and China, he remarked that without trying to sound alarmist, within the constraints of our resources, we have been trying to develop our infrastructure over the border line of India and China and that in months ahead, it is bound to increase.[21]

It would not be out of place to state here that the Indian Government's defence expenditure on Defence Services have increased by 154 per cent during

2004-2013.[22] It is a known fact that incursion and intrusion is unabated along India-Pakistan border and incursions from China. Growing volatility in the borders between India and Pakistan, India and China, India and Bangladesh, has resulted in improving our arsenal to such a great extent by spending huge sums of money. Over the years, we have added an array of sophisticated military hardware, missile systems and surveillance technology for the country's defence security.[23]

The Minister also stressed by saying, "India and China have had good relations and at times we have had strained relationship."[24] He also stated that 1960 was something and 2009 is totally different as there is a sea-change. India has become stronger and no one can brow-beat India.

He made a point that he believed when he held talks with the Foreign Minister of China, on a serious note, that China has agreed to reciprocate. And that he was pleasantly surprised when Chinese Foreign Minister himself reminded him about the five principles of peaceful co-existence.[25]

While replying to Vijay Bahadur Singh of BJP who has raised the issue of crisis of confidence and Shailendra Kumar of SP who mentioned about evaluating our shortcomings, he emphasised, "We do not have a crisis of confidence from our side; we are fully secure; we feel quite confident in what we are saying; and how we are dealing with China."[26]

While responding the vexed issue of stapled visa raised by many Members during this debate, Minister has made the stand of the Government of India very clear when he stated, "I think we have reacted to it, the only way that a strong India can react to that. We have said—anything which is not stamped on the Indian passport will not be treated as a valid visa either to go out or to come into this country. So, how can you say that our policy towards China is weakening?

About the menace of duplicate drugs, and fake currency, the issues raised by Jagdish Sharma of Janata Dal (United), he accepted that all these are menaces and that India is keeping a close eye on it in order to prevent it.[27]

While responding to the comments of some Members about India being a soft state, Minister retorted by asking: How can you say that our policy towards China is soft? He further elaborated the efforts of the Indian Government when he acceded to the fact that, we have not been hard; but we have been very correct. He stressed the fact that China must understand this and they will have to respect the way we are dealing with our visas in the last sixty years. He was vociferous when he said, "We certainly are not going to compromise with the visa policy which has been laid down by the Ministry of External Affairs."[28]

About specifically referring the remark of India being a soft State by Anant Geete, Leader of Shiv Sena in Lok Sabha, Minister rejected that kind of a contention with the contempt that it deserves. He stressed, "we are not a soft State; we are a State which has earned the respect of the entire world today. He informed the House about how India is looked upon in the outside world. Now, Indians are looked with awe, we are looked with admiration and we are looked with, shall I say, some subterranean jealousies also. That is the kind of the new found stature that our country has acquired today."[29]

Sanjoy Takam, a Congress Member of Parliament from Itanagar of Arunachal Pradesh, while participating in the debate, asked the Government—Where were we weak-kneed?[30] Minister responding to him stated China has been telling us that His Holiness Dalai Lama should not visit Arunachal Pradesh; our Prime Minister should not visit Arunachal Pradesh. For these remarks, Minister responded by saying, "Did the Prime Minister not go to Arunachal Pradesh? Did His Holiness Dalai Lama not go to Arunachal Pradesh? Did my predecessor, Shri Pranab Mukherjee not go to Arunachal Pradesh? He reiterated the resolve of India that Arunachal Pradesh is part and parcel of this great country of ours."[31]

About a query from a Member from Kashmir as to why construction of a road in Jammu and Kashmir was stopped. Minister responded, "Government of India had no role to play either in the starting of that road project or in the halting of that road project. It was purely a decision which the State Government of Jammu and Kashmir has taken, with which the Government of India was neither consulted nor was it brought to our notice. Only we came to know through the media reports about that road."[32]

Minister took Lok Sabha into confidence when he said, "We are fully cognizant of the need to protect and safeguard our borders and ensure that there is no erosion of our sovereignty. The situation in the India-China border areas is being constantly monitored. As I submitted earlier, we are strengthening the infrastructure in the border areas, and our defence system is well established and highly efficient. There is also excellent coordination between the various Departments." He rejected the argument that there was no coordination between various departments of the Government.

While concluding his reply, he emphasised, "The resolution of differences on the border with China must be and can only be resolved peacefully. The history of the last 60 years of our relations with China cannot be simply brushed aside. We must learn from the experience, which has taught us that conflict is not a solution, and dialogue and negotiation provide the best way forward."

Taking cognisance of the attacks on Indian students in Australia, in the Budget Session of 2012, a Statement[33] was laid by the Minister of External Affairs regarding attacks on Indians in Australia. Then Minister, S.M. Krishna delineated various steps being taken by the Government of India. In the beginning itself, he stated that each assault on Indian students since 2007 was taken up by the Indian Government with the Australian authorities, at the State level by the Consulates General and at the State and federal levels by the High Commission of India.[34] Almost half of million Indians (including 97,000 Indian students) and people of Indian origin live in Australia. He also stated that how India attaches importance to its relationship with Australia. It has also been conveyed to Parliament that the Australian Government has recently set up a high-level Working Group under overall charge of Foreign Minister Stephen Smith to deal with this issue on an urgent basis.

Minister is of the opinion besides law and order problem, commercialisation of Australian international education industry and laxity in monitoring/enforcing compliance of regulations were the reasons for such attacks. Already 8 Ministerial level visits from Australia to India have taken place in 2009, which primarily addressing growing concerns of safety and well-being of Indian students. Even during the visit of Prime Minister of Australia, Kevin Rudd to India on 12 November, 2009, Prime Minister Dr. Manmohan Singh conveyed our concern to him. Prime Minister of Australia reiterated the Australian Government's commitment to taking all possible measures to protect the safety and welfare of all international students including Indian students.[35] India is for further strengthening and expanding our relations, improving security and surveillance and to deal with the issues in a concerted and coordinated manner.

Discussion on the Demands for Grants of the Ministry of External Affairs gives us an insight into various aspects that concerns the Members of Parliament. As is the practice, every year only three or four or five Demands of different Ministries are taken up, out of 60 and odd Ministries and Departments of the Government.

Demands for Grants of the Ministry of External Affairs for 2010-11

Considering the growing importance of neighbours in the volatile situation, the Demands for Grants of the Ministry of External Affairs were taken up in 2010. This debate took place primarily because of the developments that took place in the region, and the growing influence of China in our neighbourhood and our borders. Many prominent Members from different political parties participated. Dr. Murli Manohar Joshi of BJP, Mulayam Singh Yadav of Samajwadi Party, Prasanna Kumar Patasani of BJD, Raghuvansh Prasad Singh of Rashtratiya Janata Dal, Madhu Goud Yaskhi of Congress, Sudhi Bandyopadhyay of Trinamool Congress, Nama Nageswara Rao of Telugu Desam Party, Prabod Panda of CPI, and others.

While initiating the debate on Demand for Grants under the control of the Ministry of External Affairs for 2010-11,[36] Murli Manohar Joshi of BJP emphasized on reviewing our foreign policy and there should be consensus on foreign policy.

Joshi reminded the Government that Pranab Mukherjee, when he was Foreign Minister said, "On the day the Chinese Naval Chief arrived in New Delhi on his maiden visit to India, China's rise was India's new security challenge. China out to clip India's wings; makes massive investments in neighbouring countries to spike nation's regional aspirations." This clearly brings out the fact that India has a challenge in the form of security with the rapid growth of China in recent past. India has neglected Russia as a potential counterweight both to the US and China and charged that Prime Minister is putting all eggs in the US basket, alluding that US would play the protector role that the USSR performed earlier.

Deepender Singh Hooda of Congress stressed on the need to strengthen our Look East Policy. Be it our association with ASEAN or the East Asian Summit. He is of the opinion that deepening of our ties with East Asian countries would help us in dealing with China and in actually gaining a better relationship out of China. Respond to what Murli Manohar Joshi said about Bangladesh opening up of Chittagong Port to China and US $ 425 million credit to Sri Lanka to build infrastructure around Jaffna in North Sri Lanka, he said that India has taken right steps towards economic integration and deepening of economic ties, but much more needs to be done. Hooda made a point that China represents a challenge as well as an opportunity; both the countries have oldest civilizations; greatest cultures; most populous nations; and by 2030, we would represent the second and third largest economies. Hence, India cannot afford to be at loggerhead with China. He highlight how China cooperated with India in G-20 Summits; and in the Copenhagen Summit; and the recent visit of our External Affairs Minister led to establishment of direct communication line between our topmost leadership. While responding to the remarks of Yashwant Sinha of BJP about the Copenhagen Summit and the reason why India and China cooperated there was because China needed us more than we needed China, Hooda said that India do not fear China; we do not need to fear China. We have confidence in ourselves.

Nama Nageswara Rao of Telugu Desam Party stressed on the need to improve our bilateral relations with China. Mohammed E.T. Basheer remarked that India is becoming a global leader[37] . There is no need to have inferiority complex about India's courage, strength and diplomacy. C. Sivasami of AIADMK stated that India is one of the biggest democracies in the comity of nations. He asked the Government to do soul searching to know whether India has succeeded in establishing cordial relationship with our neighbours. He went on to suggest that for India time has come to have a re-look, revisit and review our Foreign Policy. Asaduddin Owaisi from Hyderabad has stated that the last six months have been very eventful when it comes to the foreign policy of the country with the visit of Indian Prime Minister to Brazil for the BRICS summit, in which China is a Member-State.

Mirza Mehboob Beg of Jammu & Kashmir National Conference while talking about alternative economic method, and the banking system, he insisted that India should release that countries like Britain, China, Japan, France are entering into this field in a big way. Madhu Goud Yaskhi of Congress talked about the potentiality of Indian Diaspora like Chinese did with Chinese Diaspora. He recalled how Indians came to the rescue of the Government with India Resurgent Bonds, Indians came to the rescue of the Government. To buttress his point, he stated that remittance by the Indians, particularly in the Gulf and other countries, as per the statistics of 2005, was over 27 billion dollars compared to FDI in that particular year, which was hardly 3.7 billion dollars. He urged the Minister to look upon not only the NRIs particularly those settled in the Gulf regions but also set up a Fund to help those who are staying illegally, and who are being exploited by the companies.

Rattan Singh Ajnala of Shiromani Akali Dal of Punjab highlighted how India suffered because of its espousal of a non-aligned foreign policy. He stated, "In 1962, China stabbed us in the back. It (Indian foreign policy) was a debacle."[38] He stated that China has the audacity to claim entire Arunachal Pradesh as theirs; how Chinese put up boards on Indian soil in Ladakh claiming it to be part of China and that China has been browbeating us and Indian Government is turning a blind eye to this problem. Before ending his speech, he cautioned the Government to the evil designs of China and must talk from a position of strength. Prabodh Panda of CPI from West Bengal insisted, "India's strength can never come from being a subordinate to the USA. It comes from having a voice in the neighbourhood—West Asia, South Asia, China and Russia." He expressed his apprehension that India is getting marginalised.

Dr. Prasanna Kumar Patasani of Biju Janata Dal from Odisha articulated on China by stated how huge tracts of land were invaded by China, how Nehru's Indo-China diplomacy failed and how India has been paying heavily since then. India has been deliberately turning a blind eye to frequent incursions and clandestine occupation of strategic posts and locations in the mountainous Ladakh region. He also stated that thousands of kilometres of metalled roads were being laid on the Chinese side but on our side, there is abysmal infrastructure both in road communication and other logistical facilities; Chinese are changing the contours of Indus River which resulted in leaving enough space for intrusion.

Adhir Ranjan Chowdhary of Congress from West Bengal highlighted the hostile relationship with China. He quoted the Prime Minister of India steadfastly stating that Arunachal Pradesh is part and parcel of India. He remarked that when US President feared to meet Dalai Lama, India gave assent to Dalai Lama to visit Arunachal Pradesh, which speaks autonomy of India's foreign policy.

A Sampath of CPI(M) from Kerala insisted that there should be coordination between the Ministries of External Affairs, Overseas Indian Affairs, Home, Finance, Commerce, Labour etc. Next to China, we send more persons abroad. We receive complaints from the relatives of the people who are working abroad. He urged the Government to address this very complex issue.

Pinaki Misra of Biju Janata Dal from Odisha stated that China is encircling us from Urumqi to Kashgar and today China can bring its troops at 24 hours' notice but for Indian Government, it would take 24 days if not 24 weeks to mobilize troops and to mobilize the requisite armoury. He stated that India International Development Cooperation (IDCA) which was started in 2007-08, as an important vehicle to spread our influence abroad has been spread. He further stated that the Public Diplomacy Division of Indian Council for Cultural Relations (ICCR), which undertakes junkets and organises cultural programmes abroad cannot take on the might of the *madarsas* that are dotting the skyline in Nepal, and the extraordinary amount of foreign policy initiatives taken by think-tanks in China. Sudip Bandhyapodhya of Trinamool Congress of West Bengal insisted on having good relations with different countries of the world, whether it is the USA or China.

About Japan, Dr. Thokchom Meinya has remarked that Japan should also be included in the realm of India's Look East Policy. Nama Nageshwar Rao raised the issue of attacks on Indian students studying in Australia have attracted global attention. He is of the opinion that this rabid cultural and racial menace in Australia have attracted worldwide condemnation. He brought the case of one Sravan Kumar Theerthala from his constituency of Khammam in Andhra Pradesh who was hit with screwdriver and it has pierced through his head in his house at Melbourne in June 2009. He also raised another case involved one Baljinder Singh, another student from India studying in Melbourne, who was robbed and stabbed in his abdomen.

Since then several attacks took place against Indians in Australia. To keep up the morale of the Indian students from Andhra Pradesh and India, he informed Lok Sabha, that on the advise of his leader Nara Chandra Babu Naidu, he along with his colleague from the Andhra Pradesh Legislative Assembly visited Australia and met the affected students there and also the opposition leaders in Melbourne Parliament House to express Indian concern over the attacks in Australia. Asaduddin Owaisi of All India Majlis-e-Ittehadul Muslimeen from Hyderabad raised the issue of shortage of staff in Hyderabad Regional Passport Office and the problems being faced by Indian nationals in Australia as Australia mandated police clearance certificate. He suggested to the Government to issue a Note Verbale to all the foreign Embassies and Missions which insisted on police clearance certificate which would be valid for two years and request the Minister to consider this request of his. C. Sivasami of All India Anna Dravida Munnetra Kazhagam of Tamil Nadu brought out the issue of Indian students are being attacked in Australia, forcing them to flee and return to our motherland. If Indo-Australian relations are very cordial, Indian Government need to ask the question as to why these attacks against the Indians are continuing there. He expressed his pain to see attacks on India students in Australia particularly when our relations are smooth.

S.M. Krishan, Minister of External Affairs while responding to the debate stated that India have fiercely pursued an independent foreign policy. Stating China is our largest neighbour. While acceding that there are complex issues like boundary question in our relationship with China, he is of the firm belief that dialogue and negotiation are the best ways to resolve outstanding issues with China. He said, "Peace and tranquillity are being maintained in the border area with China. We have been open and candid in conveying our concerns to China about such issues as 'stapled visas'."[39] He further stated that the existence of such problems only underscores the need for us to resolve them not from confrontation but through dialogue and communication. He informed Lok Sabha that trade and economic content of our relationship have grown by leaps and bounds in recent years. He revealed that mechanism of high level political contact and dialogue has helped to deepen mutual understanding and co-operation on multilateral issues like climate change has also been mutually beneficial.[40]

He recalled that his defence and security dialogue with China, a fortnight ago, in China, to coincide with the 60th anniversary of the establishment of diplomatic relations between India and China, He reminded the House of the historic visit of late Rajiv Gandhi, as Prime Minister to China in 1988 to further develop relations with China, which in turn helped successive Indian Governments to build upon relationship between our two countries.

As is the procedure, Minister of External Affairs laid the statement regarding recent visits abroad by Prime Minister in November, 2010[41] , where he stated that Prime Minister visited Japan from October 24-26, 2010 for the Annual Summit with the Prime Minister of Japan, which have been institutionalised since 2006. Japan's generous Official Development Assistance (ODA) to India over the years is reflected in India's various flagship projects like Delhi Metro, Dedicated Freight Corridor Project, Delhi-Mumbai Industrial Corridor.[42] India has highlighted the attractiveness of India as an investment destination. Both the Prime Ministers announced the conclusion of negotiations on a Comprehensive Economic Partnership Agreement (CEPA) between our two countries.[43] There was a proposal from Japan for the establishment of a comprehensive Ministerial-level Economic Dialogue to drive economic relations forward between two countries. Indian Prime Minister endorsed the proposal. Dr. Manmohan Singh while complimenting Prime Minister Kan for his decision to commence negotiations with India on an Agreement for Cooperation in the Peaceful Uses of Nuclear Energy, urged to conclude such an Agreement at an early date.[44] Minister for External Affairs expressed his confidence that both countries, with their engagement, would become one of our most vital and dynamic international relationships. He further stated that India and Japan are moving ahead to work together on several regional and international issues including the merging East Asian architecture, for reform of the United Nations, including its Security Council and on climate change.[45]

A Statement[46] was made by the Prime Minister in March, 2011 regarding massive earthquake and Tsunami in Japan. While conveying deepest condolences to the Prime Minister of Japan on behalf of Government of India and people of

India, informed the August that as an immediate step, India is airlifting 25,000 blankets to Japan and India is ready to send search and rescue teams and relief material and that we stand ready to help in the relief, rehabilitation and reconstruction phase. [47] It so happened that the very next year, once again, Demands for Grants of the Ministry of External Affairs were taken up. It is very rare to see such an important debate taking place on the Demands of External Affairs considering the various developments concerning foreign affairs of the country.

Demands for Grants of the Ministry of External Affairs for 2011-12

On 15th March, 2011, prominent members like Jaswant Singh of BJP, Shashi Tharoor, a former External Affairs Minister and a Congress Member, Mulayam Singh Yadav of Samajwadi Party, Chandrakant Khaire of Shiv Sena, Prabodh Panda of CPI, Raghuvansh Prasad Singh of Rashtriya Janata Dal, Sudip Bandyapadhyay of Trinamool Congress and other Members from different political parties participated. In the end, Minister of External Affairs comes out with all the details pertaining to the foreign affairs during the period and puts forth the views and policy matters of the Government before Parliament for the consumption of the Members as well as public in general. This gives an opportunity to also state as to what the Government would be pursuing in the days to come as well as the exact situation prevailing concerning respective countries with which India is having relationship.

While initiating in the debate on Demands for Grants of the Ministry of External Affairs[48] , Jaswant Singh of Bharatiya Janata Party and a former External Affairs Minister has brought the blunder India committed when during the Independence, India accepted the domination of the People's Republic of China over Tibet for which we are continuing to pay the price. China is posing us challenge He insisted on recognizing the reality of China. He said, "A China that is unified, that has a centralized command of Government, will be an expansionist China."[49] What China is doing is a long-term threat. By saying India and China destiny's perennial twins, he remarked that China will continue to wish to dominate India,

Shashi Tharoor of Congress wondered how can we overlook the fact that China, with which we fought a war less than five decades ago, is now our largest single trading partner. He acceded to the point that India is not far behind China. He also reminded of the visits of all five of the present Permanent Members of the United Nations Security Council—China, the US, Britain, France, and Russia—to India in 2010. He brought out the fact that with the establishment of Nalanda University in Bihar, India would revive a University that till the 8thCentury AD used to receive students from China, Japan, Korea. Foreign countries used to send their students to India before Oxford or Cambridge or Harvard were even a gleam in anybody's eye.[50]

On speaking specifically about China, he said, "Today's China is a country with which we have had 51 billion dollars of trade in the last fiscal year. By the end of this month, the figure might be 60 billion dollars for this fiscal year, and the Prime Minister of China has come here and spoken of 100 billion dollars by 2015. We are talking about a China where we have 7000 Indian students studying now."[51] He has also brought to the fore the fact that China has been permitting our pilgrims to travel to Kailash and Mansarovar and that requesting China to allow Indian companies to open branches in Shanghai and Huangztiou and that Chinese companies are trying to come into India.

India is having the world's longest unresolved frontier dispute with China. By stating that our Prime Minister has visited and campaigned in Arunachal Pradesh and that Dalai Lama, despite Chinese warnings, was able and allowed to go to Arunachal Pradesh and speak there shows that India has at no point compromised its position. He is of the opinion that our defence preparedness is adequate and that China has far too much a stake in its economic relationship with India to be tempted to engage in any sort of military adventure.

While comparing with China, he acceded to the fact that China is a bigger player in Africa like the West but African leaders look at India as a country that is familiar to them; they see India as a country not unlike Africa. Jagada Nand Singh said that our foreign policy about China, which has been claiming a large part of Kashmir and Arunachal Pradesh as its own[52]. China has been posing a danger to our country by withholding and diverting the water of the river Brahmaputra and at the same time it is also involved in inciting our neighbours. R. Thamaraiselvan of DMK stated that China does not consider Arunachal Pradesh as an integral part of India. He recalled the visits of five permanent members of the United Nations to India in 2010 which reflects our importance in the global sphere. He noted that except China, all the other countries, during their visit to Delhi, have agreed that India deserves to be in the UN Security Council as its permanent member. He remarked that China is also constructing a dam on Brahmaputra to store water, which would result acute shortage of water in our country. Hence, requested the Government to take up the issue with the Chinese Government on a serious note.

Mulayam Singh Yadav of Samajwadi Party was harsh when he stated that when China blocked water flow from river Brahmaputra, Government is not talking about it; China is encroaching upon our land, Government is not opposing it. Nama Nageshwar Rao of TDP, highlighted that our relations with China is not showing any progress and that Chinese aggression and territorial claims over Arunachal Pradesh is affecting the smooth relations between the two countries. Incursions by Chinese troops into the Indian territory has been increasing every day. He mentioned that bilateral trade between both the countries is around $ 50 billions. He suggested that India should deal effectively on refusal of regular visas and stapled visas to the people of Arunachal Pradesh and Jammu and Kashmir.

C. Sivasami of AIADMK from Tamil Nadu has expressed his opinion that foreign policy issue should be taken very seriously. He highlighted that we are not having good relations with our neighbouring countries including China. Baijanti Panda is of the opinion that while dealing with China, neither of the extremes is true. He stated how China surged ahead in economic terms since 1980. Though China has become our largest trading partner, we should keep in mind China's interest in nuclear proliferation around the world and around our neighbourhood, the issue of stapled visas, etc. and use economic diplomacy as a tool. He stated how China brought back their 30,000 nationals much before Indian Government started evacuating Indians from Libya.

P. Karunakaran of CPI(M) argued that India deserves to be in the UN Security Council as its permanent member and asked India to make determined bid for permanent seat in the UN Security Council.[53] Sudip Bandhyapadhyay of Trinamool Congress stated that India now acquired enough strength and power to raise its voice in the whole world and that globally, India is now certainly a force to reckon with. He wondered if China has emerged as such a huge force by utilising their human resources, why can India not rise to the occasion whenever it is required? Bhausaheb Rajaram Wakchaure of Shiv Sena also raised the issue of India becoming a Member of the UN Security Council. S.S. Ramasubbu of Congress from Tamil Nadu highlighted how India established a peaceful friendship with China. Bismuthiary wanted to know from the Government of India what pro-active policy actions have been taken so far towards the very dangerous and very detrimental policy approach adopted by the Government of China against India. On Japan, Jaswant Singh of BJP expressed his sadness about the simultaneous cataclysmic earthquake; a Tsunami; a potential nuclear meltdown of enormous dimensions; adding to that, in South West Japan, a volcano has erupted.

Dr. Botcha Jhansi Lakshmi of Congress expressed her concern about nuclear power plants in India after the nuclear crisis in Japan in the aftermath of Tsunami and asked the Government to assure the country of the security. Dr. Mirza Mehboob Beg expressed the sympathy to the suffering people of Japan on Tsunami Prabodh Panda of CPI has recalled the horrendous earthquake that devastated Japan and highlighted the positive attitude of India towards Japan. He also brought out the emergence of a multipolar world from unipolar world after the disaster in Japan. Nama Nageswara Rao of Telugu Desam Party said that there was only an increase of 11.50 per cent increase of the Budget of the External Affairs Ministry from last year. This year the allocation is Rs.7,106 crore. Baijayant Panda of Biju Janata Dal asked the Government to extend every possible help to Japan in this hour of need. He reminded Lok Sabha how a decade back, how India was scoffed at in ASEAN but now, we could sign Free Trade Agreements with Japan.

Many Members stated that our Prime Minister Dr. Manmohan Singh travelled extensively to meet the Prime Ministers and Presidents of various countries which helped India to establish a peaceful friendship with U.S.A., Russia, Japan, China and Arabian countries. He is also creating a conducive situation to get a place for India in United Nation Security Council. On our relations with Japan, Rama Subbu of Congress stated that Japan, a developed country, is in a great danger of Tsumani and earthquake. It is very important to help these people and also to bring out our Indians from Japan. The Nuclear project is now damaged totally. The people are affected much due to the breakdown of this nuclear project. In our country we are constructing a nuclear project in Koodamkulan with the collaboration of Russia. In order to safeguard the people of our Southern Tamil Nadu, the foreign affairs ministry should take much care to establish this project with all the security measures. It is essential to tell the Russian scientists and government that the project must be free from fusion.

Shashi Tharoor while associating with the concerns expressed about the tragedy in Japan recalled how till 8th century AD Nalanda University, which is being revived in Bihar, used to receive students from Japan, China and that it would once again become a symbol of excellence in our region.

On our relationship with Australia, Jaswant Singh stated as to how he became a part of the Asia-Pacific Leadership Network on Nuclear Non-Proliferation and Disarmament and recalled the great initiative of a very prominent Australian, Mr. Gareth Evans. Dr, Botcha Jhansi Lakshmi highlighted the problems being faced by Indian students in Australia. Sher Singh Gubaya also raised the issue and request the Government to take up the issue of Indian students in Australia with the Australian Government. Nama Nageshwara Rao specifically mentioned about the killing of a girl student. He requested the Government to tackle the issue properly and immediately. Sivasami wondered why Government is not able to ensure safety and security of our students in Australia and in USA.

Many Members while debating has stated the visits to India by Mr. David Cameroon, the Prime Minister of UK, Mr. Barrack Obama the US President, Mr. Nicolas Sarkozy, the French President, Mr. Wen Jiabo, the Chinese Premier and Mr. Demetry Medvedev, Russian President. Thamaraiselvan of Dravida Munnetra Kazhagam stated that while India is extended hands of friendship with other countries, we do not have real friends and cited the Indian students flight in Australia and requested the Government to ensure safety and security of Indian students in 'Australia. Sudip Bandhyapadhyay of Trinamool Congress expressed the need to ensure safety of Indian students studying abroad, particularly in Australia. He asked, "How far are we taking steps and what sort of stern attitude are we projecting?"[54] Rama Subbu of Congress asked the Government to pay more attention on Australia and America, where our Indian students are stabbed to death and ridiculed.

On 16th March, S.M. Krishna, Minister of External Affairs while replying to the debate[55], stated that India has always pursued the path of careful deliberation, conscious always of the need to defend out security interests and to carefully monitor activities from other foreign powers including China. He further stated, "There are various areas that China and India have similar approaches on but there are others where our interests do not coincide." He accepted that issues like stapled visas for residents of Jammu and Kashmir have generated differences in recent years. In this regard, he informed Lok Sabha that Indian Government has taken it up with the Chinese Government at the highest level when I went to China and when the Foreign Minister of China was here and when the Premier of China Wen Jiabao came to Delhi and that they have assured us that the intention of Chinese Government is to solve the problem to our satisfaction. He expressed the hope that China would rise to this expectation of ours. While responding to Mulayam Singh, who raised the issue of roads, infrastructure in border areas in Arunachal Pradesh, Utharakhand, etc., he said, "Building infrastructure in the India-China borders is one of the priorities of our Government. The Border Roads Organisation is constructing 61 India-China border roads, spread over Jammu & Kashmir, Arunachal Pradesh, Sikkim, Himachal Pradesh and Utharakhand.

On Japan, Krishna stated that India share with the initiator of the discussion, Jaswant Singh, in expressing our deep sorrow and heartfelt condolences for the Government and the people of Japan at an hour when a terrible tragedy has struck that country and the people. He also informed that India share a deep friendship with Japan as strategic global partnership with that country, and that partnership has acquired strategic relevance not only to the two countries but also to the entire Region. He assured Lok Sabha that Government of India is ready to help Japan, the people of Japan in whatever way necessary at this tragic hour.

Responding to Members request for the need to augment specialised interpreters cadre, he informed that we have 19 language specialisted interpreters and specialist officers in different languages such as Chinese, Russian, Arabic, etc.

On Australia, he informed Lok Sabha that India took up the murder of Indian girl student in Australia a couple of days back with the highest authority in Australia and our High Commissioner in Australia had high level meetings with the Australian authorities and assured that law of the land will take its own course.

In these interventions in the 15th Lok Sabha, Members of Parliament sought information about varied subjects concerning the countries in focus in this paper. These interventions had brought to the fore the latest on various subjects of interest in these three countries—China, Japan and Australia—and the efforts that are being made from the Government end and to attend to such issues with these countries. Concerned Ministries come out with the authentic and factual information on the issues asked by the Members. Debates certainly throw light on the issues in vogue and helps Parliament to know as to what the Government is thinking on an issue and as to how it is going to resolve them.

Departmentally-Related Standing Committee on External Affairs

Apart from the debates in Parliament on foreign policy and discussion on demands for grants of the Ministry of External Affairs, and other related issues concerning the foreign policy of the country, Parliamentary Standing Committee on External Affairs plays a very major role in scrutinizing the Demands for Grants of the Ministry of External Affairs, various activities of the Ministry, and consider general principles and clauses of the Bills referred to the Committee and make report thereon; and discussion any other emerging issues that come up from time to time.

In the 15th Lok Sabha, there are 21 Members from Lok Sabha and 10 Members from Rajya Sabha, and currently Ananth Kumar is the Chairman. This Committee also deals with Ministry of Indian Overseas Affairs. In the Committee set up, discussions are more focused and structured, as top officials of the Ministry of External Affairs depose before the Committee and the Members of the Committee generally get all relevant information from the top officials then and there. Such information can be termed as authentic and valuable. An expert on Indian foreign policy, therefore, remarks, "With the increasing time lost in the pandemonium inside the halls of Parliament, Committees seem to be the only escape buzz in which issues involved in Bills are discussed in detail, without any disruption.[56]

This sort of exercise enhances the level and standard of proceedings of the committee and indirectly paves way to the enlightened discussions when issues relating to foreign affairs and foreign policy are discussed in the Lok Sabha. It may therefore be stated that they often act as conveyer belts for the opinion and views of the executive branch on different policies to the larger membership of Parliament[57] Members of Parliament thus get ample opportunities for expressing their views in the Committee to thoroughly examine and analyse national as well as international issues. On international issues, primarily, the Minister of External Affairs, and sometimes, concerning water related issues, the Minister of Water Resources try to respond to the views expressed by the Members and, accordingly, changes are incorporated in the foreign policy of the country. But it does not happen in the meetings of the Committee and its reports. The recommendations made in reports of the Committee are not mandatory for the Government to accept *in-toto*. They are advisory in nature. But in the Committees, Members of Parliament take up pressing issues involving the foreign policy and have healthy and threadbare discussions, which would have an impact on the Government's policies and decisions. Parliament, moreover, can influence the formation of foreign policy related to water sharing with its neighbours through the Consultative Committee of the Ministry of External Affairs also.

I would like to quote from the Report[58] of the Committee during 2009-10—headed by Sushma Swaraj, the then Chairperson of the External Affairs Committee, and other prominent Members were Karan Singh, Najma Heptulla, T.K.S. Elangovan. It is heartening to note that all the 15 recommendations made by the Committee were accepted by the Government, out of which 9 were implemented; 5 were under process of implementation and one was to be implemented.

As regards the Reports presented by the Department-Related Standing Committee of External Affairs, during 5 August 2004 to 18 May 2009, 10 Demands of Grants of the Ministry of External Affairs and Ministry of Indian Overseas Affairs of have been scrutinized; two Annual Reports were scrutinized.[59] On an average, the Committee on External Affairs has met 18 times per year during the 14th Lok Sabha—from 5 August 2004 to 31 March 2009. [60] In the 15th Lok Sabha, from 31 August 2009 to 30 August 2010, the Committee has met 24 times.[61]

Coming to the 15th Lok Sabha, last meeting of the Committee on External Affairs was held on 20th February, 2014. During the 15th Lok Sabha is that it has presented 25 Reports to Lok Sabha till February 20, 2014.[62] The huge body of work it has produced not only shows the elaborate functioning of the Committee to make the Executive accountability but also to scrutinize various activities of the Ministries of External Affairs and Indian Overseas Affairs. In the days of coalition era, with less and less days of proper functioning of Lok Sabha, the painstaking efforts of the Committee cannot be swept aside. The efforts of the Committee in the parliamentary democracy is laudable by any standards

During the 15th Lok Sabha, till 18th February, 2014, out of 114 meetings[63] held by the Committee on External Affairs, on three occasions (6th October, 2009, 13th January, 2012 and 20th January, 2012) issues concerning China was taken up. For example, Foreign Secretary brief on our relationship with China with special reference to recent border violation; briefing on 'relations with China including cultural/civilisational contacts'; and on `India's relations with China'. On all these meetings, extensive discussions took place with the participation of Members from different political strata and the detailed responses from the top officials of the Ministry of External Affairs.

On Japan, a meeting took place on 22nd August, 2013, with the Japanese Delegation of the House of Representatives of Japan, where wide range of issues and information concerning both countries were exchanged.

Consultative Committees of the Ministry of External Affairs

Consultative Committee of Ministry of External Affairs help its Members to know first-hand information and details from the Minister of External Affairs as well as briefings from the higher officials of the Ministry. As its name indicates, it is expected to perform a purely consultative function. The meetings of the Consultative Committee do, however, serve one useful purpose. Since the proceedings of the meetings are confidential, Ministers can give details of international situation to the makers of India's foreign policy, which cannot be disclosed elsewhere.

In the 15th Lok Sabha, Salman Khursheed, Minister of External Affairs is the Chairman of Consultative Committee for the Ministry of External Affairs. E. Ahamed and Preneet Kaur, Ministers of State in the Ministry of External Affairs are also Members. This Committee has 30 Members, out of which 13 Members from Lok Sabha, which includes two Permanent Special Invitees. Likewise, 17 Members of Rajya Sabha are also the Members of this Committee, which includes two Permanent Special Invitees. Two Ministers of State in the Ministry of Parliamentary Affairs, namely, Rajeev Shukla, and Paban Singh Ghatowar are ex-officio Members.[64]

The Consultative Committee held 13 meetings and discussed issues ranging from India's Neighbourhood: Security Concerns and Prospects for Overall Cooperation, India-EU relations, Pursuits of India Economic Interests Abroad, Cultural Diplomacy as a tool of Foreign Policy, India's relations with ASEAN Countries, India and the United Nations, India's Relations with West Asia and North African Countries, India-Russia relations, Look East Policy, and Public diplomacy from 3rd September, 2009 till 25th June, 2013.[65] The Consultative Committee of the Ministry of External Affairs is thus an important institutional link between Parliament and implementation of various schemes, policies, programmes and plans of the Ministry of External Affairs. If it is allowed to work properly, this can be a useful instrument for Parliament to influence the Government's decision on issues relating to women empowerment. Since the proceedings of the meetings are confidential, Ministers can part with details and situations emanating on a certain policy or issue, which cannot be disclosed elsewhere. The Consultative Committees of the Ministry on External Affairs are thus an important institutional link between Parliament and Government.

Since Parliament meets only 80-85 days approximately in a year, it hardly finds time to discuss various aspects of public policies including foreign policy. Hence, Committees—both Standing as well as Consultative—assume significance as these Committees examine Demands of Grants of various ministries as well as long-term policy documents of the Government—Annual Reports, Action Taken reports, etc. In the Committee set-up, discussions are more focused, as top officials of the Ministry of External Affairs depose before these Committees and Members generally get relevant and authentic information. Considerable amount of work is performed in these Committees.

Often, there has been a debate whether Committees are in a position to influence the foreign policy, to what extent Committees contribute in framing of the foreign policy, whether its inputs are taken into account by the Government of the day et al. If we analyse the recommendations of the 14th Report of the Standing Committee on External Affairs (14th Lok Sabha), we can see that 80.95 per cent of recommendations/observations of the Committee were accepted by the Government.[66]

In the case of the 15th Report of the Standing Committee on External Affairs, we can find that almost 100 per cent recommendations/observations contained in the 15th Report on Demands for Grants (2007-08) of the Ministry of External Affairs, presented to the Lok Sabha on April 26, 2007 were accepted by the Government.[67] Hence, we can say that Committees serve the purpose of their existence. Though recommendations of the Committee are not binding on the Government, we can see that over the years this trend has slowly been changed and at present most of the recommendations of the Committee are accepted by the Government.[68] An analyst of India's foreign policy, therefore, observes: "There is a healthy attitude that the process of securing a greater degree of accountability of the executive branch to the legislature and the people, is a continuing one."[69]

Likewise, out of 20 recommendations[70] made by the Standing Committee on the Action Taken on the II Report (15th Lok Sabha) on Demands for Grants of the Ministry of External Affairs (2009-10), 12 were accepted (60%). This shows that Standing Committee do serve the purpose and its recommendations are not only considered by the Government but also accepted.

Ministry of External Affairs

Countries in the Asia-Pacific region—China, Japan and Australia—under focus in the paper come under the purview of the nodal Ministry—Ministry of External Affairs. These countries have also evinced enough interests from other Ministries of Government of India, namely, Commerce & Industry, Railways, Finance, Defence, Coal, Textiles, Shipping, Health & Family Welfare, Petroleum & Natural Gas, Agriculture, Consumer Affairs, Public Distribution & Food, Human Resources Development, Road Transport and Highways, Steel, Chemicals and Fertilizers, Heavy Industries, Urban Development, Water Resources, Atomic Energy, Environment and Forests, Culture, Indian Overseas Affairs, Youth Affairs, Power, Tourism.

In regard to China, till February, 2013, trade and economic relationship between two countries have grown rapidly over the last decade or so. The testimony to this is that from less than US$ 3 billion in 2000, trade between India and China has grown to US$ 74 billion in 2011; it was US$ 66 in 2011.[71] It is noteworthy to state here that two countries have set a target of US$ 100 billion in 2015 for bilateral trade. Indian investment in China were US$ 441.70 million; and Chinese investments into India till December 2011 stood at US$ 575.70 million.[72]

As far as Japan is concerned, till January, 2013, bilateral trade reached $18.43 billion, which was an increase of 34.33 per cent over the financial year 2010-11, when the total bilateral trade was $ 13.72 billion. As is well known, India has been the largest recipient of Japanese Official Development Assistance (ODA) since 2003-04. On 16th February, 2011, the Comprehension Economic Partnership Agreement (CEPA) was signed between India and Japan.[73]

Speaker of 15th Lok Sabha, Meira Kumar, has led a Parliamentary Delegation to Japan from 2-6 October, 2011 at the invitation of the Japanese Parliament

(Diet).[74] She held a number of interactive meetings with Speaker of the House of Representatives; called on the Prime Minister, etc. during her visit, which had highlighted not only happenings of Indian parliament but exchanges and interactions helped both countries to know each other better.

Coming to Australia, till February, 2013, trade in goods and services between India and Australia is growing exponentially from A$ 6.54 billion in 2003-04, it has reached A$ 18.35 billion in 2011-12.[75] Many exchanges and visits by Indian Delegations at various levels had helped both countries to come closer in various spheres.[76] Commerce and economic relationship between two countries have grown rapidly over the last decade or so. The testimony to this is that from less than US$ 3 billion in 2000, trade between India and China has grown to US$ 74 billion in 2011; it was US$ 66 in 2011.[77]

Annual Report of the Ministry of External Affairs which is tabled in both Houses of Parliament every year explains various aspects of developments that took place during the year in an elaborate manner. Hence, having a look at this would be of great importance to the study.

Annual Report of the Ministry of External Affairs for 2012-13

The Annual Report has highlighted various aspects concerning countries in focus—China, Japan and Australia. During the year under review, we could find relationship between India and China progressing well. Bilateral exchanges and dialogue in various areas like counter-terrorism, trans-border rivers, policy planning and economy, defence took place. Both countries had reached an understanding to resolve the boundary questions through peaceful negotiations, in a fair, reasonable and mutually acceptable manner, as a strategic objective.[78]

Both India and China had continued to pursue its policy of developing friendly and cooperative relations in the framework of the Strategic and Cooperative Partnership established in 2005. Both countries had adopted the "Shared Vision for the 21st Century", which reflected the congruence of interests on regional and international issues, and their willingness to work together in those areas.[79] Period of 2012-13 had witnessed all round progress with the designation as "Year of India-China Friendship and Cooperation".

The Chinese incursion in eastern Ladakh in April, 2013, and later going back by China has been raised by India with the Chinese Premier Li Kequiang when he visited India in May, 2013. The Working Mechanism on Consultation and Coordination on India-China Border Affairs, which was established during the 15th Round of Special Representatives (SRs) talks on the Boundary Question in January, 2012, met twice during the year 2012-2013 on 5-6 March, 2012 in Beijing; and on 29-30 November, 2012 in New Delhi.[80] Informal round of discussion too took place with the Chinese when India's Special Representative and National Security Advisor visited China on 3-4 December, 2012.[81]

During the period, relationship between India and Japan has moved on an upward trajectory.[82] Dialogues on cross-cutting economic issues, on maritime affairs, cyber security, social security and rare earths industry took place between two countries.[83] A steady upward curve was maintained in our relations with Japan during the year under review, which marked the 60th anniversary of the establishment of diplomatic relations.[84] The 6th meeting of the Strategic Dialogue took place between our two Foreign Ministers in April, 2012.[85]

During the period under review, Australia and India had consolidated its relations with the uranium sales to India and both countries have agreed to commence negotiations on a bilateral civil nuclear cooperation agreement.[86] There has been significant transformation in India's relationship with Australia in the recent years

Apart from Parliament, Parliamentary Standing Committee on External Affairs and Consultative Committee of the Ministry of External Affairs play its part in taking forward our foreign policy in regard to Asia-Pacific Region countries China, Japan and Australia, apart from other issues brought up before it from time-to-time.

Road Ahead

Being neighbours, both countries cannot afford to antagonise each other. As we have seen in the past two decades or so of liberalisation, globalisation and privatisation, both countries have surged ahead in the growth path. China and India emerge as two ambitions trading States that prioritise growth through interaction with the outside world instead of isolation.[87] Cooperation among countries would go a long way in further the interests of both countries. Beijing regarded a more confident and prosperous India as a bothersome neighbour, a growing rival for influence in Asia and a potential anti-China partner of the U.S. Beijing, however, did not regard India as a major military threat or trade competitor.[88]

During National Democratic Alliance (NDA), the then Prime Minister, Vajpayee visited China from June 22 to 27, 2003.[89] Later a number of visits followed to further the cooperation between both countries. In this direction, it is pertinent to point out that a Joint Study Group to assess the prospects and impacts of EPA economy was set up and upon its successful conclusion and adoption of its report by the two partnership agreements, PMs in December, 2006, in Tokyo, the CEPA negotiations were launched on the trade front, export of Indian mangoes has been one of the main issues. Japan has also proposed a US $ 90 billion Delhi-Mumbai Dedicated Freight and Industrial Corridor during the visit of PM Abe to New Delhi in August, 2007.[90]

It can be seen from the records that opening up of respective markets would help each other's economy. China's and India's opening of their respective domestic markets to each other will bring an exponential increase in trade and investment opportunities, thus enhancing the tremendous gains from trade for both countries.[91] This has been proved time and again that gains are immense when we see the benefits accrued to both the countries by throwing open our economies. There is a lot of room for China and India to enlarge the scale of bilateral trade with India having a population of 1.07 billion and China having a population of more than 1.3 billion, added together, they account for one-third of the total world population.[92]

But the core area of interest between India and China is and should be peaceful co-existence, resolving the differences in an amicable manner. If we see the past, we can say that both countries have been successful to a great extent. There cannot be two opinions about that. Relationship between China and India have four aspects: the maintenance of long-term peaceful co-existence; the keeping of political and economic differences and conflicts manageable; the further opening of markets and the facilitating of economic cooperation in fields of mutual benefits; and strengthen cooperation on specific issues at regional and international levels.[93]

Way back in 1962, Indian Wise Men Committee on Indo-Japanese Collaboration was set up and Jagdish Bhagwati was appointed as Secretary, India, Japan and Asia.[94] This shows that efforts have always been attempted to smoothen the ties among countries and attempt is just a small one in that direction.

Suggestions

Strenuous efforts are on the anvil to make Parliament effective. It is to be noted that Parliament could discuss only four times during the period 1988-2003 (1988, 1990, 1992, 2003) but in the 15th Lok Sabha, in two consecutive years, 2010 and 2011 the Demands for Grants of the Ministry of External Affairs for 2010-11, and 2011-12 were taken up for discussion.. Considering the growing importance of developments that are taking place on foreign affairs, and particularly in our neighbouring countries—Pakistan, China, Bangladesh—renewed efforts have been taken to discuss the whole gamut of issues concerning issues of countries like China, Japan and Australia in Parliament more often than ever in the last over two decades.

It would be pertinent to point out here as to what happened during the Winter Session of Parliament in 2010, Lok Sabha, when Lok Sabha could transact business for a day only, that too, on the first day. It could not transact rest of the days of the Session because of lack of consensus on setting up of Joint Parliamentary Committee (JPC) between the Government and the Opposition parties. Lok Sabha Speaker, Meira Kumar has expressed her concern and anguish over collapse of question hour as it would dent Parliament's image. In this direction, Lok Sabha Rules Committee has carried out an amendment in the rules to prevent collapse of Question hour. The Committee has also taken a series of decisions to ensure that the proceedings of the House were not stalled for some reason or the other.

At present, only a miniscule portion of the policy aspect is scrutinized by the committees with the result majority of the important aspects of different ministries and departments are left out and never come in the domain of discussion and debate in the committees. This trend has to be changed for good. We should also strive for having more number of sittings of Parliament. As is well know, Parliament is bestowed by our Constitution with powers to oversee the functioning of the executive. This very purpose would be defeated if the sittings of Parliament are few and far between.

Parliament is bestowed by our Constitution with powers to oversee the functioning of the Executive. This very purpose would be defeated if the sittings of Parliament are few and far between. Efforts should be made to evolve a consensus on not only having nearly 100 days of sitting but also to ensure that there will not be any stalling of parliamentary proceedings.

Certainly, Parliament and parliamentary debates can be made more vibrant by merely bringing before Parliament more important concerns of public for discussion and for finding solutions. Parliament's time can be used in a meaningful manner to highlight peoples' issues or concerns of farmers, and having threadbare discussions on issues involving education, trade, environment, business, communications, information technology, foreign policy, health, housing et al. More participation of Members in Parliamentary debates would bring out the finer elements of issues having impact on people.

Conclusion

Discussions and debates in Parliament invariably help in finding out solutions. A general awareness is always created and a message goes out to the nation whenever parliamentary discussion takes place and the debate is telecast live in the Lok Sabha Television and highlights are shown in the national network and other prominent private channels. Debate on issues concerning China, Japan and Australia in the Asia-Pacific Region in Parliament would undoubtedly help to know the issue in proper perspective. The next day, the print media would give coverage in an extensive and elaborate manner and that too in the front page. Editorials are written and a strong public stance is formed through all parliamentary inputs in the electronic and print media. Efforts should be made to make parliamentary debates and interventions more effective. There has been consensus in Parliament on foreign policy. Of late, we could find no consensus on issues concerning Sri Lanka, Bangladesh because of assertion by regional parties in Tamil Nadu and West Bengal.

Nonetheless, renewed efforts should be made with more vigour to ensure that a fruitful resolution in resolving the long pending issues concerning China, Japan and Australia in the Asia-Pacific Region is put in place. Though Indian Parliament has a limited role in the making of India's foreign policy, on sensitive issues such as India's relationship with its neighbour China, Japan and Australia, Parliament has played its role. One can hardly deny the fact that Parliament contributes in its own ways to the Government's efforts to meet the challenges at external front by arriving at a consensus on a particular issue regarding foreign policy. In this scenario, in the present coalition era, Parliament can certainly play a prominent role in pursuing India's interests—in Asia-Pacific Region, particularly China, Japan and Australia—and in arriving at logical conclusions. Parliament helps to make great strides to increase trade and investment with China, Japan and Australia. Further and strengthening relationship with Japan would also help India to counterbalance China in the political realm of Asia-Pacific Region.

To sum up, Parliament has had a mixed record as far as its role in the making of India's foreign policy till the 1980 is concerned. While the Constitution bestows on Parliament powers to legislate on matters concerning foreign policy and the Government is responsible to Parliament, Parliament normally played only an advisory role. Parliament, of course, had an educative impact and discussions in Parliament have had the result of showing the world how Indians think. Parliament also educated people and helped in making foreign policy acceptable in many ways.

Parliament is bestowed with many constitutional provisions to bring up issues of national importance concerning the policies, schemes, programmes and plans of the government. Parliamentary debates, interventions should be made more effective to protect the interests of the country. As has been amply brought out in this paper, Parliament has invariably served the national interests.

NOTES

1. Lok Sabha Debates—Questions—parliamentofindia.nic.in, http://164.100.47.132/LssNew/psearch/qsearch15.aspx accessed on March 18, Accessed on March 18, 2014.
2. Ibid.
3. Lok Sabha Debates—Questions—parliamentofindia.nic.in
4. Debate—Lok Sabha—Motion of Thanks on President's Address on March 13, 2012
5. Lok Sabha Debates, Felicitations, dated 27th August, 2012.
6. President's Address to both Houses of Parliament, dated 21st February, 2013.
7. Ibid.
8. Ibid.
9. Lok Sabha Debates, Special Mention, dated 01 December 2009.
10. Lok Sabha Debates, Special Mention, dated 8th June, 2009
11. Ibid.
12. Lok Sabha Debates, Discussion under Rule 193, Dated 29th July, 2009.
13. Ibid.
14. Ibid.
15. Ibid.
16. Lok Sabha Debates, Discussion under Rule 193, 30th July, 2009.
17. Ibid.
18. Ibid.
19. Lok Sabha Debates, Discussion under Rule 193, dated 9th December, 2009.
20. Ibid.
21. Ibid.

22. Ministry of Defence, & Putting India on the Road to Progress, 2004-13, UPA, New Delhi, October, 2013.
23. Lok Sabha Debates, Discussion under Rule 193, dated 9th December, 2009.
24. Ibid.
25. Ibid.
26. Ibid.
27. Ibid.
28. Ibid.
29. Ibid.
30. Ibid.
31. Ibid.
32. Ibid.
33. Lok Sabha Debates, Statement by Minister, dated 25th February, 2010.
34. Ibid.
35. Ibid.
36. Lok Sabha Debates, Demands for Grants of Ministry of External Affairs 2010-11, 20th April, 2010.
37. Ibid.
38. Ibid.
39. Lok Sabha Debates, Demands for Grants of Ministry of External Affairs, 20th April, 2010.
40. Ibid.
41. Lok Sabha Debates, Statement by Minister, dated 19th November, 2010.
42. Ibid.
43. Ibid.
44. Ibid.
45. Ibid.
46. Lok Sabha Debates, Statement by Prime Minister, dated 14th March, 2011.
47. Ibid.
48. Debate—Lok Sabha—Demands for Grants of the Ministry of External Affairs on 15th March, 2011
49. Ibid.
50. Ibid.
51. Ibid.
52. Ibid.
53. Ibid.
54. Ibid.
55. Ibid.
56. Interview with A.K. Ray, Professor of Political Science (Retd.), Jawaharlal Nehru University, in New Delhi on February 2, 2008. However, K. Natwar Singh, the former External Affairs Ministers and the Rajya Sabha Member expressed the view in his interview on January 24, 2008 that "Committees have not functioned as well as they should. There is a room for improvement."
57. Kamath, n.18, p. 236.
58. Second Report of the Standing Committee on External Affairs, 2009-10, November, 2009.
59. Lok Sabha Secretariat, Bureau of Parliamentary Studies & Training, February, 2013.
60. Ibid.
61. Ibid.
62. Standing Committee on External Affairs, Lok Sabha.
63. Ibid. http://164.100.47.134/committee/committee_informations.aspx, Accessed on February 18, 2014.

64. Consultative Committee of Ministry of External Affairs, 25 September, 2013.
65. Ibid.
66. India, Lok Sabha, *Report of the Standing Committee of the Ministry of External Affairs*, http://www.parliamentofindia.nic.in – Accessed on 3.3.2008.
67. Ibid.
68. India, Lok Sabha, *Debates,* http://parliamentofindia.nic.in.164.100.24.209/newls/debtext_nls.asp, accessed pm 18.10.2007
69. P.M. Kamath, "Foreign Policymaking in India: Need for Committee System to Strengthen the Role of Parliament" *Strategic Analysis*, New Delhi, vol. 9, no.10, Jan.1987, p.231.
70. Sixth Report, Standing Committee on External Affairs (2009-10), May, 2010.
71. Ministry of External Affairs, Government of India, February, 2013.
72. Ibid.
73. Ibid.
74. Ibid.
75. Ibid.
76. Ibid.
77. Ministry of External Affairs, Government of India, February, 2013.
78. Annual Report, 2012-13, Ministry of External Affairs, p. i.
79. Annual Report, 2012-13, Ministry of External Affairs, p. iii.
80. Ibid. iv.
81. Ibid. iv.
82. Ibid. p. ii.
83. Ibid. p. ii.
84. Ibid. p. vi.
85. Ibid. p. vi.
86. Annual Report, Ministry of External Affairs, Government of India, New Delhi, 2012-13, p. ii.
87. China & India: Prospects for Peace, Jonathan Holslag, (New York: Columbia University Press: 2010). Chapter 2 – The Evolution of Sino-Indian Relations.
88. "China's Rise in Asia, Promises & Perils—Robert S. Sutter, (US: Rowman & Littlefield Publisher: 2005). Chapter 9, p. 239.
89. "India & China: Learning to Learn" (Institute of Chinese Studies, New Delhi, Oct. 2003), pp. 45-54.
90. Nagesh Kumar, K. Kesavapany & Yao Chaocheng (ed.) Asia's New Regionalism and Global Role—Agenda for the East Asia Summit (RIS, New Delhi (Research and Information System for Developing Countries) & ISEAS (Singapore: Institute of South East Asian Studies: 2008) in Japan and an Asian Economic Community by Masanori Kondi. pp. 83-93.
91. Masahisa Fujita (ed.), Economic Integration in Asia & India, (New York: Palgrave Macmillan: 2008). Chapter 3 – The Relationship between China and India within the framework of Asian Economic Integration by Zhang Yuyan. p. 74.
92. Ibid.
93. Ibid. p.86
94. Ibid. Masahita Fujita (ed.) Economic Integration in Asia & India (New York: Palgrave Macmillan: 2008).

14

Vietnam and Other Nations: Coincidental Reciprocity in Strategic Alliances

M. Pragaya

With the introduction of *doi moi* reforms in 1986 and foreign policy outlook Vietnam experienced rapid transformation through the redefinition of economic management. Once Vietnam became one of the middle-income countries and got integrated with regional and international organizations Vietnam's reforms potential to contribute to the development have been increasingly realized. Moreover, at the turn of the 21st century China's rise both economically and militarily acquired significance in global affairs in as much as China started asserting its supremacy in the Southeast Asian region. Besides, the United States has been keenly getting its relations with Asia, particularly with Southeast Asian region strengthened in the economic and strategic interests following the global economic recession. These evolving security trends do credit Southeast Asian region and Vietnam with strategic importance. Vietnam with its growing economy and proven history of its resilience is also making strategic alliances with regional and global powers. Keeping in view the converging interests of many countries in this region, this paper focuses on the strategic significance of Southeast Asia and the growing strategic alliances of Vietnam in promoting peace and stability in this area.

Strategic Importance of Southeast Asia

The visits of the US President Barack Obama and Japanese Prime Minister Shinzo Abe respectively in November 2012 and January 2013 to the Southeast Asian region obviously as their first foreign visit destinations after winning the second-term elections, clearly indicate the importance they attached to the vibrant region. In the light of the fact that Southeast Asia, a sub-region in Asia, has become pulsating with its tremendous economic growth, investment destination, strategic importance and successful Association of Southeast Asian Nations (ASEAN) in regional cooperation, it has emerged as a centre of attraction for major powers of Asia—China, Japan and India—as well as the influential global powers.

Southeast Asia's burgeoning relations in the region is the result of many factors. Southeast Asia encompasses eleven independent countries coastal nations as well as island nations—Brunei, Cambodia, Indonesia, Laos, Malaysia, Myanmar, the Philippines, Thailand, Singapore, Vietnam and East Timor—situated in east of India, south of China, and north of Australia. The Southeast Asian region is also a rich store house of natural resources like rice, palm oil, cocoa, and coffee, crude oil, natural gas, hydro power, timber and various minerals. These resources eventually led the region towards industrialization as well as the trading centres of the world.

Southeast Asian nations have most diverse socio-political systems and economic development heights, but they have been collectively striving for common interests in the promotion of regional peace, sustainable development and mutual cooperation through the spirit of ASEAN framework and also to maintain relations with the rest of the world. This region after the Second World War, significantly after the formation of ASEAN in 1967, evolved into an economic power house with a US $2 trillion economy and a population of more than 600 million people.

Some of the countries of Southeast Asia such as Singapore, Thailand, Malaysia and Indonesia followed the footprints of Japan and Korea development landscapes and made enormous accomplishments in industrial and agricultural production, exports, education, health, nutrition, consumption, and other development indicators. Southeast Asia's openness to export-oriented trade and investment makes its role in the world economy an increasingly important one. Many of its countries have followed a similar path to development, moving in the space of a generation from inward-looking economies dominated by agricultural production, to industrialised, outward looking, market-oriented economies, open to trade and capital flows.[1] Southeast Asian region with resources and geo-political location became an avenue with "undiscovered and massive" potential. The market-friendly atmosphere turned this region into a comfortable venue for investors to find their prospects in the promising markets.

Singapore's early adoption of market economic policies combined with its entrepôt facility made it competent to join the group of 'Asian Tigers' along with Korea, Hong Kong and Taiwan and elevated it to the high-income group of nations of the world. Structural changes adopted towards development in Indonesia, Malaysia, the Philippines and Thailand augmented the promising middle-income economies. The latest entry into this middle-income group is Vietnam with its economy moulded on market-oriented lines from centrally controlled socialist model. However, there is glaring discrepancy in the incomes among Southeast Asian countries such as the one between Singapore with world's third largest GDP per capita and Cambodia and Laos which are pooled in the list of poor countries. The financial crises of 1997-98 and great recession of the world in 2008-2009 awfully hit the region. Yet the countries withstood the conditions resiliently. As Vikram Nehru, a consultant of the World Bank, pointed out: "In fact, the entire sub-region performed impressively, growing at over 8 percent, as rapid policy adjustments helped soften the blows of the crisis and enabled a quick rebound that also helped the broader global recovery."[2]

In view of different intra-trade arrangements, political stability provides ground to solve regional issues through conciliatory measures. The vibrant activities like finance, investments, business climate, infrastructure and education contributed to the region's turning into a hub for development activities which is very much in evidence in the buoyancy showed in the economic recovery in the post-Global Financial Crisis (GFC) period. The 5.5 per cent average growth rate of the Southeast Asia region is projected to an average growth rate of 5.5 per cent over 2013-17, the same rate recorded during the pre-crisis period (2000-07). The success of the Southeast Asian economies in sustaining robust growth in 2012 (5.3 per cent) is a testimony to their resilience in the face of major external shocks.[3] On the economic recovery of Southeast Asian economies from great recession, Changyong Rhee, ADB chief economist noted: "The top five economies in the 10-member Association of Southeast Asian Nations—Indonesia, Malaysia, the Philippines, Thailand and Vietnam—will continue to grow by 5.9 percent this year, and by 5.8 percent in 2013."[4]

While economic growth was tardy in other parts of the world, Southeast Asia displayed buoyancy. Some analysts predict that the growing young population and middle class in this region would also promote robust economic growth in this region. Apart from merging as an engine of growth for the world economy, it has been emerging as an arena of strategic competition amongst the internal and external players.

On the face of geography, this region is situated in the vital Malacca Straits, the second busiest shipping channel in addition to being the second most popular oil tanker routes, and thus assumes greater strategic significance. Given the fact that more than half of the world's merchant fleet uses the channels each year, the closing of the Straits would be highly disruptive and possibly even catastrophic to the world trade.[5] The region became a ground for the vying interests of super powers during Cold War years and ex-regional powers involvement also increased for politico-economic and investment interests. Besides, this region is also becoming vulnerable for illegal activities such as piracy, terrorism, drug trafficking, gunrunning and illegal fishing.

However, the political map of Southeast Asia has been comparatively stable in the recent history of the region. The main exception to this has been Indochina and the reunification of North and South Vietnam and the recent emergence of

East Timor as an independent nation on 20 May 2002. Otherwise, there have been only minor territorial changes although some unresolved boundaries, particularly in the division of marine resources, continue to be a source of tension.[6] Taking cognizance of the resonance of the region, the global powers are redrawing their policies that cause power dynamics in the international system. Strategies include the fostering of political, economic, trade, cultural and defence to promote the global players' consolidation of relations with the countries of the region.

The US military involvement in Afghanistan and Iraq after the 9/11 terrorist attacks, had become instrumental in neglecting the region in its strategic equations. The rapid changes at the dawn of 21st century in Asian region with significant trade arrangements, growing skilled labour, and natural resources, pushed the region to emerge strongly. Increasing levels of intra-regional trade and investment enabled the Asian countries to feel very confident about local economic development in the face of GFC. This implies that the state of the US economy may be less significant for the region's growth than it once was.[7]

During this period, China displayed its rapid economic and military emergence through its characteristic assertiveness in the region particularly, in the South China Sea. The US again focused attention on this region to gain the support for its trade and commerce besides strategic involvement. Further, being China's 'backyard', Southeast Asia could be the venue of growing competition between China and the US, which after a period of distraction, is once again actively engaged in the region. Apart from the wider economic competition between the two, there are a number of long-running territorial disputes between China and member states of ASEAN that could draw the US in—particularly in the South China Sea, where there are thought to be large reserves of oil and gas, and the dispute between China and Vietnam over the Paracel and Spratly islands has been causing grave concern.[8] The US officials with their statements and leaders with their visits made it amply clear that Southeast Asian region is vital for their enhanced role in the Asia-Pacific. While speaking at the Shangri-La Dialogue in Singapore in June 2012, Leon Panetta, the US Secretary of Defense, said,

> As part of this rebalancing effort we are ... strengthening our presence in Southeast Asia and in the Indian Ocean region. In addition to rotating US marines and supporting aviation units through northern Australia, the US would deepen its strategic cooperation with Thailand; pursue 'mutually beneficial capability enhancements' with the Philippines, while working to improve its 'maritime presence'; forward-deploy littoral combat ships (LCS) to Singapore; and enhance security partnerships with India, Indonesia, Malaysia, New Zealand and Vietnam.[9]

Between 2011 and 2012, the Secretary of State Hillary Clinton made her diplomatic visits to all the ten ASEAN countries, as well as Timor-Leste, and participated for four times consecutively in the deliberations of the ASEAN Regional Forum (ARF), a security organization of the region. Moreover, in the course of his visit to Southeast Asia in November 2012 Obama visited Myanmar, the first ever by a serving US President. Obama's participation in the East Asian Summit remains the first of its kind for the US. His visit clearly underscored US willingness to support ASEAN's centrality in 'Asian regional multilateralism'. [10]

Another important high level visit to Southeast Asian region was that of the Japanese Prime Minister Shinzo Abe to Vietnam, Thailand and Indonesia in January 2013. Japan has attached much importance to this region for promoting peace and prosperity in Asia. Japan tends to view Southeast Asia as "a geopolitical hinterland which happens to sit astride its own critical oil and resource lifelines."[11] Abe's visit assumes importance in the context of strategic rise of China and its growing influence in East Asia. During Prime Minister Abe's visit he has not shied away from voicing his concerns over China's military modernisation and "aggressive" behaviour in the East China Sea.[12]

Strategic Significance of Vietnam

Vietnam is one of the littoral states of the South China Sea along with other countries such as China, the Philippines, Brunei, Malaysia, Indonesia, Singapore, Thailand and Cambodia. It has a long coast line of over 3,300 km. that accommodates abundance for fisheries as well as an important naval footage in the South China Sea. Many Japanese and Chinese mercantile ships bound to Europe and Middle East pass across this region. The South China Sea, which is parallel to Vietnam, also houses the Paracel islands in the north and the Spratly islands in the southern sector rich in oil and natural gas and strategically significant in the region. After the Cold war, this region became a new flashpoint in Southeast Asia. The conflicting and rival claims for sovereignty on these archipelagoes have been seen by analysts as a crucial test for peace and security in the region. Keeping in view the emerging strategic scenario of Asia, one may say that Vietnam's geographical location, political stability, growing economy and its state of being situated in the important Sea Lanes of Communication (SLOC) as well as frequent usage of maritime and air routes in the vicinity of the South China Sea elevated Vietnam as a strategically important power in the region.

Vietnam's Surging Economy

At a time when more tumultuous events in the former Soviet Union and Eastern Europe started hitting the headlines, Vietnam set off 'quieter revolution' from a centrally-planned economy towards liberal, multi-sector market economy. Vietnam's protracted struggle for independence and reunification of the country and reconstruction on Soviet-style socialist model and poor economic management led to a huge financial and economic disaster in the country. At the Sixth Party Congress, the Vietnamese Communist Party (VCP) in1986 saw the introduction of '*doi moi*' (renovation) for a range of socioeconomic and structural reforms aimed at rejuvenating the decades old moribund economy. Following the introduction of *doi moi*, unprecedented changes took place agricultural and State-owned

Enterprises. The Council of Ministers issued Resolution No.10, which reallocated land-use rights to individual and family households from co-operatives. Rice production increased and Vietnam emerged as the third largest rice exporter in the world.[13] After the fall of socialism in Europe, Vietnam prudently chose to embrace liberalization besides owing its allegiance to political power. Liberalization in foreign direct investments provided necessary stimulation for the investors to invest in different kinds of developmental activities in the country. Domestic economic reforms and international integration have brought years of development to Vietnam's economy, with average annual growth of 7.5 per cent during 2002-2007. Vietnam also achieved tremendous development in the fields of trade, investment, industry, agriculture, export and international integration. Duong Chi Dung, Vietnamese Ambassador to France, while highlighting Vietnam's accomplishments claimed that, "despite the impact of the global economic downturn, Vietnam achieved economic growth rate of 5.9 per cent and 5.2 per cent respectively. Its exports rose from US$ 15 billion in 2001 to US$ 115 billion in 2012, of which foreign-invested businesses earned around US$ 72 billion, making up 63 per cent of total export value." Vietnam's accession to WTO in 2007 has witnessed a surge in FDI inflow and trade together. Duong Chi Dung also boasted justifiably that, Vietnam has welcomed investors from 90 nations and territories with a total of 13,700 projects capitalized at US$ 200 billion. Vietnam has established economic, trade and investment ties with more than 200 nations and territories in the world as well as international organisations and non-governmental organizations.[14] The average incomes have risen nearly fourfold since 1989. Important threshold of US $1000 per capita was also achieved in 2008.[15]

Vietnam's Foreign Policy

The ushering in of liberalisation in the domestic economy under the VCP leadership and the surfacing of redesigned foreign policy of Vietnam in mid 1980s had been simultaneous. The rapid demise of the East European bloc fundamentally altered Vietnam's foreign policy in which emphasis shifted from ideological solidarity with the Communist bloc towards non-communist states and this became a pragmatic attempt to attract overseas investors.[16] Further, the withdrawal of Vietnamese forces from Cambodia led to a dramatic improvement in relations with ASEAN, China, the US and Japan. With the sustainable economic growth and rising international image, Vietnam sought to turn bilateral relations to strategic cooperation with number of countries. Vietnam has strategic partnerships with several countries, including Japan, India, China, South Korea, Spain, the United Kingdom, Netherlands and Germany, which paved the way for cooperation in areas ranging from political, trade and commerce to defence.

Vietnam-Russia Strategic Partnership

Vietnam became a beneficiary of the former Soviet Union in political, economic, defence, scientific and technological cooperation as well as in matters of mustering support in international forums, during the struggle for national reunification. Even after the unification in 1975, Vietnam received similar unstinted support from the Soviet Union until its disintegration. The fall of the Soviet Union created serious difficulties to its socialist allies including Vietnam because of their heavy reliance on the Soviet Union for development activities. The collapse of the Soviet Union was an international event that shook up the world and had a strong impact on the political, economic, military conditions of every other country, big and small.[17] With the new realities surfacing on the geo-politics of the world after the end of the Cold War, Vietnam tried to integrate itself with a number of regional organizations. With the consolidation and emergence of Russia, Hanoi continued the promotion of bilateral relations with Moscow. The visits of Prime Minister Vo Van Kiet and Deputy Prime Minister Tran Duc Luong, resulted in Vietnam and Russia signing a treaty on the 'fundamental principles of friendship relations' in 1994. Their bilateral relations developed gradually and picked up pace with Russia's economic recovery. Russia became Vietnam's first strategic partner in 2001. The elevation of relations to the level of comprehensive strategic partner was a natural development.[18]

The strategic partnership includes, oil and gas cooperation, energy cooperation for hydro and nuclear power, military equipment and technology, and trade and investment. In the oil sector, 'Vietsovpetro', a joint venture between Vietnam and Russia, extracts 50 per cent of Vietnam's oil. Moscow showed interest in supplying the Sukhoi Super jet 100 passenger planes and helicopters to Vietnam. Russian Prime Minister Dmitry Medvedev during his official visit to Vietnam in November 2012 stated: "The earlier reached agreements are being implemented, and the trade turnover between the two countries is growing. Russia and Vietnam have various spheres of interaction. One of them is the construction of a nuclear power plant in Vietnam. We'll do our utmost to ensure a high quality of products as well as safety of the facilities."[19] Underlining the need for enhanced relations between the two, Carlyle A. Thayer, analyst on Vietnam noted: "As for the South China Sea, Russian military assistance will improve Vietnam's capacity for defence and enable it to develop its own version of anti-access/area-denial in the Nansha Islands, also known as the Spratly Islands."[20]

Vietnam-Japan Strategic Partnership

After the conclusion of Paris Agreement in 1973, which signaled the withdrawal of US forces from Vietnam, the diplomatic relations between Vietnam and Japan were established. Until the signing of Paris Agreement on Cambodian problem in 1991, relations of the two were confined to the foundations of development. The high degree of diversification approach in economic and foreign policies enabled Vietnam to pursue greater cooperation with Japan. The Vietnamese Prime Minister Vo Van Kiet's visit to Japan in March 1993 brought the two countries closer. His visit was reciprocated by Murayama, the first Japanese Prime Minster to visit Vietnam, in August 1994. Exchange of high level delegations in various fields turned Japan the largest aid donor to Vietnam. Japan also assisted Vietnam in many public activities such as planning comprehensive rural development, technical assistance in the areas of insurance, public health, agriculture and vocational training. On the basis of mutual interests and equality both countries expressed their willingness to contribute to the peace, cooperation, and development in the Asia-Pacific region and the rest of the world.[21] The mounting Chinese influence in the East Sea and South China Sea, which is an important sea route for Japanese navigation, drove the two countries into strategic cooperation. In October 2006, both countries agreed to transform bilateral relations into strategic partnership. In a joint statement the two sides reaffirmed their determination "to advance cooperation on specific priority areas and economic integration toward the realization of the East Asian community through the framework of East Asia Summit (EAS), ASEAN+3 and other fora."[22] In January 2013, Japanese Prime Minister Shinzo Abe, after assuming office, chose to make his first overseas visit to Vietnam, Thailand and Indonesia. Abe made it clear that Vietnam is important partner in this region and both have a common growing concern in this region. On the relevance of his visit Abe said: "In the context of complicated strategic developments in Asia-Pacific, I and Prime Minister Nguyen Tan Dung have agreed to promote the strategic partnership formed in 2006 in a more comprehensive way." He also stated that, "I've decided to visit Vietnam, Thailand and Indonesia, the three countries playing an important role as 'centers of development' of the 21st century, in order to strengthen the ties with these three nations, contributing to development and stability of the region."[23] It was obvious that key issues of maritime security, safety of sea lanes in the region besides territorial issues with China, have been shaping the strategic relations between Vietnam-Japan.

India-Vietnam Strategic Relations

The post-Cold War period witnessed the emergence of new regional order as well as the influential regional players in the region. Particularly after the launch of Look East Policy, India has been deeply involved in engaging the attention of the ASEAN region. Vietnam became a dependable partner in India's relations with the region. The traditional relations are growing strongly in the defence and strategic fronts as demonstrated by the periodical visits and the conclusion of agreements. As strategic cooperation has much potential for both sides, India and Vietnam closely associated themselves with the ARF and East Asia Summit. India's support to Vietnam to get access to WTO and India's bid for membership of the UNSC and the APEC were duly acknowledged by both countries. Their association further increased in trans-regional cooperative mechanisms such as MGC which was founded to promote tourism, transportation, human resources development and people-to-people contacts.

On the strategic front, the long bonhomie and political solidarity between the two reached new heights when a Joint Declaration on Strategic Partnership was signed by the Prime Ministers of the two countries, Dr. Manmohan Singh and Nguyen Tan Dung in July 2007. Towards strengthening the security relations, Indian Defence Minister A.K. Antony, visited Vietnam in December 2007 and announced, that New Delhi would transfer 5,000 items of naval spares belonging to Petya class of ships to Vietnam to make many of the ageing vessels operational.[24]

As India's growth of economy and population has been fueling energy demand, energy security has become an imperative issue for sustainable development. To address the growing energy demand, India's ONGC Videsh Limited (OVL) entered into joint cooperation with Vietnam's PetroVietnam in oil exploration work in Nam Con San gas fields. The OVL also has stakes in two other exploration blocks, 127 and 128 in Phu Khanh Basin in Vietnam. Further, OVL signed a three-year deal with PetroVietnam in September 2011 to jointly explore for oil and gas in these blocks.[25] However, China has raised objections to these explorations on the ground that the areas fell within the Chinese waters and has repeatedly warned India against such moves. Indian External Affairs Ministry official spokesperson, Vishnu Prakash, averred: "This is one important area of cooperation and we would like this area of cooperation to grow. Our cooperation with Vietnam or with any other country for that matter in the world is always as per as international laws, norms and conventions."[26] Since then, OVL continued its exploration in the South China Sea. However, the OVL relinquished exploration work at block 127 on techno-commercial lines after it encountered dry wells. Vietnam was a bit disappointed with the withdrawal. Some analysts felt, "this particular move by the OVL can hamper India's international stature especially at a time when India is expanding its maritime boundaries."[27]

But, India was keen on maintaining strong relations with the members of the region. In the context of overarching attitude of China in the region, India and Vietnam have improved their strategic cooperation in safeguarding the sea lanes in the South China Sea. Vietnam has given India the right to use its port of Nha Trang just south of China's naval base in Hainan Island. The Indian Navy was perhaps the only foreign navy in recent times to have been given this privilege by the Vietnamese at a port other than Ha long Bay, near Hanoi.[28]

It has been reported that India has agreed in principle to sell Vietnam the Brahmos supersonic anti-ship missile and possibly Prithvi surface-to-surface missiles. India and Vietnam celebrated the year 2012 as it marks the 40th year (1972-2012) of the establishment of diplomatic ties between the two countries and also the 5th year (2007-2012) of the Vietnam-India Strategic Partnership. The two Prime Ministers Manmohan Singh and Nguyen Tan Dung, at the ASEAN-India Commemorative Summit to mark 20 years of dialogue relations held in December 2012 said, "they were glad to see the development of the strategic partnership between the two countries and vowed to continue cooperation in all fields, including politics, economics, national defence and security, science and technology, culture, and education and training."[29] On the need of greater strategic cooperation, political analyst Subhash Kapila, felt, that the global and regional military interdependence also merits recognition by India in Asia where an aggressive military power like China now threatens the whole region extending from The Himalayas to the South China Sea. In this context, Kapila also suggested that "India's existing strategic ties with Vietnam now need to be put on a higher level than the platitudes on economic, cultural and scientific cooperation. The crux of the matter in the Vietnam-India Strategic Partnership is strategic and military."[30]

Vietnam-China Relations

The Vietnam-China relations were under severe strain following Hanoi's military intervention in Cambodia in December 1978, which resulted in the replacement of Chinese backed government by a pro-Vietnamese government. The incident was a tremendous blow to the power and prestige of China. The deteriorated conditions led to border war between the two in February 1979. China sought to subject Vietnam to increasing pressure through international isolation besides its military threats. However, Vietnam, compelled by the challenging domestic economic crisis, heightened by decades of foreign embargo and the waning up of financial support from the Soviet Union and East Europe, made a determined bid for developing relations with China. The termination of Cold War was proved to be catalytic in fortifying the relations between the two. The foreign policy changes in both countries were characterized by a series of exchanges of official and unofficial visits and enhanced trade and economic relations besides normalization of relations in 1994. Since then, the economic relations between Vietnam and China developed significantly. China is Vietnam's largest trade partner for the eighth consecutive year, with two-way trade exceeding US $41 billion in 2012. Despite the Vietnamese perception of threat from China, one could notice a transformation of relations between the two neighbours and mutual interdependency on the economic front.[31] On the strengthening of multilateral relations between the two, Liu Yunshan, a member of the Standing Committee of the Political Bureau of the Communist Party of China Central Committee, remarked thus: "China treasures the development of strategic partnership with Vietnam."[32]

Despite growing bilateral relationship in the wake of normalization, the South China Sea dispute has been figuring prominently in Vietnam-China relations. Vietnam along with Brunei, Malaysia, the Philippines and Taiwan is disputing China's claims over the Paracel and Spratly islands. Though, China a signatory of the United Nations Convention on the Law of the Sea (UNCLOS), Beijing periodically demonstrated and indulged in aggressive actions against Vietnam and other Southeast Asian countries over these islands.[33] In a naval skirmish in 1988, China sunk Vietnamese ships over Spratlys causing death of as many as 70 sailors. This incident became a common concern for Southeast Asian countries in this region. In the recent years, China continued to indulge in its usual claims and resorted to strengthen its presence in the region. In September 2011, Chinese Navy warned Indian naval vessel INS *Airavat* when it was travelling in open international waters in the South China Sea.[34] In the same year, Chinese ships disrupted the commercial activities of Filipino and Vietnamese oil exploration vessels which point to an escalation of Chinese assertiveness. On these belligerent actions, Thayer, while answering a question said,

> Chinese ships deliberately and with premeditation used force to interrupt lawful commercial activities in Vietnam's exclusive economic zone. In the case of Filipino exploration vessel Chinese ship maneuvered..., live firing at Filipino fishing boats stands out as a singular act of aggression. China's use of heightened rhetoric is a new and worrying feature. [35]

China's growing geopolitical ambitions and military capabilities naturally have been pushing Southeast Asian countries to revise and redraw their security relations within the ASEAN and with the US also.

Vietnam-US Relations

The turbulent relations during the Cold War era ended with the normalization of relations between Vietnam and the US in July 1995. Since then, the multilateral relations were established with each other. The United States has been Vietnam's largest export market, and exports to the United States represented about 18 per cent of Vietnam's total exports. US firms have become one of Vietnam's largest sources of foreign direct investment. On the security matters both countries are longing for mutually beneficial relations in the South China Sea. Commenting on the US interests in the region E. Manyin, specialist in Asian Affairs felt, "voices favoring improved relations have included those reflecting U.S. business interests in Vietnam's reforming economy and U.S. strategic interests in expanding cooperation with a populous country—Vietnam has over 90 million people—that has an ambivalent relationship with China and that is asserting itself on the regional stage." He also said that, the Vietnamese leaders have sought to upgrade relations with the United States in part "due to the desire for continued access to the U.S. market and to worries about China's expanding influence in Southeast Asia."[36] On the mutual interests, Capt. Ross Myers, commander of the George Washington's air wing, felt, "The strategic implications and importance of the waters of the South China Sea and the freedom of navigation is vital to both Vietnam and the United States."[37] Both wish to translate the multilateral relations to strategic cooperation.

Besides, extra-regional powers in Southeast Asia, ASEAN countries including Singapore and Thailand proposed to have strategic cooperation with Vietnam. Singapore is the fourth-largest foreign investor in Vietnam after Japan, South Korea and Taiwan, with cumulative investments of US$ 24 billion (S$ 30 billion) in more than 1,000 projects. Both governments are working for the signing of strategic cooperation. Nguyen Phu Trong, General Secretary of the Communist

Party of Vietnam, and Prime Minister Lee Hsien Loong of Singapore agreed in 2012 to work towards signing a strategic partnership agreement in 2013 on the occasion of the 40th anniversary of the establishment of their diplomatic relations. The strategic partnership agreement between them would open up new vistas of cooperation in education, training, finance, defence, and security.[38] If Singapore seals such a partnership with Vietnam, it could be one of the first countries in ASEAN to do so.[39]

Vietnamese Prime Minister Nguyen Tan Dung and his Thai counterpart Yingluck Shinawatra showed interest to raise their relationship to a strategic partnership at the second Viet Nam-Thailand Joint Cabinet Retreat, held in Hanoi in October 2012. They also agreed to promote cooperation in the fight against trans-national crimes and terrorism, in both bilateral and multilateral frameworks.[40] Italy and France are also maneuvering to turn their bilateral relations to strategic cooperation with Vietnam.

Conclusion

In view of Vietnam's resurgent economy, geo-strategic location, gallant history and huge population Hanoi is regarded as a strategic power to be reckoned for promoting peace and stability in this region. Like many emerging economies, Vietnam, with its young and relatively well-educated population, has a demographic advantage in the developing world. On the other side, China has been increasing its military presence in the East Sea which is causing strategic concerns for the ASEAN countries as well as Japan and the US. Besides, China's strategy was evident at the ASEAN Ministerial Meeting held in July 2012. For the first time in its history ASEAN failed to issue the joint communiqué of the meeting which also discussed disputes in the South China Sea. China's assertive stance has provoked Vietnam and ASEAN to have strategic tie-ups with the US, India and Japan for sea lanes safety in the South China Sea. Thus, it is not for nothing that Vietnam has acquired strategic significance. Its very geo-strategic location, its competence and above all its state of preparedness besides contributing to its serving as a bridge between ASEAN nations and other extra-regional powers, enable Vietnam to maintain stability, maritime security, freedom of navigation on high seas and peace and tranquility in this region. It is these potentialities of Vietnam that inspire as many countries as possible, to court the strategic alliance of Vietnam. Incidentally, Vietnam too gets its ardent desire fulfilled and hence the coincidental reciprocity in matters of strategic alliances in Southeast Asia.

NOTES

1. Jon Lunn and Gavin Thompson, "Southeast Asia: A political and economic introduction," Research Paper, 11/78 (House of Commons Library), 14 December 2011, p. 2.
2. Vikram Nehru, "Southeast Asia: Crouching Tiger or Hidden Dragon?," *International Economic Bulletin*, 7 JULY 2011, http://carnegieendowment.org/ieb/2011/07/07/ southeast-asia-crouching-tiger-or-hidden-dragon/2wc7

3. http://www.oecd.org/dev/asiaandpacific/SAEO2013%20E-Executive%20summary.pdf
4. Dion Bisara, "ADB Remains Bullish on Southeast Asia's Economy by Raising Its Forecast," *Jakarta Globe*, December 08, 2012, http://www.thejakartaglobe.com/ business/adb-remains-bullish-on-southeast-asias-economy-by-raising-its-forecast/560401
5. Nehru, n. 2.
6. Vivian Louis Forbes, "Geopolitical Change: Direction and Continuing Issues," Chia Lin Sien (ed.), *Southeast Asia Transformed: A Geography of Change*, (ISEAS, Singapore, 2004), pp. 71-76.
7. Xiaosong Tang, "The future role of the United States in the Asia-Pacific region: dead end or crossroads?," *Australian Journal of International Affairs*, Vol.66, No.5, November 2012, p. 593.
8. Jon Lunn and Gavin Thompson, n. 1, p. 1.
9. "US rebalance: potential and limits in Southeast Asia,"(http://www.iiss.org/publications/strategic-comments/past-issues/volume-18-2012/december/us-rebalance-potential-and-limits-in-southeast-asia/).
10. http://www.iiss.org/publications/strategic-comments/past-issues/volume-18-2012/december/us-rebalance-potential-and-limits-in-southeast-asia/.
11. William T. Tow, *Asia-Pacific Strategic Relations: Seeking Convergent Security*, (Cambridge University Press), 2001, p. 82.
12. Bhubhindar Singh, "New Japanese premier's first foreign trip: Why SE Asia?," The Nation (Thailand), January 16, 2013.
13. Laurence J Brahm, *Vietnam Banking and Finance*, (Butterworths Asia, Singapore, 1995), p. 5.
14. "Vietnam—A New Dragon of ASEAN," http://businesstimes.com.vn/vietnam-a-new-dragon-of-asean/
15. Jonathan Pincus, Vietnam: Sustaining Growth in Difficult Times, *ASEAN Economic Bulletin*, Vol.26, No.1, 2009, p. 11.
16. http://www.nationsencyclopedia.com/World-Leaders-2003/Vietnam-FOREIGN-POLICY.html
17. Luu Van Loi, *50 Years of Vietnamese Diplomacy: 1945-1995*, (The Gioi Publishers, Hanoi, 2006), pp. 515-516.
18. Carlyle A. Thayer, "Vietnam's regional growth tied to renewed Russian relations," http://www.globaltimes.cn/content/735031.shtml
19. Ilya Kharlamov, Russia, "Vietnam-Multipurpose Partnership," Nov. 7, 2012, http://english.ruvr.ru/2012_11_07/Russia-Vietnam-Multipurpose-Partnership/
20. Thayer, n.18.
21. Luu Van Loi, n. 17, p. 538.
22. "Japan-Vietnam Joint Statement, Toward a Strategic Partnership for Peace and Prosperity in Asia," 19 October 2006, http://www.mofa.go.jp/region/asia-paci/vietnam/joint0610.html.
23. "Japanese PM pledges more ODA for Vietnam," January 18,2013, http://english.thesaigontimes.vn/ Home/business/other/27550
24. "India, Vietnam to Boost Defence, Strategic Cooperation," http://www.india-defence.com/reports/3652; also see, Subhash Kapila, "Vietnam-India: Time to Make Partnership Truly Strategic," http://www.southasiaanalysis.org/%5C papers22%5Cpaper 2169.html.
25. Abhishek Shukla, "Oil's not well on South China Sea," *The Hindu Business line*, 3 May 2012.
26. *The Economic Times*, 16 Sep 2011.
27. Teshu Singh "The Curious Case of India's Withdrawal from the South China Sea," http://www.ipcs.org/article/india/the-curious-case-of-indias-withdrawal-from-the-south-china-3632.html

28. Baladas Ghoshal, "Why India should look at Vietnam more keenly," 10 December 2012, http://strategicstudyindia.blogspot.in/2012/12/why-india-should-look-at-vietnam-more.html
29. ASEAN and India aim for strategic partnership, *Vietnam Investment Review*, 24 December 2012.
30. Subhash Kapila, "Vietnam-India Strategic Partnership 2012: A Contextual Analysis," 14 December 2012, http://www.southasiaanalysis.org/node/1093
31. http://dangcongsan.vn/cpv/Modules/News_English/News_Detail_E.aspx?CN_ID=566434&CO_ID=30253
32. http://talkvietnam.com/2012/11/china-treasures-strategic-partnership-with-vietnam/#.UQv6GR04sSM.
33. Vijay Sakhuja, *Asian Maritime Power in the 21st Century: Strategic Transactions China, India and Southeast Asia*, (ISEAS, Singapore, 2011), pp. 51-53.
34. *The Times of India*, 2 September 2011.
35. Carlyle A. Thayer, Background Briefing: South China Sea: Prospects for Armed Conflict, 28 June 2011, p.2, http://www.scribd.com/doc/59084631/Thayer-South-China-Sea-Prospects-for-Armed-Conflict
36. Mark Mark E. Manyin, "U.S.-Vietnam Relations in 2011: Current Issues and Implications for U.S. Policy," *Congressional Research Service*, 18 May 2012.
37. "U.S.-Vietnam Military Relations: Former Enemies Now Military Mates," http://www.huffingtonpost.com/2010/08/09/us-vietnam-military-relat_n_675202.html
38. Vietnam, Singapore work towards strategic partnership,http://www.diplonews.com/ feeds/free/13_September_2012_130.php
39. http://www.mfa.gov.sg/content/mfa/media_centre/singapore_headlines/2012/201204/news_20120428.html.
40. Viet Nam, Thailand Aim for Strategic Partnership, http://www.asean-cn.org/Item/6384.aspx.

15

Post-Jiang Leadership of China: Fourth Generation

Ravindra Sharma

Background

The 16th Party Congress (8 to 14 Nov. 2002) was one of the cardinal events in the history of the CPC, which elected a new leadership changing from third to the fourth generation. Tentatively, Sinologists largely have identified with Mao as the first, Deng Xiaoping, as the second, Jiang-Zemin as the third and Hu Jintao as the fourth generation, leadership forgetting a splendid contribution of Li Dazhao and Chen Duxiu in the history of the CPC. Historically, the CPC was founded by Li Dazhao and Chen Duxiu, it needs to be mentioned that at the 7th Party Congress held in 1945, Mao quoted Chen Duxiu as saying that "those who are sitting in this Congress hall are the students of Chen Duxiu."[1] More importantly, the term "Fourth generation" was coined by the CPC in Deng's era. The term "political generation" is also very confusing and arbitrary, as Chessington remarks," it is rather arbitrary to define where one generation begins and another ends. For instance, Hu Yaobang is usually seen as a member of the second generation of the Chinese leaders, although he took part in the long March."[2] The point, I am trying to argue is this: While dealing with the leadership of the CPC, under no circumstances, Li Dazhao and Chen Duxiu's, name should be excluded. As regards the "Political generation," two more points need to be discussed: First, Post-Deng China's ruling elite has vividly ignored the role of Hu Yaobang and Zhao Ziyang. However, the fact of the matter is that Hu Yaobang and Zhao Ziyang had played a cardinal role in the life of the party in the 1980's. Both were picked up and purged by Deng. Objectively, with the help of Hu Yaobang, Deng had laid the foundation of modernization curricula, upon which the edific of modern infrastructure was built by Jiang Zemin and others; and more importantly, Hu Jintao was promoted by Deng with the concurrence of Zhao Ziyang. While Zhao Ziyang was put under house arrest, Hu Jintao wept but in vain. The irony of succession politics in Communist set up is that the rules of the successions are not scientifically defined yet and the CPC is no exception to this regard. Tentatively, the succession/generation of the CPC may be divided into four eras: First, pre-Mao era, second, Mao's era; third post-Mao era and fourth, Post-Deng era. Compare to Mao's era, Deng and his successors have been very careful in staging the succession drama. Deng purged his own handpicked successors, however, consciously avoided the bloodshed and Pandemonium of the late 1960's; and the post-Deng succession has been more smoothly than post-Mao. Politically, Jiang Zemin was unwilling to relinquish power at the 16th Party Congress. However, under the pressure of the "fourth generation", Jiang Zemin had to step down paving the way for Hu Jintao to take over China. However, Jiang at the closing session of 16th Party Congress succeeded in appointing five of his protégée to the new member Politburo Standing Committee of the CPC, (Huang Ju, Wu Banguo, Qinglin, Zeng Qinghong, and Li Changehun). As the "fourth generation" of the CPC was dedicated to the task of economic modernization with the formulation of "building a well off society by the mid of the 21th Century", no harm seems to be in discussing an overview of the fourth generation of the CPC. Jiang's era came to an end at the 16th Party Congress coining the idea of "Three Represents". Now the cardinal question is what were the primary features of the "fourth generation"? Was there any continuity between the fourth and previous generations of the CPC; and what were the class origins, educational background and ideology of the fourth generation? In what sense, the fourth generation's definition and nuances of "Communism differed to the classical definition of Communism"? To begin with, as Li Cheng aptly remarked, "The fourth generation is composed of those grew up, or had their formative years, during the Cultural Revolution, and usually acquired first political experience during the same time. They are the youngest group listed in who's who in China; all born between 1941 and 1956."[3] While dealing with the fourth generation, two points must be kept in our mind: First, the leadership of the fourth generation of the CPC was born, when the Chinese Revolution had swept the countrywide. Second, the fourth generation grew during the storm and upheaval of the Cultural Revolution. As the Central Committee, Politburo, and the Standing Committee of the Politburo constitute the nucleus of The Communist system, the first part of this study is primarily based on the profile of the fourth generation of the CPC occupying prominent position in the upper echelons of the party and the state. And the second part basically deals with the theory of "scientific out-look of development" propounded by Hu at the 17th Party Congress held in 2007.

An Overview of the Fourth Generation

Academically, in the official document of the CPC, the term "Fourth generation" began to appear with the elevation of Hu Jintao as a Vice President at the Ninth National People's Congress (held in 1998) was the first signal of grooming the fourth generation. The fourth generation attained the supreme power of China at the 16th Party Congress (2002-12), which elected a Central Committee consisting of 356 members (198 full members, 158 alternate members) a Politburo of 21 men-members, and a Standing Committee of Politburo of a nine-members; at the 16th Congress, a new Central Commission for Discipline Inspection was also elected, which is composed of 121 members; almost 180 out of the 356 members and alternate members of the 16th Central committee were new faces. At the 16th Party Congress, Jiang Zemin was re-elected as Chairman of the Central Military Commission (was replaced by Hu Jintao in March 2003 at the 10th NPC) and Hu Jintao, Guo Boxiong and Cao Cangehuan were elected Vice-Chairman of the Commission; Xu Caihou, Liang Guangli, and Li Jianai were elected members of the Commission.

Younger in age: Humorously, in politics one hardly retires and Communist ruler's rules till the last breath. However, the post-Deng ruling elite, keeping in view the role of younger generation consciously inducted and promoted the younger people into the organizational structure of the 16th Central Committee. A Chinese commentator named Li Jiangguo provides a detailed information about the age of the members of the 16th Central Committee, telling us that the average are of the 16th Central Committee members was 55.4 years, which was half a year younger than that the 15th Central Committee and more than one fifth ware below the age of 50."[4] Further, a few officials below the age of 50 were also inducted into the Central Committee and at the provincial level, the average age of the Party Secretary was 58 years and the average age of Governor was 55 years."[5] In the new leading groups, 65 percent Secretaries of Party Committees were 59 years or younger of the 15th Central Committee. Many young officials such as Qinghai province Governor Zhao Leji (45), Henen province Governor Li Keqiang (47) and Zhe Jiang province Governor Xi Jinping (49) were elected to the CPC's 16th Central Committee. Significantly, a considerable number of officials below the age of 40 had also entered the new Central Committee."[6]

Influence of higher Education: Significantly, the fourth generation of the CPC did not suffer from the ideology of the Cultural Revolution. The influence of the higher education was vividly visible in the structure of the 16th Central Committee. As per the information provided by Li Jiangguo, 98.6 percent members of the Central Committee have received a junior College education, which is 6.2 percent higher than that of the 15th Central Committee and 15.2 percent higher than that of the 14th Central Committee."[7] A few eminent scholars such as Xu Kangdi, Lu Yongxliang and Pan Yunhe were also made members of the 16th Central Committee. While going through the profile of the fourth generation, one tends to argue that post-Mao China's ruling elite has made the university education compulsory to lead China into the 21th Century. Sources from the Organization Department of the CPC Central Committee confirm the fact that even at the provincial and the county level, the influence of higher education had increased from 16.4 percent in 1981 to 27 percent in 2001. It needs to be pointed out that even some provincial leaders graduated from prestigious universities, Such as: the Governors of Liaoning and Hunan graduated from Beijing University and the Governors of Fujian and Yunan graduated from Qinghua University."[8]

Further, at the provincial level, the fourth generation of the CPC, with a master's degree or doctorate accounted for 18.4 percent; out of 62, top provincial leaders, Six obtained master's degree and the remaining 56 have obtained Bachelor's degree. The 16th Central Committee represent a wider section of the Chinese society consisting of provincial leaders, core officials from provincial and ministerial levels and major military area commanders, and the representation of corporate sector. The 16th Central Committee has 33 representatives from different section of society, including writers and entrepreneurs, make 9.3 present of the total membership. Additionally, 27 female officials and 35 officials from different minority groups had occupied a prominent place in the 16th Central Committee."[9] In sum, one may argue by saying that the formal, education carried a serious influence in shaping the post-Mao Chinese politics and society so much so that even "private owners" had started obtaining degree from the universities. Significantly "private owners" constitute a new force in China. The average age of "private enterprise owners" was 42.9 years; as more than 70 present running from the age 30 to 49."[10] The educational level of private enterprising owners has been steadily improving in Post-Deng China; as more cadres and intellectual shifting to business, and overseas students returning to start their own business, the higher education is getting prominence day by day in China. In 1993, in China the proportion of university graduated in "private enterprises" was only 16.6 percent however, it rose 35.5 percent in 2002, more than doubled. The proportion of post-graduate students also increased from 0-6 percent in 1999, and 4.6 percent in 2002."[11]

Influence of Corporate Sector: Importantly, with the advent of economic reforms, the "corporate sector" has been highly benefited in Chinese Society. The Corporate sector is yet to from a separate force in Chinese politics. However, China's ruling elite keeping in view of the theory of (Sanga Daibiao) had provided a reasonable place to corporate sector in the 16th Central Committee. Zhi Yuebo provides a detailed account of the growing influence of corporate sector in China's political system. He remarks, "Corporate Sector carries more influence in the 16th Central Committee. There were 18 corporate leaders in the 16th Central Committee: 2 full members and 16 alternates. One full member Li Yizhong Chairman of the Board and President of Synoptic Corporate was promoted from an alternate member. Zhang Kingwie, president of China Aero space and technology corporation was made full member of the Central Committee because of his enormous contribution of the successful launching of satellites for Chinese clients as well as for foreignness."[12] Factually, the influence of corporate sector in recent past has been enormous in China's political setup. While the 15th Central Committee inducted only three corporate leaders, the 16th Central Committee promoted sixteen as, Lowell Dittemur's remarks, The 16th Party Congress represents a continuation of "Marketization, privatization and globalization."[13] Not only that the fourth generation of the CPC was so much opposed to Marxist ideology, that it suggested to re-incorporate' of "Confucianism" into Chinese nationalism.

Technocrat Turned Statesmen

Significantly, while going through the profile of the Politburo members of the Standing Committee of the 16th Party Congress, one is stunned to see that all top leaders of the fourth generation of the CPC, hold the degree of engineer; none of them had obtained the degree in social science; A sort of cursory survey of the educational background of the nine members of the politburo of the Standing Committee certainly proves the point: Hu Jintao, graduated from the Hydraulic Engineering Department of Qinghua university, where he majored on the study of hydro power stations. University educated, Hu Jintao had the title of engineer, and Second, Wu Banguo graduated from the Radio Electronic Department of Qinghua university also obtained degree of engineer. Third, Wen Jiabao graduated from the geological structure of Beijing Institute of Geology. A post-graduate Wen Jiabao, also obtained the degree of engineer. Fourth, Jia Qinglin graduated from the Electric Motor and Hubei Appliances design and manufacture of the department of the Electric Motor and Hubai Engineering Institute; Jia Qinglin also had the title of engineer. Fifth, Zeng Qinghong, graduated from the Automatic Control Department of the Beijing Institute of Technology. Zeng Qinghong, also had the degree of engineer. Sixth, Huang Ju, graduated from the Electrical Engineering Department of Qinghua university, where he majored in electrical machinery manufacturing; Huang ju, also had a degree of engineer. Seventh, Wu Guangzheng graduated from the specialty of Thermal Measurement and Automatic Control of the Power Department of Qinghua University; a post-graduate, Wu Guangzheng also had the title of engineer. Eighth, Li Changchun graduated from the Industrial Enterprises Automation of the Department of Electric Machinery of Harbin Institute of Technology; university trained Li Changchun was also identified as engineer. Ninth, Luo Gan graduated from the Machine Casting Specially of the Fireburg Institute of Mining and Metallurgy from the Democratic Republic of Germany; a foreign degree holder Lu Gan also had the title of senior engineer in the PRC. Shall I remind to the readers, that Jiang Zemin, a representative of "third generation" and a handpicked successor of Deng was also an engineer; Jiang Zemin graduated from the Electrical Engineering Department of Shanghai Jiaotong University in 1947 and worked as a trainee at the station automobile works in Moscow till 1995."[14] In sum, while in Mao's era, "peasants and workers" with the background of professional revolutionaries were inducted and promoted in the apex bodies of the Party and government, in Deng's era, well qualified, career conscious leadership was promoted to take over China. The educational back ground of nine-men politburo

Standing Committee of the 16th CPC is cumbersome enough to argue that radar of the Chinese state in post-Jaing China was no longer in the hands of "workers and peasants", but instead in the hands of technocrat turned statesmen'.

Political Career: As far as career of the fourth generation is concerned, two facts need to be stated; First all Politburo members of the Standing Committee joined the Chinese Communist Party either Just before or during the storm of the Cultural Revolution; and out of nine, four Politburo members of Standing Committee obtained the degree of graduation from the prestigious universities of China in the mid 1960's, while the Cultural Revolution was at peak. Significantly, at the 12th Party Congress (1982), Deng consciously picked up the anti-Cultural Revolution leadership to lead China. The year 1982 appears to be land mark in the political career of the leadership in China. It needs to be pointed out that in September 1982, the historic 12th Congress was convened under the leadership of Deng, when radical Maoism began to lose its philosophical sheen; Deng at the 12th Party Congress introduced "non-socialist policies" arguing that China urgently needed "experts not reds". Deng at the 12th Party Congress promoted developmental oriented leadership of the 3rd and 4th generation. While Jiang Zemin representing the 3rd generation of the CPC was elected as a Central Committee member at the 12th Congress, Hu Jintao, representing the world view of the 4th generation was made an alternative member at the 12th Party Congress. Importantly, five politburo members of the Standing Committee of the fourth generation were inducted by Deng at the 12th Party Congress. Moreover, Jiang Zemin (3rd generation) and Hu Jintao (Fourth) were picked up by none other than Deng Xiaoping.

A brief Survey of fourth generation's political career will prove the point: Hu Jintao, was alternate member of the 12th Central Committee and was subsequently elected as a permanent member at the 13th, 14th and 15th Central Committee and finally promoted as a Politburo member of the Standing Committee at the 16th Party Congress. Additionally, four other leaders of the fourth generation, Wu Banguo, Wu Guangzheng, Li Changchun and Luo Gan were inducted by Deng as an alternate members of the Central Committee of the CPC at the 12th Party Congress; Wen Jiabao and Huang Ju were inducted by Deng at the 13th Party Congress, and Jia Qinglin and Zeng Qinghong were elected as a member of the Central Committee at the 14th and 15th Party Congress respectively. A cursory survey tells us that the 12th Party Congress was a turning point in shaping the world view of the third and fourth generation of the CPC, arguing that the primary contradiction in socialist China lay not between the "bourgeoisie and proletariat" but instead between the "backward productive forces" and the "advanced industrial system". Factually, Deng's thesis of "Advanced industrial system", approved at the 12th Party Congress was absolutely in tune with the fourth generation of the CPC, as all the nine Politburo members of the Standing Committee hold the degree of engineering.

Ideology

Ideologically, the CPC in its history over the years has proposed three major theories to mobilize the Chinese masses: Mao Zedong thought was the first theory of "Marxism with Chinese Characteristic," Deng Xiaopong's theory was the second theory of socialism with Chinese characteristic, the "important thought of three represents" put forward by Jiang Zemin is the third theory of "Marxism with Chinese characteristic, In fact, the third generation of the CPC with Jiang Zemin as the core had initiated the theory of the "three represents" and the fourth generation of the CPC under the leadership Hu Jintao had endorsed the Ideological underpinnings of the third generation without any reservation. The closing session of the 16th Party Congress remarks "The three represents calls for the Chinese Communist Party to represent the development trend of China's advanced social productive force, the orientation of China's advanced cultural and the fundamental interest of the overwhelming majority of the people of China."[15] As China under the guidance of second and third generation (Deng and Jiang Zemin) moved from command economy to private economy, a senior spokesman of the fourth generation and also a Chairman of the All China Society of Private economy Research named Bao Yunjun supported the existence and promotion of "private" enterprises saying," all this indicates that in primary period of socialism, encouraging, supporting and guiding the non-public economy is not contradictory to the development of the public economy but instead it promotes the common progress of both public and non-public sectors."[16] In the era of the Primary Stage of Socialism, the agenda of the fourth generation of the CPC was vividly clear: Hu Jintao, soon after the 16th Party Congress while addressing a press conference pointed out that in the years to come, "the Communist party of China will show the rest of the world its sound image of keeping peace with the times and its pioneering spirit. The whole party and people from all ethnic groups will unit more closely and concentrate on construction and development so as to continue pushing forward China's reform opening up and modernization drive.[17]

Factionalism

Factually, Post-Deng leadership was not free from factionalism. Hu versus Jiang was well known fact of Post-Deng Chinese politics. Jiang's protégée Zeng faild to rise at the fourth plenum of the 16th Party Congress held in September 2002. On the contrary, by promoting Xu Caihou as a Vice-chairman of the CMC, Hu consolidated his power. Zhi Yuebo identified four major factions in the fourth generation of the CPC. He remarks, "Qing hua clique and the CCYL group have been competing with each other for power. There are 20 graduates of Qinghua university in the 16th Central Committee: 16 full and four alternate members and among nine standing members of the politburo, four are Qinghua graduates, Hu Jintao, Wu Banguo, Huang Ju and Wu Guangzheng. Another politburo member, Zeng Peiyan is also a Qinghua graduate."[18] Interestingly, Hu Jintao enjoyed the confidence of Qing Hua Cliqua as well as of CYL faction.

Problems: Factionalism apart, the fourth generation of the CPC faced several problems such as "Formalism, the bureaucratic style of work, falsification, extravange and waste are still serious problems among some leading cadres in our party and corruption is still conspicuous in some place"[19] declared the Document of the 16th Congress. The journal of Human Rights in China (No 1, 2005) had printed a chronology of social unrest in China causing the deep anxieties and fear for the post-Jiang leadership. The chronology provides us detailed information about the social unrest influencing in Chinese society from June 2003 to December 22, 2004. The same issue of Human Rights in China also published a detailed report of Hanyun incident which rocked the entire Sichuan province. A report by the He Qing Lian tells us that, "in October and early November 2004, tens of thousands of villages from the Hanyun reservoir area in Sichuan province protested against the relocation to make way for the Rubugon dam. During the protest, as many as 10,000 soldiers were deployed against the protesters."[20] In September 2004, while preparing the document of the 11th Five Year Plan (2006-10) the official Chinese intellectuals also identified 10 major problems to be solved by the post-Jiang leadership of China. The problems are as follows. (1) Unemployment, (2) Widening gap between rich and poor, (3) Environmental decay, (4) Corruption, (5) Aids, (6) Lack of faith in government, (7) Balance between financial sector and capital, (8) Threat from globalization, (9) Issue of Taiwan, (10) Crisis of faith."[21] At the fourth Plenum held (from September 16 to 19, 2005), the third generation of the CPC led by Jiang was replaced by the fourth generation of the CPC, led by Hu and Wen echoing Deng and Jiang in toto.

17 Party Congress: (2007)

Hu's Elevation with "Scientific Outlook on Development"

While Hu and Wen came to power at the 16th Party Congress (2002), the two most prominent leaders of post-Jiang China consolidated power at the 17th Party Congress, held in October 2007 (from 15 to October 27) with the ideological formulation of "Scientific outlook on development". Hu and Wen were considered as the representative of the fourth generation of the CPC. In Hu-Wen era, China became a very powerful country trying to compete with the USA. When Hu had attained the supreme authority of China, China had just joined the World Trade Organization (WTO). In the Hu-Wen era, China became the second largest wealthy nation of the globe having 3 trillion in Hu's era, the per capita of an average Chinese increased from 800 to 4000.

Chinese Dream

Hu at the 17th Party Congress was re-elected General Secretary of the CPC and coined the idea of "harmonious socialist society" which was not included in the Constitution. However, Hu's Chinese dream was acclaimed by the party veterans as Hu pleaded for making China as a "prosperous, strong, democrat, culturally advanced and harmonious modern socialist country."[22] Significantly, despite of using pro-people jugglery, Hu throughout in his tenure remained committed to the "development of non-public sector along with the public sector". Hu as a follower of Deng and Jiang was not uncomfortable with the emerging *Noveau Rich* and middle class in China. However in Hu's dream, China successfully uplifted 300 million Chinese people out of poverty.

As a leader of the Communist party, Hu throughout his tenure could not ignore the role of the Chinese people in attaining the Chinese dream. Hu at the end of 17th Party meet reiterated the policy of "putting people first", to make China a global power. Factually, Hu became a prominent leader of modern China in 2007. However, he was inducted by none other than Deng Xiaoping in 1992 at the 14th Party Congress as the "youngest member" of the CPC's politburo's Standing Committee. In terms of "generation", Hu won the political favour of Second generation (Deng) and worked with the third generation (Jiang) as well to develop the vision of "harmonious socialist society". Politically, Hu's predecessor, Jiang had coined the "Theory of Three Represents" which was dubbed by China watchers as a "capitalist theory" particularly in the West, perhaps this seems to be the reason that Hu carefully coined formulation called "scientific outlook on development". Hu was aware of the fact that "inequality" is growing in Chinese society year by year, as 10 percent families of China own more than 40 percent of nations, wealth which impelled Hu to argue the social development with the focus on improving peoples livelihood to ensure that all the people "enjoy their rights to education, employment and medical housing to build a harmonious and socialist countryside."[23] The growing disparity between "rural and urban" area, also perturbed Hu.Hu at the 17th Congress argued that economic reforms initiated by his mentors, Deng, will certainly create conducive situation to raise the income of "low income groups" on the one hand, and "set up a mechanism of regular pay increase" to provide the comfortable material life to the rural area. Post-Jiang leadership of China also faced a serious problem of migration from countryside to the "urban area", as an Indian journal commented, "the long work weeks, irregular employment and low wage rates specially among migrants, have stagnated fuelling unprecedented huge migration into the cities, over the past 25 years, some 150-200 million persons, including women have migrated from the countryside to the urban areas in search of job."[24]

In Hu's view, as China's 60 per cent, population still live in the rural area, China's "poverty alleviation program", will be properly taken care of, declared Hu. Hu at the 17th Congress showed serious concern over the "growing, regional imbalance" in China as China's economic reforms in the past two decades have created a huge gap between "wealthy province and the poorest province". Importantly, Hu was not opposed to the wealthy section of the Chinese society. Following the dictum of Deng, to be rich is glorious; Hu protected the "lawful income" of prosperous citizens. Hu by profession as a technocrat was not averse to the idea of "borrowing and buying the latest science and technology from the western world", to carve a new path of "industrialisation with Chinese characteristics". Retrospectively, while Mao was fond of equality, Deng was found of "prosperity". While Mao had an obsession for "class struggle", Deng had passion for wealth. Following Deng's dictum that idealisation of poverty is not socialism, the post-Deng as well as post-Jiang leadership of China dedicated to achieve the goal of socialist society with Chinese characteristic. Now the cardinal question is, what is the socialist society with Chinese characteristic? In the view of Deng and his successors as China is passing through the phase of Primary Stage of Socialism, only the goal of "moderately prosperous society" can be achieved. At the 17th party meet Hu declared that the "efforts would be made to attain the goal of moderately well off society"[25] by 2020.

Hu's attitude towards Democracy, Environment and Defence

Politically, during the Tiananmen episode, China was globally criticized for violating and suppressing the human rights. Hu's "scientific outlook" also included "respect and safeguard for human rights" along with the free airing of views. Factually, the idea of multi party system was bulldozed by Deng and Li Peng, yet, the demand continued to influence the mind of intellectuals and the students as well. Hu's idea of "democracy with Chinese characteristics", included more "judiciary rights" than the "political rights" so that an average Chinese "can use" the courts to seek justice easing their grievances. While presenting the political report at the 17th Party Congress Hu pronounced the word "Democracy 60 times."[26] With the implementation of Deng's developmental strategy, China witnessed a serious environmental decay as a result post-Jiang leadership including Hu Jintao paid a serious attention to the environmental problems of China. At the 17 party meet, Hu proclaimed that the CPC is dedicated to building a "new socialist countryside making China an innovative country and an environment friendly society."[27]

Historically, Chinese rulers since the Qing dynasty (221) has shown serious concern to the 'safeguard of motherland', when China was defeated in the Opium War (1840) and was forced by the western powers to sign several unequal treaties, China's Sino Centrism was hurt and China's two prominent intellectuals, such as Liang Qichao and Kang Yuwie proposed to king to "buy and borrow" science and technology from the barbarians (west) to defeat barbarians. Normally, Deng is considered as antithesis of Mao, yet, Mao and Deng both had a soft corner for China's defence programme. Deng on the eve of Mao's demise, with the concurrence of Zhou implemented the package of "four modernizations" which included the curricula of military modernization. Hu as a bona-fide member of the CPC, and staunch supporter of Deng, included his mentor's vision highlighting a proper role for military in the document of the 17th Congress. Hu declared, "the CPC ensures that the People's Liberation Army accomplishes its historical mission at the new stage in this country."[28] Moreover, Hu's "Scientific outlook" gave full play to the PLA's role in consolidating national defence defending the motherland and participating in the socialist modernization drive.

From the point of view of factionalism, the CPC in Hu's era was divided into "elitist *vs* populist". Hu and his fellow traveller Wen Jiabao and others were widely known as "populist". As a populist, Hu's idea of "harmonious society" was based on strategy which worked to "narrowing the widening chasm"[29] in urban rich and rural poor on the one hand and wealthy coastal areas and underdeveloped interior provinces on the other. Retrospectively, both Mao and Deng were in search of global power and prestige, however both of them operated in two different eras while in Mao's era socialism was offensive and imperialism was defensive. Conversely, in Deng's era imperialism was offensive and socialism was on retreat. While Mao's search for global power began by blowing imperialism, Deng accepted the terms and conditions of imperialism at least economically. Deng introduced the role of "non-public sector" to make Chinese socialism rich and vibrant. Hu as a bona-fide follower of Deng inducted more non-Communists in to the upper echelons of the CPC. Soon after the 17th Party meet, Louyangvice head of the CPC's Central Committee Organization Department declared in a press conference saying that "as the CPC is operating in different eras, induction and promotion of non-communist is the desire of time."[30] Mr Wan, an automobile technologist was appointed as Minister of Science and Technology and the world famous haematologist Chen Zhou was named as Health Ministers in Hu-Wen era.

Hu and Religion

Religiously, following the dictum of Karl Marx that religion is an Opium, Communist China in 1949 declared itself as an "atheist country". Historically, religion as such had never dominated China, what influenced Chinese society was Confucianism which guided the cultural and social milieu of China. Confucianism a part, Buddhism, Daoism, Christianity and Islam also operated in China. China as a country of Han race had respected and honored Confucianism since centuries, however Mao as a radical Communist was allergic to Confucianism from the May Forth Movement (1919) to the pandemonium of the Cultural Revolution. Mao seriously bashed up Confucius. However, with the advent of Deng, the Confucianism revisited China. The revival of Confucianism or religion was initiated in China for several reasons which does not need to be discussed in detail here, however the point needs to be pointed out is this that "The word" religion" for the first time was used in Hu's China at the 17th Party Congress, amending the Constitution of China with a pragmatic massage keeping in view the increasing numbers of religious people in the "Atheist China."[32] A prominent member of the CPC of Shan Nan of South-Western Tibet Autonomous region was quite happy while reading the report of the 17th Party Congress, which allowed the citizens of China to follow or practice the religion of their choice. The amended Constitution of the 17th Party Congress stressed on "harmony" as one of the important objective of modern China along with prosperity, democracy and cultural advancement. **Hu's** political formulation that "the scientific outlook on development" was described by several as a continuation of Marxism-Leninism Mao Zedong thought, Deng Xiaoping theory and the theory of Three Represents propounded by Jiang at the 16th Party Congress held in 2002. As China was passing through the "primary stage of socialism", the concept of the "scientific outlook on development" has been formulated to meet the new requirements of China's developmental strategy proclaimed Hu Jintao at the 17 Party Congresses.[34]

Hu and the Structure of the CPC

Organizationally, the 17th National Congress elected a Central Committee of (204) members and 167 alternative members. While Hu Jintao, Wu Bangguo, Wen Jiabao, Jia Qinglin and Lichangchun were elected to the party's apex body, Zeng Qing hong, Wu Guanzhong and Luo Gang protégée of Jiang Zemin Were excluded from the 17th Central Committee. Mr Zeng (68), Mr Wu Quan Zhong (69), and Mr Luo (72) were honourable members of the Standing Committee of the 16th CPC. The 17th National Congress also elected a 127 member Central Commission for Discipline Inspection.[35] Significantly, with the exit of Jiang's protégée, Hu along with his reliable colleague Wen Jiabao became the most powerful and prominent leader of the 21st century China in 2007.

Importantly, Wu Yi an "Iron lady" of Jiang's China and the defense minister General Cao Jangchuan were also not included in the 17th Central Committee. The exclusion of Wu Yi as the only women in the core leadership sent a massage throughout the country that the CPC still suffers from the hangover of male dominated political party. Factually, form the point of view of women empowerment, since 1949 to 2007, only three women had been part of China's core leadership including Mao's wife of Jiang Qing who committed suicide in 1991.

The seven day Congress of the 17th Party elected Hu Jintao to the status of Mao, Deng and Jiang with the concept of scientific outlook on development to decide the destiny of China for 10 years with the world's second largest economy. The 17th Congress also elected nine members of the polit bureau of the Standing Committee with Hu Jintao as the radar of the CPC. In the view of Hu, the 17th Party Congress was the congress of "unity victory and progress" along with a resounding success.[36] Additionally, keeping in view of the post-Hu-Wen succession, the 17th Party Congress in its first Plenary Session held on 22nd October also inducted two prominent members, Xi Jinping (54), and Li Keqiang (52) to the Standing Committee. Soon after the 17th Party Congress, Hu Jintao while addressing the media said "we will always hold high the great banner of socialism with Chinese characteristic, follow the guidance of Deng Xiaoping theory and the important theory of three Represents and, we will adhere to scientific, democratic and law based governance"[37] declared Hu. Culturally, when Hu was striving to achieve the status of Mao and Deng, China's ruling elite was busy in making the preparation for "Beijing Olympics". Significantly, while Jiang Zemin had received 16 applause during the 16th Congress, Hu Jintao was applaud by the delegates 40 times. Moreover, in March-April 2008, Hu Jiantao was also elevated as President and the Chairman of the Central Military Commission of China. Hu's team included Yu-Zhengshang Party Chief of Shanghai, He Guoqing head of Central Commission of Discipline impaction, Jia Qinglin head of the People's Political Consultative Conference, Xu Caihou, Vice-Chairman of Central Military Commission, Guoboxiong Vice Chairman of the Central Military Commission, Wen Jiabao Premier of the State Council, Bo Xilai Party Chief of Chongqing, and Wang Yang Party Chief of Kuangdong, and Wang Qi-shang Vice Premier of China.

Significantly, Hu-Wen's leadership was widely commented by the global media. Hu's December 18, 2008 Speech was considered as the most important one, in which he used the phrase of "Sinicization of Marxism". Following Mao, Hu declared on December 18th 2008, "China should continue to host high the great flag of Socialism with Chinese Characteristics and push forward the Four Cardinal Principles."[38] Willy lam, a most prominent scholar of Chinese studies in East Asia commented on Hu's December 18th Speech saying Mr. Hu's hard line speech has confirmed disturbing tendencies that add up to a great leap backward in China's modernization programme, and that the unemployment rate in urban areas is much higher than the 9.4 percent and close to thirty three million urban resident lost their job in a second half of 2008.[39] In the opinion of willy, while Hu's leadership has forbidden the media to "mention Charter 08", State Security Department had "detained writer dissident Liu Xiaobo"[40] in early December.

Sino-US Relation in Hu's Era

Briefly, Deng had invaded Vietnam in January 1979, at the behest of US. Post-Mao Chinese leadership initiated a serious dialogue with the US. Both sides willy-nilly came forward to shake hands. However on the issue of Tibet, Taiwan and Tiananmen both differed fundamentally. After the collapse of the Soviet Union (1991) China-US rapprochement rapidly increased as a result in Hu's era Sino-US relationship witnessed the faze of "collaboration and confrontation". An analyst Commented on Sino-US relationship of Hu's period. "The idea that collaboration and confrontation support one another is moored deep in both the American and Chinese political traditions, confusions argued 2,500 years ago that "harmony" a term much in favour with the Hu Jintao government arises when there is disagreement and diversity of opinion.[41]

Concluding Remarks

In sum, Hu-Wen leadership remained committed for the economic modernization of China, it was opposed to Cultural Revolution, and was determined to carry forward China's poverty allevation programme; it out rightly rejected the idea of "Western style of democracy" and re-incorporated Confucianism.Hu, allowed its citizens to follow Western life style, restricting the role of Marxism. Hu-Wen leadership upheld the Charter of "four cardinal principles. The CPC, in Hu-Wen era, moved toward US and Europe for trade with caution and care, expended trade, and investment with the other developing countries.Hu shook hands With the Muslim world, yet, seriously dealt with radical Islamists, operating particularly in Xin Jiang and the Central Asia. Hu-Wen remained Chummy with Pakistan but continued to bully India on several issues. The Beijing Olympic (2008) enhanced the image of China. The per capita income of an average Chinese increased, yet, the disparity between rich and poor widened in Hu's era. Mass incidents, peasants uproar, urban unrest, and intellectual discontent continued to upset the ruling elites of China. In Hu's era, the PLA's budget increased, however, higher education and health became quite costly. While the tiny *noveau rich* enjoyed the pink evenings and rosy nights, the wealth became a new mantra for the upcoming middle class in Hu-Wen era. The idea of "Marxism" was replaced by the idea of "Modernization" yet, the CPC remained a strong Leninist ruling party. Hu-Wen polit bureau launched serious campaign against "corruption" yet, the issue of corruption became a chronic ill for the Chinese society. Unfortunately, crime increased and divorces rates thrived in Hu-Wen era. China's family institution, despite the growing living standard witnessed a sort of rupture and crises between husband and wife and moreover China's "younger generation" became the victim of "Me". The influence of money alcohol, open sex, drugs and competition made the Chinese teenager more negative than creative.

A China watcher, summed up Hu's era by saying" the Hu decade, will perhaps be remembered most for heralding China's rise as a global, economic political and military power, with China influence in all three spheres rising considerably in the period"[42] Lastly, Hu provided leadership to the most turbulent period of China. Hu was aware of the problems facing China. He aptly remarked just on the eve of the 18th Party Congress saying "we must not be afraid of any risks and not be confused by any destruction."[43]

REFERENCES

1. See, The Political Report of the 7th Party Congress, in Tony Saich, *The Rise of Power of the Communist Party*, An East gate Block, 1996, p. 73.
2. Ruth Chessing on "Generation Issue in China: A case study of the 1980's generation of young intellectuals," *British Journal of Sociology*, Vol. 48, No. 2, June 1997.
3. Li Chang, "Jiang Zemin's Successors: The Rise of the Fourth generation of the leaders in the PRC", *The China Quarterly*, March 2000, No. 161, p. 4.
4. Li Jiangguo, "Hu elected to the Top Post", *Beijing Review*, December 5, 2002, p. 13
5. Ibid, p. 5.
6. Ibid, p. 7.
7. Ibid.
8. Ibid.
9. Zhang Zhiwei, "Chief Engineer of Successful Transition", *Beijing Review*, March 2001, p.10.
10. Ibid.
11. Ibid.
12. Zhi Yuebo, "The 16th Central Committee of the Chinese Communist Party: Formal

Institution and Factional Group", *Journal of Contemporary China* (2004), 13 May, pp. 223-256.

13. Lowell Dettmer, "Leadership and Chinese Political Development", *The China Quarterly*, December (2003), No. 176, p. 903.
14. See, "The Profile of Top Leaders", *Beijing Review*, November 28, 2002, pp. 14-19.
15. See, the Document of the 16th Party Congress 2002.
16. See, the Interview with Bao Yu Jun, Chairman of the all China Society of Private Economy, *Research, Beijing Review*, March 20, 2003, p. 14.
17. *Beijing Review*, December 5, 2003, pp. 13-14.
18. See, Zhi Yubo, the 16th Party Congress.
19. See, the Document of the 16th Party Congress.
20. See, A Chronology of Unrest: Reported case of uprising in China over the past 18 months; He Qinglian, the Hanyan incident, daring the pond of the fish, the *Journal of Human Rights in China*, No. 1, 2005, pp. 23-26.
21. See, the Document of the 11th Five Year Plan, Foreign Language Press, Beijing, 2005.
22. See Hu Jintao's Report delivered by him at the 17th Party Congress, Foreing Language Press, 2007.
23. Ibid.
24. See, China at 60, the *Economic and Political Weekly*, October 24, 2009, Vol. XLV, No. 43, p. 6.
25. See, the Document of the 17th Party Congess.
26. See, Xin Hua, October 22, 2009.
27. See, the Document of the 17th Party Congress.
28. Ibid.
29. See, Pallavi Aiyar, "Shaping the Future of China at a Challenging Time," *Hindu*, October 15, 2007.
30 Xin Hua, 22 October, 2007.
31. Ibid.
32. See, CPC's amended Constitution using the world "religion" at the 17th Party Congress, op. cit.
33. Zhou Yan, Ji Ming and Quan Xiaoshu's report in Hindu, CPC constitution adopts scientific development, October 22, 2007.
34. See, the Document of the 17th Party Congress, op. cit.
35. See, Xin Hua, October 22, 2007.
36. Ibid.
37. Ibid.
38. See, Hu's Speech of December 18, in Xin Hua, December 19, 2009.
39. See Willy Lam "Hu Jintao's Great Leap Backward", *Far Eastern Economic Review*, Jan./Feb. 2009, p. 20.
40. See, Willy Lam, op. cit.
41. See, John Delury, "China and US Collaborate, Comfort", *Far Eastern Economic Review*, Jan/Feb., 2009, p. 26.
42. See, Ananth Krishnan's, Analytical Report on China, *Frontline*, October 19, 2012. p. 46.
43. See, Hu's speech, July 2012, delivered by him at a workshop, *Frontline*, quoted in October 19, 2012, p. 46.

16

Indian Foreign Policy: Change and Continuity

Satish Kumar

Introduction

This article is designed to focus on the structures of Indian foreign policy. Its ideals, philosophy, and basic parameters are being attempted to include. The changing route in Indian foreign policy is also mapped out from Nehru to Manmohan Singh. The leadership factors impact on FP that is why a brief identical niche and persona of each prime minister is being wrapped up. The Economic Foreign Policy has become a strong underpinning of foreign policy, therefore, a brief summary of international economic tenets were properly pinned up. This chapter also runs to focus on the different kinds of challenges of foreign policy. The association with neighbors and world powers are also discussed. Unfolding of the world politics and a continuous free falls of challenges before the foreign policy are also covered.

Foreign policy is an instrument to a country that promotes its national interests. There is broad agreement on the concept of national interest, namely that it compromises the obligation to defend the country's national security, to maximize economic benefits for its citizen from international trade and commerce. The tool of foreign policy is to export ideology or religious fervor. Recently the some of the western countries are exporting democracy in the Third World countries. India today impinges on the world in unprecedented ways. At the same time it is increasingly dependent on the rest of the world for its own security and prosperity. This sets the stage for an ever larger Foreign policy grows out of the interplay between internal and external environments. The role of leaders becomes equally important. Nehru placed non-alignment at the centre of Indian foreign policy to break away from the colonial rule and beginning of the cold war. Shortcomings in India's post-Independence grand strategy based on non-alignment and a 'socialistic' economy were evident by the 1980s. The policy of non-alignment was adopted by Nehru to enable and underline India's strategic autonomy.[1] The objective of the foreign policy of a country should be to create space and options for itself in the international arena. India has become one of the power centers of the world. There has been discussion in India in recent times about an independent foreign policy. Indian foreign policy especially in its neighborhood moves from cooperation to conflict to joint ventures. In fact, in the last few years internal and external factors are twisting and buffering the threshold of Indian foreign policy. Federal tinge from inside and multiple external factors from different corners of the world, are maneuvering the agenda of foreign policy. Pakistan, China and US are in the first line to weigh credentials of the foreign policy.

Philosophy of Indian Foreign Policy

A policy cannot sustain without underpinning of a strong philosophy. Indian foreign policy is also supported by a strong philosophy. How this philosophy has become a part of Indian foreign policy, needs an explanation. Indian renaissance of 18th and 19th centuries provided an opportunity to locate its geopolitical identity and cultural individuality. Raja Ram Mohan Roy as well as Dwijendranath Tagore, the founder-leaders of the Brahmo Samaj movement, advocated India's modernization and its establishing relations with other societies to meet the foregoing objectives. It could be said that this was the first phase of India's developing an international consciousness and acquiring aspirations to become a part of the modern world.[2] The second phase in the evolution of India's international consciousness could be traced back to the aftermath of the Mutiny of 1857. In the second half of the 19th century and in the first half of the 20th, an Indian religious-cultural integrity and an urge to define a nationhood in Western terms, but rooted in Indian history, became the hallmarks of the Indian value system and Indian religious and intellectual renaissance that characterized the subcontinent which comprised two broad strands in terms of attitudes and reactions towards other countries and foreign societies. The period between1920 and 1946[3] was crucial in that India became more aware of international political and economic trends as well as the ideological undercurrents influencing them. The list of such persons who later emerged as national leaders in India in the 1940s and 1950s are many. The prominent among them such as Jawaharlal Nehru, M.N. Roy, Zakir Hussain and Jinnah. The major political events also impacted to influence the Indian policy of the world. Momentous events such as Bolshevik Revolution, radical political trends generated in Muslim countries, manifested in the overthrow of the Ottoman Empire by Kamal Ataturk, the early military successes of Japan against Czarist Russia in the first decades of the 20th century attracted the attention of Indian intelligentsia and the political circles. The responding to the rise of Fascism and Nazism in the early 1930s, Jawaharlal Nehru pronounced "These movements based as they are on hatred and violence and dreams of war would lead to a world war unless they were checked in time. The Congress firmly opposed German occupation of Czechoslovakia and Franco's overthrow of the representative republican government in Spain. India's response to the Balfour Declaration aiming at the displacement of the Palestinian Arabs from their homeland signified the Indian National Congress giving full support to the Palestinian people long before Israel came into existence, for the establishment of a united, independent Palestinian state. Early in 1939, at the Tripura session of the Indian National congress, party affirmed that world peace and progress depended on the "imperative destruction of Fascism".[4]

Drafting of Indian Foreign Policy

Obviously, Nehru became the first choice of Gandhi to structure Independent India's grand foreign policy. It was on Nehru's return to India at the end of this European visit that Gandhi entrusted him with the responsibility of formulating the foreign policy terms of reference of the Indian National Congress. Nehru created the Foreign Policy Cell of the INC, and brought in people such as Ram Manohar Lohia and Dr. Syed Mehmood to work with him in this cell. He also involved Maulana Abdul Kalam Azad in shaping Congress's foreign policy vision, particularly in respect of India's relations with the Islamic world in the context of India's own large Muslim population. The segment of time between 1933 and 1946 crystalized India's views on foreign relations manifesting in them India's foreign policy in the immediate aftermath of India attaining independence.[5]

The newly created foreign policy cell went into scrutinizing intensively and extensively the factors which fit into India's understanding of the international system. Several questions were raised; what were our perceptions of international equations? What did we think of our positions in the emerging scheme of things? What were the equations which we fashioned? How did we define the terms of reference of our policies to cope with the international situations for the first time? Who are going to frame the policy? Will it be feasible to go against the established structures of the bipolar world? There were volumes of questions raised to establish Indian foreign policy in the right directions.

Several factors have been instrumental in shaping India's foreign policy. First, perceptions of the Indian leadership of international politics were deeply influenced by the freedom struggle of the people of India against colonialism and imperialism. Secondly, Indian leaders viewed the world through the prism of the political, economic and ideological contradictions that resulted in two world wars which many of them had witnessed. Thirdly, they were convinced that political contradictions and economic inequalities could not be confined or compartmentalized in order to prevent tendencies of competition, conflict and violence affecting the entire international community. Fourthly, the unique nature of their non-violent struggle for freedom, contrasting with the nature of other similar movements along with their resisting aggression and domination, led them to realize that each people and each society conceive their own aspirations. Fifthly, in consequence of the above realization they were convinced that international harmony, peace and stability could be achieved only through factors such as a process of reasoning together, a commitment to cooperation rather than confrontation and an attitude that differences and diversities need not automatically result in adversarial stances between states and societies. Sixthly, their national experience and their perceptions of international relations convinced them that foreign relations, if they were to contribute to peace, stability and well-being of the international community, had to be responsive to the profound aspirations of common people all over the world.[6]

The moral high ground, which figures such as Swami Vivekanand and Mahatma Gandhi envisioned for India, influenced articulate sections of Indian public opinion in their perceptions of India's position in the international community. Vivekanand had repeatedly stressed that India's future role in the world was that of "a messenger of peace, that of a catalyst for creating a just and moral world order". He also pointed out that the basis of Indian influence need not be power or military might or economic riches. Jawaharlal Nehru's statement on relations with other nations during the first decade of our freedom consolidated these intellectual undercurrents in India's foreign policy. In a radio broadcast from London, on 12th January 1951, he declared "what we need is a passion for peace and for civilized behaviour. It is not the temper of war that we want."[7] Then again speaking at the Dyanamo Stadium in Moscow, on 22nd June 1955, he clarified: "peace in our view is not merely abstention from war but an active positive approach to international problems and relations, leading first to the lessening of the present tension through an attempt to solve our problems by methods of negotiations, and then, to a growing cooperation between nations in various ways.

The second characteristic of the collective Indian foreign policy mindset was that India had an ideological as well as operational role to play in world affairs to eradicate imperialism, colonialism and all forms of discriminations. The support extended by India to Indonesia, to other countries of South-east Asia and later to the African countries in their freedom struggles reflected this attitude. India felt both a responsibility and an obligation to be supportive of liberation struggles and to oppose all forms of domination.

Major Objectives of Indian Foreign Policy

The objectives of India's foreign policy are many. It keeps changing the track. At present India's first objective is to pacify the northwestern part of the subcontinent, or the AfPak region, as it is known in Washington. All of India's great empire-states throughout the last 2,500 years, from the Mauryans to the British Raj, have had trouble controlling these turbulent lands across the Indus River that frame the subcontinent's western frontier. India's second objective is to become an indispensable power in the littorals of the Indian Ocean and southwestern Pacific. For nearly two centuries until partition, the British Raj was the source of stability and the main provider of security in these regions. But after independence in 1947,[8] India chose an inward economic orientation and focused on the global mobilization of the Third World during the Cold War. In the past, India balanced Beijing through a de facto alliance with the Soviet Union. Today, it needs a strategic partnership with the United States to ensure that China's rise will continue to be peaceful. With Washington yet to make up its mind on how best to deal with Beijing, India has no option but to hedge against growing Chinese power as well as the dangers of a potential Sino-American condominium.[9]

India's third objective is to increase its weight in global governance and eventually emerge as a "rule-maker"[10] in the international system. But U.S. support for India's bid to become a permanent member of the U.N. Security Council has been elusive. The United States, instead, wants to test whether India is a "responsible stakeholder" in the negotiations on issues ranging from climate change to international trade. India is prepared to engage on these issues and participate more fully in global decision-making bodies on the basis of its own enlightened self-interest, but is not prepared to take tests from anyone. India's fourth objective is to strengthen the factors that are critical for becoming a credible power on the regional and global stages. This involves sustaining its current high economic growth rate, consolidating its advantages in knowledge industries, providing education and skills to its younger population, and modernizing its armed forces and security agencies.

India's relations with the world have seen a fundamental transformation over the last decade and a half. A number of factors were at work in India. The old political and economic order at home had collapsed and externally the end of the Cold War removed all the old benchmarks that guided India's foreign policy. Many of the core beliefs of the old system had to discard and consensus generated on new ones. The collapse of the Soviet Union and the new wave of economic globalization left India scrambling to find new anchors for its conduct of external relations. Most Indians agree that its first Prime Minister Jawaharlal Nehru had defined a unique foreign policy for India at the very dawn of its independence.

Structural Changes in India's World View

Underlying India's current foreign policy strategy is a set of important transitions in India's world view. Not all of these were articulated self-consciously or clearly by the Indian political leadership. A few of those changes stand out and are unlikely to be reversed. The first was the transition from the national consensus on building a "socialist society" to building a "modern capitalist" one. The socialist ideal, with its roots in the national movement, had so dominated the Indian political discourse by the early 1970s that a Constitutional amendment was passed in 1976 to make the nation into a "socialist republic". But 1991 saw the collapse of the Soviet Union, the veritable symbol of socialism, and the edifice of India's state-socialism began to crumble. Adapting to the new challenges of globalization now became the principal national objective. The change in the national economic strategy in 1991 inevitably produced abundant new options on the foreign policy front. A third transition in Indian foreign policy is about the shift from being a leader of the "Third World"[11] to the recognition of the potential that India could emerge as a great Power in its own right. The 1990s, however, brought home some painful truths. There was no real third world trade union that India believed it was leading. After a radical phase in the 1970s, most developing nations had begun to adopt pragmatic economic policies and sought to integrate with the international market. Finally, the fifth transition in Indian foreign policy in the 1990s was from idealism to realism. Idealism came naturally to the Indian elite that won independence from the British by arguing against colonialism on the basis of first principles of Enlightenment.

Major Challenges of Foreign Policy

The first and most important challenge for India is the creation of an area of peace and prosperity in the South-Asian subcontinent. Since the late 1970s, the north-western parts of the subcontinent have seen disturbances and violent conflict that has affected not only India but also the entire world. India's ability to cope with this turbulence has been undermined by its tense relations with Pakistan. India is determined to work with its neighbours in the region as well as with the world's major powers to defeat the scourge of violent extremism that has taken root in the subcontinent's north-west. Recently Pakistan has under gone a democratic election to choose the new prime minister. Nawaj Sharif has been declared victorious. But the apprehensions remains the same, will the prime minister of Pakistan be taking the India specific decisions. For many years this has been the turf of the Military with the deep connivance of ISI in Pakistan. The Pakistan Army expressing constant enmity towards India is the single most powerful institution. Indians also feel threatened by Pakistan's close diplomatic, economic, military and nuclear cooperation with China that includes China building a deep water port at Gwadar in Baluchistan, and stationing troops in the northern districts of Kashmir while upgrading the highway linking that area to Xinjiang. Unless there is radical change within Pakistan, away from the military-jihadi nexux, the prospects for peace in the subcontinent are not encouraging. India will have to be patient and overcome conflict with Pakistan if it is to play the global role it envisages for itself.

India has devoted much energy—both diplomatic and political—over the last decade to transforming its relations with Pakistan. Three prime ministers, representing three different political trends—Inder Kumar Gujral, Atal Bihari

Vajpayee and Manmohan Singh—have persistently attempted to normalise the country's ties with Pakistan. The effort has begun to pay off. India and Pakistan are now implementing a road map for the comprehensive normalisation of bilateral trade relations. They also signed an agreement in September 2012 to liberalise a four-decade-old restrictive visa regime. India is committed to supporting the Afghan people's efforts to reconstruct their war-ravaged economy. Its interest in the security of the Afghan state is reflected in the strategic partnership agreement signed a year ago. The quest to normalise India's relations with Pakistan and to deepen its strategic partnership with Afghanistan are part of a single vision that seeks political stability, economic modernisation and regional integration in the subcontinent's north-west. Nepal has been another eyesore for India. It has been working on equi-distance policy between India and China. The recent visit of Prachanda in China proved this fact that Nepal is gradually shifting its base line from India to China. Patience also characterizes India's current dealings with China. As outlined earlier, relations between the two Asian giants improved substantially after 1988, both economically and politically. Several cooperative agreements and MOUs were signed on the occasion of ex-premier Wen Jaibao's visit to India in April, 2005, including an optimistic one on political parameters and guiding principles for settlement of the boundary question. China still claims to all of Arunachal Pradesh, calling it 'southern Tibet'. China has also intensified the level of its presence in Nepal, Sri Lanka and other Indian neighbours significantly, raised its cyber, military, missile and space technological capabilities to challenge those of the US and surpass India's embarked on an ambitious expansion of its navy with a declared intention of policing the Indian Ocean, and greatly enhanced its logistical capabilities and military strength in the Tibet Autonomous Region. Fearing a Chinese repetition of 1962 armed attacks, India too has moved to strengthen its air and ground defences in Ladakh and Arunachal Pradesh while carefully refraining from rhetoric that Beijing could consider provocative. It needs to be noted, however, that the Ministry of External Affairs routinely denies newspaper reports of Chinese incursions across the LOAC and continues to engage in dialogue at multiple levels while standing firm on India's known positions and pressing for mutual respect of territorial integrity and core interests. The Chinese too see a 'trust deficit' on the Indian side. The new India-US strategic partnership and India's growing ties with Indonesia, Japan, Korea, Singapore and Vietnam on China's perimeter that include joint naval exercises also alarm Beijing; its fears of 'encirclement' are deep seated. Equally strong is Beijing's resentment of India's hospitality to the Dalai Lama and his followers.

The second challenge for India lies in making an effective contribution to the construction of a stable architecture for peace and cooperation in Asia. The idea of Asian unity and solidarity deeply influenced the Indian national movement in the early decades of the 20th century, while promoting political solidarity and economic cooperation within a newly liberated Asia was one of independent India's diplomatic initiatives. These ideas were far ahead of their time in the 1940s and 1950s.

Third, more than six decades later, many of those ideas have become a reality. Asia has never been as integrated within and with the world as it is today. This has generated unprecedented levels of prosperity and the continent is once again becoming an important driving force for the world economy. Asia's extraordinary accomplishments in the last few decades, however, could easily be reversed if the region falls prey to great-power rivalry, national chauvinism and unbridled arms races. India needs to help prevent such an outcome by accelerating its own economic integration in the region, deepening its bilateral and multilateral security partnerships, promoting an inclusive political and security order for Asia and finding a balance between the interests of the major powers. Above all, India must help Asia rediscover the 'universalism' of Rabindranath Tagore and other pioneers who made the region aware of its shared cultural identity but refused to define it in opposition to the West.

The emerging negative trends in Asia express themselves most clearly in the maritime domain. The intensification of territorial disputes over small islands has begun to threaten Asian waters. China's growing assertiveness and America's 'pivot to Asia' are likely to herald a tense period in the region's international relations. At precisely the time when Asia needs to strongly adhere to the principles of the Law of the Sea, the legal framework for maintaining good order at sea appears to be breaking down. Competing interpretations of the principle of freedom of navigation are threatening the vital lines of communication linking the different parts of Asia and connecting it to the rest of the world. Meanwhile, as the role of seaborne trade in the economic life of Asia rises, all the major powers in the region, including China and India, are strengthening their maritime capabilities. The rise of new naval powers in Asia is bound to generate inevitable friction with the US that has long been the dominant maritime power in the Indian and Pacific Oceans. India does not agree with the proposition that the maritime politics of Asia are a zero-sum game. Nor does it see an inevitable confrontation between China and the US in the Indo-Pacific.

India already cooperates with the US in wide-ranging maritime security activities. It is also planning to initiate a maritime dialogue with China and to build on the first steps towards a coordinated anti-piracy policy in the Gulf of Aden. India has supported the proposal of the US Secretary of State Hillary Clinton for a trilateral engagement between Washington, Beijing and Delhi and hopes that sooner rather than later China will agree to begin talks in such a trilateral framework. Strong and sustained cooperation between the US, China and India holds the key for the peaceful management of Asia's maritime commons.

Strategic Divergence and Convergence with America

The new post-Cold War strategic and geopolitical bases to warming Indo-US relations are complex and problematic to verify. The success of a strategic accord rests *BJP and Nehruvian tradition* significantly on the measure of agreement between Delhi and Washington on nuclear non-proliferation. Pokhran drew instant condemnation and sanctions from the Clinton administration and threatened to jeopardise the new socio-economic currents slowly drawing the two countries closer. In the pre-1998 phase, America was interested in promoting greater regional stability in South Asia as an incentive to prevent India from going overtly nuclear. After *Shakti* and Pakistan's nuclear tests, US policy shifted to capping an arms race by getting both countries to unconditionally sign the CTBT and to halt weaponization and theatre deployment.

The possibility of a "deal" on CTBT was hinted at after Jaswant Singh, perhaps the staunchest pro-American Foreign Minister ever, met Deputy Secretary of State Strobe Talbott over ten rounds of negotiations and promised accession to the treaty provided there was national consensus. National consensus, however, might be difficult to achieve because of the accumulated domestic political antipathy to the CTBT, particularly among Congress and left parties.

Vajpayee's Asia policy is to encourage America to see India as a democratic, pluralistic and *status quo* alternative and counterweight to authoritarian, aggressive, unpredictable and revisionist China. Washington might play a great geopolitical game of hemming in China and containing its long term ascent via Taiwan, South Korea, Japan and India. Conversely, the US may continue the last administration's "better off working together" with the dragon approach, recognise it as the unrivalled leader and overseer of Asian security, and The weight of geography and history compel India and Russia to continuously upgrade defence and military co-operation. Nehru had the vision of harnessing the immense scientific, technological and military reservoir of the USSR to meet India's developmental and defence needs. Russia's role as principal defence supplier to India suffered disruptions immediately after 1991, but is now back on track with a host of new contracts, joint military exercises and a Strategic Partnership vowing to carry multifaceted ties to higher and qualitatively new levels. Disproving Western underrating of Russian military-industrial technology, Indo-Russian joint ventures are producing state-of-the-art weaponry like the just-unveiled Brahmos cruise missile.

Last, The third challenge is to build consensus around a coherent and grand strategy to safeguard national security and advance India's interest abroad. Contemporary analysts discern three central paradigms underlying India's international behaviour that are not mutually exclusive in practice and can be called Nehruvian, hyper-realist and neo-liberal. India is today lending uncritical support to a liberal international economic order in the belief that it will help sustain high growth rates, while this move enhances opportunities for India through greater integration with the global economy. India FEP has moved away from Nehruvian policies that were framed to pursue 'an independent and self-reliant path of development' using coalitional instruments such as the Non-Alignment Movement (NAM) and G-77. Indian FEP is today lending uncritical support to a liberal international economic order, which, while it allows greater integration with the global economy, involves compromises with the policies of the developed countries leading to among other things. India's new internationalism is likely to be shaped by two factors. The first is India's deepening integration into the global economy. Two decades ago the rest of the world was not critical to India's inward-oriented economic strategy. After two decades of reform, more than 40 per cent of India's GDP is now linked to international trade. India needs massive amounts of imported energy and mineral resources to sustain the high growth rates that are so vital to its people's well-being. This is only one example of India's increasing interdependence with the rest of the world. In turn, this makes India's commitment to internationalism less of an ideological conviction and more of a vital self-interest.

Inter Play between Economic Foreign Policy and Foreign Policy

India needs to accelerate efforts underway towards improving national capabilities and widening its international reach. Because economic growth depends on reliable sources of energy and India imports about 30 per cent of its commercial energy requirements.[12] India's main sources of energy caol, oil, gas, hydro, nuclear and more recently, solar and wind. Coal is produced domestically. India now imports oil from several producers (Saudi Arabia, the United Arab Emirates, Nigeria, Kuwait and Iran), has acquired assets in Russia and the Sudan, and hopes to do so in Indonesia. Thus, India has a double stake in peace and stability of the Persian Gulf region from which it imports most of its oil and where some 5 million Indians work and vital interests in keeping sea lines of communication open across the Indian Ocean. Various pipelines have been under consideration for years but not yet built. These are the Iran-Pakistan-India (IPI) Pipeline that has become hostage to insecurity in Pakistan and Afghanistan. The Myanmar-Bangladesh-India pipeline now perhaps is more feasible than before because of improved relations between Bangladesh and India. Despite strong commercial cultural links with Central Asia, India has not yet established strong commercial ties there, though it offers modest training facilities and credits and maintains an air base in Tajikistan. Partly because Pakistan prevents direct overland connection, the immense potential of Indo-central Asian relations is yet to be tapped. Projects financed by India in Bhutan, Nepal and Tajikistan produce valuable hydroelectric power, and maintaining good relations with these neighbours is vital. Exploration and production of clean, renewable, sources of energy such as bio, nuclear, solar and wind power offer enormous potential for Indian science and technology in cooperation with others similarly engaged as in Europe, Japan and the US.

There is undoubtedly an inextricable link between domestic structures and foreign policy including foreign economic policy. The foundations of Indian FP lay in the course of the freedom struggle. The conduct of an independent FP, with anti-imperialism at its core, was its central feature. Its concomitant attribute was the principle of economic self-determination and the pursuit of self-reliant development as India had inherited a colonial economy. The fact that independent India was from the very beginning a functioning democracy imposed its own constraint. But realist' critics were unhappy with India's unwillingness to have close relations with the US. The Bangladesh liberation war in 1971 and the influx of 10 million refugees strengthened the realist orientation. In 1974, India carried out a peaceful nuclear explosion and was confronted with a sanctions regime. The Soviet intervention in Afghanistan in 1979 and India's refusal to condemn it also transformed the regional geo-political situation with Pakistan becoming a firm ally of the US, receiving from it substantial military aid. India had to respond by further enhancing its own military capabilities, including pushing ahead with its nuclear weapons programme.

It is often suggested that the country's inward-looking domestic economic policies, the matter of FEP did not receive adequate attention in the first two phases of Indian FP, that is, there was no systematic thinking on the matter. India's support for decolonisation in Asia and Africa had a critical economic dimension. It was accompanied by the demand for aid for development to newly independent states. More significantly, India played an important role in the 1960s and 1970s in shaping the thinking on a new international economic order (NIEO) culminating in the famous UN General Assembly resolution, with appropriate coalitional strategies, including the instruments of G-77 and NAM. India was also active in GATT and UNCTAD to reconfigure international trade relations by laying emphasis on the preferential or special and differential treatment principle, especially in GATT of which it was a founding member. India also played a role in the attempt to make the UN, through the economic and Social Council (ECOSOC), coordinate the global development agenda. In short, during much of the Cold War era, India was a forceful leader of the developing states and represented their views through the Group of 77 and the non-aligned movement.

Second, in order to meet difficulties confronted in the first decades after Independence, India had to seek external economic assistance, including food and technology imports. It also had to bring in necessary foreign investment. The third phase of Indian foreign policy began with the end of the Cold War. It initiated a debate on the relevance of NAM. Slowly but surely, Indian FP moved from the policy of non-alignment to what the present National Security Advisor has termed 'un-alignment' in an attempt to break free of ideological concepts to build mutually beneficial relationship with principal countries and regions. A shift in Indian FP was compelled by the fact that, in May 1998, India carried out a second series of nuclear tests. It saw India isolated and facing sanctions, including a restrictive technology-licensing regime. A key aim of Indian FP now was to break out of this nuclear isolation. It required India to pursue closer relations with the US. This was eventually helped by the fact that included access to India's huge domestic market and the containment of China, sought greater strategic engagement with India, a policy that Obama has continued. In 2005, India entered into a new framework for the US-India Defence Relationship,' sealing a strategic relationship. It was followed in 2008 by the landmark Indo-US civil nuclear deal.

Prime Ministers and their Imprints on Indian Foreign Policy

Nehru as the Prime Minister and Indian Foreign Policy

The foreign policy of a country is determined by the times in which it is conducted. It is also influenced by its history and its geographical positions. Jawaharlal Nehru himself said, India's foreign policy was rooted in India's civilization and traditions, India's struggles for freedom, India's geographical position, and India's quest for peace, security, development and a place in the sun. To quote Nehru, "it is completely incorrect to call our policy 'Nehru policy' I have not originated it. It is the policy inherent in the circumstances of India, inherent in the past thinking of India, inherent in the whole mental outlook of India, inherent in the conditioning of the Indian mind during the struggle for freedom and inherent in the circumstances of the world today."[13]

Primarily two important approaches, defined Nehru's Foreign Policy; the awareness of current weaknesses and the belief in India as a potentially great power. One lead to remaining in the commonwealth and keeping intact India's economic links with the west and other to nonalignment, thought Nehru. However, Nehru realized that the country needed some security from the hostile winds that were blowing in the world. Nehru was also of the opinion of creating multi-forum organizations. In Nehru's words, "we maintain our old ties with those countries because no certain things that we cannot get from elsewhere. That some people obsessed by nation can live in isolation. We wanted certain things that we cannot get from elsewhere." Nehru believed in principles and ideas in the power of ideas but he was against the ideololisation of foreign policy. Nehru rejected fundamentalism in foreign policy, weather of the Western or the Soviet variety. He was accused of preaching, but in fact he was against moralism in foreign policy. As early as March 1949, he told an audience of the Indian Council of World Affairs that he disliked moralizing and preaching in international relations. He felt that it was the Western and the Soviet leaders who were most of the time preaching the virtues of their respective system.

He was too a large extent a pragmatist, though he was accused of the idealist. Once Nehru told his people that India's interests were paramount in the interactions in foreign relations. He told the Constituent Assembly on 4th December 1947, "whatever policy we may lay down, the art of conducting foreign affairs of a country lies in finding out what is most advantageous to the country". It was Nehru who first used the words "enlightened self-interest", so as to harmonize the differing interests of various countries. Nehru made at least a visible contribution to the Indonesian struggle by organizing an Asian conference to oppose Dutch efforts to reoccupy the island known as Indonesia. Nehru was very concerned about its neighbourhood policy. To begin with India's foreign policy priorities did not concern developments in Europe but were focused nearer home. It was the neighbourhood that claimed first attention. As early as 1949 Nehru spelt out the natural directions of India's foreign policy. The nearby countries always had a special interest for India. Necessarily India's foreign policy first turned its attention towards countries bordering it by land and sea. Nehru strongly believed that next to the neighbours the place comes for the Asian countries. Indeed India's geographical position made it important whether one thought in terms of China or the Middle East, or Southeast Asia. Nehru wanted to dismantle dominance of any block on international politics. He wanted to initiate a process of pluralism. As Nehru put it, "the only truth about the world was that truth not confined to one country, one people, one ideology and one world." Nonalignment was not foreign policy but a tool of foreign policy in a given situation.

Indira Gandhi: India's Foreign Policy

Mrs. Gandhi began her innings in foreign relations first with a visit to Yugoslavia and the UAR (now Egypt) to reemphasize their special relationship and the continued adherence to non-alignment. During the Mrs. Gandhi regime the world politics was very adverse. It was time of Nixon-Kissinger duo was creating a wave against India. They were clubbing with Pakistan and China to pin down India. Kissinger secret visit to China was mapping a new road map to end the Chinese isolation. The immediate implication of this change was to side-line India with the proper instruction of the US. The Bangladesh episode was an acid test for Indian foreign policy. It was under the circumstances that the Indo-Soviet Treaty of Peace Friendship and Cooperation was signed in August 1971. Again, Mrs. Gandhi had set the agenda. The Soviets agreed, perhaps reluctantly, that if there was aggression against any of the two parties, they would immediately consult each other on how to meet the aggression. Since there was no question of any aggression against the Soviet Union, the treaty served as a warning to both Washington and Beijing not to think of military action against India in the unfolding Bangladesh crisis. The treaty also praised India's policy of nonalignment.

India recognized the new state of Bangladesh on 6th of December and Bangladesh had become a reality and soon afterwards Sheikh Mujibur Rehman was restored to power in his sonar Bangla. This was Mrs. Gandhi's finest hour and won her tribute of being India's John of Arc. Both China and US made threatening noises and Nixon even sent the aircraft carrier "Enterprise" into the waters of the Bay of Bengal but they had been constrained by the Indo-Soviet Treaty. Mrs. Gandhi also tried to improve ties with China. Having understood the geographical proximity that was imperative to make a friendly move, she sent an Indian ambassador to Beijing in 1977 and she chose a career diplomat known for his sobriety and maturity, K.R. Narayana who subsequently rose to be the President of India. When she came back to power in 1980, she continued the policy of improvement of relationship with China. It was Mrs. Gandhi who initiated the "look east" policy, later pursued by succeeding prime ministers. She took special steps to improve relations with the Southeast countries. She visited Malaysia, Indonesia, Singapore, Thailand and the Philippines during her two tenures as Prime Minister. Gandhi's handling of foreign policy was firm, realistic and dignified. Indira Gandhi's foreign policy shared many of Nehru's assumptions about the civilizational and moral greatness of India, the necessity to remain wary of western neo-colonialism, the imperative of championing decolonisation in Africa and Latin America, and about the benefits of a highly protected mixed economy. But the 1962 Indian military defeat by China and domestic political turbulence caused a transformation in attitudes on the use of force such that Indira Gandhi projected a symbolic militancy and toughness.

Rajiv Gandhi as a Prime Minister

Rajiv Gandhi (1984-89) signalled a complete throwback to Nehruvian posturing by proposing a much-touted "Action Plan" at the United Nations for phased elimination of all nuclear weapons. At the same time, regional tensions with Pakistan and growing signs of Pakistan-abetted militancy in Kashmir led to an unprecedented peacetime military build-up in 1987 (Operation Brasstacks), and Rajiv Gandhi also burnt his fingers intervening in Sri Lanka. Thus, the post-Nehruvian Congress era witnessed many seesawing foreign policies calibrated to changing times although.

I.K. Gujral: Gujral Doctrine

The Gujral Doctrine is a set of five principles to guide the conduct of foreign relations with India's immediate neighbours, notably Pakistan, as spelt out by Gujral. The doctrine was later termed by journalist Bhabani Sen Gupta in his article, *India in the Twenty First Century* in International Affairs as Gujral Doctrine. The United Front Government's neighbourhood policy now stands on five basic principles: First, with the neighbours like Nepal, Bangladesh, Bhutan, Maldives and Sri Lanka, India does not ask for reciprocity but gives all that it can in good faith and trust. Secondly, no South Asian country will allow its territory to be used against the interest of another country of the region. Thirdly, none will interfere in the internal affairs of another. Fourthly, all South Asian countries must respect each other's territorial integrity and sovereignty. And finally, they will settle all their disputes through peaceful bilateral negotiations. These five principles, scrupulously observed, will, I am sure, recast South Asia's regional relationship, including the tormented relationship between India and Pakistan, in a friendly, cooperative mould. He wrote in his autobiography of the doctrine: "The logic behind the Gujral Doctrine was that since we had to face two hostile neighbours in the north and the west, we had to be at 'total peace' with all other immediate neighbours in order to contain Pakistan's and China's influence in the region. As Indian External Affairs Minister he continued with his initiatives in the realm of foreign policy concerning with Asia and Eurasia. It was Gujral who first mooted the idea of close cooperation between Russia, India and China, in the post-Cold War-era.

Vajpayee as a Prime Minister

Nuclear explosion was the hall mark of BJP's foreign policy. The grand strategy of Vajpayee proved to be a new mile stone. All the weakness, vulnerability, "lack" and effeminacy of the past are behind India after Pokhran, according to the Foreign Minister, with a "transformation from the moralistic to the realistic" and India's self-centered pursuit of strength. A pro-BJP news-editor has gone so far as to say, "India has arrived on the threshold of superpower status, literally with a bang." The Prime Minister concedes, "India has never considered military might as the ultimate measure of national strength," but adds, "it's a necessary component of national strength" that will earn the respect of the world. Vajpayee established a National Security Council in April 1999 "to analyse the military, economic and political threats to the nation and render continuous advise to the government."[14] Two new offices have been created—Chief of Defence Staff (CDS) and Defence Intelligence Agency (DIA)—to integrate weapons acquisition, logistics and strategy, hitherto performed compartmentally by the Chiefs of Army, Navy and Air Force. Pursuant to the BJP mantra of "security first and the rest will follow," a massive military modernization drive is underway with party claims of "the largest ever increase in defence budget." In Advani's words, a "comprehensive systemic overhaul to meet security challenges of the 21st century" is being carried out for the first time in independent India's history.

Vajpayee's dramatic Lahore bus ride for a summit with Pakistan's Nawaz Sharif in February 1999 was the first visit by an Indian head-of-government to its most nettlesome neighbour since Nehru's visit forty years before. When Vajpayee was the Janata Foreign Minister in the late 1970s, India's neighbourhood diplomacy garnered an unprecedented degree of goodwill causing Vajpayee to declare "a new era of understanding and friendship" between India and Pakistan.

Manmohan Singh's Foreign Policy

Prime Minister Manmohan Singh not only stated his government's continued commitment to the peace dialogue but efforts was made to intensify the peace process. The foreign policy of Manmohan Singh has made solid imprint on many occasions. He in subsequent speeches and statements, emphasised the need to work towards a situation in which borders would become irrelevant. He initiated the process of composite dialogues with Pakistan. Along with Kashmir issue, differences over the boundary in the Sir Creek area the only maritime dispute between the two countries were discussed. In India's federal, parliamentary, cabinet form and now coalitional government system, foreign policy remains, as it always has been, the prerogative of the Prime Minister alone. Fully appreciative of the limits within which a Prime Minister could function in the kind of set-up that he had inherited, Dr. Singh was quick to draw red lines at home, as his first Foreign Minister, Natwar Singh, discovered early during his term in office.

The most dramatic event occurred when the Left Front government informed the Centre that it would not be able to ensure law and order at the Kalaikunda air force base where a group of CPI(M) protesters had planned to gather to disrupt joint air exercises between the Indian Air Force and the United States Air Force. Reminding Chief Minister Buddhadev Bhattacharya that no State government can prevent the Centre from conducting defence and foreign policy, Dr. Singh threatened to impose President's rule in West Bengal if the State government failed to discharge its constitutional responsibility of maintaining law and order, especially near a defence installation. More recently, there was a comment that the same Dr. Singh failed to impose similar discipline on West Bengal Chief Minister Mamata Banerjee when she blocked a bilateral agreement between India and Bangladesh on Teesta river water sharing.[15] One can give several other examples where Dr. Singh may have initially stepped back in the face of opposition at home but eventually walked the talk. Faced with criticism at home, even from his own party, for the famous India-Pakistan joint statement at Sharm-el-Shaikh, in July 2009, Dr. Singh not only defended his initiative twice in a month in Parliament but also continued his dialogue with his Pakistani counterpart.

Externally also, Dr. Singh has not shied away from drawing red lines. When President Barack Obama sought to send Richard Holbrooke to India as a special envoy to discuss Kashmir, the U.S. was told in no uncertain terms that Mr. Holbrooke would not be welcome. On another occasion, when the Chinese government publicly warned India against permitting the Dalai Lama's visit to Arunachal Pradesh, Dr. Singh made bold to let China know that it cannot dictate which part of India the Dalai Lama can or cannot travel to. A similar red line was drawn on the issue of the attendance of the Indian ambassador at the ceremony where a Chinese dissident was to be awarded the Nobel Peace prize and on China stamping its version of India's map on Indian passports.

Conclusion

Indian foreign policy has many successes and failures. Liberation of Bangladesh, Nuclear Tests, Strategic ties with the US and many others could be regarded as mark of achievements. But there are many failures which are holding India as a limping power in its own region. The international agenda have fissile out from the hands of India. China has been showing its aggressive postures against India. Pakistan continues to burn the pockets of India. Smaller neighbours of India irritate India on many occasions. The hot seat of UN is still eluding from India's reach. Terrorism haunts and kills thousands of Indians. Multilateral International bodies are not working on the frame work of Indian interest.

NOTES

1. Bajpai, Kanti P. (2002), 'Indian Strategic Culture' in Michael R. Chambers, ed., South Asia in 2020: Future Strategic Balances and Alliances, Stanford.
2. Rajan, M.S. (ed) (1976), *India's Foreign Relations during the Nehru Era*, Asia Publishing House.
3. Dixit, J.N. (2042), *Makers of Indian Foreign Policy*, Harper and Collins.
4. Ibid.
5. *Times of India*, 17th January, 1978.

6. Tellis, Ashley J. (2011), *Doughtful India's Role in World Politics*, Report Washington D.C., Carnegie Endowment.
7. Mohan, C. Raja (2006), *The Impossible Allies*, New Delhi, Indian Research Press.
8. Dixit, J.N. (1996), *My South Block Years: Memoirs of a Foreign Secretary*, New Delhi UBS Publisher.
9. Prasad, Bimal (1962), *The Origin of Indian Foreign Policy*, The Indian National Congress and World Affairs, Bookland Private Limited.
10. Pardeshi, Manjeet Singh (2005), 'Deducing India's Grand Strategy of Regional Hegemony from Historical and Conceptual Perspectives' working paper series, Singapore.
11. *Indian Express*, 12th June 2011.
12. Dubey, Muchkund (2009), *New International Economic World Order and India*, Delhi Lancer Publications.
13. Basu, Kaushik (2008), 'The Enigma of India's Arrival': A Review of Arvind Virmani's Propelling India.
14. *Foreign Affairs*, Record, 2011.
15. *The Times of India*, Sept., 2012.

17

India and the Indian Ocean: A Post-Cold War Human Security Perspective

Suresh R

The protection and promotion of national interests is the most significant concern of any nation state. Though the national interests of nation states are mainly to maintain peace, security and prosperity, they differ on the means applied for the protection and promotion of these interests. In the Cold War period, the clashes of ideology prompted nation states to overtly or covertly support either of the two blocs at the international system to protect and promote their respective national interests. Thus, nation states enjoyed only limited choice in the pursuing their national interests, especially their security interests. During this period the most important security concern of developed and developing nations was military security. Though there were other grave issues in the economic, social, and environmental fields, they were either side tracked or overshadowed by military security concerns. However, a marked change is visible in the security concerns of nation states in the post-Cold War period.

Security in the post-Cold War Period

The disintegration of Soviet Union and the consequent end of super power rivalry provides nation states an opportunity to pursue new means to achieve their national interests. The security perceptions of the nation states had also underwent a radical change in the post-Cold War period. Economic security appears to be the foremost concern of all nations, both developed and developing. Though the traditional security perception based on pure military security has not been abandoned outright, it has lost much of its significance.[1]

The emergences of new forms of threat pose by the transnational terrorist groups add new dimensions to the security of nations. The operations of these groups demonstrated that traditional approach to national security has become redundant. No nation whatsoever powerful can single handedly tackle the threat pose by these non state entities. This again demands multilateralism in international relations to meet the challenges posed by transnational and non state actors.

Another major problem before international community is the environment degradation and the consequent climate change. Over consumption of available resources on the one hand and lack of resources for the fulfillment of basic necessities on the other hand pose a challenge in the management of available resources and the environmental protection. Thus environment security has become a major security concern of nation states. However, environmental protection demands joint effort from the developed and developing nations.

The globalization process which pervades in every nook and corner of the world brought together all nations into a common platform. The globalization process have not only brought the nations together at the global platform but also strengthened regional cooperation. Another notable feature of the globalization process is the growth of powerful transnational and multinational corporations which poses a threat to the Westphalia state system. Some of these corporations are more powerful than nation states in terms of area of operations and possession of resources. The gradual withdrawal of the state from welfare services such as education would aggravate the prevailing social and economic inequality in the developing countries.[2]The gradual withdrawal of state from the social and economic sphere would further worsen the existing social and economic inequality prevalent mostly in the developing nations.

The growth and development of non state actors in international relations is a new phenomenon in the post-Cold War period. Along with this development international civil society organizations are gaining strength as a player in intra national and international levels. The existence of these international and national civil society organizations to protect and promote human rights and the environment also accelerate the pace of the ongoing global democratization process. The interaction among people as a result of information and communication technology (ICT) revolution further strengthened the bonds of universal brotherhood and understanding among people about the basic problems before them. A better understanding among the people of their basic problems transcending the artificial boundaries would further weaken the role of state as a player in international relations. Further the huge administrative cost involved in implementation of welfare programmes by bureaucracy and bureaucratic corruption prompted several international funding agencies to rely on civil society organizations rather than governmental agencies. This again resulted in the shrinking role of nation states in welfare activities.

In the post-Cold War period the strength of a nation appears to be based not solely on the possession of destructive weapons it possess but on many other nontraditional factors including the strength of its economy, the functioning of the democratic institutions, and the human security situation. The security of the people living in a nation is as important as security of a nation state. Thus in the post-Cold War period the human security is gaining significance in international relations. This new dimension of security has also been driven by the globalization.[3]

India's Security in the post-Cold-War Period

In the Cold War period, in addition to the threat from Pakistan and China, major security concern of India was presence of external powers especially the US presence in the region. This prompted India to support the Sri Lankan initiated proposal to declare Indian Ocean as a Zone of Peace by the UN in 1971. The entry of the US naval fleets into the Bay of Bengal in support of Pakistan during the Indo Pak war of 1971 again prompted India to take strong stand against external power presence in the region especially the US presence. Throughout the Cold War period India's Indian Ocean policy was mainly based on this stand and in all international and regional platforms India strongly maintained this position.[4]

India's traditional security concerns revolve round the threat from Pakistan and China. However, in the post-Cold War period a major threat from Pakistan have only remote chance because of two major developments in the region. Pakistan's decision makers both military and civilian are well aware of the fact that they may not get any support which they had received in 1971 war, from their Cold War defense ally, the US. Secondly since Pakistan becomes a nuclear weapon power, no major players at the international level or the UN would allow the outbreak of a nuclear war in South Asia. With regard to the threat from China, though there is an unresolved border problem, China may not initiate a 1962 type war with nuclear India due to nuclear deterrence. Here again the global players and the UN would not allow a nuclear war in Asia. Thus in the post-Cold War period India's traditional security concerns have undergone a marked change, though the defense establishments in India and the external affairs ministry pay least attention to these developments.

In the post-Cold War period the major security concern of India emanate mainly from cross border terrorism. All other traditional security concerns were overtaken by economic issues. The challenges posed by international terrorism, global economic meltdown and environmental degradation including climate change are also security concerns before India. In the domestic front India faces many challenges including poverty, illiteracy, social and economic inequality, communalism, regional imbalance, and development based displacement etc. Thus in the post-Cold War period the human security challenges before India are more in number as well as grave in nature.

India's Quest for Security

India's quest for security has incorporated the traditional concept of security and also the new dimension of security. India placed equal importance to security of the nation as well as security of the people. In the Cold War period there was a competition among nations to accumulate more and more weapons. Though the competition for weapons continues in the post-Cold War period it has lost much vigor and popular support. This appears to be the reason for the shift in focus from military security to economic and environmental security in security studies. The plea for a human security approach is also a post-Cold War development.The positive as well as negative impacts of globalization process have also appears to accelerate the momentum for human security approach. On the positive side, globalization process has helped the growth of civil society organization at the national and international levels. These organizations make democratic system more participatory and people friendly. With regard to the negative impact of globalization process, the withdrawal of state from welfare activities further worsened the position of poor and marginalized section in the society. In a globalised international system greater interaction among people has created a better understanding of the common problems before the deprived sections in each society and pursuing a concerted effort in resolving these problems in a time bound manner. Thus in the quest for security India appears to have placed equal importance to both the human security and national security.

In order to strengthen India's economic and military power it has taken strong policy decisions toward achieving a growth rate of 8 percent by focusing on agriculture, infrastructure development along with its quest for modernization of defense forces. Again India's reluctance to compromise on nuclear weapon option, its strategic interaction with the US, and strengthening the naval forces to the level of blue water force are part of this strategy. These steps are also appears to be based on a new security perception.

The international and domestic situations are favorable to India to initiate the new security strategy. At the international front the post-Cold War international power structure, which is mostly a multi polar system, and the US initiative to curb international terrorism and actions against state sponsored terrorism also suite India's foreign policy objectives. The emergence of two major political fronts at the federal level accelerated competition in the Indian polity. Each front tried to formulate domestic and external policy to gain maximum popular support. This trend again prompted each front to pursue a realist foreign policy. India's decision to break the shell and declare as a nuclear weapon power and the signing of Indo US Civilian Nuclear Agreement and a number of policy decisions in the domestic and external fields marked this change. In the 2009 federal election the strong popular support for the ruling front to form a stable government without the conditional support from minor ideology based political parties, reflects popular support to the new policy initiatives of the decision makers.

Indian Ocean and India's Security

Indian Ocean is very important to India's military, economic, energy, environment, and human security. India has a coast line of 7516 kms and an exclusive economic zone (EEZ) of 2 million sqkms. The significance of this Ocean has long been recognized. The famous words of Alfred Tyler Mahan testifies this "whosoever control Indian Ocean dominates Asia. This Ocean is important in the seven seas, in the twenty first century the destiny of the world will be determined in its waters."[5]

India occupies a central position in the Indian Ocean region, a fact that exercises an increasingly profound influence on India's security environment. Writing in the 1940s, K. M. Pannikar, noted the importance of the Ocean to India that "while to other countries the Indian Ocean is only one of the important oceanic areas, to India it is a vital sea. Her lifelines are concentrated in that area, her freedom is dependent on the freedom of that water surface. No industrial development, no commercial growth, no stable political structure is possible for her unless her shores are protected."[6] In tune with the above observations the first Prime Minister of India, Jawaharlal Nehru observed "History has shown that whatever power controls the Indian Ocean has, in the first instance, India's sea borne trade at her mercy and, in the second, India's very independence itself.." The significance of the Indian Ocean to India has also been emphasized in the Annual Report (2004-2005) of India's Defense Ministry, which noted that "India is strategically located vis-a-vis both continental Asia as well as the Indian Ocean Region."[7]Again the Indian Maritime Doctrine asserts: "All major powers of this century will seek a toehold in the Indian Ocean Region. Thus, Japan, the EU, and China, and a reinvigorated Russia can be expected to show presence in these waters either independently or through politico-security arrangements." There is, moreover, "an increasing tendency of extra regional powers of military intervention in [IO] littoral countries to contain what they see as a conflict situation."[8] Thus the Indian Ocean and its littoral and hinterland area have a direct bearing in safeguarding India's security interests.

India's Indian Ocean Policy in the Post-Cold War Period

In the post-Cold War period, nations are very careful in their interaction with others. The international politics of the post-Cold War is not the same as the one in the Cold War period. There are no ideological confrontations. Nations are more concerned about resolving their basic problem. International cooperation is required for the protection and promotion of national interests, concerning peace, security and development. No nation whatsoever powerful can protect its national interests by pursuing an isolationist policy. This understanding among nations forced them to unite and work together to resolve domestic as well as external problems through international cooperation. Such cooperative efforts are also visible among the countries in the Indian Ocean region (IOR).

India's maritime policy also underwent a sea change in the post-Cold War period. The policy of exclusive engagement and elimination of outside powers has given place to overt engagement with extra regional powers. This has been well reflected in India's joint military exercises along with the US, Japan, France, and Australia. India no longer considers the external power presence as a threat to its security. Rather it considers a joint effort is required to wipe out the major threat to India and international community posed by terrorism. It is not possible for any single nation whatsoever powerful to address the menace of international terrorism singlehandedly. India began to realize the importance of a realist approach in framing its foreign policy objectives and pursuing it through increased naval power and active collaboration with extra regional as well as intra regional powers. This policy shift in India's stand is visible in the maritime doctrine as well as in the Navy's vision document published by the Indian Navy.

It essentially encompasses:

(i) Shaping a favorable maritime environment in the IOR for operations in peace as well as during conflict.
(ii) Preventing incursions by powers inimical to India's national interests by actively engaging countries in the IOR littoral, and rendering speedy and quality assistance in fields of interest to them.
(iii) Engaging extra-regional powers and regional navies in mutually beneficial activities to ensure the security of India's maritime interests.
(iv) Projecting the Indian Navy as a professional, credible force and the primary tool for maritime cooperation.[9]

India has also ear marked the area which falls within its immediate concern. "India's growing international stature gives it strategic relevance in the area ranging from the Persian Gulf to the Strait of Malacca..." While enumerating the basic features of India's post-Cold War Indian Ocean policy the Prime Minister, Manmohan Singh has stated: "India has exploited the fluidities of the emerging world order to forge new links through a combination of diplomatic repositioning, economic resurgence and military firmness." [10]

It appears that India has adopted a three pronged strategy to protect and promote its national interests. Firstly through diplomatic means, India has pursued a policy of cooperation with all major players in the Indian Ocean, including extra regional powers. This policy would help India to increase further its international stature. The Indo-US civilian nuclear agreement can also be viewed as an attempt to do away with nuclear isolation. The process of globalization has also accelerated better and cordial interaction with outside powers as the movement of people as well as commodities would further cement relation between nations.

India has developed a friendly and cordial relation not only by bilateral exchange with nations but also strengthened the bilateral cooperation through interactions in regional organizations, such as ASEAN, EAS, SCO, BRICS, ASEM, IBSA, APTA, and IOR-ARC. India is vigorously pursuing the objective to become a developed nation by 2020. This requires the Indian economy to maintain an annual average growth rate of 8 percent per annum. India has adopted a reinvigorated "Look East" policy in pursuance of this objective. Now the look east policy is a vital part of India's foreign policy.More than an external economic policy or a political slogan, the look east policy was a strategic shift in India's vision of the world and its place in the evolving global economy. It was also a manifestation of India's belief that developments in East Asia are of direct consequence to its security and development. Therefore India actively engaged in creating a bond of friendship and cooperation with East Asia that has a strong economic foundation and a cooperative paradigm of positive inter-connectedness of security interests.India becomes a member of the ARF in 1996 and considers it as an experiment in fashioning a pluralistic, cooperative security order reflective of the diversity of the Asia-Pacific region. India has also successfully clinched a free trade agreement with the ASEAN which had come into force on 1 January 2010. India is also a member of the East Asia Summit (EAS) which includes the ASEAN members and India, China, Japan, Republic of Korea, Australia, and New Zealand. It focuses on energy, environment, climate change, and sustainable development. The look east policy of India has included not only vigorous interaction with ASEAN but also improved relation with China. The ultimate objective,it appears, is to evolve an Asian Economic Community on the lines of EU.

India has also pursued a policy of strengthening its economic and military power. It appears that in order to increase the national power India not only declared itself as a nuclear weapon power but also augmented its non nuclear defense capabilities manifold. India is the largest importer of weapons as per the SIPRI reports.[11]Again the maritime doctrine of India focuses mainly on building blue water navy.[12] India's role in ensuring the security of Indian Ocean region has been recognized by major players in the region mainly because of the major shift in its external policy.As a result India was not hesitant to cooperate with any regional and extra regional powers. India has undertaken several innovative steps towards economic resurgence of the country. India's initiative to interact with nations at the bilateral and multilateral levels through various regional groupings appears to be based on this policy initiative.

India's foreign policy is to be adapted to the demands of the rapidly changing global, regional and domestic environments. The main drivers for reshaping India's foreign policy appears to have been the sustained dynamism of the Indian economy, emergence as a responsible Nuclear Weapon State, global expectations of India's role on the international stage and the capability to shoulder both regional and global responsibilities. India's engagement with the world community has grown to ensure a peaceful and supportive international environment that contributes to India's development goals. India advocates the need to evolve a new paradigm of cooperation, relevant to the contemporary world, in which global threats are addressed by global responses, and multilateralism becomes the preferred norm for addressing global challenges including terrorism, environmental degradation and economic meltdown.

India and the Human Security

With the end of Cold War the concept of security has increasingly come under scrutiny from scholars of international relations. In the classical formulation security is about how state use force to manage threat to their territorial integrity, their autonomy and their domestic political order, primarily from other states. Some critique of classical formulation of security opined that the protection and welfare of the individual citizen or human being is central. The conception of security that is centered above all on the sanctity of the individual may be called human security.[13]

Though the idea of human security in its rudimentary form may be traced in 1960s, it was the Independent Commission on International Development Issues in its North-South Report of 1980 highlighted the changing thinking on development and security. The chairman of the commission Willy Brandt observed "Our Report is based on what appears to be the simplest common interest that mankind wants to survive, and one might even add has the moral obligation to survive. This not only raises traditional questions of peace and war, but also how to overcome world hunger, mass misery and alarming disparities between the living conditions of the rich and poor."[14]

Another notable development in the idea of human security was the Common Security Report of the Independent Commission on Disarmament and Security Issues chaired by Olaf Palm. It acknowledges that Third world security was also threatened by poverty and deprivation by economic inequality. The report noted "common security requires that people live in dignity and peace, that they have enough to eat and are able to find work and live in a world without poverty and destitution."[15]

With the end of superpower rivalry the call for new thinking in security matters gained momentum. In 1991 the Stockholm Institute on Global Security and Governance issued a call for " Common Responsibility in the 1990s ",which maintained a" wider concept of security, which deals with threats that stem from failures in development, environmental degradation, excessive population growth and movement, and lack of progress towards democracy." Again in 1995, the Commission on Global Governance's report, *Our Global Neighborhood*, stated that "The concept of global security must be broadened from the traditional focus on the security of states to include the security of people and the security of the planet."[16]

The above commission reports may be considered as precursors to human security thinking. However, a human security perspective was developed by the UNDP (United Nations Development Programme) in the Human Development Report of 1994.This report contains a section on 'Redefining Security: The

Human Dimension'.[17] It proposes an alternative to traditional security and a necessary supplement to human development.

The Human Development Report of 1994 offers an alternative to traditional security. The report discusses in details the question of security for whom by reference to traditional notion of security. These were concerned with security of territory from external aggression, or as protection of national interest in foreign policy or as global security from the threat of nuclear holocaust. It has been related more to nation state than to people. What this conception overlooked was the "legitimate concern of ordinary people who sought security in their daily lives". [18]Human security, on the other hand, is people centered.

The Human Development Report maintains that human security means protecting vital freedom of the individuals. It means protecting people from critical and pervasive threats and situations, building on their strengths and aspirations. It also means creating systems that give people the building blocks of survival, dignity and livelihood. Human security connects different types of freedoms—freedom from want, freedom from fear and freedom to take action on one's own behalf. To do this, it offers two general strategies: protection and empowerment. Protection shields people from dangers. It requires concerted effort to develop norms, processes and institutions that systematically address insecurities. Empowerment enables people to develop their potential and become full participants in decision-making. Protection and empowerment are mutually reinforcing, and both are required in most situations. Human security complements state security, furthers human development and enhances human rights. It complements state security by being people-centered and addressing insecurities that have not been considered as state security threats. By looking at "downside risks", it broadens the human development focus beyond "growth with equity". Respecting human rights are at the core of protecting human security.[19]

In the age of globalization protection of the vulnerable groups in the society, who are affected by development based displacement or by loss of job and income, assumes great significance. India had taken several steps to ensure human security or the security of the people. Being the largest democratic system in the world it has a strong democratic structure to implement human security measures at the national level. Though the political foundations of India are strongly based on a parliamentary system in the economic and social fields it confronted with many challenges. It includes poverty, unemployment, illiteracy, social inequality communalism, casteism, the economic disparity between haves and have-nots. All these factors have an implication on human security.

In a democratic system human security assumes great significance. Since the support of the people is required for the government formation no political party can ignore human security. The globalization process has also contributed towards the inclusion of human security in the national and international sphere. The awareness of the people regarding their own basic problems and the increased interaction among people across the man made borders as a result of the development in information and communication technology, has also promoted the move towards human security.

At the national level India had initiated several programmes for providing security of the people. It includes measures which are aimed both protection and empowerment of the vulnerable section in the society. The major programmes initiated are the Mahatma Gandhi National Rural Employment Guarantee Programme (MGNREGP), right to education act, right to food, programmes for improvement of slum, National Rural Health Mission, right to information act, food security bill passed by both houses of Parliament.[20]

Though, reforms are aimed at making the government more accountable, transparent, and responsive to the needs of the people, the implementation of these reforms is undermined by high levels of corruption, the criminalization of politics, and weak institutions especially a colonial system based bureaucratic machinery. Again there is lack of clear understanding about the elements of human insecurity that are manifest in India. Whenever there is unrest in the society as a result of their loss of dignity or access to land, the government views this only as a law-and-order problem that requires police action, rather than implementing responses that are as multidimensional as the causes themselves. Thus in the many policies in India continue to be driven by state-centric frameworks.

During the Cold War period India had taken the initiative to ensure peace and security of the IOR through the elimination of external power presence from the region. In the post-Cold War period the globalization process and the increased multilateral cooperation has provided an opportunity to India to initiate a regional forum for greater economic interaction among the countries in the IOR. Most of the countries in the Indian Ocean are developing countries and they are facing many common problems in realm of ensuring human security. A nuanced understanding of the common domestic problems of the countries in the IOR could help them to incorporate human security issues as one tactic for reducing national security threats. Thus any move to ensure human security would mould and strengthen the bonds of interaction at the regional level. A common strategy to address the problem related to human security would also lead to evolving common strategy in ensuring national and international peace and security.

Conclusions

The shift in international power structure from bipolar to multi polar or 'non polar' after the disintegration of former Soviet Union has posed many challenges to the erstwhile non aligned nations. In the Cold War period nation states were deprived of a wider foreign policy option to promote their national interests. Thus the end of Cold War marked the end of strict international discipline imposed by the super power rivalry on nation states. Today there is 'de hyphenated relations' between nations and they are free to engage or disengage with anyone. The pure military security concerns were overtaken by economic interests. The balance of power proposition has been replaced by balance of interests. The globalization process and challenges posed by international terrorism, global economic slowdown, and environmental degradation including the climate change has placed 'collective actions' and multilateralism in the forefront of international relations.

The protection and promotion of national interests, namely, peace, security and prosperity, is the foremost concern of any nation, though they adopt different means to achieve these objectives. The changes that had taken place at the international setting placed India in a new security environment and compelled to adapt its foreign policy to the changing needs. India appears to have adopted a two pronged strategy to meet the new security concerns.[21] India has consolidated and projected its power and also initiated engagement with global powers and regional groupings hitherto considered as taboo under 'enlightened national interests'.

The present global order demands a pragmatic approach from the decision makers to protect and promote the national interests. When the options are limited before the decision makers to pursue their national interests a common perception would evolve in all areas including security. This happens mainly because of two important factors. Firstly it happens due to the fundamental changes that are taking place in the domestic and external settings. And secondly it is because of the blurred boundary between human security and national security on the one hand, and national security and international security on the other. However, much depend on the ability of the Indian political leadership to make use of the emerging situation through timely and pragmatic policy initiatives. Resolving the domestic social and economic problems including poverty is not as important as defense of the border[22] to the political leadership because the latter is perceived to be a prerequisite of the former. Notwithstanding, the focus on human security issues not only would enhance India's domestic strength but also ensure its national security through better understanding among the regional and extra regional countries in the Indian Ocean.

NOTES

1. With the end of Cold War the concept of security has increasingly come under scrutiny from scholars of international relations. In the classical formulation security is about how state use force to manage threat to their territorial integrity, their autonomy and their domestic political order, primarily from other states. Some critique of classical formulation of security opined that the protection and welfare of the individual citizen or human being is central. The conception of security that is centered above all on the sanctity of the individual may be called human security. For a detailed analysis of security perception see Suresh R, Nuclear Proliferations and Security of South Asia: A Post-Iraq War Scenario, in G. Gopakumar (ed.) Iraq War and the Future World Order, Icon Publishers, New Delhi, 2006.
2. Suresh R., *Foreign Policy and Human Rights: An Indian Perspective*, Madhav Books, Gurgaon (Haryana) 2009.
3. Human Security—people centered approach to security. The Human Development Report

of 1994 offers an alternative to traditional security. The report discusses in details the question of security for whom by reference to traditional notion of security. These were concerned with security of territory from external aggression, or as protection of national interest in foreign policy or as global security from the threat of nuclear holocaust. It has been related more to nation state than to people. What this conception overlooked was the "legitimate concern of ordinary people who sought security in their daily lives".[5] Human security, on the other hand, is people centered. For details of Human Security approach of the UN as well as Canada See Suresh R, Human Security: A Canadian Perspective, *Holistic Thought*, Vol. V, Nos. 1 & 2, Jan-Dec 2006, pp. 103-113.

4. Suresh R., *Peace in the Indian Ocean: A South Asian Perspective*, Serials Publishers, New Delhi, 2012.
5. Ibid.
6. Ibid.
7. Annual Report 2004-05 Ministry of Defence, Government of India, New Delhi 2005.
8. India's Maritime Military Strategy, Ministry of Defense, Government of India, New Delhi. Also see The Indian Navy's Vision Document, May 2006. www.indiannavy.nic.in
9. Ibid.
10. Ibid.
11. "India's imports of major weapons increased by 38 percent between 2002-06 and 2007-11," SIPRI said Asia tops other regions when it comes to weapon imports, according to a study released Monday by the Stockholm International Peace Research Institute (SIPRI) India is the world's largest recipient of arms while South Korea is second and Pakistan and China are tied in third place, says the Stockholm International Peace Research Institute (SIPRI) in a study on international arms transfers.
12. India's Maritime Military Strategy.
13. Indo-Soviet Peace and Friendship Treaty of 1971, though not a defense treaty some of its provisions are termed as components of a defense treaty. For details see n. 4 Suresh R., pp. 75-87.
14. The Independent Commission on International Development Issues, North-South: A Programme for survival, Cambridge, 1980 p. 9.
15. The Independent Commission on Disarmament and Security Issues, Common Security: A Blueprint for Survival, 1982.
16. The Commission on Global Governance, Our Global Neighbourhood, Oxford University Press, New York, 1995, p. 306.
17. UNDP Report 1994, Oxford University Press, New York, 1994.
18. Ibid.
19. Ibid.
20. See for details India 2013, Publication Division, Govt. of India, 2013.
21. See the statement of Dr. Manmohan Singh the PM of India in the Maritime Military Strategy Document of Indian Navy. "diplomatic repositioning, economic resurgence and military firmness."
22. The Defence Minister of India stated that India's annual expenditure for Defence is Rupees 1,93,000 Crores see www.indiannavy.nic.in, 21 Aug 2013.

18

Indo-Iran Relationship: Challenges and Opportunities

S.N. Singh

The ties between India and Iran date to the Persian Empire of Cyrus the Great. The nations have long influenced each other in the fields of culture, art, architecture, and language, especially during the 1526-1757, when the Mughals ruled India. India and Iran also shared a border until 1947. For many centuries, Persian remains the language of Indian judiciary. The first Persian newspaper was carried out not by any Iranian but Raja Ram Mohan Roy, an enlightened Indian social reformer of 19th century. However after independence India's relation with Iran could not sustain the same warmth due to gamut of prevailing compulsions. Iran, along with Pakistan and Turkey joined American led capitalist block after Second World War and in contrast India adopted the dogma of non-alignment and tilted towards the Soviet Union led socialist block. Pakistan has remained a factor between India and Iran. But after the end of the cold war many changes have taken place at the bilateral as well multilateral level and these changes have brought India and Iran closer than ever despite the fact that there are gamut of divergences of interests between the countries.

But these divergences are manageable therefore despite many odds India and Iran relations have strengthened into the aftermath of the end of the cold war and cold war days' memories have become the materials of the archives.

Long back, Kautilya has opined that convergences of interests are the basic determinates of foreign policy. Growing India-Iran relationship has vindicated the fact. It has also rejected the traditional notion that religious similarity could be a common bond between co-religious countries. Saudi Arabia is the self proclaimed harbinger of the global Islam and Iran also considers herself fit for the same role but both never had cordial relations at least after the end of the cold war. So is the case of Pakistan and Iran. The fact remains that there are more divergences of interests between Saudi Arabia and Iran and some lesser status is between Iran and Pakistan. Major bone of contention between Saudi Arabia and Iran is treatment of Shia Muslims in Saudi Arabia and elsewhere. In the southern provinces of Saudi Arabia, which is the hub of oil production, Shias are in majority and additionally these areas are the important contributors of Saudi oil production. Beside that, Saudi Arabia has propelled Wahabism, which perpetuates intolerant Islam and even considers Shia's as non Muslim. Being the richest country of the Muslim world, Saudi's have propagated this ideology of Wahabism throughout the globe. Iran started protesting export of Wahabism by Saudi Arabia particularly after 1979 revolution and since then sustained its protest.

General Zia-ul-Haq had captured the power after throwing an elected government in July 1977 led by Zulifikar Ali Bhutto (a Shia) therefore through implementation of Nizam-A-Mustafa (Rule of the Prophet), Zia was consolidating his position. Shias of Pakistan took this initiative as the beginning of their marginalization within Pakistani society as had been mooted to Ahmadis by declaring them as non-Islamic. Since than more than 10,000 Shias have been killed in Pakistan in sectarian violence. Pakistan is a Sunni majority country but Shias are around 20-25 per cent of overall population and they are educated, wealthy and possess big land holdings. There are ample proofs that Pakistani state and particularly army is nurturing Sunni sectarian groups to eliminate the sphere of influence of Shias.

Iran considers herself as the custodian of global Shias. Saudi Arabia considers herself for the same role, but for the Sunnis. The bitter enmity between both is accelerating violence within the countries where both sects are dominant by all counts. For the last three decades Pakistan has been converted into the battleground between Saudi Arabia and Iran to propagate their interests. We are aware about the interrelationship between the Taliban and Al-Qaeda with Pakistan. The elimination of Osama Bin Laden in May 2011 at Abbotabad (Pakistan) has vindicated the fact that both have been working with tacit understanding. Interestingly the Taliban and Al-Qaeda both are claiming themselves as the harbinger of global Islamic Ummah but they are killing Shias in Pakistan. Taliban ruled over Afghanistan from 1996 to 2001. During this period, they killed Shias in thousands and tried their level best to divide the ethnic and sectarian mosaic of Afghanistan. In Mazar-A-Sharif many officers of the Iranian consulates have been killed during the Taliban period and bring both Afghanistan and Iran at the brink of the war. Due to mediation of Prime Minister (Pakistan) Nawaz Sharif (1997-99) it was managed. Even at this juncture Shias are under serious threat of the Taliban and their sustainable elimination is going on both in Pakistan and Afghanistan and even elsewhere also. We are aware about the fact that Saudi Arabia and Pakistan are two important countries out of three, who gave recognition to

Taliban government as required under the provisions of the international law. The third one was UAE.

Since March 2011, violence in Syria is on between government and the opposition forces and according to the United Nations till June 2014 around 1,50,000 people have been killed. The Tehrik-A-Taliban Pakistan has declared in July 2013 that they have dispatched their fighters to wage Jihad against the government forces in Syria. One of the most important motivating factors behind this decision of the TTP is that the government of President Asad is Shia.

Saudi Arabia along with their supporters is with opposition forces and Iran along with China and Russia is supporting President Asad government.

Afghanistan is a matter of utmost concern both for India and Iran. During the Taliban period India and Iran along with Russia extended their all round support to Northern Alliance. By 2014, NATO forces are withdrawing from Afghanistan. Since last ten years Karzai regime, an elected one is ruling in the country and tried to build the strength of Afghan National Army (ANA) but there are apprehensions that after the NATO withdrawal the ANA would not be able to properly contain Taliban. In this prevailing situation, Taliban may take over and given its previous governance record, it could be detrimental for the national interests of both India and Iran. In this situation they must forge a strong alliance to protect and promote their national interests in Afghanistan. Needless to say that Pakistan will not like this to happen therefore India and Iran must formulate a combined strategy to cope with this situation. Saudi Arabia, traditional arch rival of Iran will also support Pakistani position to export its narrow version of Islam as it had done during the previous Taliban regime. Needless to say that the Taliban is the harbinger of the conservative version of Islam in Afghanistan.

Iran is traditionally a peaceful country. Iran established a national army only recently, under the Pahalavis. The country has no martial tradition unlike its western neighbor Turkey. After Iraq war, Tehran has avoided direct military conflict ever since, and its military expenditure is slight high compared to that of a smaller Gulf countries.[1] India also never initiated any war but has only responded till date. In case of India and Iran there are less divergences and more convergences of interests therefore they must cooperate. The changing security architecture of South and South West Asia has also pushed both countries at the same platform. There are many critical areas where both countries national interests are converging. Drug trafficking and terrorism is a major concern for both countries. Since last three decades more than 5,000 Iranian border guards have been killed while containing drug traffickers. Iran share large border with Afghanistan and Pakistan therefore drug traffickers find Iran a route convenient to export drugs to Europe. There are strong inter linkage between drug trafficking and terror network and India and Iran is the worst affected form this menace. Pakistan and Afghanistan are the dens of drug trafficking and terror network. For preventing this situation to spill over to India and Iran, it is must that they should do some concerted groundwork much before end of 2014 to prevent this possibility.

Since independence Pakistan remains a mortal enemy of India. Iran extended its all round support to Pakistan during 1965 war. In 1979, the monarchy of Iran was thrown out by an Islamic revolution led by Ayatuallah Khomeini. He is considered as one of the leading Islamic ideologue along with Maulana Maududi of Pakistan and Md. Qutub of Egypt. Iran has been supportive to the rights to self determination of Kashmir Muslims.

Cold War has changed many things within the system of international relations. Iran-India relationships have grown manifolds due to many compulsions brought by the end of the cold war. Many interests started to converge and as Kautilya has lamented that it is the real cementing force of foreign policy. Three Indian Prime Ministers have visited Iran since the end of the cold war. In 1993, Prime Minister, Narasimha Rao visited Tehran and opened a new vistas of deepening relationship. In 2001, Prime Minister, Atal Behari Vajpayee visited Tehran. This visit was unique because it had started cooperation in many areas which was unexplored previously. Cooperation in Central Asia, energy related cooperation, military cooperation, cooperation in Afghanistan had also started along with strategic security. Iranian leaders had reciprocated these top visits. Many other dignitaries' visits were also made by both the sides. In 2003, Iranian president visited India and became Chief Guest for the Republic Day, a rare respect only reserved for the closest Indian friends. In August 2012, Prime Minister, Dr. Manmohan Singh visited Iran to participate in 16th Summit of the NAM. During this visit many rounds of negotiations were held with high voltage delegations. It was agreed that along with Afghanistan India and Iran must work together on the areas of common benefits.

In April 2013, Foreign Minister, Salman Khursheed, visited Tehran and it was agreed that Chah Bahar port facility will be expanded. India and Iran has already connected Central Asia through this port while making Delaram-Jarnej road in western Afghanistan. It has also reduced Afghanistan's dependence over Karachi port for trade and other necessities. During this visit many bilateral agreements were inked ranging from energy supply to defense cooperation. India by all available calculations will become third energy consumer by 2020. Iran has enormous energy reserves therefore relationship took a natural way of deepening. India has more than double Muslim population of Iran and one forth among them are Shias. They are peaceful, remain far away from any anti state activities and are contributing enormously in national developmental process.

The United States and India has been in good relationship since last one decade. The atomic agreement called 123 treaties of 2008 and gamut of deepening efforts of relations is the testimony. This is a hurdle in deepening Indo-Iran relations. Particularly nuclear issue has widened the gap between Iran and the western world. This issue was discussed during Prime Minister, Dr. Manmohan Singh's Tehran visit in August 2012. Iran is the chairman of the NAM for next three years. Dr. Singh visited Tehran despite huge protest by U.S. led block. Tension still prevails between Iran and western countries over the nuclear issue despite truce made by President Obama and President Roohani after their telephonic conversation in the last leg of 2013. In the backdrop of this tension, Dr. Singh's visit was path breaking. Many bilateral treaties were inked during the visit. This visit gave new phillip to Iran and negated the notion that it has been isolated at the international level.

Afghanistan remains the top agenda between India and Iran because of convergences of interests. Iran never supported Taliban and forged Northern Alliance along with Russia and India. During its five years [1996-2001] of rule, the Taliban killed thousand of Shias in Afghanistan. Being the only Shia majority country of the globe and immediate neighbor of Afghanistan, it was a great worrying point for Iran. Because Pakistan was among only three countries of the globe which recognized the Taliban according to the international law as the legitimate ruler of Afghanistan and became illegitimate father of the Taliban, Iran started to make distance from Pakistan. Here it is of utmost important to mention that in post-cold war scenario the clash for the supremacy over Islamic world is prevailing between Iran and the Saudi Arabia. In recent decades, Iran was compelled to understand that Saudi Arabia is getting closer to Pakistan therefore it has set a new tone for its relationship with Pakistan.

As Kautilya has said that enemy's enemy is friend therefore trust deficit between Iran and Pakistan has widened due to many prevailing factors and that has pushed India to cooperate with Iran on variety of issues. Iran has cooperated with several other regional countries, notably India and Russia, to gain influence in any post-American Afghanistan. During the Afghan civil war in the post-Soviet period, the three countries constituted the bloc that supported the Northern Alliance in opposition to the Pakistani and Saudi-supported Taliban forces.

Strategic Imperatives for the Development of Chahbahar for India and Iran

In order to address its need to secure energy routes, and to contain the growing Chinese influence in the Arabian Sea, Persian Gulf, and the Indian Ocean, India brought Iran into an economic and strategic alliance. India spent huge amount on the Iranian Port of Chahbahar. Iran was already working on Chahbahar port in Sistan-Baluchistan, which will be easily accessible for Indian imports and exports through road and rail links to Afghanistan and Central Asia. The development of Gwadar in Pakistan by China just 70 KM east to Chahbahar, resulted not only in open rivalry and competition between the two countries in the region, but also raised contention for the economic and natural resources of Central Asia.

Chahbahar's geo-strategic location plays an important role in connecting India to Afghanistan and Central Asia both militarily and economically. India sees Central Asia, Iran, and Afghanistan situated at the crossroads of overland trading routes as a potential consumer market for India products. Similarly, Iran wants to get India's cost effective source of high technology inputs.[2] India's ultimate objective is to by pass Pakistan, and also cooperate with Iran on a highway and rail system that leads from Chahbahar port into Afghanistan and Central Asia. Highway connecting Afghanistan and Central Asia has been in order since last many years. Rail system has to be restored.

On the other hand, active Chinese cooperation in the Port of Gwadar, since it is the only port, which can serve the best interests of both China and Pakistan in the region. The Port will, therefore, enable China to keep a strict watch on India's growing influence in the Indian Ocean, the Arabian Sea, and Persian Gulf. Hence, the possibility of any future economic and military collaboration between India and the US in the region can be effectively dealt with. Another geographical advantage of the port is that it will reduce the distance for energy imports from Persian Gulf to China. Gwadar also holds a geo-strategic significance for China because of its proximity with the sea lane between the West Asia and China. It is vital for oil trade. As a gateway to the Indian Ocean, Gwadar will provide Beijing with a listening base from where the Chinese may exert surveillance on hyper-strategic sea links. The military activities of the Indian and American navies in the region can also be closely watched. Gwadar port will also provide a strong base for Chinese ships and submarines. Since Gwadar Port can fulfill its political, security and commercial objectives vis-a-vis India, China has spent a huge amount on its construction. More significantly, Gwadar Port provides both Pakistan and China an opportunity to strengthen its security vis-a-vis India. The port will also help both China and Pakistan to promote trade with Gulf states possessing 63 per cent of world's oil reserves.[3]

China has acknowledged the strategic significance of Gwadar no less than that of the Karakoram Highway.[4] This will further strengthen the relations between China and Pakistan. China is also interested to turn Gwadar into an energy-transport hub by building an oil pipeline from Gwadar into Chinese Province of Xinjiang. The proposed pipeline will carry crude oil from Arab and African states. Gwadar's strategic advantage to China is due to its close proximity with the Strait of Hormuz. The presence of the US forces in the region poses not only a threat to Chinese navy but, also to its commercial interest. Gwadar provides China with a strong base where it can monitor US naval activity in the Persian Gulf, India in the Arabian Sea, and the future of Indo-US maritime cooperation in the Indian Ocean. China has already set up electronic posts at Gwadar for monitoring maritime traffic through the Strait of Hormuz and the Arabian Sea.

Chahbahar is a part of the Indian grand design to apparently develop transportation infrastructure. It is however viewed with suspicion to sabotage Pakistan's future strategy of expanding its influence in Central Asia and beyond. Chahbahar provides India easy access to Afghanistan and Central Asia through Indian Ocean. India's ultimate desire is to connect Chahbahar with Central Asian countries through roads and a network of railway system to bypass Pakistan, and to reduce the dependency of Central Asian countries on the Pakistani port of Gwadar. Iran is already enjoying close socio-cultural and economic relations with the Central Asian countries. Iran is working on several projects in Tajikistan including the Anzob tunnel, and constructed a bridge over the Amu Darya that connects Chahbahar with Khojent route. In addition, the construction of 218 km long Zaranj-Delaram highway that now links Afghanistan to the Iranian port of Chahbahar also connects Herat and Kabul via Mazar-e-Sharif in the north and Kandhar in the south-thereby providing easier access to Afghanistan and possibly even further, to Central Asia via Iran.[5] Because of the fact that Central Asian countries are land-locked, they depend on Iranian ports, especially, on Chahbahar for trade and commercial relations with the rest of the world. Moreover, Afghanistan is more friendly and close to India than Pakistan. In this regard, with its eco-strategic positioning in Iran, India gets a pivot opportunity to have an access to warm waters through this region. The creation of North-South Corridor is the best prospect for Iran to expand its transit corridor to India. The idea of North-South Corridor has multiple purposes and is, therefore, seen an opening to bypass East-West Silk Road Project.[6]

Thus, India gains more security, political, economic and strategic advantages depth from Iran, Afghanistan and Central Asia as compared to China. Iran is more stable than Pakistan. It has better relations with Afghanistan and the Central Asian states. Bordering Azerbaijan and Turkmenistan, Iran has a natural geographical advantage by providing access to Sea for the Central Asian States. However, intensifying competition between India and China in Arabian Sea and Central Asia, the growing US concerns about China's offensive capabilities, made the global and regional security environment more complex and sensitive.

If one has to be focused than it is crystal clear that stability of Afghanistan, containment of terrorism, containment of drug trafficking, integration of Central Asia with larger world, energy security, Pipeline issues and development of commerce and cooperation in energy sector are some of the important cementing points of bilateral relationship between India and Iran. Nuclear issue and western sanctions on Iran and Kashmir issues are irritant factor between both countries.

There are gamut of divergences between India and Iran. These divergences need to be narrowed down. The most important among them is nuclear issue. Due to 2008 nuclear treaty, India and United States have been converted into cold war era Estranged Allies to Engaged Allies in 21st century. This development vindicates Kautilya's theory that only convergences of interests are the decisive factor in the realm of international relations. Nuclear issue is one of the most mischievous bones of contention between both countries. Iran is of the opinion that it is building nuclear power for its peaceful use. India must tell the Iranian that they must adhere to the requirements of the international law. In the meanwhile India must convince United States that its own engagements with Iran are in the interests of US too. United States and Iran both needs to understand that new security architecture of the Middle East requires their cooperation. This cooperation will bring durable peace and cooperation in this most volatile part of the globe. India today is perhaps the only capable country to convince both of them on this issue. But instead of doing mediation with Iran and the United States, India has become party against Iran while voting on nuclear issue against Iran in the United Nations. Bringing closer to United States and Iran on the same page on diverse conflicting issues is in the larger national interests of India. It will also provide stability to the security of South West Asia. India must convey to the United States that Iran is mutually beneficial for us. India must also advice Iran that instead of confronting US, it must cooperate with the western world. Iran has been doing its efforts to free Shia places of worships in Iraq but it has yielded no adequate results till it was not vacated due to American military operation. After the elimination of Saddam Hussain in 2003, it was known that the one of the most pious places of Shia worship, Najaf and Karbala is in Iraq not in Iran. Iran must also shed its mindset of opposition for the sake of opposition to the United States. It is also equally applicable for the United States. India is better positioned today to mediate between two bitter rivals probably first time after the end of the Second World War.

Second most important irritant between India and Iran is Kashmir issue. Recently Iran has not extended its support to the cause but previously it had extended its support to the Kashmir independence from India. Iran must understand with its experience in Iraq war that religion could not be promoter of national interests. Since many decades Iran is competing with Saudi Arabia on gamut of issues. Both are harbingers of Islam then why are they fighting against each other. Only convergences of interests are cementing friendship in foreign policy. It is an open secret that in majority of the cases India and Iran's national interests converges therefore they must cooperate not only for the protection and promotion of their national interests but for peace and stability in the region.

Iran is yet another point of contention between India and the United States although recently India has been motivated by the US to participate in UN led western sanctions against Iran. Global concern over Iran's nuclear weapon development program, and the potential for subsequent proliferation, has driven US efforts to coordinate a coercive international sanctions regime. India, however, has a long historical and mutually beneficial relationship with Iran centered on trade, commerce, and cultural diffusion, with India currently importing significant amounts of oil from and facilitating the financing of Iranian energy companies—the targets of Western sanctions. India and Iran are two important oldest civilizations and have been connected to each other since millennia. There are many convergences and fewer divergences between both countries. Beside Afghanistan there are many other convergences between both.

After the end of the Cold War, there has been a shift in the global distribution of power; from the West to the East. While the political system globally can still be described as unipolar, Asia is characterized by multipolarity. The powers of

Asia compete for power, influence and resources. Amongst the great powers on the rise is India. India is the seventh largest country in the world, the second most populous and the world's largest democracy.[7] It has one of the world's most powerful economies and highly professional armed forces, which have made India emerge as an entity that can help shift the global balance of power. In this changing political environment, India has struggled to define itself and comprehend its power capabilities as well as the possibilities and limitations of that power. Indian global thinking is characterized by a lack of consensus on a strategic framework that can structure its foreign relations.[8] India could change the game while invoking real spirit of NAM in the context of Iran. Given the pressure of the United States on India in this context India must take the principle stand and advise both to settle their thorny issues through amicable means of settling disputes. Fortunately the situation is emerging to help India's ideal line on Iran.

Concluding Remarks

What complicates India's Iran policy is that the US and Iran are adversaries. The US wants to isolate Iran, partly through imposing strict sanctions on the country, and it wants other countries, including India, to follow suit. This forces India to engage in a delicate balancing act between on the one hand pursuing its regional goals and beneficial policies towards Iran, and on the other hand ensuring that the relationship with the US does not suffer. The question is how big a part the US has played in the Indian foreign policy decisions that concern Iran. After the took over of the President Roohani, Tehran has perhaps understood realist aspects of the delicacy of its diplomacy particularly towards the west led by the United States. The truce has been worked out. Still it is early to say that it will be certainly positive but the fact remains that after many decades window of opportunity has been visible. It is the compulsions also of both the parties to resolve the crisis. Things are going on positively at least till date and one must hope that a win - win situation will be achieved by both the parties. At the outset of 21st century the contours of international system has changed radically. It has provided an opportunity to both countries. India is growing rapidly and all set to become third global energy consumer country by 2020. The sustainable growth of India could not be ensured till the ensuring of energy security. Iran is one of the top five energy producing countries and not far away from India physically too therefore Iran could be an excellent energy security guarantor to India. In Central Asia too, Iran and India have gamut of convergences. They wish to connect Central Asia with the Iranian port of Chah Bahar. The road is ready and rail needs some more time to furnish. It will give a new Phillip not only to Central Asian Republics but India and Iran also. Iran is energy producer country and its growth depends on the sustainable sale of this precious resource. Due to growing requirements India is and will be an important buyer of Iranian energy products.

Eminent Indian security analyst, Raja Mohan has rightly stated in November 2013 "Any nuclear deal between Washington and Tehran will immediately bring down oil prices, relieve the current macroeconomic pressures on India, and improve Delhi's energy security calculus over the longer term. US-Iran rapprochement will help to strengthen Afghanistan against the Taliban and Pakistan and expand India's room for regional maneuver after 2014."[9] The interim deal between Washington and Tehran has already been concluded and it is the time when Indian diplomacy must act and bring Iran and United States on the same page to ensure peace and stability in Afghanistan in particular and Southwest Asia in general. Iran is an important player and it had been part and parcel of Indian efforts along with Russia and Central Asian Republics to contain Taliban and formation of the Northern Alliance during Taliban rule over Afghanistan (1996-2001). In the backdrop of NATO withdrawal by the end of 2014 this proximity is utmost required.

India will be extremely beneficial with its growing relationship with Iran and vice versa. Both countries have convergences of interests on many arenas be it economic, strategic etc therefore they must minimize the divergences. In August 2013, Vice President of India was present in the swearing in ceremony of new Iranian President, Roohani. It is an excellent goodwill gesture. Both countries are availing good relationships but to cope up with the emerging challenges they urgently need to enhance it. Deepening India-Iran bonhomie is therefore must for peace and stability in Southwest Asia. The basic requirement for a country is to provide human security for its people. Both India and Iran could do it with better way through deepening of their relationship. It is of utmost need of the hour for both the countries to promote their bilateral relationship. The newly elected Modi government is expected to forward its previous NDA government policies led by PM Vajpayee with timely modifications.

NOTES

1. Shahram Chubin, Is Iran a Military Threat?, *Survival,* Vol. 56, No. 2, April-May 2014, 66.
2. Juli A. MacDonald, Rethinking India and Pakistan's Regional Intend,' *The National Bureau of Asian Research Analysis,* 14(4), 2009, 5-26.
3. Rajeev Ranja Chaturvedy, Interpreting *China Grand Strategy at Gwadar,* Institute of Peace and Conflict Studies, 14 February, 2006.
4. *Dawn,* Karachi, July 4, 2006.
5. *Tehran Times (Tehran)* November 28, 2011.
6. Mohammad Arifeen, Chahbahar Port: Its Importance for India. *The News International* (Rawalpindi), November, 22, 2011.
7. Brzezinski, Zbigniew. (2012). *Strategic Vision.* New York: Basic Books, pp. 20, 162.
8. Pant, Harsh V. (2008). *Contemporary Debates in Indian Foreign and Security Policy: India Negotiates its Rise in the International System,* UK: Palgrave Macmillan, p. 1.
9. C. Raja Mohan, The Great Game Folio, *The Indian Express,* New Delhi, 20 November 2013.

19

Indo-Pak Relations: Post-NATO Withdrawal from Afghanistan

Sudhir Singh

India and Pakistan are neighbors and biggest countries of South Asia as well. Pakistan came into being in 1947 after the bifurcation of united India into two units called India and Pakistan. Like India Pakistan inherited a secular state ruled through a bureaucracy led by a civil service elite recruited and organized on merit. There is little evidence that Jinnah wanted to effect major changes on many of these fronts.[1] . Indian leadership established military, bureaucracy and political elite balance just after independence. But Muslim League, unlike the Congress in India, failed to make the transition from a national movement to a ruling party and soon fragmented as it failed to move quickly towards drafting a new constitution and lost both of its founding leaders, Jinnah and Liaquat Ali Khan. Muslim League used religion to garner political support and thus created third stake holders popularly known as Mullah. The troika of military, bureaucracy and the Mullah captured the canvass of national building process and instead of egalitarian state they formed a theocratic state which was detrimental for the minorities in particular and development in general. General Zia-ul-Haq (1977-88) military regime further consolidated the power of this troika over the destiny of the country. This makes the domestic political environment detrimental for good relations with India. Either military or civilian every ruler is known to use India card when ever they are in crisis.

In this backdrop since its inception both countries' relations have been turbulent. Both fought limited war over Kashmir just few months after the independence. Till date both have fought three full and one half wars and three among them were fought for Kashmir. We are aware about the fact that India has grown phenomenally since the end of the cold war at the international level. Three US Presidents have visited India from independence to 2000 but since then three US President have already visited India. Between January to June 2010 all five permanent United Nations Security Council member countries' Prime Minister/ Presidents have already visited India. India is gaining space at global table of governance also. India has been maintaining the growth rate of 7 per cent since last two decades. In contrast, 55,000 people have been killed in Pakistan between 2007 and 2014, i.e. after the assassination of former Prime Minster, Benazir Bhutto in December 2007. Its economy has remained stagnant. One thing is extremely important that since 2000 the United States has started to maintain cordial relation simultaneously with India and Pakistan while maintaining neutrality on Kashmir. It is in contrast with the cold war era when the United States was inclined towards Pakistan and even after the end of the cold war but before 2000, Rabin Raphel, US Deputy Secretary of State (first President Clinton regime, 1992-96) gave controversial statement about Kashmir which had dented Indo-US relations.

The post-Pokhran (1998) situation has raked up Indian status at the global level. Boosted with sustainable economic development, India has done good progress at the strategic level as well. The end of the cold war and post-9/11 situation has further brought Asia as a dominating continent at the global table of governance. Asia is biggest in terms of geography and continent at the global level. India has emerged as an important Asian power and without India Asian balance of power is not stable. These developments have however put India under stress. In the given prevailing circumstances India could not be obsessed with Pakistan. The forefathers of Indian national movement had given adequate mandate to Indian foreign policy formulators to promote the tenets of justice based international order. But as Kautilya has stated that without power, a country is not an important player in the shaping of the global order. Today in contemporary global system India has the capability as well as will power to implement the mandate of its founding forefathers.

In this prevailing situation how India could reformulate its Pakistan policy? There are many divergences and fewer convergences between both traditional rivals of South Asia. How diplomacy could be used to reduce divergences and increase convergences? This focal point will be widely debated within the ambit of this paper. It has been also discussed that how far Afghan tango will make imprint on this thorny bilateral relations in the backdrop of NATO withdrawal by the end of 2014. In April 2012, Pakistan's President, Asif Ali Zardari visited New Delhi although for pilgrimage of famous Sufi Dargah of Ajmer, Rajasthan but he had a lunch session with Indian Prime Minister, Dr. Manmohan Singh. All outstanding issues have been discussed and it was decided that irritants will not be preventing the normalization process. It was a maiden visit of any Pakistani President after a long time. It is an open secret that President Zardari was representing Pakistan People's Party (PPP), which were ruling the country since March 2008 till March

2013 and despite many odds completed its tenure of five years. It is the first democratic government of Pakistan to do so. It should also be noted that military still holds the key as far as Pakistan foreign policy is concerned but after the deadly avalanche in Siachen in April 2012 in which more than 130 Pakistan's military personnel had been killed, the Chief of Army Staff (Pakistan) General Pervez Asfaq Kayani had suggested that India and Pakistan must inked an agreement on Siachen because this terrain is inhospitable for human being and weather has killed more soldiers than the actual fighting. He also expressed his concern that more military activities in Siachen will erode environmental security and water flow in Pakistan could hurt the most.[2]

Former Prime Minister, Dr. Manmohan Singh had retreated many times that a strong Pakistan is in Indian interests. He has expressed his desire to strengthen the relationship despite many hazards. In May 2014 after the general election, BJP in the leadership of Narendra Modi has taken over. The BJP and PM Modi are known for their nationalist temper. Modi invited all SAARC head of the state to participate in his swearing in ceremony on May 26. Pakistani PM, Nawaz Sharif had also participated alongwith other SAARC leaders. Modi and Sharif had 50 minutes conversations and expressed their desire to resolve all outstanding issues.

For that purpose many arena could be taken up gradually. The trade could be the first. The present trade (2012) volume between both countries is $ 2.7 billion and the target is $ 10 billion by 2015. Both countries have expressed their desire to adopt China-India model of relationship. India and China have done the trade of $ 67 billion in the financial year of 2012-13 but till January 2014 despite 17 rounds of high voltage bi-lateral talks they could not resolve the most turbulent question of boundary. They have many other divergences but in spite of this they have agreed that they will cooperate in the arena of economy. Since last one year, trade related activities have increased many folds between both countries. Pakistani commerce Minister, Makhdoom Amin Fahim had visited India in January 2012 and Indian commerce Minister, Anand Sharma also visited Pakistan in later part of 2012. There was trade expo in Lahore and Delhi within first three months of 2012. Granting of Most Favored Nations (MFN) status to India by Pakistan is also under active consideration. Wagha border has been modernized which could facilitate many rounds of exiting trade. More places like Wagha could be started at Punjab, Rajasthan and Gujarat border as well. But again the million dollar question is what the basic irritants between India and Pakistan are and how they could reshape their policies which could be a push factor for their mutual benefits. These points will be debated within this paper.

One thing could be said about the recent trends of India-Pakistan relationship that it has been decided by both the governments that they will pursue in converging domains and in the meanwhile will try to resolve divergent issues including the core issue of Kashmir through bilateral dialogue. In January 2004 Islamabad SAARC Summit it was agreed upon by both countries and despite devastating Mumbai terror attacks in 2008 through many summits and other high voltage meetings it was agreed that dialogue is the only mechanism to resolve all outstanding issues.

After May 2013 general election the government has changed in Pakistan. Nawaz Sharif led PML-N has taken over and Sharif has become Prime Minister third time, which is a unique record given the fragile nature of democracy in Pakistan. During election process, ruling PML-N and other parties have refrained from their pet rhetoric of anti India propaganda. Sharif had promised during election campaign that if elected he will promote cordial relationships with India. His government has released over 350 fishermen in August 2013 as a goodwill gesture. In a interview given to *Telegraph* (London), Prime Minister, Nawaz Sharif asserted that his victory in May 2013 elections as a mandate for peace with India. He further added that "We have been in very unfortunate arm race with India ever since partition and I think we are a very unfortunate country from that point of view". He stressed that trust deficit should end and we both countries must settle all outstanding issues through dialogue and remain with peace and development.[3]

In this regard the first bilateral meeting between the Indian Foreign Minister, Salman Khurshid and Pakistan's Prime Minister's special adviser, Mr. Sartaj Aziz took place on the sidelines of the 20th ASEAN Regional Forum on 2nd July 2013. Pakistan is facing acute power crisis since last few years. The government of India is working on a deal to supply 5 million cubic meters of gas to Pakistan for five years initially. This would enable Pakistan to generate power to narrow down the gap between power generation and its demand. The GAIL has laid down a 110 KM pipeline from Jalnadhar in Punjab up to the Wagah border and it will be connected by the Pakistani side to Lahore.[4] If it will goes well, it will create more ambience of cooperation. Government of India keeps repeating that it is intended to engage Pakistan in a comprehensive way.

I must return on the focal issue now. What are the basic irritants between both traditional rivals of South Asia. It keeps on changing but more or less it has been sustainable. When Benazir Bhutto's PPP took over in 1988 and became first women Prime Minister of Pakistan, the Pakistani army took three assurances from her, where she agreed not to intervene. Kashmir, Afghanistan and Nuclear issue were the three arenas, which were agreed upon between Prime Minister, Benazir Bhutto and Chief of Army Staff, General Aslam Beig. More or less these three issues are still preventing cordiality based relation between nuclear armed two biggest nations of South Asia. Terror has remained as an instrument of Pakistan's foreign policy and since early 1980s Pakistan has extended support to cross border terror activities in India. First it was done in the case of Punjab and later on in Kashmir. However in later part, Pakistan has revised its policy and now extended support to terror activities in entire India. Strengthening of participatory democracy could be pivotal for cordial relations between both hostile neighbors. When Nawaz Sharif was trying to accelerate the peace process, five Indian soldiers were ambushed and killed at the LOC in August 2013. Who was accountable for both provocative incidents? It is the Pakistani army. Army and the terror network have been pursuing one thing as common agenda and that is anti-India megalomania. According to Stephen P. Cohen a leading American expert on Pakistan, "A full blown democracy, in which the armed forces come under firm civilian control, will be impossible until Pakistan's strategic environment alters in such a way that the army retreats from its role as guardian of the state."[5] Army will not allow any government either democratic or military to do so, because Pakistani army has only one agenda and that is sustaining its monopoly over the system.

Presently the situation in Pakistan is extremely grim and even President or Prime Minister is not safe. Daily wise dozens of people are massacred in gamut of violence be it sectarian violence, be it targeted killing, be it terror attacks or secessionist violence. In April 2014 one of the top TV journalist, Hamid Mir of the Zeo TV was attacked in Karachi and he has accused ISI for this attack. Since 2008 with the restoration of democracy according to 2014 reports of the Amnesty International 34 journalist have been killed.[6] Years before an eminent journalist, Saleem Sahzad was also assassinated by the security agencies because he was working on Osama Bin Laden and ISI linkage in the backdrop of his elimination in May 2011. Mir was attacked in April 2014 at Karachi while going to his office from the airport. Mir was hosting 'Capital Talk' show and discussed many issues which were not gone well with the army and the ISI. These incidents vindicates the fact that there is utmost monopoly of the army in the helm of affairs and India-Pakistan relations remains hostage of this power struggle because an anti India megalomania suits army to sustain its traditional holds. Afghanistan is still boiling and it suits also to the army.

It has proved the argument that if violence will occur in Afghanistan it will spill over to Pakistan. Due to porous border and ethnic and religious commonality, both countries are prone to the violence of another country. Sustainability of NATO forces in Afghanistan and survival of Afghanistan's own democratically elected government led by Hamid Karzai has created the question of survival for Pakistan. Since 1979, Afghan war, when entire capitalist world came into Afghanistan to contain expansion of communism, Pakistan had been nodal platform of this Afghan Jihad. Militants right from Morocco to Mindanao (the Philippines) have been recruited to establish the supremacy of the Ummah. In this process, terror factory originates and after elimination of the Taliban and Al-Qaeda from Afghanistan, it has shifted its bases into Pakistan.

By the end of 2014 the NATO led forces will be withdrawn from Afghanistan. Pakistan is mad for regaining its position which it was enjoying during Taliban rule (1996-2001). It is also an open secret that Pakistan had given recognition according to the tenets of the international law to the Taliban regime along with UAE and Saudi Arabia. In fact, Taliban is the illegitimate child of Pakistan. Since the Afghan war (1979), Pakistan has adopted terror as an instrument of its foreign policy. Afghanistan has been crucial for this project because of strategic purposes. After operation Enduring Freedom (Since October 2001 till today), the United States gave around $ 20 billion to Pakistan. Since the inception of Pakistan and before 2001 this equal number of amount was not given to Pakistan by the United States despite their much hyped cold war comradeship. Despite this huge largesse Pakistan provided patronage and safe heaven to Osama Bin Laden (OBL). In May 2011 he was killed at Abbottabad, just few hundred meters away from prestigious Kakul military academy, which is also not far away from Islamabad. The Pakistani commission which was constituted for its investigation has revealed many things which proved the allegation that OBL had a protection from the army. Abbottabad is a garrison town hosting Kakul Academy which is British era military academy. Just weeks before the killing of OBL,COAS General Pervez Asfaq Kayani was announcing from Kakul that we will eradicate terror but within 100 meters of the Academy, army protected safe heaven was hosting OBL. It has also been revealed by the commission that OBL was in Pakistan since his ouster from Afghanistan after operation Enduring Freedom (October 2001). The billion dollar question arises that how he was living in Pakistan without the knowledge of intelligence agencies? Pakistan was protecting OBL merely to protect terror networks and used him to blackmail the United States.

Needless to say that it has soured Pakistan-United States relations. Pakistan feels that Afghanistan must be under the umbrella of her dominance and it is necessary for the strategic depth of Pakistan over India. The NATO presence in Afghanistan since last thirteen years has immensely benefited India. It has reduced the terror export to India in particular and rest part of the world in general. Today if any terror act occurs in any corner of the globe the link goes to Pakistan and Afghanistan. It has also raised Afghanistan National Army (ANA) which is intended to defend the country after the withdrawal of the NATO forces. India has already contributed more than $ 2 billion into the reconstruction process of Afghanistan. India has also provided training to ANA personnel and slated to increase it due to prevailing circumstances in Afghanistan.

Afghanistan remains a hot spot not only between Pakistan and India or United States and Pakistan but entire globe has its genuine stakes in Afghanistan. It is producing over 80 per cent of the global production of drugs. Drug trafficking has threatened the societies across the globe in general but adjoining to Afghanistan it has leased unprecedented harm to the younger generation. In the backdrop of NATO withdrawal Pakistan will try its level best to maximize its interests. It will wish that its pet Taliban must be in helm of affairs in Afghanistan. One must remember that whenever there was stability in Afghanistan, it had thorny relations with Pakistan. Afghanistan was the first country to oppose Pakistani demand of plebiscite in Kashmir in the United Nations. The issue of Pakhtunistan is raking high with the stability in Afghanistan. Pakistan feel worried in this situation therefore intended to keep Afghanistan as its satellite country. India, Iran and

Russia oppose this possibility along with the like minded countries of the western world. On Afghan front India and Pakistan must cooperate because Pakistan has witnessed the unprecedented violence at the domestic level, which has tarnished the developmental process. Peace in Afghanistan will be push factor for the sustainable development of Pakistan. Sustainability of Hobessian State of Nature in Afghanistan will be detrimental for Pakistan first.

Another issue is Kashmir. Since last 67 years it has been the core issue between India and Pakistan. Pakistan is claiming over Kashmir due to its religious and geographical proximities. It is also an open secret that despite many wars and cross border terror in Kashmir, Pakistan has not been able to snatch Kashmir from India. Pakistan's economy is at the verge of collapse. This has helped to the Pakistani military to remain most important and powerful institutions of the country. In May 2014, COAS, Raheel Sharif has stated that the Kashmir is jaguar vein of Pakistan. Due to Kashmir the army will avail lion share within resource less Pakistani economy. This process has helped to militaries the country and thus negated fundamental freedom and human rights. Since March 2008, democracy prevails in Pakistan not merely because after the passage of 18th Constitutional Amendment, but also due to the fact that it is not feasible for the army to impose martial law. Prior to this amendment the provision is already in 1973 Bhutto Constitution. Article 6 of this constitution prohibits military takeover and provide case of treason in case of violation to this system. It is also very obvious that many times this breach has occurred and nothing has happened. The military is aware about the fact that due to international recession and American presence in Afghanistan, imposition of military rule is not feasible. Constitution is merely piece of paper for the Pakistani army. Kashmir, weak Afghanistan, Nuclearisation and terror all are pet projects of the army. These projects are the lifeline of the army because it provides a kind of legitimacy to the illegitimate aspirations of the Pakistani army. For the promotion and protection of these projects hostility against India is must therefore army never allowed any civilian government to encroach this space and perhaps will not allow in foreseeable future too.

Aysha Siddika, an eminent military expert of Pakistan has opined in her famous book '*Pakistan Military Inc*' that even if India will hand over Kashmir to Pakistan in a silver plate, there is hardly any guarantee that animosity between both rivals will end. For the time being both countries must sustain the dialogue process on Kashmir till its final resolution and in the meanwhile cooperate on the areas where there are hardly any divergences like trade and commerce.

According to Munir Akram, Pakistan's former Ambassador to the UN, "The hostility between Pakistan and India has deep historical and popular roots in both countries. Despite cultural, linguistic and ethnic affinities, the mutual hostility between Hindus and Muslims of the sub-continent is real and endemic. It was the *raison d'être* for the creation of Pakistan. The history of last fifty years has, if any thing, further intensified this hostility and given a structural expression in the relationship between the two states. The Kashmir dispute, in essence, is but one expression of this divide and hostility, (Bangladesh relations with India displays the same dynamic). Thus, even if outside issues like Kashmir, are resolved, and some semblance of civility restored between Pakistan and India, their relationship will remain competitive for the foreseeable future. Those who argue that, with goodwill and conflict resolution, peace and harmony can descend on the sub-continent are either ignorant or self-serving."[7]

Whenever the crisis of democracy/military regime started they are singing the saga of Kashmir to rescue themselves. The PPP led coalition (2008-2013) did the same thing. President Asif Ali Zardari pledged to work for good relations with India earlier but in September 2012 while addressing United Nations General Assembly he raised six decade old Kashmir saga. PM Nawaz Sharif is known to promote trade with India but he also sings the raga of Kashmir in March 2014 when he met US President, Barack Obama.[8]

The growing tentacles of terror have created an alarm well about the security of nuclear arsenals in Pakistan. In the aftermath of killing of OBL, many military installments were attached by the terror network. In June 2014, Karachi Jinnah International airport was attacked by suicide attacker's resulted into the death of 38 people. It was also revealed by the investigations that there was insider information to the attackers. If such a kind of loopholes will exist in the security protection system of the nuclear devices then it could be dangerous for the human existence. Being the most targeted neighbor, India will be first casualty. Another aspect is nuclear weapons first use. There must be consensus between both countries in this issue. India must engage Pakistan in dialogue process and these pertinent issues will be solved mutually. It is in the interests of both the countries.

Cross border terror in India has been supported by Pakistan. Pakistan has understood the reality that even after 3-1/2 war they could not gain the desired results therefore they have adopted the tactics of thousands cuts propelled first by Z.A.Bhutto. In 1980s it was started from Punjab, later on Kashmir and now spread all over India. Due to presence of the NATO forces in Afghanistan, terror network has shifted to Pakistan and created havoc within the country. This network has killed former Prime Minister, Benazir Bhutto, Former Governor of Punjab, Salman Tasser and gamut of high profile people. The prevalence of terror violence has reduced in India but there is a possibility that it could increase sharply after the withdrawal of the NATO forces in 2014. First of all India must gear up its security preparedness, must stop politics in terror related incidents and must deal it with an iron hand. A better and time bound judicial system is also necessary. Beside that it should advise Pakistan that it has lost thousands of lives in terror related violence therefore they must stop supporting terror networks. Till date the master mind of Mumbai attack, Hafiz Saeed is enjoying full freedom and spreading hatred against India. Dawood Ibrahim is also rooming in Pakistan. Pakistan must understand that sustainability of its support to the terror groups has been proved detrimental for the stability of the country. Comprehensive dialogue is on after 2009 Sharam-AL-Seikh (Egypt) Summit between both Prime

Ministers. In August 2012 Prime Minister Dr. Manmohan Singh met President Asif Ali Zardari at Tehran during 16th NAM Summit. During September 2013 UN summit in New York both Prime Ministers met. It needs to be sustained.

There may be terror incidents in future to derail the process. Pakistani army will never like cordial relations with India. It could hamper its monopoly over the system which it have been availing since independence. According to Wilke Boris "The people in charge—-bureaucrat's on the one side, army officer on the other—were at great pains in protecting and dominating the state field against adversaries from in and outside the official borders. Internally, they had to confine their effort to some 'core' state ; secular and most essential rules inside narrowly drawn boundaries, they had to prepare for war, since Pakistan's territorial status (if we include—as we must—following official ideology-Jammu & Kashmir) was not clearly determined. More importantly, external and internal matters were mixed right from the start, giving the army a key state building role."[9]

This is the reality but since we cannot remove neighbors therefore we have to make our region at least a place to live with peace and harmony. But we needs to be alert and must promote gamut of people to people interactions to promote comprehensive dialogue process.

Economic cooperation on India-China module could be emulated by India and Pakistan also. India has already extended MFN status to Pakistan long back in 1995 but despite WTO requirements, Pakistan has not reciprocated it till date. By 2015 India and Pakistan bilateral trade projected to reach $ 10 billion but it has the capability to cross $ 20 if proper will power will be applied. Prime Minister, Nawaz Sharif persuaded Prime Minister, A.B. Vajpayee for Lahore Bus Trip (1999) culminated into Lahore Declaration which was another consensual declaration by both countries after Shimla (1972) that they will resolve their bilateral problem on bilateral level. The process was derailed by the Pakistani army by Kargil incursion. Now after 14 years, Nawaz Sharif has become Prime Minister. He has also promised for better ties with India. Let's hope that he will implement his promises. One has to understand the limitations of the electoral mandate in Pakistani context.

Prime Minister, Nawaz Sharif was removed by the army 14 years before in 1999 and the same army is extremely powerful even today. It has been said about Pakistani army that it is not within the state as usual but state is within the army. Many analysts have given their opinion that ouster of Sharif in 1999 was due to hostile relations with COAS, Pervez Mushrraf but the fact remains that Pakistani army act like one united institution. Any action of this nature of the army is only taken when there is consensus among top corps commanders. The focal truth of the story is that Pakistani army could not tolerate good India-Pakistan relations because it could be detrimental for the sustainability of their dominance over system. Army is all powerful in Pakistan. In the words of former army chief, General Jehangir Karamat, " Whenever there is a breakdown in ...stability, as has happened frequently in Pakistan, the military translate its potential into the will to dominate, and we have military intervention flowed by military rule."[10] Since independence out of 67 years of history, Pakistani army has ruled 32 years and even when it is not ruling it is shaping the policies related to core issues of foreign policy like Kashmir, Afghanistan, United States, China and Nuclear etc. when civilian regime is ruling over Pakistan our empirical experience vindicates that more anti Indian megalomania prevails in the Pakistani system in comparison with the periods directly ruled by the army. The civilian regimes have no role to play in these matters.

Due to lopsided budgetary system where army is bound to utilize maximum national budget for its affairs a civilian government is bound to fail simply because it has no money on its disposal to meet with the aspirations of the common masses. It is happening in Pakistan since independence and even after the passage of CoD and famous 18th amendment of the constitution, army remains most powerful within Pakistani system. Many efforts were made to implement real notion of good governance. Given the fractured nature of politics, the growing power of the vested interests, and the greatly diminished ability of the civilian bureaucracy to function, these efforts, commendable as they are, may well be a case of too little too late, for they do not address the problem at its foundations. Pakistan needs a state strong enough to stand above primordial and religious pressures and deliver on promises or order and progress.[11]

We have to keep in mind that US led coalition forces is going to withdraw from Afghanistan by the end of 2014 and by all counts, Taliban will be the key player. We are aware about the intense relations between the Taliban and the Pakistani army. Since 1989 unrest in Kashmir, Pakistani army has used terror as an instrument of their foreign policy. Just after Soviet army withdrawal from Afghanistan, bloodbath started in Kashmir. In the upcoming situation it has to divert terror network focus on Kashmir if they will make good space in Afghanistan. Pakistan has remained committed being the part of the international coalition for global war against terror. But gamuts of reports have appeared which proves that including Haqqani Pakistan has maintained tacit understanding with the number of terror groups. Pakistan was repeatedly saying that Osama Ben Laden is not there but finally he was killed just near 100 meter from the prestigious Kakul military academy at Abbottabad. Till date Pakistan has not taken any concrete steps to bring perpetuators of Mumbai carnage to justice. Pakistan has been anxious about Indian presence in Afghanistan despite the fact that India remains the 5th largest contributor into the reconstruction process. Pakistan's ISI has been instrumental for terror attacks on Indian assets in Afghanistan and post June 2014 elections, Afghanistan will achieve relative stabilization, ISI may replicate the violent modules against India in Afghanistan again. In the meanwhile including Hafiz Saeed, Mullah Omar and Maulana Azhar, many icons of global terror is rooming in Pakistan.

These non state actors are hell bent to radicalize bilateral relations between both rivals merely because it converges with their core interests. Mumbai (2008) was executed by the LET for this purpose.[12] They are trying to provoke incidents which could trigger extensive violence. It is vindicating from January 2013 beheading of two soldiers at the LOC and August 2013 killing of 5 Indian soldiers at the LOC. It may occur again.

Pakistani army is now trying to create anarchy in Kashmir and thus through provoking India, its game plan is to push composite dialogue between both countries in the dustbin. Democracy is ruling the roost in Pakistan since March 2008. It has created an embarrassing situation for the army therefore army has to show that it is the only cementing force of the country. The trust deficit between the Pakistani military and the democratic government has increased in last few years and army may try to capture power. For the compliance of that purpose, violence in Kashmir and thorny relations with India is the essential requirements.

We need to be alert to safeguard our national interests in the given situation. We have to keep high arrangements to meet with any urgent situation. But I will argue that at the same time, India should not derail dialogue process. Simply because through this response we will be serving the wishes of the Pakistani army and the terror network.

Pakistan has a long border with India which could have reached to all geographical arenas of Pakistan. India is also an emerging global market. In reciprocal way Pakistan is also crucial for ensuring energy security to India. India is presently 5th global consumer of energy and slated to be on 3rd by 2020. Diversification of energy supply is must for energy security. Pakistan could be pivotal for this purpose because of its geo strategic position. Pakistan could take the benefits and must garner the benefits provided under the framework of SAARC. Economic theory emphasizes the gains from trade. Sino-Indian module is an excellent example that despite thorny relations on strategic front they are cooperating on economic front and making an ambience to resolve outstanding issues. Sino-Japan, Sino-United States and Sino-ASEAN relations could also be invoked in this context. PPP government led by Asif Ali Zardari (2008-2013) did ground work for emulation of India-China model but it did not work because Pakistani army did not allow due to mainly Afghan problem. Indian growing presence in the infrastructure building activities in Afghanistan has been viewed by Pakistan detrimental to their strategic interests of strategic depth. It has not only blocked India-Pakistan economic relations but Afghanistan-India, India-Iran and India-Central Asia as well. Various gas pipeline projects like IPI, TAPI etc have become victims of this power struggle. According to an expert " while India and Pakistan fight each other for the expansion of their prospective influence in Central Asia, other states gain actual economic and political power in the region. More precisely; 'Thus, to consider the problem of lack of adequate transport corridors between Central and South Asia...will depend entirely on the fact whether these corridors reach India or not."[13] This process has been slowed down also due to non-reciprocal attitude of Pakistan on the isses of MFN and relevant trade issues. The positive aspect is that there is an influential section in Pakistan who is willing to expand economic relations with India. Again the billion dollor question remains unanswered that all powerful army will allow the civilian government to do this?

Concluding Observations

Since its inception, Pakistan has perceived India as their immortal enemy. But since 2001 till 2013, Pakistan has witnessed killings of thousand of innocent citizens. This has triggered a smaller debate in Pakistan that its western border is more dangerous than its eastern border for national security. According to BBC, defence analyst Talat Masood "Pakistan army for the first time has admitted that the real threat is emanating internally and along the western borders and not from India, which was previously considered as number one enemy of the state.[14]

Through emulating China-India model, Pakistan could earn the financial leverage to eradiate its fundamental problems. But again all powerful army has prevented it to realize. There is a fear in Pakistan that due to huge in size India will be the ultimate beneficiary. But question remains that Pakistan has already accorded MFN status to China, which is superior economy than India. Pakistan can learn some lessons from this experience. It is an era of globalization and despite rhetoric it is clear that every country has to cooperate with another to sustain their developmental process. Pakistan could not ensure sustainable development without ensuring peace with India. As nuclear power both countries are aware about the consequences of conflict. As pointed out by E. Sridharan "Explicit nuclearization with a demonstrated missile capability has assured Pakistan's security in a way that reduces the sensitivity to relative gains in the military sphere... Pakistan is more secure vis-à-vis a possible Indian military threat than ever before... Therefore, it has less to fear and much to gain from greater economic engagement with India."[15]

It is also true with lesser sense for India. It is well perceived by the Modi led BJP government. The fact remains that despite its hawkish posture, the BJP government has the capacity to deal with Pakistan properly. PM Modi gave this message to Nawaz Sharif during summit meeting in May 2014 at New Delhi. Nawaz has also reciprocated but the question remains unanswered that how long army will allow him to sustain the process. But Modi government must sustain its engagement policies with Pakistan. India has emerged as an Asian power and aspiring for global power. India must shed its elder brother mentality within South Asia and must prove that it is a responsible and peace loving country. Through this process India can not only sustain its developmental process but also convince the global community that despite all odds it is also abided by reconciliation and international norms in South Asia. This particular scenario will strengthen Indian space on global table of governance. Modi government has set the tone while calling all SAARC leaders in his swearing ceremony.

At this juncture the nature of international politics is shaky and for taking the benefits of this situation it is must for India to decentralize its focal attentions towards all directions of the globe. Still despite all-round diplomatic presence there are certain arenas where our presence needs to be upgraded.

France and Germany fought many bitter wars and both World War's even they fought from different poles. But they have learnt a good lesson from their bitter experience. The youth of France and Germany have played a vital role to bridge the gaps between the two countries. Both countries exchanged six million youth, who got education in each other's country. The Elysee Treaty of 1963 brought the two rivals closer for progress and prosperity. Both are cooperating in a massive way under the framework of the EU. India and Pakistan share not only common border but common fate as well therefore they must forget the past and cooperate with emulating France-Germany model.

Pakistan must understand Indian security needs in the context of Chinese growing military might. Instead of making efforts to come parallel to India in terms of military might, Pakistan must focus of its socio-economic development. Establishing peace with Pakistan will be a push factor in this direction of achieving bigger goals of Indian foreign policy as narrated by Kautilaya.

NOTES

1. Iqbal, Rana Saleem, (ed), *The Quaid on Civil Servants; Speeches and Statements, October 1947 to August 1948,* National Documental Centre, Islamabad, 2007.
2. *Dawn,* Karachi, 18 April, 2013.
3. Blame Game between India, Pak has to stop, *The Indian Express,* New Delhi, August 24, 2013.
4. Punjabi, Raiz, India-Pakistan Bilatreal Relations; Opportunities and Challenges, *Journal of Pecae Studies,* Vol. 20, Issue 2, April-June 2013, p. 1.
5. Cohen, Stephen, *The Idea of Pakistan,* Oxford University Press, New Delhi, 2006, p. 278.
6. Pakistani Journalist under Siege, Amnesty International, *Dawn,* Karachi, 30 April 2014.
7. Munir Akram, Reversing Strategic Shrinkage in Maleeha Lodhi (eds) *Pakistan; Beyond the 'Crisis State',* Columbia University Press, New York, 2011, pp. 287-288.
8. *Dawn,* Karachi, 29 March 2014.
9. Boris, Wilke, 'State Formation and the Military in Pakistan; Reflections on the Armed Forces, their State and some of their Competitors, *Working Paper,* No. 2, Research Unit of Wars, Armament and Development, University of Hamburg, 2001, p. 26.
10. Nawaz, Shuja, *Crossed Swords, Its Army, and the Wars Within,* Oxford University Press, Oxford, 2008, pp. xxvii-xxviii.
11. Niaz, Ilhan, Identities and The State in Pakistan; A Study of Mentality, *Asian Affairs,* Vol. XLHI, No 111, November 2012, p. 469.
12. Burke, Jason, Pakistan Intelligence Services Aided Mumbai Terror Attacks, *The Guardian,* London, 18 October 2010.
13. Rudenko, Yelena I (2013) 'Problem on the way to closer interaction between Central and South Asia' ' in Rashpal Malhotra, Sucha Singh Gill and Neetu Gaur (Eds), *Perspectives on bilateral and regional cooperation*; South and Central Asia, pp. 425,427, Chandigarh, CRRID.
14. *Dawn,* Karachi, 9 January, 2013.
15. Sridharan E, 'Improving Indo-Pakistan relations; International Relations Theory, Nuclear Deterrence and possibilities for economic cooperation, *Contemporary South Asia,* Vol. 14, No. 3, September 2005, p. 322.

20

Indian Diaspora in the United States: A Bridge Between Two Democracies

S. Manivasakan

Introduction

Diaspora comes from the Greek word "Dia"—through and "Sperio"—to scatter.[1] Hence the term literally means scattering or dispersion. The term Diaspora can be used to describe people's migration or a section of it outside the boundary of their homeland. There is a clear distinction between mere migrations, because while migration is about the sheer numbers diaspora and their impact created in the particular region.

The concept diaspora includes connotation of violence, catastrophe, alienation, loss exile and return,[2] but it is to be noted that the concepts are not static. The World History of Diaspora can be traced back to the expulsion of the Jewish from their homeland. There is extensive literature available on the diaspora of the Greeks, the Chinese, the Africans and the Americans, but over last decade there has been more research and work on the Indian Diaspora worldwide. An individual can be termed as a diaspora only if he/she fulfills at least one if the following criteria:[3]

(a) Family tradition of the origin country, eclipsed by the social, political and cultural tradition of the host nation.
(b) An acute awareness of the origin, but don't go much further than sympathetic curiosity about them. However, a personal identity that is affected by awareness.

(c) A perpetuation of significant features of the cultural and tradition of the home land.

(d) Regular communication with kin in the homeland.

(e) Influence the host to pursue policies that are favorable to the homeland.

Post-independence, overseas Indians have served as a bridge of friendship and cooperation between India and their adopted homes abroad. Regardless of whether they are successful professionals, traders and entrepreneurs, or second generation Indians, comfortably reconciling their two identities, or workers toiling hard to build a future for their families, they are at all times a most effective window for the world to India's heritage and its progress.[4]

The Indian Diaspora is estimated to be second largest in the world and has a diversified global presence. The Diaspora, estimated at over 25 million, is spread across more than 200 countries with a high concentration in regions such as the Middle East, the United States of America, Malaysia and South Africa.[5]

Spread of Indian Diaspora

The Indian Diaspora has not only increased in numbers but has been gaining universal recognition for the unique contributions to its host countries, be it skilled and semi-skilled work force in the Gulf region or technocrats and educated professionals of Indian origin. Members of the Indian Diaspora do play a significant role in mobilizing political support for in their country of residence on issues of vital concerns to India.[6]

Indian Diaspora (Region-wise)

S.No.	*Country*	*Percentage*
1.	Southeast Asia	31%
2.	Gulf	19%
3.	US	10%
4.	UK	7%
5.	Latin America & Caribbean	7%
6.	South Africa	6%
7.	Mauritius & Reunion	6%
8.	Canada	5%
9.	Asia-Pacific	4%
10.	Other Europe	4%
11.	East Africa	1%
12.	Israel	0.03%
13.	Central Asia & Maldives	0.01%

Source: Global distribution of the Indian Diaspora (NRIs and PIOs) by world regions.
ICWA, Report of the High Level Committee on the Indian Diaspora, New Delhi: Indian Council of World Affairs, 2001.

The Table presents the regional distribution of an approximately 20 million-strong stock of the Indian diaspora at the close of the twentieth century. It is common knowledge that the earlier migrants who formed the basis of an Indian diasporas were mainly 'cheap' manual workers who left India in large numbers to meet the enormous demand for indentured labour that arose in the plantations, mainly in the Southeast Asia and the Pacific, immediately after the British abolished slavery in 1834, leading to what is sometimes also called the 'brawn drain'. The 'brain drain' a quality exodus of the cream of India's highly skilled professionals comprising doctors, engineers, scientists, teachers, architects, entrepreneurs and more recently the Information Technology workers, as well as nurses, appeared a century-and-a-quarter later. From the post-mid-1960s, this brain drain has continued into the twenty-first century, flowing westward and contributing inter alia to the 10 per cent concentration of the Indian diaspora is now in the USA.

The History of Indian Migration to the US

From time immemorial, the Indians have migrated to different parts of the world for trade and religious purposes. The country has also established contacts with great civilizations such as the Mesopotamia. India was the chief producer of slaves in the 15th and 16th century, of which most of these slaves were migrated to Europe. It was during this period that the European expansion had started. The immigration of India may be examined in terms of three phases:

- The Ancient and the Medieval.
- The Colonial.
- The Post-Colonial Phase.

The institution of slavery was banned by the British in 1830 and as a result, they introduced two kinds of labour system. The "Indenture Labour"—largely focused on North India labours, while in South India it was the "Kangani System". Both the labour system had provided cheap labour to the far flung British colonies thereby establishing a diaspora population in many parts of the world. The Indian Diaspora does not include the migration of Indian people alone, but also their culture, religion, social norms, political thought, ethical supposition and artistic behaviour. The first Indian migration to the US can be dated 1790, a maritime worker from the Madras Presidency. Indians have worked very hard to maintain their identity in the host country.

The Punjab peasant in 1890, were the first pioneers to Washington and California working in the Lumber mills and agricultural field. The Sikhs were referred to as "Hindus", and were subjected to racial discrimination. The Indian community later sought to protection and security from their host country. Over the years the Indian community in the United States grew in size and started a weekly newspaper Ghadr, based out of San Francisco. The political party of the same name was also floated. The newspaper and the political party supported the independence movement, back in India and this was conceived to be a vehicle that expressed seditions ideas by the local authorities[7]. The Punjabi pioneers were followed by the Indian Students to the United States. In 1901, the first Indian Student arrived; a decade later hundreds of student came to the United States to seek higher education.

Since 1930's Indians have been migrating from South India, Vishakhapatnam, Coimbatore, Tanjore, South Arcot and Madras Presidency to many parts of the world. North India was the largest supplier of Indian labourers to the rest of the world. While the West India comprising of Bombay, Poona, Rathanagiri and Nagpur had very low migration. During the 19th century, the practice of indentured labour was introduced by the British. This resulted in the introduction of Indian labour in places like Fiji, Mauritius, Guyana, Trinidad, Surinam, Malaysia, South Africa, and Sri Lanka.

In 1917 the United States introduced the Immigration Act that barred the entry of all Asians. Naturalized citizenship was only granted to "whites". This as noted by the Supreme Court referred to people of European origin. The Alien Land Law of 1913, amended in 1920-21, denied land ownership and leasing by non-citizens. To circumvent this law the Indian community transferred their land holding to their associates. The net fall out of these two legislations was a drastic fall in the Indian population in the United States and in the case of the state of California alone, the community that was 10,000 strong in the year 1914, shrunken to 1,476 persons by 1940. This was despite the best efforts of the community to demonstrate their "Aryan origins".[8]

Migration after World War II

The Indian Welfare League and the India League of America had chosen a new path to obtain and support for the demands against the British. Between 1948 and 1965, around 7,000 Indian's immigrate to the United States. During same period 1,780 Indians who were residents of the United States were also granted American Citizenship. A quota of 20,000 immigrants was set for each country by the Immigration and Naturalization Act of 1965.The earlier nomenclature of "Hindus" for all Indians had long been abandoned, but their designation as "Indians" was scarcely more acceptable, since what are now known as "Native Americans" were also known as "Indians".

The Indian community was subjected to racism since they were perceived to be part of the "black" community. During the last two decades of the 19th century there were many religious leaders who visited US. From the beginning of the 20th century there were many intellectuals and many students who started migrating to the US and Canada. During the first war period many Indian returned to India either voluntarily or by deportation. Post the Second World War most migrants were professional men along with their families. The immigration act of 1965 was a landmark in Indian migration to the US. Indians gradually migrated in large numbers from the 1970'when the impact of this act actually dissipated and reached the people.

Hence the present day Indian Diaspora dates to the following: [9]

(a) The decedents of the migrants of the 18th and 19th century
(b) The descendants of the migrants after 1965—The Hart Celler
(c) Act was passed in 1965
(d) All the Persons of Indian Origin (PIO) staying in the US

The Census Bureau, in 1980's reclassified the Indian immigrants as "Asian Indians" since the unemployment rate was five times that of other Asian communities.[10] Indian immigration to the United States grew rapidly since the 1990's. Additionally, people with Indian ancestry have also immigrated to the United States from the Caribbean, East Africa, Canada, and the United Kingdom. In 2011, the Indian community in the United States as a whole, numbered 1.9 million making it the third largest immigrants group, only behind Mexico and China. Between 2007 and 2008, the number of Indian immigrants surpassed the number of Chinese and Hong Kong-born immigrants for the first time since 1960.[11]

Indian Diaspora is the migration of Indians in different phases to the United States. The major proportion of Indian Diasporas to the US dates back to the post-1960's during the 18th and the 19th century. In 2011, nearly 1.9 million Indian immigrants resided in the United States. Indian-born immigrants accounted for almost 5 per cent (1.86 million) of the country's 40.4 million immigrants. This population has grown to over 150 times its size since 1960, when there were more than 12,000 Indian immigrants, who represented less than 0.5 per cent of the total immigrant population of 9.7 million immigrants.

The overall growth of Indian's in America from 1990-2000 was 105.9 per cent, the largest growth on any Asian American community.[12] The Indian Americans represent almost 4.6 per cent of the total immigration population of the United States and constitute about 16.1 per cent of the Asian immigrants (see Table 1 and Figure 1).

Table 1: Indian-Born Share of All Asian Immigrants 1960-2011

Year	*All Immigrants*	*Immigrants from Asia*	*Number*	*Share of All Immigrants*	*Share of All Asian Immigrants*
1960	9,738,100	491,000	12,300	0.1	2.5
1970	9,619,300	824,900	51,000	0.5	6.2
1980	14,079,900	2,539,800	206,100	1.5	8.1
1990	19,767,300	4,979,000	450,400	2.3	9.0
2000	31,107,900	8,226,300	1,022,600	3.3	12.4
2010	39,955,700	11,283,600	1,780,300	4.5	15.8
2011	40,377,800	11,562,000	1,856,800	4.6	16.1

Source: US Census Bureau's 1960-2000 Decennial Censuses, 2010 and 2011 American Community Survey (ACS)

Figure 1: Number of Indian Born in the United States 1960-2012

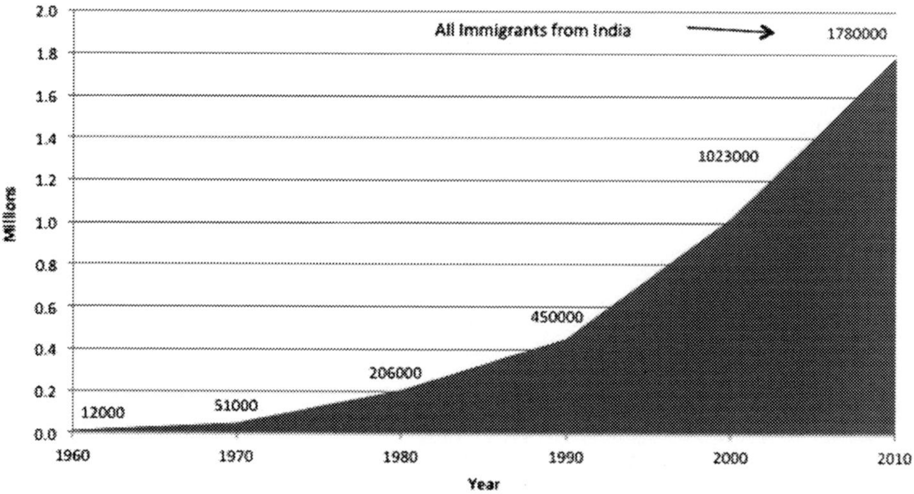

Source: US Census Bureau's 1960-2000 Decennial Censuses, 2010 ACS.

The India-born men aged 16 years and above are employed in various sectors in the US: 29 per cent of Indian male workforces are engaged in the IT sector; finance and management account for 21 per cent of the male workforce); and about 11 per cent in sales. The Indian working in the science and technology sector are more compared to the overall immigrant, specifically in information technology and other science and engineering occupations and in business and sales occupations. There are a very small proportion of Immigrant Indian in the field of construction, extraction, and transportation; service and personal care; and manufacturing, installation, and repair occupations. The Indian-born women prefer to take up professions as management or in the financial sector. (See Table 2)

Table 2. Occupations of Employed Workers in the Civilian Labour Force (Ages 16 to 64) by Gender and Origin, 2011

	Indian Born		*Foreign Born (Total)*	
	Male	*Female*	*Male*	*Female*
Number of persons ages 16 to 64 employed in the civilian labour force	717,000	415,000	12,892,000	9,580,000
Total (per cent)				
Management, business, finance	21.4	19.2	10.5	10.6
Information technology	29.3	15.5	4.6	2.2
Other sciences and engineering	9.5	5.3	3.8	2.0

	Indian Born		*Foreign Born (Total)*	
	Male	*Female*	*Male*	*Female*
Social services and legal	0.8	1.3	1.0	1.9
Education, training, media, and entertainment	4.3	8.0	3.6	7.2
Physicians/Surgeons/Dentists/Podiatrists	4.2	5.3	1.2	1.0
Registered nurses	0.4	5.3	0.5	3.7
Other healthcare practitioners	2.0	5.5	1.2	3.2
Healthcare support	0.4	2.1	0.8	5.9
Service and personal care	4.1	5.8	19.1	26.9
Sales	10.6	11.3	7.7	10.0
Administrative support	4.1	10.3	5.4	13.4
Farming, fishing, forestry	0.1	0.1	2.9	1.2
Construction, extraction, transportation	4.9	1.4	23.6	3.1
Manufacturing, installation, repair	3.8	3.8	14.2	7.6

Source: Authors' analysis of the US Census Bureau's 2011 ACS.

The Importance of Indian Diaspora

The Indian Diaspora is large, becoming more visible and powerful. However, we need to be cautious while talking about this in singularity, in truth there are many diaspora attached to the Indian Diaspora—The 'Dollar Diaspora' of the west and the 'Desperate Diaspora of the developing world. There are the Diasporas formed by 'Brawn Drain' and 'Brain Drain'.[13] There are also Diasporas within Diasporas whose relationship to India is marked by memories, these relationships are influenced by distances from India, initial reasons for leaving our country, points of convergence and divergence like food, fashion, clothes, art, music.

The origins of the Indian Diaspora can be traced back to the incorporation of India into the British Empire. Over two million Indian men have fought on behalf of the empire in numerous wars, including the Boer War and the two World Wars. In the post-World War II period, the dispersal of Indian labour and professionals has been a nearly world-wide phenomenon. Indians, and other South Asians, provided the labour that helped in the reconstruction of war-torn Europe, particularly the United Kingdom and the Netherlands, and in more recent years unskilled labour from South Asia has been the main force in the transformation of the physical landscape of much of the Middle East.

Meanwhile, in countries such as the United States, Canada, and Australia, Indians have made their presence visibly felt in as skilled professionals.[14] The Indian Diasporas has earned a reputation for itself in the world. They have won laurels for their competence in various fields including academia, science, politics, economics, sports, arts, culture and literature. India has contributed very little towards the shaping of their spirits or intellect. Nevertheless, their birth or ancestry alone is reason enough for us to revel in their glory and invent patriotic attributes to their success.[15]

The Indian Diaspora in the US is very clear from the various structures and festivals celebrated. The Mahatma Gandhi memorial in Washington, The Gandhi Marg in Devon with Indian Restaurants and stores that specialize in India groceries, The Swami Vivekananda memorial at greater Chicago, The Krishna Consciousness that is famous in many cities of the US are all various examples to show the impact of Indian Diaspora in the United States.[16]

Swami Vivekananda also referred to as "Cyclonic Monk of India" visited Chicago on July 1893, to deliver a religious speech, Parliament of Religion at the Harvard University. The Orator addressed the gathering as "Sisters and Brothers of America" and he received a standing ovation from a crowd of 7000.[17] The speech of swami Vivekananda evoked the spirit of Hinduism and a sense of universality in the country. Swami Vivekananda spent almost two years lecturing at different places in Eastern and Central parts of the United States, but mainly in Chicago, Detroit, Boston and New York. Swami Vivekananda was considered as the representation of Mother Religion of India. The visit of Swami Vivekananda was funded by Raja of Ramanathapuram (Ramnad) under whose Zamindari Katchchatheevu island formed a past,[18] which included the Katchchatheevu island, which was later given to Sri Lanka by then Prime Minister of India Indira Gandhi in the year 1974.

Mahatma Gandhi was an inspirational role to the Americans in the country with his non-violence movement and Satyagrah during the late 1940's. He was an instrument of peace and his policy of gaining independence was acknowledged by the Great King Martin Luther King in the fight between the black and the Whites, who argued that the Gandhian philosophy was "only the morally and practically sound method open to oppressed people in their struggle for freedom". During his visit to the US, the people were greatly impressed by his humbleness and simplicity.

In the 1960's CN Annadurai, the Tamil Nadu Chief Minister was the first non-American to receive the prestigious Chubb Fellowship at the Timothy Dwight College in the areas of public life and governance. A Yale University Press had described Anna as 'one of the few charismatic leaders in post-Nehruvian India. In many centuries of having been a literary and cultural reality, 'Tamil Nadu' became a political reality as well.[19] These three incidences helpful the American academician and people to get better understanding about Indian cultural values and society. Moreover it changed the outlook of Americans towards Indian diaspora and created a positive impact.

Achievements of the Indian Diaspora

The Indian Diaspora is the second largest and has a diversified global presence in the world.[20] The Americans have eaten at Indian restaurants, and have visited the religious shrines of India. Indians have influenced America in the field of Science and Technology, Bio Technology and Medicine. About 300,000 Indian works in technology firms in Silicon Valley. There about 600-700 Indian companies in Silicon Valley and the numbers are still increasing. Many American Universities have a number of Indian faculties specializing in the areas of research. The Indian group is one of the highest paid groups in the country.

Most Indian immigrants are well educated with a strong knowledge of the English language. The Indian-community when compared to other immigrant groups in the United States is well off in terms of social-economic parameters. Very few lives below the federal poverty. They are also more concentrated in the working ages than immigrants overall, and Indian-born men out number Indian-born women. As of the 2011, India's, second only to the Chinese in the terms of international students who peruse their higher education in the United States. The Indians have excelled in various fields in professional fields like medicine, engineering and IT. The Indian print media has also been recognized widely by establishing a web presence and is readily available to those interested in following the news of their own region.[21]

In terms of culture, the country has attracted many American citizens towards learning its art and culture such as Bharatanatyam, Yoga and Ayurveda. Indian immigrants are heavily concentrated in California and New Jersey. Compared to other immigrant groups, the Indian foreign born are much better educated — nearly three-quarters of Indian-born adults have a bachelor's degree or higher degrees.

Educational Attainment:2010
(25 and Older)

Ethnicity	*Bachelor's Degree or Higher*
Indian	71.1%
Chinese	52.4%
Filipino	48.1%
Total US Population	28.0%

Source: http://www.indolink.com/displayArticleS.php?id=111912084143

The U.S. Census Bureau uses the term Asian Indian to avoid confusion with the indigenous peoples of America commonly referred to as American Indians. In the Americas, historically, Indians had been most commonly referred to as the indigenous peoples. Qualifying terms such as American Indian and East Indian were and are frequently used to avoid ambiguity. While the East Indian remains in use, the term South Asian is often chosen instead. The U.S. government coined Native American to refer to the indigenous peoples of the United States, but the American Indian remains popular among the indigenous and general populations.

Asian Indian Organizations

The Indian community is the fastest growing Asian community in America. There are a number of Indian organizations formed on the basis of religion, profession, caste and on many other unique characteristics. The Indian diaspora had its shared sense of discrimination that every first generation immigrant group encounters. Since 1980s important professional organizations and groups has been reorganized by the community and the same has been formed by members of the diaspora. These organizations have lobbied for the welfare of the community and have their share of success and failures.

One of the lobbying efforts of the community that has hit a road block is in the city of Los Angeles. The Little India Chamber of Commerce, in the city has been unable to persuade the municipality to put up signs guiding visitors to "Little India", in localities that are predominantly dominated by the diaspora.

A school has been named after Mahatma Gandhi in Jersey City, and the same town recently renamed a portion of one of its streets after Dr. Babasaheb Ambedkar, Statues of Gandhi are to be found in numerous American cities, including New York City and Atlanta, and the US Congress has recently approved the construction, for which the expenses will be borne entirely by the Indian government and the Asian Indian community, of a memorial to Gandhi in the diplomatic enclave of the capital city not far from the hallowed grounds where are to be found the memorials to Lincoln, Roosevelt.[22] Some of the notable Indian Organizations are:

1. The American Association of Physicians from India (AAPI).
2. The Federation of Indian American Associations (FIA).
3. The National Federation of Indian American Association (NFIA).
4. The National Federation of Americans of Asian Indian Descent (NAAAID).

Influence of Indian Politics in Asian Indian Diaspora

The Indian community since 1990 had started growing in size and made a creditable influence among congressional members. Positively, there is an increase in the political mobilization among the Indians in America. Politically, Indians are likely to play an enhanced role in the future. They have begun realising the importance of it in getting recognition and in redressing their grievances. Being intellectually gifted and financially sound they can accomplish their political goals through concerted efforts. They would achieve this as a single ethnic group in the U.S. Above all; such a political achievement will be the foremost manifestation of their identity.[23]

The complexities of South Asian politics has made its presence felt in the United States. When a portion of Chicago's Devon Avenue was renamed after Gandhi, the Pakistani businesses lobbied successfully for the adjoining section to be named after Jinnah. A number of political groups and movements in India have benefited from the support that they receive form the diaspora. The case of Sikh separatist movements in Punjab have received financial aid and support from the Sikh organization in the United States is well documented. Within the Sikh community in the United States, there has been reports of clashes and violence between moderate Sikhs and their more militant and orthodox brethren.[24]

While Indian Muslims in the United States, whose numbers are in any case relatively small, have not been similarly vocal in stating their views on the insurrection taking place in Kashmir, the same can scarcely be said for those Hindus who continue to give their unstinting support to India. The Hindu community rejoiced the destruction of the disputed site in Ayodhya in 1992 and has supported the efforts of constructing a temple in place of the Mosque that was demolished. They have contributed generously to the activities of the Vishwa Hindu Parishad (VHP), a world-wide organization to promote the Hindu culture and the Bharatiya Janata Party (BJP), a political party that aims to serves Hindu interests in India. Indians also play a prominent role in the American politics, and have funded the both the Republicans and Democrats. Dilip Singh Saund, became the first Indian Congress men from California.

Asian Indians in Obama's Administration

For long the Indian community in the United States, seldom engaged itself in American political discourse. However, over the years the community has taken a keen interest in the domestic politics of the United States. The Indian-American Leadership Initiative Public Action Committee (IALIPAC) one of the major aims of the forum is to train young Indians in political activism,[25] goes to show political participation of the community. The India caucus of the Congress in 2004 had the largest membership of any such political group.

In recent years, the Indian community actively participates in politics. A number of Indian's have stood for American elections. The legacies of the Ghadr movement, the struggle for Indian independence and the civil rights movement has stir greater political awareness despite the political attitude of the community. Few prominent personalities in American public life include the likes of Raj Shah who was appointed by President Obama, as an administrator of USAID—the highest ranking Indian American in any administration. During Obama's first presidential year the administration estimated that the list of Indians could be counted easily at least a few dozens or even touch the half a century mark.

The US-India Political Action Committee (USINPAC) "provide a national platform for local leaders and organization and give them the ability to leverage their activities and co-ordinate their efforts with like-minded people in our community and country".[26] This is a far cry from the Regan Administration when the first Indian Americans were appointed to a senior administration post. In 1987, Regan appointed Joy Cherian for the Equal Employment Opportunities Commission. He later on went to become its Commissioner from 1990 to 1994 and 1990. Sambhu Banik, a psychologist, was appointed as the executive director of the President's Committee on Mental Retardation.

The Indian Americans have come a long way since then and have travelled quite a distance under the Obama Administration. Vinai Thummalapally, the US Ambassador to Belize, became the first Indian-American Ambassador in the history of US. The highly talented, Vikram Singh in his capacity as the Deputy Assistant Secretary of Defense for South and Southeast Asia (SSEA) is the highest ranking Indian American official in the Pentagon.[27] The anti-terrorism and anti-Wall Street crusade of Preet Bharara, the US Attorney, who is another Obama appointee, is well known. Subra Suresh in his capacity as The Director of the National Science Foundation, the agency is responsible for promoting science and engineering through the research programs, education projects, and funding overseas billions of dollars in scientific research.

Early this year Obama appointed Paula Gangopadhyay Member of the prestigious National Museum and Library Services Board. Sonny Ramaswamy, the Director of the National Institute of Food and Agriculture (NIFA). Romesh Wadhwani was appointed as the board of trustees of John F Kennedy Center for Performing Arts. Anuj C Desai, Associate Professor of Law at University of Wisconsin Law School, was appointed by Barrack Obama as member of the Foreign Claims Settlement Committee.[28] However; this is not a comprehensive list of Indian Americans serving in the Obama Administration.

Education and Politics

Indian diaspora spans the globe and stretches across all the oceans and continents. It is so widespread that the sun never sets on the Indian diaspora. The population of the Indian diaspora is estimated to be about twenty million. They live in different countries, speak different languages, and are engaged in different vocations. What gives them their common identity is their Indian origin, their consciousness of their cultural heritage, and their deep attachment to India.[29]

Even as vernacular politicians have replaced the earlier, more sophisticated generation, the number of American-educated Indian legislators across the political spectrum is growing.[30] Reflecting increased cooperation between American and Indian legislators,[31] a recent parliamentary delegation included Milind Deora, who earned a bachelor of science degree in business administration from Boston University; Sachin Pilot, who has an MBA from the University of Pennsylvania's Wharton School; B.J. Panada of the Biju Janata Dal, who majored in scientific and technical communication at Michigan Tech; and the Bharatiya Janata Party's Manvendra Singh, son of former external affairs minister Jaswant Singh, who is an alumnus of Hamp-shire College.[34] Other prominent Members of Parliament educated in the United States include Ajit Singh, son of former Prime Minister Charan Singh, who actually became a U.S. citizen, before renouncing his American citizenship in order to return to India and run for Parliament, and, of course, Palaniappan Chidambaram, finance minister in and again in the Congress led government in 2004, who earned a Harvard MBA.

Who have studied in the United States include Congress leader Rahul, who studied at Harvard, as did Dayanidhi Maran, the son of former Industries Minister Murasoli Maran of the Dravida Munnetra Kazhagam (DMK); Jyotridaya Scindia, who earned an MBA at Stanford; and Dushyant Singh, the son of Vasundhara Raje, who attended Boston University. While an education in the United States does not guarantee support for Washington's policies, it does impart an understanding and transmission of American values and culture. Students, as well as an increasing number of other immigrants to America, serve as a bridge between the two countries.

The new Indian elite that have emerged in both countries had a significant impact on Indo-American relations. Indian economists have routinely been educated abroad and worked at institutions such as the World Bank and International Monetary Fund. Many did not return home after completing their education. Economists trained in Britain tended to endorse the command economy model. Some of the initial dissenters from the state-dominated economic strategy were economists who tended to locate in the United States, such as Jagdish Bhagwati at Columbia University and T.N. Srinivasvan of Yale.

In recent years they have been reinforced by a new generation of American-educated scholars who have returned to India and assumed positions of influence, these include Arun Shourie, whose dissertation at Syracuse was critical of India's licensing regimes; Rakesh Mohan and Suman Bery, two Princeton-trained economists who both headed the National Council of Applied Economic Research (NCAER); S. Venkitararamanan, a champion of liberalization who did his doctoral work at Carnegie Mellon and was a member of the IAS; and Vijay Kelkar, who earned a PhD from Berkeley before becoming finance secretary.[33] Others have moved from India to the American financial sector. Jayant Sinha, son of former Finance and Foreign Minister Yashwant Sinha, joined Citibank in New York before moving to Bear Sterns, and then Lehman Brothers. It is believed his endorsement of free enterprise affected the evolution of his father's economic thinking.[34]

In March 2004, a thirty-five member "Friends of India" grouping was formed in the Senate in con-junction with the Indian Embassy, the first such country—focused grouping in the history of that body—a development made easier by the departure of legislators with a broader agenda than ethnic politics, such as the late Daniel Patrick Moynihan and John Glenn (D-OH). Co-chaired by John Cornyn (R-TX) and Hilary Rod-ham Clinton (D-NY), its membership includes Senate Majority Leader Bill Frist (R-TN), Senate Minority Leader Tom Daschle (D-SD), former Judiciary Committee Chair Orrin Hatch (R-UT), Finance

Committee Chair Charles Grassley (R-IA), Appropriations Chair Thad Cochran (R-MS), and other influential senators such as Joe Lieberman (D-CT) and Edward Kennedy (D-MA).[35]

The net result of these diverse developments as been a remarkable turnaround in congressional attitudes toward India and US-India ties.[36] "The transformation of congressional attitudes from indifference or deep-seated hostility to their current positive state on Capitol Hill confirms the necessity for a foreign country to have a strong domestic base of support in the American political system if it intends to be influential in Washington."[37]

It reinforces the administration's disposition for improved ties with India in light of the threat of global Islamic terrorism after September 11, 2001, and the prospect of the challenge presented by China. Yet, even though the image of Indians in the United States has been dramatically and positively transformed, the delicate nature of bilateral relations remains inhibited from achieving partnership by their residual pattern of ambiguity and mistrust. This wariness is evidenced by India's unhappiness with America's renewed commitment to Pakistan as a frontline state, and American anxiety over outsourcing service jobs to highly-educated, but lower-paid Indians. The irony of the evolution of the Indo-American relationship was not lost on Congressman Gary Ackerman. He bemoaned what he called "India bashing," arguing that "for years we told the Indians they were too aligned with the Soviet Union, they were too socialist; they had to free their economy and be entrepreneurial. Now that India is free and entrepreneurial, we are telling them you are coming on too strong."[38]

Diaspora Inter-Linkages

These diaspora relations encompasses wide gamut of activities: business networking, remittances, political lobbying, marriage relations, pilgrimages, tourism, socio-cultural exchange programmers etc. Inter-diaspora relations also encompass all such activities giving rise to trans-nationalism, which broadly refers to sustained ties of persons, networks and organizations across nation state borders rising out of international migration and refugee flows. Globalisation and new information technologies and communication have served as catalysts in promoting new transnational kinship groups, transnational social circuits and transnational communities. Indian diaspora is no exception in this regard. In which case a number of Indian sub-diasporas based on region and language, religion and even caste have been formed in different parts of the world.[39]

Transnational organizations such "Global Origin of People of Indian Origin" (GOPIO) have emerged to preserve and promote their identities and cultures uniting India and the Indian diaspora in a transnational context. Conceptually speaking, both diaspora-homeland and inter-diaspora linkages have been consolidated horizontally as well as vertically. In Asia-Pacific region both Pan-Indian and Sub-Ethnic diaspora are actively involved in various activities directed at India and among them. Thus, Indian diaspora in Malaysia, Singapore and Fiji are very active members of GOPIO which is non-partisan, non-sectarian and global organization engaged in promoting wellbeing of non-resident Indians and people of Indian origin, enhancing cooperation and communication between groups of Indians living in different countries and in furthering their cooperation with India.

Through GOPIO as well as independently Indian diaspora communities have been the active participants in Pravasi Bhartiya Divas (Overseas Indian Day) celebrated in India on 9th of January each year since 2003. Business networking apart, transnationalism among Indians can also be seen in religious and socio-cultural activities in Asia-Pacific region. A number of Indian religious sects, such as Swaminarayan, Chinmaya Mission, Ramakrishna Mission, Bramha Kumaris, International society for Krishna consciousness and etc. have extensive global networking. Similarly, Indian festivals like Deepawali, Holi, Dushehra, Shivaratri, Thai Poosam and etc. have acquired universal status among Indian diaspora. Indian diasporic writings too are part of not only local or regional literature but also of Indian and the world literatures.

Schemes for Indian Diaspora

The Indian Diaspora refers to those people who migrated from territories that now constitute a part of the Republic of India. The term can also refer to their descendants, Non-Resident Indian's (NRI's) and People of Indian Origin (PIO's). The Indian Diaspora is a representation of India, its people, regions, values and diverse and appealing range of culture.[40]

The Government of India for the Diaspora

Date	*Scheme*
1983	Mahatma Gandhi Parvasi Sureksha Yojana
2008	Pravasi Bhartiya Bina Yojana
2006	Overseas Citizenship of India card scheme
2012	Study India Program
2007	Scholarship Programmer for Diaspora Children
2003	Pravasi Bhartiya Divas

Source: Annual Report 2012-13, Ministry of Overseas Indian Affairs, New Delhi: Government of India, pp. 8-9.

The Indian diaspora is spread across regions of the Middle East, USA, Malaysia and South Africa. The concentration of the diaspora in eleven countries of the world numbers more than a million people each; while at the same time a smaller concentration of around hundred thousand ethnic Indians can be found in 22 other countries. As a result of this the diaspora has engaged in a process of the sharing ideas, culture, social and economic interests amongst themselves and with both the host country and also with India. Given the wide spread of the diaspora, Government of India has taken a keen interest in their welfare; though much needs to be done.

The Indian origin individuals have made a name for themselves in their chosen profession while at the same time they have retained their emotional, cultural and spiritual linkage with the country of their origin, India.[41]

Conclusion

The first Indian immigration to the country dates back to 1700's. India has achieved, arguably the world's most diverse and complex migration histories spread across 6 continents and 125 countries with an estimated number of 25-30 million people as its diaspora. According to the 2009 department of Home Land Security, India was ranked 2nd for illegal immigrants entering the US. The Indian diaspora is like a mass of variegated strands with differing forms and textures, its own needs and expectations.[42] The Indian culture plays a key role in influencing the country. The rise of Indian organization supports their native individuals politically and culturally.

There are also a series of challenges and threats the Indian Diaspora also face in the country. Hence it is the concern of the Indian government to deal with issues that protect its citizens in the host country. The India and America are democratic countries based on the principles of pluralism, tolerance and equal opportunity. At present, the numbers of Indians migrating to the United States are more associated on linguistic and religion bases. The Indian immigration to the US includes an active community of students and professionals to pursue their higher education and career. Over the years, the educational and the economic status has changed the position of the Indian community in the country. Hundreds of thousands of Indian have worked in the United States with H1-B visas. The Indian community has occupied a place of considerable prestige.

In recent years, India's have become a target of racial attacks. This is partly because of the declining economy and the concentration Indians into clusters that visibly put them apart of the rest of the society. The Indian women also called as "dot busters" have been victims of violence.[43] The Indo-American relation has transformed the historical bilateral relation between Washington and the New Delhi. The Diaspora has influenced the United State's skill, education size and income. The prosperous and successful Indian communities in Washington act as a vibrant bridge between the two countries and act as a catalyst of change.

India today has one of the world's largest and most successful "diaspora" populations, with approximately 25-30 million expatriate Indians and people of Indian origin living across a wide range of countries with an estimated combined wealth of US$ 1 trillion. Despite the success of the diaspora community the India has not been able to capitalize and mobilize the diaspora well enough to help in the countries in its long term development. Efforts that were taken by India to reconnect and benefit from the success of the diaspora have lost its steam in the past couple of years. There is an urgent need to outlive old pessimism and re-energize the India story and a greater interaction with the diaspora will definitely help India in terms of its economic, socio and political progress.

Indian origin people are well placed in the United States and many among them are directly part and parcel of the decision making process at the highest level. Given the fact that Asia-Pacific is going to be important in global politics and the United States has already declared its Asia Pivot Policy. Indian Diaspora due to its leverage in the US internal system is influencing its policies to include India as an important part of these policies. India is all set to gain in the larger canvass of the Asia-Pacific given the changing security architecture of the region. US could be facilitator of the process because its suits US interests as well. Of course our Diaspora in the United States have emerged as the bridge of the two largest global democracies but beside that Indian Diaspora has emerged as important pressure groups in this direction and through that way they are playing their rôle as undeclared Indian Ambassador.

NOTES

1. Members' reference service, Lok Sabha Secretariat, Parliament Library and Reference, Research, Documentation and Information Service (LARRDIS), http://www.indian diaspora.nic.in.
2. Lal, V. Brij (Ed.), (2007), *The Encyclopedia of the Indian Diaspora*, Oxford University Press, Singapore.
3. http://www.tie.org/.../indian-diaspora-past-present-and-future-ashok-raoý
4. http://www.pmindia.nic.in (official website of Prime Minister's Office)
5. "Engaging Diaspora: The Indian Growth Story," Eleventh Pravasi Bhartiya Divas (http:// www.ficci.com/publications(studies), p. 32, 2013.
6. http://www.tie.org/.../indian-diaspora-past-present-and-future-ashok-raoý
7. John Bale (1991), "The Brawn Drain: Foreign Student-athletes in American Universities." Available at www.books.google.co.in/books?Isbn0252017323
8. Shodhganga.inflibnet.ac.in/bitstream/10603/1827/9/09
9. http://www.sscnet.ucla.edu/southasia/Diaspora/diaspora.html.
10. http://newindianexpress.com/opinion/Undue-claims-over-diasporas-success/2013/10/21/ article1846180.ece.
11. Ibid.
12. Lal,V. Brij. (Ed.), (2007), *The Encyclopedia of the Indian Diaspora*, Oxford University Press, Singapore.
13. http://www.sscnet.ucla.edu/southasia/Diaspora/diaspora.html.
14. http://www.indolink.com/displayArticleS.php?id=111912084143 op.cit.
15. http://factfinder2.census.gov/faces/tableservices/jsf/pages/productview.xhtml?pid=DEC_10_ DP_DPDP1&prodType=table, *op. cit.*
16. Amit Gupta (2004), *The Indian Diaspora Political efforts in the US*, ORF, New Delhi.
17. http://www.vivekananda.gujarat.gov.in/international-visit.aspx
18. www.new.modernrationlist.com/Kachcha-theevu-right-of-tamilnadu.fisherman.
19. Kannan, R. (2010), *Anna: Life and Times of C.N. Annadurai* (Chapter 24, The Clorious end), UK: Penguin Publications.

20. 64.100.47.134/intranet/Indiandiaspora.pd
21. http://www.indolink.com/displayArticleS.php?id=111912084143 op.cit.
22. http://www.indiandiaspora.nic.in/diasporapdf/chapter28.pdfý
23. Ibid.
24. Ibid.
25. www.ricpac.org/uploads/India.Abroad.01.15.10.pdf
26. Vijay Prasad (2004)., "An Indian American Election," *Frontline*, Vol.21. Issue 14.July 3-16, 2004.
27. http://www.defense.gov/bios/biographydetail.aspx?biographyid=340
28. ignca.nic.in/id_aboutdiaspora.html
29. Sanjay Chaturvedi (2005), "Diaspora in India's Geopolitical Visions: Linkages, Categories, and Contestations," *Asian Affairs*, Vol. 32, No. 3 (Fall, 2005), pp. 141-168, http://www.jstor.org/stable/30172876.
30. See Arthur G. Rubinoff, "The Changing Nature of India's Parliament," Indian /Pakistani/ Canadian Reflections on the 50th Anniversary of India's Independence, (ed.) Reeta C. Tremblay *et al.* (Delhi: B.R. Publications, 1998), 251-65.
31. See Arthur G. Rubinoff, "Legislative Perceptions of Indo-American Relations," in India and the United States in a Changing World (ed.) Ashok Kapur *et al.*, 412-57. 64.
32. Aziz Haniffa, "Young MPs Wow Capitol Hill," *India Abroad*, September 17, 2004. 65.
33. Kapur, *Ideas and Economic Reforms in India*, 14-15.
34. *Ibid.*, 20.
35. Aziz Haniffa, "Friends of India Formed in US Senate," http://rediff.com/, March 31, 2004.
36. "Swaminomics: Foreign Policy Impact of Indian Americans," http://syndication.indiatimes.com/articleshow.cms?msid=20448957.
37. Arthur G. Rubinoff, "Changing Perceptions of India in the U.S. Congress," *Asian Affairs*, 28, no. 1 (Spring 2001): 57.
38. *India Abroad*, February 13, 2004.
39. Sahoo, Sadnand (2006), "Socio Cultural Linkages between Indian Diaspora," in Prakash C.Jain (Ed). Diaspora and Transnational Communities (Book-2). New Delhi: Indira Gandhi National Open University (Text Book).
40. Members 'reference service, Lok Sabha Secretariat, Parliament Library and Reference, Research, Documentation and Information Service (LARRDIS). Indiandiaspora.nic.in
41. Elizabeth Gutierrez (1996), *The "Dotbuster" Attacks: Hate crime against Asian Indians in Jersey City*, Philadelphia: Middle States Geographer, 1996, 30-38.
42. Lal, V. Brij. (Ed.), (2007), *The Encyclopedia of the Indian Diaspora*, Oxford University Press, Singapore.
43. Ibid., p.314.

21

Maritime Security in the Asia-Pacific and Role of Private Partnership: A Study of Indian Experience

S. Utham Kumar Jamadhagni and Ramakrishnan Ramani

Introduction

The Asia-Pacific Region

The Asia-Pacific region is situated on the Western board of the Pacific Ocean. By popularly accepted definition it encompasses much of East Asia, Southeast Asia, and Oceania.[1] Since the 1970s, the region has seen rapid growth of regional economies that are today making an impact on the global economy. This growth has lead to the creation of inter and extra-regional forums and bodies such as the Asia-Pacific Economic Cooperation, ASEAN, EAS, PIF, and SAARC.

The Region Consists of the following Countries and Island Territories

Australia, Brunei, Cambodia, Indonesia, Laos, Malaysia, Myanmar, Philippines, Singapore, Thailand, Vietnam, China, East Timor, Hong Kong, Japan, Macau, Mongolia, South Korea, Taiwan, Cook Islands, Federated States of Micronesia, Niue, Kiribati, Nauru, New Zealand, Samoa, Solomon Islands, Palau, Papua New Guinea, Marshall Islands, Vanuatu, Tonga, Tuvalu, Nepal, Bhutan, Bangladesh, India, Sri Lanka, Maldives, Pakistan, Afghanistan, Fiji, French Polynesia, Guam, New Caledonia, Northern Mariana Islands, North Korea, Tokelau, Wallis and Futuna.[2]

The Maritime Security Issues of the Asia-Pacific Region

The Asia-Pacific region is characterised by the vast expanse of bays, seas and the mighty Pacific Ocean. A large portion of the economies of the regional states thrive on the bounty of the seas, such as fishing, oil exploration, mining, and marine tourism. The geographical demarcations and boundaries of the water mass of APAC encompass territorial waters, Exclusive Economic Zones and International waters. These boundaries and demarcations are closely grouped and often overlap. Thus states tend to violate boundaries knowingly and unknowingly. This makes the maritime security environment of this region volatile.

The major maritime security issues of this region include:

- **Criminal activities** such as smuggling contraband, narcotics, small arms, human trafficking, art and antiques, banned wildlife products money laundering.
- **Terrorist activities** by mushrooming Islamic fundamentalist groups.
- **Aggressive aspirations** by regional countries such as China on maritime assets of other countries (for example, Spratly and Diaoyu/Senkaku Island issues).
- **Environmental security** issues such as increasing abuse of resources (fishing and minerals), tourism, pollution, etc.
- **Increasing maritime traffic** which leads to adverse impact on the environment and livelihood.

The current volatile situation in the South China Sea presents both a challenge in countering Chinese ambitions as well as an opportunity for other states to cooperate and for countries like India to be actively engaged with both sides.[3]

The Indian Scenario

India is a leading economy and an established regional military power in the Asia-Pacific region. India is a peninsular country with seas covering the landmass on all three sides. Its coastline stretches for over 7,517km (5,423km of peninsular India coastline and 2,094km of the Andaman, Nicobar, and Lakshadweep island groups).[4] For over two millennia India has conducted trade and commerce with countries as far as Rome and Persia.[5]

The country's maritime domain encompasses the territorial waters and the EEZ, which is about 2.172 million sq. km.[6] The waters are rich in natural resources—both living and non-living. The Bay of Bengal, Indian Ocean and the Arabian Sea is the source of livelihood for the lakhs of coastal communities stretching from West Bengal to Gujarat. Protecting this huge source of precious resources in the EEZ falls under the Indian Navy, Indian Coast Guard and the coastal police.

The Indian Navy's main mission is to protect India's maritime borders and to enhance the country's international relations through unilateral and multilateral activities such as joint exercises, port visits and humanitarian missions.

The Indian Coast Guard is the fourth branch of the armed force of India and is under the Ministry of Defence. Its mission is "to protect our ocean and offshore wealth including oil, fish and minerals; to assist mariners in distress and safeguard life and property at sea; to enforce maritime laws with respect to sea, shipping, poaching, smuggling and narcotics; to preserve marine environment and ecology and protect rare species; to collect scientific data and back-up the navy during war."[7]

Coastal Police forces come under the ambit of state governments. Thus all states from Gujarat on the western coast to West Bengal on the eastern end have coastal units of their respective police forces.

Till the 1980s, the armed forces of India were supported largely by the Public Sector highly controlled by the Central Government. Since the late 1990s, private organizations have also started contributing towards the nation's security preparedness at various levels—from small arms components to guidance chips of cruise and ballistic missiles. However, the Indian defence market is highly regulated. Private organizations, both Indian and foreign, that offer products and solutions to governments' coastal security forces need to not only understand the politico-economic scenario of India, but also the requirements of the Indian Government. The following sections explain the various drivers of the Indian maritime security market, in context of protection of India's territorial waters and the EEZ. It does not take into account the larger, more strategic, requirements of the Indian Navy and its war fighting requirements.

Outlook of the Indian Market

While, the Indian maritime security market is driven by multiple parameters and requirements, it is also restrained by policies, processes and budgetary constraints.

General Market Drivers

Increased threat perceptions: India's recent surge in criminal and terrorist activity on India's territorial waters, coupled with the exorbitant number of fatalities/casualties within the country's borders (such as in the aftermath of 26 November 2008 Mumbai attack), has led to an increase in threat perceptions. This is expected to lead to significant levels of spending on maritime security arrangements. This has consequently resulted in the Indian Coast Guard looking to expand its capabilities and become a deep water force in order to combat smuggling and terrorist attacks penetrating the coastline.

Privatisation of the Indian defence industry: Since 2001, the Indian government has been initiating the privatisation process of the Indian defence industry. This has created greater investment opportunities as there has been an increasing investment from private sector defence participants and the scope for joint ventures in the Indian maritime security market is greater due to the offset policy of the Indian Government.

Growth of the Indian economy: The Indian economy has been growing at an average rate of 8 per cent during the 11th Five Year Plan (2007-2012)[8] and this growth rate is expected to continue over the forecast period. This has created opportunity for the Indian government to increase investment in defence, especially maritime security. India's drive to create an increasingly sophisticated maritime security force is expected to create greater investment opportunities in this security category.

General Market Restraints

Budgetary Constraints: One of the most important obstacles to investment in the Indian security market, in general, is the absence of continuity in investment opportunities. Certain threat domains, such as airport and transportation security, present greater opportunities for investment. However, with growing maritime interests and greater knowledge about the boons of our maritime zone, stakeholders in national maritime security are showing increased interest over the recent past.

Security measures remain manpower intensive: The paramilitary forces still handle a majority of the security operations with regard to internal security in the country. The reliance on manpower is still quite heavy because of the prohibitive costs involved in procuring more sophisticated security measures. However, the seas present a different picture. Large, wide and open, the territorial waters and the larger EEZ cannot be effectively secured through increased manpower alone. Advanced surveillance technologies are imperative to secure national interests on the seas.

Varied investment opportunities across threat domains: With threat perceptions varying across domains, the levels of security-related spending across the threat domains are expected to vary considerably as well. For instance, while investment opportunities are bright in airport security and mass transit security compared to other domains.

Country Analysis

Coastline	7,517km (Peninsular India: 5,423 km—Island territories: 2,094 km)
Size of EEZ	2.172 million sq. km
GDP	\$2.13 trillion (2013) – Growth by 4.5% (2012-13)[9]
Military Expenditure (% of GDP)[10]	2.5
Size of Indian Coast Guard*	
Ships	93 of all classes; 156 under construction/order
Aircraft	38 fixed wing; 27 rotary
Public Debt (% of GDP)	51.8% (2013)[11]
Industries	Textiles, Chemicals, Food, Processing, Steel, Transportation, Equipment, Cement, Mining, Petroleum, Machinery, Software

* *Approximate figures.*

Political Analysis

India is the world's largest democracy. It has a secular constitution, framed in 1950, and guarantees justice, liberty and equality while aiming to promote fraternity among its citizens. According to the Election Commission of India, the electoral population of India is more than 814.5 million—the largest in the world.[12]

The fight against terrorism within India itself is not considered to be a political issue. All the major parties have pledged to do what they can to ameliorate the occurrence and effects of terrorism.

Large coalition governments complicate policy-making at the centre as regional parties pursue their own local agendas.

The competence of state government varies enormously across the eight maritime states and 5 union territories. This is expected to have an impact on the decision-making process for maritime security procurement, although the MHA is still expected to be the main fund-holder.

The recent general elections saw the National Democratic Alliance (NDA) lead by the Bharatiya Janata Party (BJP) forming the next government. The primary issues of this election were the bad state of the national economy, prise rise, infrastructure issues, increasing corruption at all levels including at the highest ministerial levels, statehood for Telengana, and personal capability of candidates. A change in guard at the centre will definitely mean a revisit of India's defence and security policies and if needed, a revision too. This will have a ripple effect on every related activity including research & development and procurement of military equipment.

Economic Analysis

The Indian economy, the eight largest in the world by nominal GDP and the third-largest by purchasing power parity (PPP).[13] According to Moody's, the Economic Growth Rate of India would be 5.5% in 2014-15.[14] However, the country's services-led boom has not yet had a significant effect in raising living standards of the poor, with more than a third of India's over one billion population still living on less than a dollar a day. It is unclear how much of a priority extensive maritime security spending will be relative to social spending to alleviate poverty.

A vast supply of relatively cheap, skilled labour has turned India's service industry into one of the world's largest. More than half of the population is under the age of 25. Booming exports of IT-enabled services, from call centres to software developers, continue to be a valuable source of foreign exchange. This supply of labour is expected to affect the level of manpower employed in security (in relation to technologies and systems) and the country's technological sophistication (which is expected to increase soon).

India has a skilled workforce, but its business environment is crippled by excessive government interference. Foreign investment remains restricted in many sectors with greater liberalisation opposed by the left of the Indian political spectrum.

Indian economy showed high growth rate averaging 9% from 2003 to 2007. The global financial crises starting in 2008 also affected India. Over ten years ago, Goldman Sachs prophesied that India's GDP (in current prices) would overtake France and Italy by 2020, Germany, UK and Russia by 2025 and Japan by 2035, making it the third largest economy of the world, behind the US and China. Economists view India as a rising economic global power and will play a decisive role in global economy.[15,16]

In 2012, Indian economy began a phase of anaemic growth slowing down to just 4.4%. This brought to the fore other economic problems that were besetting the country: a plunging Indian rupee, a persistent high current account deficit and slow industrial growth. The Indian economy was affected by the US Federal Reserve's decision to decrease quantitative easing. Consequently, foreign investors began rapidly pulling out money from the country. This brief trend is now reversing and the current account deficit is narrowing substantially.

Social Analysis

Despite the high levels of economic growth experienced by India over the past decade, a significant proportion of the country's population lives beneath the poverty line (i.e. less than US$ 2 a day).

India still has the world's largest number of poor people living in a single country. Of its nearly 1 billion inhabitants, an estimated 350-400 million are below the poverty line, with 75 per cent of them in the rural areas.

The main causes of poverty are illiteracy, a population growth rate by far exceeding the economic growth rate for the better part of the past 50 years, and protectionist policies pursued since 1947 to 1991 which prevented large amounts of foreign investment in the country. Each of these causes of poverty will have a different effect on overall security spending in India over the forecast period.

Poverty alleviation is expected to make better progress in the next 50 years than in the past. Increasing stress on education, reservation of seats in government jobs and the increasing empowerment of women and the economically weaker sections of society are also expected to contribute to the alleviation of poverty. As an increasing number of people enter the Indian social middle class, an increasing emphasis on technology-intensive security measures is expected.

Technological Analysis

India possesses one of the largest and most sophisticated defence industries in the developing world. Much of this technological sophistication has grown from political links with countries such as Russia, Germany the United States, France and Israel. In turn, this development of India's home-grown military production capabilities has overflowed into the type of electronics used for security applications.

India is expected to continue to use technology transfer agreements, license agreements and close political alliances to further increase its technological prowess. While the country's defence industry will still be partly restricted by the export regulations of foreign countries, India's burgeoning defence industry is most likely to affect the capabilities of its security industry as well.

The growth of the Indian software industry is expected to increase the level of sophistication of defence equipment production. This is expected to encourage greater partnerships with the Indian software industry.

Terrorism Analysis

India's vast coastline is very porous and an open gateway for intruders. This has been most aptly demonstrated by Ajmal Kasab and his group of terrorists who sailed into India by sea. Down south, Insurgent fighters of the banned Liberation Tigers of Tamil Eelam commuted to India and back with ease due to the open shores of southern Tamil Nadu. Threats from Bangladesh too can use this means to enter India anywhere from West Bengal to Tamil Nadu.

The threat from the seas is real and often goes undetected. Despite the ever vigilant work of the Indian Coast Guard and the presence of over 42 Coast Guard Stations, 5 Coast Guard Air Stations and 10 Coast Guard Air Enclaves,[17] the Coast Guard is still inadequate to secure the coasts, let alone promote India's interests.

Smuggling of contraband, gun running, drug exchange, illegal fishing on Indian waters and other such illegal activities will increase over the decades as terrorist groups, criminal gangs and international mafia become stronger and expand areas of operation.

Natural Disaster Analysis

In December 2004, over 10,000 people were killed and hundreds of thousands were rendered homeless in India when a tsunami triggered by the Indian Ocean earthquake near the Indonesian island of Sumatra hit the southern peninsular coast. The earthquake registered 9.0 in magnitude and was the biggest in four decades. The state of Tamil Nadu was the worst affected on the mainland, with a death toll of over 7,000.

Indian Maritime Security Market

Market Overview

The total security-related spending for maritime areas in India is expected to be approximately US$ 1 billion by the year 2016. The expansion of the Indian Coast Guard (ICG), coupled with the increase in budget, has significantly increase capital spending before 2012.

The presence of the Coast Guard along the country's coastline is expected to involve the installation of approximately another 20 Indian Coast Guard stations in the next 10 years, along with all the relevant systems, technologies and equipment. However, once the capital spending round is over, operational spending is expected to remain relatively stagnant while capital spending on security systems and equipment is expected to fall significantly after 2013.

Recent Market Developments

The Coast Guard is helping the various state police forces in setting up new marine police stations that will be equipped with latest surveillance equipments. The Indian Coast Guard is looking to procure early warning systems. In an interaction with the media in January 2011, Indian Coast Guard Director General Vice Admiral Anil Chopra had stated that the Coast Guard will triple its fleet size from the existing 100 vessels to 300 ships by 2020. Organizations such as Northrop Grumman and Embraer of Brazil have submitted proposals. However, a press release by the Indian Coast Guard puts a more conservative number - 200 surface platforms and 100 aircraft by 2018.[18] These numbers clearly indicate that the organization has planned a clear-cut strategy to make itself "a new, modern and far more capable Coast Guard."[19]

The total expected capital investment in comprehensive coastal security by 2013 is about $ 740 million. The funds are expected to be utilised to purchase medium altitude ship-borne UAVs, unmanned combat helicopters, medium range maritime reconnaissance aircraft, new advanced offshore patrol vessels (AOPVs), interceptor boats, advanced light helicopters and pollution control vessels.

The Coast Guard has installed identification transponders in all vessels plying the West Bengal coastline in order to detect illegal boats entering into Indian waters.

Funding levels for the Coast Guard for 2006-2007 was $ 3 million, but this is set to increase to $ 35 million in 2015-16.

Planned force levels by 2016-17 will include 173 small patrol craft, 113 aircraft, 18 Nishanth UAVs, additional aerostat and OTH radars, 60 helicopters, 35 Do-228 aircrafts for coastal surveillance, 11 medium range reconnaissance aircraft, 40 interceptor boats and 6 deep sea patrol vehicles.

Market Drivers and Restraints

Analysis of Market Drivers

Coast Guard Modernisation Programme: The biggest driver for this market is the Coast Guard Modernisation Programme. Ever since the Coast Guard was established as a separate arm of the armed forces in 1978, it has continued to grow in stature. With India's growing economic importance, the Coast Guard has become a significant part of the Indian Navy's modernisation programme. The navy is looking to expand its capability to become a blue water force. Therefore, a significant portion of that programme has been targeted to modernise the Indian Coast Guard. The latter is expected to acquire deep water capability as a result of the modernisation programme.

Scope for Long-term Investment: The Coast Guard is procuring a mix of platforms and surveillance equipment in order to make it a deep water force. There exists a well defined five-year plan for the Coast Guard and there are allocations available for security equipment. Therefore, the scope for long-term investment partnerships is very positive in the case of maritime security. There is expected to be a trend toward rising investment up to 2018 and then investment opportunities are expected to stabilise thereafter.

Joint Exercises with Coast Guards of Developed Countries: The Indian Navy and Indian Coast Guard constantly conduct joint naval exercises with the navies and Coast Guards of developed countries and neighbours. This gives a clear indication to the rising stature of the Indian Navy and is likely to have additional effects in the form of new investment opportunities and greater restructuring of procurement policy.

Increased Maritime Threats: The Coast Guard modernisation programme aims to mitigate coastal terrorist threats and threats posed by smugglers. This threat stems from India's growing economic strength and a greater amount of strategic emphasis being laid on internal security. India's large coastline on either coast makes it especially vulnerable to the threat of terrorist attacks. The role of the Coast Guard therefore assumes greater importance in this regard and therefore is likely to drive investment opportunities in maritime security.

Increased Budget for Navy: The Navy has seen a significant rise in its budget. Given the Navy's involvement with overall maritime security provision, this is likely to have a positive effect on the Coast Guard in terms of procurement.

Analysis of Market Restraints

Budget is Spread out: The Indian Coast Guard has laid out a budgetary plan until the year 2020. However, investment opportunities are not expected to be constant throughout the period. Furthermore, delays in implementation of projects and lengthy proposals period is expected to delay security procurement.

Critical Success Factors

Given the list of purchases that the Coast Guard is going to make by the year 2018 especially, cost will be the overarching deciding factor in the ultimate competitor analysis. Therefore, companies that will be able to provide cost-effective equipment will stand a better chance of penetrating the market.

Given that the Coast Guard is purchasing platforms as well as surveillance equipment, systems integrators firms will stand a greater chance of successfully penetrating the market. Bigger firms can look to local market participants to enter into private industry partnerships to provide surveillance equipment.

Cost: Cost is likely to prove to be the most critical factor when analysing investment opportunities in the Indian homeland security market. Despite the relatively high levels of funding that the relevant security authorities have made available, there is an identifiable trend of cost competition across almost all procurement decisions. Only in certain niche markets where indigenous companies have no industrial capabilities and where security capabilities are absolutely vital, cost is likely to become less of a factor.

Implementation Pipelines: Some threat domains have greater budgets, such as airport security and mass transportation security. Here, the critical success factor is to understand the implementation pipelines. In the mass transportation sector, for instance, metros are being expanded in Kolkata and Delhi, while there are plans in effect for Bangalore and a pipeline plan for other major cities. This indicates that investment opportunities are expected to rise and decline and that their patterns will vary as the investment pipeline varies.

Partnerships With Indian Companies: In order to expand the number of potential market opportunities, to fulfil any FDI regulation requirements and to negotiate the potentially difficult Indian homeland security market, a strategic partnership with an Indian company is expected to be a major critical success factor. Without a strategic partnership, foreign companies are not likely to succeed to any significant degree.

Stakeholder Analysis

The Indian Coast Guard falls under the Indian Ministry of Defence. The Indian defence ministry decides the procurement policies and acquisition mechanisms for each of the respective divisions of the armed forces. The Indian Coast Guard is the apex institution that handles maritime security on India's Exclusive Economic Zone. The Ministry of Defence is the authority that handles all Coast Guard regulatory mechanisms and all aspects dealing with procurement and budgetary issues of the institution. The Indian Coast Guard is subdivided into five Coast Guard Regions:

Western Region (W) Mumbai
Eastern Region (E) Chennai
North East Region (NE) Kolkata
Andaman & Nicobar Region (A&N) Port Blair
North West Region (NW) Gandhi Nagar

These are further divided into Coast Guard Stations, Coast Guard Air Stations and Air Enclaves.

The Indian Coast Guard (ICG) is responsible for the policing of over two million square kilometres of India's EEZ. The area under its control includes nearly 1,200 islands and a coastline of 7,517 kilometres. The Indian Coast Guard is part of the Indian Armed Forces and is not a part of the Indian Paramilitary Forces.

Competitive Environment

The Indian defence industry is dominated by large public sector undertakings (PSUs). The Indian economy was a closed economy up to the early 1990s and even after the liberalisation of other sectors in 1991, the defence industry did not liberalise until 2001. The government allowed foreign direct investment and greater participation from the private sector, and the leading private sector companies began to emerge in the Indian defence / security industry.

The Indian maritime security market falls under the joint purview of the Ministry of Home Affairs (MHA) and the Ministry of Defence (MOD). While the borders and coastline is under the purview of the MHA, security of the EEZ and the country's larger security interests are the subjects of the MOD. The MHA and MOD set the procurement-related regulatory environment and handle the budgets for the various security forces under their control. The foreign direct investment (FDI) regulations that apply to the Indian defence industry also apply to the maritime security market as well, indicating that partnerships with indigenous companies are expected to become de facto standard method for foreign companies to do business.

The commoditised security products (such as surveillance systems) are provided by a large number of indigenous companies that offer an extensive range of configurations. However, more sophisticated and costly technologies (such as screening technologies and radar systems) are generally provided by foreign companies in partnership with Indian companies. And although system integration capabilities have generally been provided by western companies, the increasing sophistication of Indian industry is expected to result in Indian companies gaining an increasing competitive advantage over western-based companies.

The large-scale security systems have been provided by countries that have experience in this arena, i.e. the United States, Europe and Russia. However, Israeli companies (such as Elbit) have achieved a significant level of market penetration in the meantime, while Russian security products have generally fallen out of favour.

The prospects for systems integrators are quite high, given the number of platforms that the Indian Coast Guard is looking to purchase. Therefore, companies such as Embraer and Northrop Grumman would stand a greater chance to penetrate the maritime security market.

Another strategy that international firms could use is to form industry partnerships with Indian PSUs such as Hindustan Aeronautics Limited (HAL) and Bharat Electronics Limited (BEL). The prospects for long-term investment will be more assured.

Conclusions and Recommendations

Market Opportunities

The **Maritime Security** sector is expected to present significant demand for the following technology types:

- Surveillance technologies such as Unmanned Aerial Vehicles (UAVs) and maritime radar systems.
- Platforms such as sea vessels and aircraft that will constitute the basis for the aforementioned surveillance technologies.
- Integration capabilities will be in high demand.

Maritime Security offers major opportunities for investment, which will come in the form of demand for early warning systems, identification systems and transponders.

Recommendations

A common successful path to the Indian maritime security market is difficult to recommend. One has to look at individual market verticals to identify viable opportunities. In general, it can be said that potential suppliers of security systems in India need to adhere to certain conditions in order to succeed in this market. These conditions are:

- Become a 1st tier partner to an established Indian vendor/integrator.
- Subcontract with a local supplier with an established record, e.g. radar and other surveillance industry participant.
- A pre-existing track record in the Indian market to provide government references.
- Evolution, i.e. developing value-added capabilities in an established technology to distinguish it from other less advanced technology types.
- Revolution, i.e. development of a highly innovative product that can cover the security gaps in specific threat domains.

This can be extrapolated to the entire Asia-Pacific region where more diverse and competitive private players could help strengthen the security of the maritime region of individual countries as well as collectively.

NOTES

1. http://en.wikipedia.org/wiki/Asia-Pacific
2. Ibid.
3. China evacuates thousands of citizens from Vietnam after deadly attacks, CNN, May 18, 2014, http://edition.cnn.com/2014/05/18/world/asia/vietnam-china-tensions/ also Dr. Amit Singh's South China Sea Dispute and India, http://www.maritimeindia.org/article/south-china-sea-dispute-and-india.html
4. Kumar, V.S.; Pathak, K.C.; Pednekar, P.; Raju, N.S.N. (2006), "Coastal processes along the Indian coastline," *Current Science*, 91 (4): 530–536.
5. https://www.newworldencyclopedia.org/entry/Roman_trade_with_India
6. http://www.nio.org/index/option/com_newsdisplay/task/view/tid/4/sid/23/nid/35
7. http://www.indiancoastguard.nic.in/Indiancoastguard/mission/mission.html
8. http://articles.economictimes.indiatimes.com/2014-02-20/news/47527212_1_growth-rate-gdp-growth-negative-growth
9. http://www.livemint.com/Politics/burPSwwZ4JstNqkBGGWXCP/Economy-grows-45-in-fiscal-2013.html

10. http://en.wikipedia.org/wiki/List_of_countries_by_military_expenditures
11. https://www.cia.gov/library/publications/the-world-factbook/fields/2186.html
12. "Number of Registered Voters in India reaches 814.5 Mn in 2014". news.biharprabha.com. Indo-Asian News Service. Retrieved 23 February 2014.
13. http://www.imf.org/external/pubs/ft/weo/2013/01/weodata/weorept.aspx?pr.x=38&pr.y=13&sy=2 011&ey=2018&scsm=1&ssd=1&sort=country&ds=.&br=1&c=534&s=NGDP_RPCH %2CNGDPD%2CNGDPDPC%2CPPPGDP%2CPPPPC&grp=0&a=
14. http://news.biharprabha.com/2014/02/indian-economic-growth-rate-to-be-5-5-in-2014-15-moodys/
15. Wilson, Dominic; Purushothaman, Roopa (1 October 2003). "Dreaming with BRICs: The Path to 2050". Global economics paper No. 99. Goldman Sachs. Retrieved 2007-10-04.
16. http://www.un.org/en/development/desa/policy/wesp/wesp_archive/2010annex.pdf
17. "The Indian Coast Guard—"Committed to Serve-Making a Difference"", *Press Information Bureau*, Government of India, 31 January 2011.
18. http://indiancoastguard.nic.in/IndianCoastGuard/Press%20Release/Press%20Release%20%20on%20Coast%20Guard%20Day%202011.pdf
19. Ibid.

22

Emerging Powers in the Security Architecture of the Asia-Pacific Region: A Prognosis of India's Status

Tridib Chakraborti

If the 20th Century was the 'American Century', it is appropriate today to state the 21st Century as the 'Asian Century', with India an important actor in global politics. In April 2002, the Indian Prime Minister, Atal Behari Vajpayee in his 21st Singapore Lecture on "India's Perspectives on ASEAN and the Asia-Pacific Region" said: "India's belonging to the Asia-Pacific community was a geographical fact and a political reality, which did not require formal membership of any regional organization for its recognition or sustenance". India today, accurately, "seems to be a beautiful radiant bride, with many bridegrooms" prepared to bind the knot by deepening the areas of cooperation with it. Today, India has become an inseparable part of the South, Southeast and East Asian regions by consolidating its stature as a Summit-level partner of ASEAN in 2002, East Asia Summit partner in 2005, and the founder member of SAARC in 1985 respectively. Although India has not been able to become a member of APEC, a pivotal economic organization in the region, yet, given the present circumstances and international milieu of an interdependent world economic order, it may be contended that India's essentiality will be a part and parcel for others' economic momentum. In the 1990s, India was yearning to be a part of the international economic system. But that scenario has presently reversed in its entirety when other countries feel India's indispensability and consider it an indivisible component of the Asia-Pacific region by consolidating its stature as an emerging power in this region.

The concept of Asia-Pacific, as a regional identity is a term, which has been coined in the text of international relations in recent years. However, during the Cold War period, the regions Asia and Pacific never functioned in an amalgamated manner, on account of the then global politics. In fact, the identity of Asia and its significance in world politics was first painted by Jawaharlal Nehru at the Asian Relations Conference, on 24 March, 1947 at New Delhi. Likewise, the identity of Pacific as an entity was mainly coined by the United States, fused with the countries of South Pacific, Australia, New Zealand, Northeast, Southeast Asia etc, on account of deep-seated security and strategic reasons. As a result, the coining of this Asian and Pacific, as a combined identity lost its rhythm over the years, due to Great Power politics and involvement of some regional actors in the power game. However, this state of power relations in the Asian region re-generated its momentum since the abrupt fall of former Soviet Union and the emergence of a New Global Order, based on the processes of globalization and liberalization. This sudden withering away of the Soviet Union and the inevitable acceptance of globalization became a major challenge for most of the developing countries, including India. But slowly and steadily, since the last two decades, most of the developing countries are adjusting and thereby managing their economic survival in the ongoing process of globalization and day by day, gaining their economic strength. Among these developing countries in the Asian region, the rise of China, India, Singapore, South Korea etc and other fast-growing economies took economic interdependence to a new level. The overall effects of their performance due to rapid globalization prompted them to demand more effective global governance. This led to economic interdependence become a major feature of globalization. The growing economic vitality of the fast-developing countries of Asia, led the Pacific counties to evolve a new regional concept which is presently known as Asia-Pacific. Geographically speaking, this new emerging region includes all the littoral and island states of South Pacific, Australia, New Zealand, Northeast, Southeast and South Asia. In other words, the Asia-Pacific region has been defined somewhat narrowly to include the two Super Powers, the United States and the former Soviet Union (which demised in 1991), two regional Great Powers—China and Japan, few emerging economically strong sub-continental powers like South Korea, Singapore and India and other vibrant economies and smaller countries of the region. The major ground behind the magnitude of this region is the occurrence of some countries, which are emerging as economically vibrant ones in the current global politics, where more than one third of world's population lives and the strategic dimension owing to the importance of gas, energy and natural resource endowment. In this new map of Asia-Pacific, India along with China, obviously deserves a place on the radar screen of world politics—not just because of the size of its population, but also due to its socio-economic development process in the last two decades. It is a fact that after the end of the Second World War, India was driven by strong anti-colonialist impulses—opposed great-power politics and what was viewed as "superpower hegemony," calling instead for a multi-polar world. But since the end of the Cold War, India has become increasingly integrated into the emerging global order. It recognized that this order has created a peaceful external environment within which it can safely develop, and thereby see globalization as a positive and, to some extent, inevitable trend. In fact, India in the post-Cold War international environment, acquiescent to expansion of its bilateral ties with all the major powers concurrently, has thus followed a strategy of 'poly-alignment'—which means seeking to be a 'bridging power' between the sometimes competing poles of the United States, Russia, China, the European Union and others.[1]

As a result, India has abandoned its past calls for a complete refurbish of the global order and instead has come to participate in the process. This active participation has provided India a better space in the emerging global system and its status as a global power is not only recognized but increasingly institutionalized, even as geopolitical shifts create both opportunities and challenges. India experienced rapid development through chipping in the existing multilateral order—now its development approach makes it dependent on this order. With critical interests in almost every major multilateral regime and vital stakes in several emerging ones, India has no alternative but to persuade the evolving multilateral order if it is to sustain its own national interests. How India could become an important factor in the politico-strategic connotation of this region remains a serious subject matter of study. Moreover, how has India's multilateralism policy in the post-Cold War years, gradually made her status more dynamic in the Asia-Pacific power configuration? Besides this, if India seeks to affect the multilateral order, how will it do so? In the past, it had little option but to be contented with rule taking—sticking to accessible international norms and institutions. Will it now focus on rule flouting—challenging the present order primarily for effectiveness and seek larger space in existing global institutions? Or will it focus on rule shaping—contributing in partnership with others to silhouette emerging means and systems, particularly in playing an effective role in various regional and multilateral institutions on a number of issues? Whether India's role in multilateralism is a full measure or substantial in the context of Asia-Pacific? It is in this backdrop that this article proposes to discuss India's emerging status and role in multilateralism especially with reference to regional organizations in the Asia-Pacific region (mainly towards ASEAN, SAARC, Sub-regional Organizations and United Nations etc).

India in the Cold War Years

In the Cold War years, India's involvements in regional and global politics were based on three parameters. **First,** India, under the leadership of Jawaharlal Nehru followed a mixed economic policy and concentrated on infrastructure development programme at the domestic level and pursued the democratic principles to make it particularly relevant in the then peace building process. We are enjoying the dividend of this Nehruvian economic thinking even in the present century. **Secondly,** Nehru's initiative of Non-alignment brought most of the Third World countries under one umbrella, which made the United Nations General Assembly a "voice of protest against the developed world". In fact, the South-South Cooperation movement against the North-South divide was an outcome of this vision, where NAM acted as a catalyst of integration of the oppressed South. India's role, especially in the UN Peacekeeping operations was widely appreciated by the countries of the South. **Finally,** India had taken an indifferent outlook towards the process of regional multilateralism mainly in Asia, on account of Cold War power politics.

Actually, during the Cold War days, India did not give much importance to multilateralism especially with reference to regional economic organizations. When ASEAN was established in 1967, India fully ignored the formation of this regional organization, on account of India's closer linkages with the former Soviet Union based on its national interest as well as its bitter ties with Pakistan since 1947 and with China since 1962. Along with this, India's relations with US during much of the Cold War era were not cordial following Washington's consistent armaments supply to Pakistan, due to their security alignment and New Delhi's unwillingness to join directly any military bloc. Like ASEAN, India never initiated a similar type of regional economic organization in the South Asian region. In fact, the SAARC was established under the leadership of Bangladesh in 1985, where India took part as a facilitator of its South Asian partner. During these years, SAARC, as a regional organization failed to prove its effectiveness on account of several factors and they are: the perennial conflicting ties between India and Pakistan; New Delhi's occasional display of strength to its geographically disadvantaged smaller South Asian neighbours and the latter's alignment, time and again, with India's adversary.[2] In these years, initially India under the tutelage of Nehru followed a mixed economic policy and remained self-reliant due to its huge domestic population base. It also pursued democratic principles, which was the baseline of its true identity as a nation. Unfortunately, during this time India experienced two major wars with Pakistan, as an ill-fated history from the perception of Mahatma Gandhi's non-violent dictum. Simultaneously, India being the largest geographical entity in South Asia also played a responsible role with reference to peacekeeping in Sri Lanka and Maldives, which can be termed as "Rajdharma" of Mahabharata. Besides the South Asian region, during this era, India with its limited ability, played a prominent role in the UN-General Assembly and thereby, brought the Third World countries under one umbrella, known as a voice of protest against the developed world. The idea of Asia and its significance in world politics was first painted by Jawaharlal Nehru at the Asian Relations Conference, on 23 March, 1947 at New Delhi, when he said: "All over Asia we are passing through trials and tribulations....We find a new vitality and powerful creative impulses in all the peoples of Asia. The masses are awake and they demand their heritage. Strong winds are blowing all over Asia. Let us not afraid of them but rather welcome them, for only with their help can we build up the new Asia of our dreams. Let us have faith in these great forces and the dream which is taking shape. Above all, let us have faith in the human spirit which Asia has symbolized for these long ages past."[3] He believed that 'Standing on our own feet' and 'not being a plaything of others' was the essence of the policy of non-alignment. Based on this outlook, it was India, which, along with the other newly independent countries commenced the South-South Cooperation movement against the North-South divide and thus, tried to generate confidence among the developing countries to make their voices heard for their own survival. This resulted in that during the Cold War years, India's role had been widely acclaimed by the developing countries especially in UN General Assembly and to them New Delhi appeared as a symbol of resistance for the oppressed people of the South. Not only that, its active involvement in peacekeeping operations has been widely acknowledged and respected by most of the countries of the developing world. India stands solidly committed to assist the UN in the maintenance of international peace and security and this remains quite amenable in its entirety. Besides this, India's unique combination of being the largest democracy in the world with a strong tradition of respect for rule of law and the successful experience in post-colonial nation-state building makes it particularly relevant in the context of twenty-first century peace building. Its smooth democratic transfer of power from one government to another gives New Delhi additional bargaining power when espousing democratic values to the outside world. Thus, India's outlook towards the international multilateral institutions, mainly UN, remained one of the positive outfits of its foreign policy. However, that optimism was found lacking with reference to regional economic organizations like SAARC and ASEAN on account of trust deficit among the South Asian countries and lack of positive mindset towards the Southeast Asian countries, in spite of its historical and cultural linkages with the region.

India's Multilateralism in the Post-Cold War Years

The sudden rumple of the former Soviet Union and the emergence of a New Global Order, based on the processes of globalization and liberalization made most of the developing countries face a dilemma of economic adjustment. India, in that context felt the imperative of accommodating and thereby managing its economic survival in the ongoing process of globalization. As against such backdrop in July 1991, India announced its 'New Economic Policy' and initiated the opening up of its economy to the global market. Within a few years, many of the developing countries not only made necessary adjustments with the process of globalization, but also evolved as hubs of economic attraction to the developed countries of the world. Among them, the rise of China, India, Brazil, South Africa,

Singapore, South Korea and other fast-growing economies took economic interdependence to a new level. The overall effects of their performance due to rapid globalization prompted them to demand more effective global governance and raised issues like climate change, resource scarcity, effects on environment, economic meltdown (mainly in 1997 and 2008), reforms of World Trade Organization (WTO) and the United Nations Security Council etc. To these countries, these issues have posed interwoven domestic and foreign policy challenges at the intra and inter levels, and thus, their performing economics led them to establish economic clout of potential emerging powers. Moreover, to these countries the non-state actors came into limelight as a major agenda of global governance, either as facilitators or hindrances to cooperation. On a positive note, transnational non-governmental organizations, civil-society groups, multinational corporations, other business bodies and interest groups have been equally, if not more effective than states at reframing issues and mobilizing public. Many developing countries—which are likely to play an increasing role at the regional and global levels—also suffer from a relative paucity of non-state actors, that could help newly emerging states and their governments to deal with these problems.

In addition to the difficulties created by the current global economic situation, there are a number of important challenges that India faces since 1990s to the current century like poverty reduction at the intra level. The first challenge is poverty reduction, the main agenda of which remains providing opportunities for a better life for the economically weak Indians. Poverty reduction is important not only from a humanitarian viewpoint but also from a human resources development point of view: reducing poverty means empowerment of people; it contributes to strengthening the capacity of members of society as valuable resources. Better-developed human resources means tomorrow's social and economic development. Empirical evidences in India and elsewhere clearly show that poverty has been reducing slowly but not rapidly during these years. In fact, since the 1990s, more than 400 million middle class has emerged in Indian society, which has strong purchasing power. Besides this, India is one of the fastest growing economies of the world. So far its geographical size is concerned it is the seventh largest country with the second largest population of 1.2 billion, in the world. The Indian economy has clocked an average growth rate of 7 percent in the last decade. In the third quarter of 2011, GDP of India increased 6.9 percent. Between the years of 2000 and 2011 India's average quarterly GDP was 7.45 percent. It reached an historical high of 11.80 percent in December of 2003 and a record low of 1.60 percent in December of 2002. Over the last few years, industrial production in India increased 1.8 percent in December of 2011. Industrial production measures changes in output for the industrial sector of the economy which includes manufacturing, mining, and utilities. Likewise, agriculture India has a large and diverse agriculture and is one of the world's leading producers. It is also a major consumer, with an expanding population to feed. Energy India's rapid economic growth has made it the second fastest—growing energy market in the world. India is the world's eleventh-largest energy producer, with 2.4 percent of energy production, and the world's sixth-largest consumer, with 3.5 percent of global energy consumption. India is trying to diversify its energy sources increase India's equity stake overseas, and try to avoid destructive commercial competition with China. As far as, India's technology is concerned, the Indian industry group NASSCOM estimates that in 2008, the country's software product revenues totaled \$1.64 billion. It forecasts that this will grow to \$11 billion per year by 2015. With reference to telecommunication, India possesses the world's fifth largest public sector telecommunications network and Asia's third larges, behind only China and South Korea and the present trends created a sign to grow and prosper more and more in the coming days.[4] Summarily then, there are four important features of India's growth trends. **First**, its population; **Secondly**, despite the economic crisis, the prospects of long term growth are around 5-8 percent based on demographics and the government's education policy. **Thirdly**, due to increasing foreign exchange reserves and greater global integration, India will acquire greater stakes in its own global power as trade as a proportion of the GDP rises. And **finally**, the emergence of Indian multinationals and the global activities of Indian companies will add depth to India's global activities. In fact, it is to be noted here that Indian economy remains a less sufferer than others in 2008 financial crisis. India's performance in soft infrastructure, with its exceptional growth in the IT sector, has changed the perception of the Indian economy to a major extent. India, with its good legal structure, corporate governance, banking system, financial sector, property rights security, skilled manpower and young work force, has become the new economic icon of the emerging powers. Until recently, it spent a mere 1.99 percent of GDP on defense. This increased to about 2.5 percent of GDP in 2013. While presenting the Union Budget 2013-14 to Parliament on 28 February, the Finance Minister hiked the defence allocation by 5.3 per cent to Rs. 2,03,672.1 crore (US\$ 37.4 billion) This nominal increase in the latest defence allocation—which is quite modest in comparison to the growth rates of 17.6 per cent and 11.6 per cent in the previous two budgets.[5] Thus India's military might is not considered to be source of its rising international influence, although its regional power in South Asia and its possible role as a bridging power in East and South East Asia are increasingly recognized.

Beside this, within a short span of time, it has increased its foreign exchange reserves and a number of Indian multinationals surfaced, which added depth to its global economic clout. Furthermore, the Indian Diaspora presently numbers over 20 million, who are relatively affluent, successful, and well-integrated community spreading India's 'soft' cultural influence. Approximately 3.7 million Indian nationals now living in the six Gulf (GCC) states remit around \$8 billion annually. Indian economy is the12th largest in the world. Despite India's meteoric economic development, it can be said that India now has 410 million people living below the United Nations' poverty line—37.2 per cent of its population and actually 100 million more people than in 2004. Millions of India's rural poor are faced with food price inflation of up to 17 per cent.[6] Besides this, presently 60 per cent of Indian labour is still agricultural, and the integration of millions of peasants into a modern economy could be an extremely critical economic security challenge for her. India has to overcome such imbalances to emerge as an economic power, though the main point of India's rising as a global power has been its growing economic strength.

As against such background, India faces a number of threats from within and outside, both traditional and non-traditional in nature. The most important threats are the nuclear order or nuclear stability; nuclear proliferation among states and thereby potential danger of non-state actors gaining access or acquiring nuclear technologies; transnational terror networks and sectarian violence led by various terrorist groups, religious sectarianism; the growth of Islamic fundamentalism; arms race; human rights violation, environmental degradation, competition over the procurement of energy resources, ethnic unrest, gender issues, etc. These diverse threats often act as obstacles in its overall development process. In this context, India views that absence of coordinated development mindset among some of the regional countries (like China and Pakistan) and other extra-regional powers as a prime barrier for achieving the common developmental objectives.

India in the Domain of Multilateralism

India, in the context of changing global order, has taken multilateral regional institutions as a vehicle to develop better linkages with the countries of South, Southeast Asia and other parts of the world. At the South Asian level, India in recent times has been playing an active role to generate the momentum which it had not initiated in the Cold War years. At the South Asian level, India in recent times has been playing an active role in the SAARC process. India's ineffectiveness due to Pakistan-centric hurdles and uncomfortable ties with other neighbours led SAARC not to gain its economic strength and this situation was honestly confessed by the Indian Prime Minister, Manmohan Singh when he said at the Thimphu SAARC Summit held in April 2010, "In looking back at these two and a half decades we can claim the glass is half full, and compliment ourselves, or, we can admit the glass is half empty and challenge ourselves. I believe we should challenge ourselves by acknowledging that the glass of regional cooperation, regional development and regional integration is half empty",[7] while comparing the performance of other regional organizations in East and Southeast Asia with SAARC. This honest confession of the Indian Prime Minister clearly exhibits the weakness of SAARC in spite of its 25 years of existence.

India in South Asia

Globalization and growing interdependence generates a regular movement of problems from South Asia to the global arena and vice-versa. India, occupies a paramount position and a major player in the political management of this region. The Cold War rubric no longer limits India's ability to assert itself, and as India's own awareness about its role changes its status as a major player, according to the given environment. For India, the challenge to engage its neighbors is complicated by a periphery ringed with conflict. Because India has not yet made itself a partner of choice in regional conflict management and this regional instability offers opportunities for a range of actors to intervene. The security dilemma in South Asia severely hampers regional cooperation at all levels. The failure of regional cooperation is particularly visible in the realm of economics. So, strengthening the regional dynamics through mechanisms of cooperation that go beyond its immediate neighborhood would enhance India's visibility and presence, and also display its commitment to regional stability. It also calls for the development of specific capacities—diplomatic, civilian, and military—able to undertake such activities, which in many ways are hampered by the domestic challenges to India's economic and social development. With reference to SAARC, over the years, this regional organization has not at all performed competently, if we compare with ASEAN and other regional organizations in the Asia-Pacific region and beyond. In spite of the establishment of South Asian Free Trade Area (SAFTA) in 2004, SAARC countries as a regional bloc remained least integrated with the world economy. The major rationales behind this slow progress of the SAARC economic performance over the years are as follows:

> **First**, the regional politics overwhelms to dilute economic issues in the SAARC agenda. The key political impediment is the Indo-Pakistan conflict and their internal political problems have always affected the SAARC common work programme;
>
> **Secondly**, there are too many poor countries in SAARC;
>
> **Thirdly**, India's geographical advantage (nearly 72 per cent occupation of territory in the region) and its conflicts with its neighbours ranging from sharing of river waters, border problems, the presence of illegal immigrants, ethnic dissonance, nuclear arms race with Pakistan, etc;
>
> **Fourthly**, persistent promotion by regional and extra-regional powers of smaller neighbours of South Asia against India;
>
> **Fifthly**, occasional superiority complex mindset of individual leaders of this region;
>
> **Sixthly**, weak transit and communication facilities among SAARC countries;
>
> **Seventhly** weakness of proper policies and uniform strategies has not been adopted to coordinate production, quality and pricing; and
>
> **Finally**, SAARC has been always congested by 'soft issues' and 'housekeeping matters' in the agenda that dominate the SAARC deliberations.

Therefore, SAARC's performance over the years has been appeared quite tardy and to overcome the existing scenario, the members of this regional organization should respond to the emerging situation in a holistic manner by forging a common strategy by exploring options to safeguard regional interest through joint venture and technology transfer among its member countries. Cohesive and economically integrated South Asia would be better positioned to negotiate globally for advantageous terms of trade with WTO regime and development institutions. Currently, India is playing the role of a benevolent responsible initiator in order to accelerate the development process of the weak economies of South Asia and thereby, reschedule the train, which was derailed in the Cold War years. It was pragmatically felt by Indian policy makers that economic development and prosperity of the SAARC partners will be the essential guideline of India's economic progress. Interestingly enough, in recent times there have been signs that regional integration may have a somewhat brighter future in SAARC region. Of late, India has picked up the pace of greater engagement with its SAARC neighbours, and in a pragmatic attempt to counter Chinese presence, it has embarked upon a proactive South Asia policy, particularly in the wake of the 16th Thimphu Summit of SAARC. India's pro-activism towards the South Asian countries has been reflected by a slew of recent developments, including, India's trade and transit agreements with Pakistan and Bangladesh, which could lead to New Delhi's gain of Most Favoured Nation (MFN) status vis-à-vis Pakistan and the resumption of India and Pakistan cricket match series after five years in late 2012; India's Strategic Partnership agreement with Afghanistan, signaling the former's amenability to playing a more involved role in Kabul after US' withdrawal in 2014; India's commitment to offering impressive credit lines to Nepal, Sri Lanka, Bangladesh, Bhutan and the Maldives for infrastructure and holistic development; support for Pakistan's non-permanent membership in the UN Security Council, a US $ 1 billion concessional Line of Credit to Bangladesh, its unilateral gestures and extended economic concessions such as the facility of duty free access to Indian market for imports from Bangladesh, Nepal, Bhutan and Sri Lanka, its proposed offer by the Reserve Bank of India (RBI) in May 2012 for a swap arrangement of US$ 2 billion to all SAARC member states for the purpose of alleviating the economic condition of its poorer SAARC partners, etc can be termed as a positive initiative from India's end. In fact, India, under the leadership of Dr. Manmohan Singh, the Prime Minister of UPA Phase II years has taken a very dynamic, comprehensive and positive outlook towards its neighbours, working towards "fostering inter-connectivity and mutual confidence in multiple areas for promoting trade and investment", and thereby trying to play a more pro-active and flawless crew position towards its South Asian countries. This positive outlook of India was evident from the speech delivered by Prime Minister Manmohan Singh, delivered at the three-day Conference of Indian High Commissioners and Ambassadors from nearly 120 countries, held at New Delhi in September 2012, where he said: "The imperatives of our foreign policy have not changed. Emphasizing the idea of establishing greater connectivity in South Asia to promote the movement of goods, services, investment and technology would be essential, so that India's growth provided the engine of progress for its neighbours."[8] However, notwithstanding these positive traits in the realm of Indo-SAARC relations, a number of challenges still exist including the China factor, on account of the latter's entry as an Observer member of SAARC in 2007, which has emerged as a serious boulder and overlapping determinant deterring the smooth exercise of India's neighbourhood policy. Moreover, the prospects for an increase in regional economic integration depend critically on the future of Indo-Pakistan relations to a great extent. Thus, taking this into cognizance, India, being the largest country in the region, presently tries to play a more effective role in order to accelerate the pace of the region's economic integration by minimizing bilateral strains to the maximum extent, based on its role as a benevolent and responsible friend, as opposed to its past, re-active mindset. This is no doubt a watershed initiative of India to establish a better historical record of India's neighbourhood regional policy in recent times.

India in Southeast Asia

India's multilateralism beyond SAARC was reflected in its relationship with the countries of Southeast Asia, through its 'Look East' Policy.India's participation in regional multilateral process of Southeast Asia was evolved on account of its uncomfortable situation in the SAARC region in the early part of its New Economic Policy led it to develop better economic, cultural and strategic linkages with these countries, through ASEAN. The announcement of New Delhi's 'Look East' Policy was actually propelled on account of past solidarity experience of the South-South movement, which made it comfortable to develop better, ties with the region. India was also attracted towards ASEAN, because through its principle of non-intervention, this regional organization had attempted to resolve many of their internal problems which New Delhi had not experienced in the South Asian region. Furthermore, the growing economic strength of these countries also attracted New Delhi to initiate this policy, since the integration process of this region teach us the useful lessons about how a highly diverse set of countries some democratic and emerging, some despotic and stagnant— seek economic integration and a better insertion into the world economy with a strategic weight for the coming years. Within a short span of time, India was considered by these countries as an economic and strategic balancer against China and it was uplifted in status from Sectoral Dialgue partner to Summit-Level Partner of ASEAN and finally promoted to East Asia Summit partnership. Within this more than two decades, India's economic ties with this multilateral institution, ASEAN, has now become a prime factor for the countries of this region. India, through its economic clout, and positive mindset being the member of ASEAN Regional Forum (ARF) has provided amenable confidence in diverse areas such as counter terrorism, transnational crimes, maritime security, natural disaster relief like Tsunami in 2004, pandemics and nuclear nonproliferation and disarmament etc., to these countries.

India in Sub-Regional Organizations

One of the important goals of India's Multilateralism is the connectivity policy, which remains a prime vehicle of its Look East policy. Before, New Delhi joined in 2002, as a Summit Level Partner of ASEAN, it remains one of the chief regional architect for the establishment of few sub-regional organizations, because that will tacitly strengthen its position in the Southeast Asian region and East Asia countries. Actually, the years between Full Dialogue Partner and Summit Level Partner of ASEAN, New Delhi has initiated several transnational and sub-regional fora between parts of India (including its Northeast) and Southeast Asian countries to promote cooperation between the economically dynamic regions. In 1997, India and Thailand proposed a new organization, known as BIST-EC (Bangladesh, India, Sri Lanka, and Thailand-Economic Cooperation)—whose primary goal was to act as a vehicle for promoting trade and tourism in the Bay of Bengal region. The members of this Trans-regional grouping have agreed to cooperate on trade and investment, technology, energy, transportation and communication, tourism and fisheries. The establishment of this Bay of Bengal Initiative for Multi-Sectoral Technical and Economic Cooperation (BIMSTEC) in its First Summit held in July 2004 at Thailand, which later included two more nations of South Asia (i.e. Nepal and Bhutan) together with two countries of Southeast Asia (i.e. Myanmar and Thailand), to strengthen regional cooperation among countries on the rim of or those seeking access to the Bay of Bengal. India's interests in fostering the establishing of BIMSTEC has opened up the possibilities of enhancing its trade linkages with Myanmar and Thailand as well as the opportunity to counter China's strategic designs within the region. This sub-regional organization might also act as a bridge of mutual understanding and cooperation between South and South Asia,[9] and could generate mobility of India's 'Look East' Phase II policy, which India announced in 2003. Moreover, one of the important reasons behind the announcement of New Delhi's 'Look East' Phase-II policy, has been the road diplomacy and transportation links with Southeast Asian countries. In the context of rapidly changing global order, establishment of air and land links to East and Southeast Asia has emerged as an essential ingredient to Phase II of the policy. Hence, as part of its road diplomacy, New Delhi tries building up its transport corridors with the region. These include the India-Myanmar-Thailand trilateral highway and the Delhi-Hanoi railway line. As part of this outlook, in November 2000, India floated the Mekong-Ganga Cooperation (MGC) proposal with five of its eastern neighbours, namely—Cambodia, Laos, Vietnam, Myanmar and Thailand. Through this initiative, the six countries agreed to increase cooperation in tourism, culture and education, and further accelerated the development of bilateral relations between India and the less developed countries of Southeast Asia.[10] In fact, by taking advantage of Myanmar as a bridge to Southeast Asia, New Delhi initiated to transform the Northeast India from a security burden precinct into a land of economic opening. Thus, through these two sub-regional multilateral initiatives, India has opened the window for the first time since 1997, to break out of the political confines of the South Asian subcontinent that have poorly limited India's grand strategic options. In fact, the 'Look East' diplomacy, for the first time, has allowed India to break the artificial political barriers between the South and Southeast Asia. In other words, India has gained a natural gateway to the east through the territories of Myanmar and Thailand to reach the heart of the Southeast and East Asia and where the BIMSTEC and MGC have appeared as a major vehicle of connectivity. This would most certainly help India in the integration process with the countries of ASEAN.

India in East Asia

The region of East Asia is dense with production arrangements. This region accounts for roughly 50 per cent of global production network or supply-chain trade with China and the ASEAN countries in the lead. Such networks have contributed to deepening regional economic integration and brought unprecedented prosperity to the region. Along with this growing economic strength, this region has emerged a sensitive strategic point to the other powers also. As a result, in recent times this region has emerged a prime component of regional multilateralism global politics, and where Japan, China, South and North Korea, Taiwan etc figures prominently in this regional discourse. In security terms, in the overall context of East Asia, the focus is changing more towards this part, than the Southeast Asia and to a lesser extent to the Indian Ocean region. The unabated tensions between Japan and China on Island claims and the simmering Taiwan question are other issues that could have far-reaching impact. Additionally, there is considerable uncertainty because of changing American military strategy towards East Asia even as it prepares to re-engage its military deployment in East Asia and beyond. Besides this, the institutionalizing the role of the United States through alliances, new partnerships, non-ASEAN-led forms of multilateralism such as mini-lateral forums like the Six-Party Talks, Asian Maritime Forum and other functional efforts by Obama administration, are remains the most comprehensive articulation instruments of American rebalance theory in the East Asian region. Moreover, in recent times the row between Japan and China on island issue reaches a new heights and US re-engagement in the region, followed by the new bonhomie between India and the US, on the one hand and between India and Japan, on the other, has not been favourably looked up by China. This new power configuration suddenly placed India in huge strategic demand among all major powers because of its potential to tilt the balance decisively in the East Asian emerging balance of power equation. So, India is going to be much more substantial and important in the coming years than others to balance, not only in the East Asian region but on the world at large. However, multilateralism either at the global or the regional level will succeed only as long as major world powers extend their full support and this will happen only if they perceive that their interests are advanced in such an initiative, based on dialogue and transparency in security and military matters.

India in other Emerging Multilateral Organizations

Besides this, India's pro-active mindset of multilateralism has made it an active participant of several other regional organizations like Indian Ocean Rim

Association for Regional Cooperation (IORARC), the Shanghai Cooperation Organization (SCO), the Bangladesh, China, India and Myanmar (BCIM), Kolkata to Kunming (K-to-K) etc. Furthermore, it's growing co-relations and expanding networks with West Asia, Central Asia, Latin America and Africa (on account of energy security), naval presence for anti-piracy escort operations to ensure maritime security in the Gulf of Aden and its importance to G-8 and G-20 are significant achievements in recent times. Additionally, the growing strategic and economic understanding with the US, France, Japan, Russia and other EU countries and the Brazil-Russia-India-China (BRIC), and the Russia-India-China (RIC) Cooperation Forums have also helped India engage more closely with these countries, thereby strengthening its economic clout in the 21st Century global politics. It may be mentioned here that the formalization of the trilateral partnership, consisting of India-Brazil-South Africa Dialogue Forum (IBSA) in June 2003, was essentially an outcome of South-South cooperation and has acted as a positive factor to advance human development by promoting potential synergies among the members. The prime purpose of this IBSA forum is to share views on relevant regional and international issues of mutual interest as well as promote cooperation in the areas of defense, multilateral diplomacy, international trade, technology, social development, environmental issues and so forth. It also talked about issues related to multilateralism and the proposed reforms of the UN, peace and security, terrorism, globalization, and sustainable and social development. Therefore, these multilateral institutions are essential for India's enhanced regional and global interactions.

India's Alienation in APEC Orbit

Unfortunately, in spite of these major achievements of India since 1991, with reference to multilateral institutions and various regional organizations in the Asia-Pacific, New Delhi has not yet obtained its Asia-Pacific Economic Cooperation (APEC) membership. The APEC was initiated in 1989 and formulated on the basis of three important goals: it sought to resist protectionist pressures which would jeopardize Pacific growth by maintaining the momentum of liberalization in the face of uncertainty about the global trading system; it aimed to counter inward-looking regionalism, especially in Europe and North America; and it sought to provide better ways to deal with economic conflicts that pervade the area and agreed that it should not discuss security issues in the forum.[11] Presently, APEC has crossed more than two decades of its existence and its membership extended to 21, but its viability as a regional economic organization in the Asia-Pacific has not at all been formidable in nature. During this long period, APEC has conducted several Summit meetings, among which, the Vancouver Summit held in November 1997 was very significant. In this meeting, three new members were included, namely Vietnam, Russia and Peru and it froze its membership for ten years. India, which in the context of its liberalized New Economic Policy expressed its willingness to become an APEC partner, unfortunately was not granted membership due to its lack of political clout, the then instability of governments as well as absence of strong supporters within the APEC group. This rejection of India's membership of APEC was, no doubt, a severe blow to the mindset of the Indian policy makers in spite of its process of economic liberalization.

The importance of India's membership of APEC today is not as vital as it would have been in 1997, because during that time, India wanted to legitimize its self-declared 'Look East' Policy and New Economic Policy by gaining APEC's membership. India, at that juncture, had failed to obtain APEC's membership mainly as pointed out earlier, because of the fluctuation of permanent governments at the Centre, due to coalition politics at the domestic level, on the one hand and the non-convincing performance of New Delhi's economy, which was unable to imprint a positive image on the mindset of APEC leaders, on the other. However, within a decade, India had overcome the blemishes, which obstructed the gaining of APEC membership, and its growth rate in the economic sphere and political stability of the government since 1998 clearly exhibited its burgeoning strength, legitimizing its potentiality as a budding economic powerhouse of the 21st Century in the Asian region. Today, India has emerged as an important component of this regional organization of the Asia-Pacific region, on account of several factors:

First, India is an important investment destination, with many sectors open for foreign investment;

Secondly, its trade with many of the countries of the Asia-Pacific region has increased manifold, encompassing both goods and services, as a positive outfit of New Delhi's effective 'Look East' and 'Move East' policies;

Thirdly, India's signing of Free Trade Agreements with ASEAN (on goods and services) on the one hand and Comprehensive Economic Cooperation Agreements with Singapore, Thailand, Malaysia, Japan and South Korea on a bilateral basis on the other, has accelerated the pace of reaching its economic destination in New Delhi's extended neighbouring vicinity;

Fourthly, as testimony to its economic importance, at the 2007 East Asia Summit at Cebu, the Philippines, Japan proposed a pan-Asian free-trade zone that would include India, Australia and New Zealand along with China, Japan, South Korea and the ASEAN members and this was viewed as a pertinent step in further integrating India within the Asia-Pacific orbit;

Fifthly, the strength of the emerging more than 440 million Indian middle class and its increasing economic clout offers the APEC members a better market to cultivate and develop their economic mobility;

Sixthly, India's growing relations with Australia, China, Japan, South Korea, Russia, and the US have never been as strong and multi-faceted as of now, particularly after the Civil-Nuclear Deal was signed with Washington in 2006;

Finally, while the 2008 global economic meltdown had severely affected many countries of the world, including Europe and US economy, India

> was affected nominally due to its strong economic base. This growing and sound economic base as well as its huge emerging middle class appears too many countries all over the world that India could become a future destination of economic market. The recent consecutive visits of US President Obama, French President Sarkozy, Chinese Premier, Wen Jiabao, the Russian President and other important leaders from Japan, South Korea, Australia, etc are examples of New Delhi's growing economic prowess in global economic scenario.[12] Although India was swiftly treading on the path of liberalization of markets for foreign investments, and it believed that it would soon be considered for membership of this forum. Although, India is not an APEC member, but its trade relations with APEC nations are growing by leaps and bounds. India is an essential part of the vision for an economically integrated Asia-Pacific region that generates not just more growth, but better growth; strong protections for workers, the environment, intellectual property, and innovation; the free flow of information technology and the spread of green technology; and the efficiency of regional and global supply chains. In fact, in the present juncture, New Delhi is a strong contender for the portfolio of APEC membership and it is just a matter of time and judicious consideration before the present members induct India within the realm of this exclusive regional forum. In other words, India has sufficiently created the space for its membership in APEC, which was asserted a decade ago by missing the APEC train, in spite of its foothold through political, economic and strategic means in Southeast and East Asia steadily since the beginning of the new millennium.[13]

Besides this, this new global economic-strategic ambience has its pros and cons, which made the countries of the Asia-Pacific region, consider a number of important threats from within and outside, both traditional and non-traditional in nature. Among these threats, the nuclear order or nuclear stability; the threat of nuclear proliferation among states and thereby potential dangers of non-state actors gaining access or acquiring nuclear technologies; transnational terror networks and sectarian violence led by various terrorist groups, religious sectarianism; insurgencies and transnational linkages; the debates between Democracy and Authoritarian rule; the growth of Islamic fundamentalism and emergence of various armed Islamic groups and its terror outfits, arms race; unprecedented economic growth and development of some countries, wealth and affluence and thereby the digital gap among people; procurement and preservation of energy; power politics, military coup de etats and separatist revolts, civil-military power struggles, centre-periphery relations, and insurgency and low-intensity conflicts, human rights violation and the strong state debate, environment, ethnic unrest, gender issue, impact of globalization, Asian values syndrome and the state, are the most important. These diverse challenges in the developing world including India, have acted as obstacles in the process of their overall development. In this context, India viewed that the existing global governance was essentially based on an "absence of an internal equilibrium in Asia-Pacific domain to ensure stability."

Moreover, New Delhi perceived that India is not well positioned to help to a maximum level for development of regional institutions for Asia-Pacific, on account of extra-regional powers' continuous influence and interference and China and Pakistan's preponderant role in the South Asian region. However, given these internal constraints, India in the context of emerging global order, still persists the policy of multilateralism as a prime vehicle in its foreign policy domain.

India and United Nations

The importance of multilateralism remains "a highly demanding institutional form", and the United Nations (UN) represents the global symbol and embodiment of multilateralism. The United Nations was created chiefly as a collective security organization, and yet hundreds of conflicts have beset the world since 1945, and even with significant multilateral attention to weapons of mass destruction, the use and proliferation of nuclear, chemical, and biological weapons remain highly threatening for the human mankind. In fact, the existing multilateral arrangements are unable to guide states to a workable framework as to how to deal with widespread abuses of human rights, terrorism, environmental degradation and civil war and other issues like the UN Security Council's failure to constrain the US misadventure in Iraq. This resulted in that in recent times the United Nations has faced a number of security challenges. India is a charter member of the United Nations and as a founding member of the United Nations powerfully supports the functions and principles of the UN and has made noteworthy contributions to implementing the goals of the Charter. India viewed its membership at the United Nations as a key assurance for maintaining international peace and security at the height of the Cold War especially by working towards eliminating the causes of war and conflict. It stood at a vanguard during the UN's turbulent years of struggle against colonialism and apartheid, struggle towards global disarmament and the ending of the arms race, and towards the making of a more reasonable international economic order. Over the years, India has contributed troops to peacekeeping efforts in Korea, Egypt, Congo, Somalia, Angola, Rwanda, Haiti etc and has created a widely acclaimed image in the domain of global order. During this nearly seven decades of the work of the United Nations, India has supplied over 1, 60,000 troops to 43 of 64 UN peacekeeping operations since its inception in the 1950s. Over 160 Indian armed and police forces personnel have laid down their lives while fighting for the UN's blue flag. Moreover, in fact, the first all women contingent in any UN peacekeeping mission, a Formed Police Unit from India, was deployed in Liberia in 2007 as part of the UN peacekeeping mission. Besides this, India's status as a founding member of the Non-Aligned Movement and the Group of 77 promoted its position within the UN system as a leading advocate of the concerns and aspirations of developing countries and the creation of a more equitable international economic and political order. Moreover, India is persistent in its efforts to work with the Committee of Nations in the spirit of multilateralism to achieve comprehensive and equitable solutions to all problems facing us including development and poverty eradication, climate change, terrorism, piracy, disarmament, peace building and peacekeeping, human rights. Also, India remains the only State possessing nuclear weapons to call unambiguously for a Nuclear Weapons Convention to ban and eliminate nuclear weapons. India is committed to achieving a nuclear weapons-free world in a time-bound, universal, non-discriminatory, phased and verifiable manner as reflected in the Rajiv Gandhi Action Plan that was presented to the Special Session of General Assembly on Disarmament in 1998.[14] Thus, India over the years tries to keep its diplomatic and progressive existence felt in the UN on account of pragmatic understanding that the successful implementation of multilateralism and economic prosperity would remain the main vehicle for establishing its footing on a strong base in global politics. This pro-activeness of India with reference to UN led it, supported by many Southern countries to demand that New Delhi be a permanent representative in the UN-Security Council. This demand for India's inclusion as a permanent UNSC member is a dividend, which it has reaped from its past activities in the United Nations. Even India's contribution in the UN was widely acclaimed some years back by UN Secretary General, Kofi Annan, when he said: "Over the decades, India has made an enormous contribution to the United Nations, through the efforts of its Government, and the work of Indian scholars, soldiers and international civil servants. India's has been one of the most eloquent voices helping the United Nations shape its agenda on behalf of the developing world. And the experience and professionalism of its armed forces has proved invaluable, time and again, in UN peacekeeping operations—in which over a hundred Indian soldiers have given their lives."[15] In fact, presently India is considered a prime voice advocator of the Southern counties in this multilateral international platform and where India has adopted multilateralism as a prime component of its foreign policy dynamics in order to understand as well as to find ways for resolving transnational issues, under the auspices of the United Nations. In fact, India's display and confidence on the UN system is once again reflected with the statement, when the Indian Prime Minister in the General Debate of the 68th Session of the United Nations General Assembly, held on 28 September, 2013, said: "At a time when the world is facing multiple challenges, there is renewed attention on the role of the United Nations in advancing international peace, security and prosperity. However, never has skepticism about the UN's capacity to do so been higher, or the external environment less propitious for multilateralism." He further added that, "Multilateral efforts must guide our quest for peace and security, wherever they are threatened and for that the centrality and contribution of the UN system to development must be restored."[16]

Presently day-by-day, the hard power is increasing in the emerging security architecture of the Asia-Pacific region, on account of number of reasons including the involvement of regional and extra-regional powers and which could subtly able to shape the agendas of this region in coming years also. Besides the economic issues, the international institutions pragmatically realized its emerging role through its United Nations Security Council, the International Monetary Fund, the World Bank and the World Trade Organization. With reference to the UN Security Council issue on restructuring, a little progress has been made to include Japan and India as permanent members and as the deadlock among UN members still persist. Likewise, on the economic front, the current negotiations for a Trans-Pacific Partnership, for example, reflects an American interest in ensuring open markets in areas suited to the US such as investments, competition policy, labour standards, government procurement and intellectual property rights and that does not favourably looked upon by some countries of this region. Besides this, the emergence of proliferation of Regional Trade Agreements (RTAs) has created a widespread debate on the advantages or disadvantages of regionalism over multilateralism in this region. The debate actually twigs from the increased use of RTAs in a world, which is now ruled by an improved and disciplined multilateral trading system. The key question is whether these agreements will ram the world toward discriminatory regionalism, or can be used as a medium for promoting multilateralism in the emerging architecture of the Asia-Pacific region. Quite naturally, therefore some pertinent questions have evolved in this juncture with reference to this Asia-Pacific region. The questions are—what role India would play in this Asia-Pacific region remains a million dollar question. Whether, India's emerging security and economic profile could play the role of a balancer or would tilt in favour of strong regional powers to contain China's growing presence in the region? How India visualizes the Asia-Pacific region against the backdrop of its existing foreign policy domain? What role India would play with reference to RTAs? The fact remains that to do so India requires cautious deliberation of its place in the global economy, and the impact of possible trade diversion on its domestic industries. Generally, India has been a supporter of the multilateral system, but given the slow pace of negotiations and the developmental needs of its economy, it has recently joined in this RTA process. Given that position, what benefit will India gain through this process? Being a marginal player in the global economy, with its global share in exports is just above 2 per cent, which conduit India would follow -the regional path or the multilateral route with reference to this region, are prime question of the day.

It is a fact, that the region of the Asia-Pacific is presently termed as the core of world economy. Starting from securitization of politics and economic relations in the region together with exacerbating arms racing, all craft this region's unique position as the sanctuary of trade and growth on the one side, and tensions and ruthless balancing on the other. Here, China remains a major determining component along with other regional and extra-regional actors. Beijing's growing military posture in East Asia and beyond and its notable power projection capabilities through People's Liberation Army Navy (PLAN), appears to many countries, like Japan, Vietnam and to some extent Russia as threatening, problems with India, severe tensions in the South China Sea region, the issue of Taiwan etc, in the Asia-Pacific region causes severe anxiety. The evolution of China's security doctrine prompted the American military presence in the region, in order to tacitly contain the growing Chinese presence in Asia-Pacific and which also constantly infuriates the Chinese leaders. As a result, there has been increasing Chinese official military budget, like in 2011, it was roughly US$ 915 billion, whereas the SIPRI estimated its 2010 budget as US$ 114,3 billion, in comparison to US$ 687,1 billion, by the US for the same period.[17] However, this growing US commitment to regional security in this region, has been fiercely opposes by China and this China's new security doctrine and its growing multifarious presence in the South, Southeast, Central Asia and East Asian regions had led some sort of uncertain security complex to these countries, and as a reaction to this, many of them were extremely sensitive to changes in their relative security outlook and more prone to react, either with balancing or even some sort of confrontational attitude in the emerging security architecture of the Asia-Pacific region.

As against such background, how India can project herself remains a million dollar question? Presently India is not yet a global power, but it is one of the top contestants for becoming a prime one. India has the prospective—and possibly also the aspiration of becoming a global power. India's path to global power status is however not smooth. It is forced by a number of internal and external restraining factors. In spite of these precincts, a clear expansion of India's area of interest has been visualized. Determined by great power intuitions and the quest for strategic raw materials, India's immediate area of interest now extends well beyond the sub-continent. India currently tries to maximize its influence globally, politically, economically, strategically and to some extent culturally. As a reflection of this, relations with other major powers are becoming more important, notably China and the US, along with other regional powers of the Asia-Pacific region, and where India is likely to avoid the alliance principles and favours upholding the balancing role.

Conclusion

Having discussed the past and present historical preview of India and its status in the emerging multilateral regional organizations, based on constraints and possibilities that India's attachment to multilateralism is marked by an effortless fact that whether New Delhi has at all achieved, exert the actual power that it perceived itself to deserve in emerging international affairs. Until recently, India was perceived as a poor, low-income country and had a low visibility on the global political and especially global economic front and took on the role of spokesman for the Third World in international organizations and was active with its soft power approach with a significant role it played in the decolonization process. However, that trajectory has changed presently and today, India declines international aid, seeks a UN Security Council seat, and negotiates with the US in most multilateral forums not as a Third World nation, but as an emerging power with a possibility of dynamic new future image. This will lead to a greater exertion of India's power outside its borders, not only for its own economic development, but also to play a more constructive responsible role in emerging global order. India sees itself as an emerging power in a multi-polar world, which will maintain a strategy of multi-alignment, obviously determined by the calculus of its national interests. Today, India casts itself as emerging power intent on exerting the bilateral and multilateral influence that the country's founding leaders had long aspired. Past foreign policy instruments such as nonalignment and developing world leadership have mostly been discarded in the present global structure and the prime questions remain about India's motivation and competence to take on global responsibilities to match its global objectives. In the post-Cold War years, New Delhi's approach to multilateralism largely constitutes a sober and silent, but as yet incomplete uprising. From idealist moralizer to frequently pragmatic decision making led its emerging mirror on the rise—second only to China. Currently, India's influence carries more weight in multilateral forums largely due to its enhanced economic power, political stability, and nuclear capability. In fact, almost in every international forum, India has explicitly engaged with smaller groups of powerful nations to affect outcomes at the expense of the more broad-based regional and international issues. Here two important questions are relevant in this juncture for India to emerge as a premier global interlocutor. First, what kind of power does India aspire to be, and how will it engage with others in years to come? Secondly, is the Indian foreign policy establishment attuned to engaging with the multilateral system, not just on India's own terms but also on terms that will appeal to others and contribute to positive outcomes?

Over the years, India has been constrained to remain generally selective rule taker in the multilateral system, by believing it should have been a rule maker. This has led to a number of apparent constrains in its overall foreign policy, not least with respect to its strong attachment to sovereignty and the nonuse of force, its feeble promotion of its own attractive values of democracy, its internal struggle for the attainment of human rights, but many of its internal economic and social challenges and feeble stand towards its some South Asian neighbours, unresolved territorial issues and rivalry with China and occasional irritants with others on several regional and international issues, which intermittently limit it's ability to take a more active global role. Given this political gamut and limitation, on 5 November 2004, the Indian Prime Minister Manmohan Singh, in a speech clearly outlined India's global philosophy, which he described as "Cooperative Pluralism."[18] However, in spite of these constraints, there exists a space between theory and practice of targets for a more truly multilateral management of international relations on the one hand, and India's conferring position and approach in a variety of forums and issue by issue on the other. What are major challenges in the present global order for India is to assume a more independent pro-active role of a responsible stakeholder in the international system, based on good governance, multilateralism, human rights, financial crisis, proliferation, terrorism, other non-traditional issues etc or even inducing other emerging powers to take the role of responsible international actors and where to exercise its diplomatic leverage, it is essential that engagement rather than balancing and containment should become its long term strategy diagram. However, to sustain its present growth curve, India needs an environment that is free from transnational threats like terrorism and other disturbing issues.

India began adjusting to the new realities in the Asia-Pacific region in the early nineties, through its 'Look East' policy which aimed at deepening its engagement with the ASEAN countries and beyond. Today, India holds for the future of Asia and other countries of the globe, a template for democracy, inter-faith coexistence, secularism, gender equality, active member of multilateral regional organizations and a dynamic cum expanding middle-path economy that can become a model for a large number of nations to follow and where it sees itself as an emerging great power in a multi-power world, which will maintain a strategy of poly-alignment, based on national interest. India is a paradigm of pluralism, which is the urge and aspiration of those who seek a modern future. In fact, India's approach to the Asia-Pacific region, through multilateralism is still evolving and will take many forms in the years to come. So, ignoring India will carry a price already today, not to mention tomorrow. In this context, three broad measures should be urgently pursued by India for peace and harmony in the present global order and they are: **First,** to build Asian security architecture anchored round Asian values and interests, which will benefit the entire world; **Secondly**, a commitment to foreign, economic and security policies, based on multilateralism that would enhance regional security, abjure interference in the internal matters of states, while respecting human rights and promote trade and commerce within Asia and with the outside world; and **Thirdly,** India should initiate a more pro-active constructive mindset in global politics and thereby pursue the proposal for greater pan-Asian economic cooperation, with a human face.

Summarily then, while exploring emerging India's status in multilateral platform in the evolving security architecture of the Asia-Pacific region, it is evidently clear that presently, security and economic diplomacy is developing its thrust day by day. India's cooperative and pragmatic mindset—be it in economic, political and security spheres—is expanding quite rapidly, since it would not only promote the best interest of herself, but also balance the entire Asia-Pacific region, as a whole. It is clearly evident that New Delhi has taken a pragmatic, constructive gesture towards its historical friends on account of the changing global order, and thereby modified its earlier outlook from political rhetoric to economic and strategic imperatives and reveals clearly that any part of Asia-Pacific and other areas can no longer be monopolized by any single power. India's broad-based multifarious cooperative mindset and increasing understanding with many countries of the Asia-Pacific region, through regional and sub-regional organizations could provide in future a new mini-security ambit in the evolving dynamics of the Asia-Pacific security architecture and, could help to build up the broader frame of this scaffold to contain evolving tensions, which remains the major coin of the 21st Century for ushering in ultimate peace, progress and stability in the Asia-Pacific strategic architecture.

NOTES

1. Harsh V. Pant, "A Rising India's Search for a Foreign Policy", *Orbis*, Vol. 53, No. 2, 2009, p. 264.
2. For details analysis see Tridib Chakraborti, "SAARC expands its Wings: Insinuations in the New Global Order", *World Focus,* Vol.29, No5, May 2008, pp. 201-208.
3. *Selected works of Jawaharlal Nehru*, Second Series, Vol. 2, Jawaharlal Nehru Memorial Fund, Teen Murti House, New Delhi, 1984, pp. 508-509.
4. For details see Murat Akcanba, Country Report-April, 2012, McBDC Business Development and Consultancy Services Co. Ltd, pp. 3-5, www.mcbdc.com/wpcontent/uploads/INDIA_APRIL_2012.pdf+&cd=3&hl=en&ct=clnk&gl=in (accessed on 13 October, 2013).
5. http://www.indiastrategic.in/topstories1929_India_Defence_Budget_2013_2014.htm (accessed on 15 October, 2013).
6. David A. Robinson, "India's Rise as a Great Power, Part One: Regional and Global Implications", Associate Paper, 7 July 2011, p.3, for details see http://www.futuredirections.org.au/files/FDI%20Associate%20Paper%20-%2007%20July%202011.pdf (accessed on 13 October, 2013)
7. Opening Statement by Prime Minister Monmohan Singh, at the 16th SAARC Summit, Thimphu, 28 April, 2010, see http://www.mea.gov.in/Speeches-Statements.htm?dtl/533/Opening+Statement+by+Prime+Minister+at+the+16th+SAARC+Summit (accessed on 15 October, 2013)
8. Ashok Tuteja, "PM Calls for Friendly Ties with Neighbours", *The Tribune* (Chandigarh), 14 September, 2012.
9. For details see http://www/mofa/gov.bd/bimstec (accessed on 16 October, 2013).
10. Tridib Chakraborti, "India's New Regionalism in Asia: Look East and BIMSTEC Interface," in T. Nirmala Devi (ed), *India and Bay of Bengal Community: The BIMSTEC Experiment*, Gyan Publishing House, New Delhi, 2007, p. 108.
11. Tridib Chakraborti and Mohor Chakraborty, "India and the Asia-Pacific Region: Dilemma of a Changing APEC Mindset", *Asia-Pacific Journal of Social Sciences (Tirupati),* Special Issue on Asia-Pacific, No.1, December 2010, p. 2.
12. *Ibid,* p. 9.
13. *Ibid.*
14. http://www.mea.gov.in/india-and-the-united-nations.htm (accessed on 13 October, 2013)
15. http://www.mea.gov.in/in-focus-article.htm?22231/India+and+the+United+Nations(accessed on 13 October, 2013).
16. http://www.mea.gov.in/SpeechesStatements.htm?50/Speeches_&ampamp;_Statements (accessed on 13 October, 2013).
17. Pawel Bienkowski, "Potential Game Changers and 'changing of the game' in the Asia-Pacific", 21 November 2011, see http://www.eu-asiacentre.eu/pub_details.php?pub_id=18 (accessed on 13 October, 2013).
18. Manmohan Singh, "India and the World: A Blueprint for Partnership and Growth," speech at the Hindustan Times Leadership Initiative Conference, 5 November 2004, http://pmindia.nic.in/lspeech.asp?id=42. (accessed on 16 October, 2013).

23

India-China Geopolitical Rivalry and Advent of the 'Asian Century'

Tej Pratap Singh

Long back Rabindranath Tagore spoke about the emergence of Asian Century in spiritual terms. Chinese foremost leader Deng Xiaoping also spoke about Asian Century but unlike Tagore, Deng spoke in terms of materialism. However, both the leaders and other analysts have emphasized upon the centrality of Sino-Indian ties for the advent of Asian Century, whether spiritual or materiel. Coming together of two Asian giants will expedite the advent of the 'Asian century'. India and China will occupy prominent place and play leading role in the emerging 'Asian century'. We cannot think of 'Asian century' without the emergence of India and China as global powers. India-China relations will influence and determine emerging regional and global order. Their bilateral relations will be a significant factor in regional and global peace, stability and security. However, India feels threatened by the rising Chinese strategic-military power and assertive foreign policy. To address asymmetric power relations with China, India is cosying up with the US. Warming Indo-US relations is perceived by China as US led effort to counterbalance and contain rising China. To contain India in South Asia, China has befriended Pakistan and other neighbours of India. Sino-Indian geopolitical rivalry is creating strains in the bilateral relations and adversely impacting advent of the 'Asian century'.

I propose to examine in this paper how India-China geopolitical rivalry is impacting their regional and global partnership? What implications does it have for the dawning of the 'Asian century'? How will it impact evolving regional and global order? What is the role of the US in India-China geopolitical rivalry? Why is India suspicious of increasing Chinese presence and role in South Asia and Indian Ocean? Why does China resent increasing Indian presence and role in Southeast Asia, East Asia and particularly South China Sea? Why does China view increasing Indian engagement with Vietnam, Japan and other Southeast Asian and East Asian countries as mainly directed against China? Is Chinese string of the pearls strategy against India a myth or reality? These and other geopolitical questions related to Sino-Indian rivalry, I intend to address in this paper.

Rise of China and India

'Let China sleep, for when China wakes, she will shake the whole world', Napoleon famously said about China but this applies to India too. For almost two hundred years, China and India seemed to follow Napoleon's instruction, staying dormant and serving as arena for geopolitical rivalry among great powers. China in 1979 and India in 1991 began the process of coming out of long slumber and world began shaking. China and India's reawakening is reshaping the global economic and political landscape. Economic and technological pressures are pushing New Delhi and Beijing toward a cooperative integration into the world. Growth also means that China and India becomes more assertive, casting a larger shadow on the region and the world (Zakaria, 2008: 88).

China has marched far ahead of India on a whole gamut of development indices. The two countries were, by and large, on a par when they set out on their different development paths sixty years ago. India recognising the reality, is not aiming to catch up with China. The more likely scenario is that China will stay well ahead of India. But India can still capitalize on its advantages—a growing economy, an attractive political democracy, a vibrant model of secularism and tolerance, and a special relationship with America (Zakaria, 2008: 165). India's ambitions compared to China are modest. It simply aims at consolidating its power as a benign regional power with global influence.

India and China—the two oldest civilisations, for the first time in more than half a millennium are simultaneously marching upward on their relative power trajectories. Both see Asia's rise on the world stage as bringing about the end of Western dominance. Both have a long history of bitter rivalry and a contested border. Both have their weak points- regional conflicts, poverty and religious divisions for India; the contradiction within the 'Market-Leninist' system for China. Both are plagued by domestic linguistic, ethno-religious and politico-economic faultlines that could be their undoing if not managed properly (Malik, 2009:163).

Conceptualizing Sino-India Relations

Regarding Sino-India relations, there are two major school of thought, one overly pessimist and other overly optimistic. 'The Eternal Enemy School', paints a very gloomy picture of Sino-India relations. China's all out support to Pakistan's ambitions of strategic parity with India and China's consistent effort to undermine Indian influence in its immediate and extended neighbourhood are well thought out Chinese strategies to thwart and delay the rise of India as a significant global power in Asia and compel India to accept China as the hegemon that must not be engaged in the regional competition. 'The Chindia School' is too optimistic and indulges in the wishful thinking. The cooperation between these two Asian giants will hasten an end to the western domination of the world leading to the dawning of the Asian Century. Sino-India cooperation will shift the centre of gravity of the world from the occident to the orient and will herald the emergence of the era of oriental powers.

In the contemporary unipolar global structure, China is trying to emerge as another important pole of global structure and thus convert the contemporary unipolar structure into the bipolar one. Rise of China has brightened the prospect of China emerging as a rival centre of power to the US in near future. Revival of bipolarity where China is another pole in the international system suits the Chinese aspirations. However, the current distribution of power in the world suits the US. Naturally the US wants the perpetuation of the present world order. The US subscribe to hegemonic stability theory, where one benevolent global hegemon ensures global peace, security and stability. Great Britain did it in the nineteenth century and the US wants to do it in the contemporary world.

The US is a status-quoist power, whereas China is a revisionist power, challenging the global status quo. It is because of this possibility; the US strategic thinkers are suggesting containment policy towards China. In this business of containing or counter balancing China, the significant Asian powers like India and Japan assume importance for the US. John Mearsheimer argues, 'in the not-too-distant future, the United States may need other Asian countries to help it contain China. It would be difficult to fashion an effective coalition of Asian countries without India as a central pillar' (Mearsheimer, 200). Hence neocons of Bush era argued that India must be helped to emerge as great power and Indian power will strengthen American power rather than posing any challenge to the US in Asia.

In this background, the US and its allies like Japan has come with the idea of concert of democracy against the authoritarian regimes. Former Japanese Prime Minister Sinzo Abe advocated the 'arc of democracy' or 'concert of democracies' in Asia consisting of the US, Japan, India, Australia, Singapore and other democracies of the region. The US despite not being part of Asia treats itself as a resident Asian power. China is alarmed by all these moves and has denounced it as efforts to contain China. Japan and the US have denied any such motives. It is in this context, China condemned the expansion of annual US-India bilateral Malabar naval exercise in 2007, when apart from the US and India, navies of Japan, Australia and Singapore also participated. Because of Chinese sensitivities, from next year onwards Malabar exercises were scaled down to bilateral Indo-US level. There was also talk of 'quadrilateral initiative' consisting of US, Japan, India and Australia but because of Chinese opposition to the idea and change in governments in Japan and Australia, it was quietly dropped.

Containment and Engagement

Since India's independence in 1947 and advent of communist China in 1949, both the Asian giants have been involved in the great game of engagement and containment. Because of globalize world it has become imperative for both the nations to engage each other for trading and commercial reasons and because of Asian geopolitics they are trying to contain each other. Rising China and India are finding difficult to accommodate the interest of each other despite the India Prime Minister Manmohan Singh's assertions that world is vast enough to accommodate the interests of both India as well as China. Despite being together on several global issues, they often end up at loggerheads on bilateral and regional issues.

At global level Sino-Indian interests converge. In multilateral forums like Doha round of trade talks, G-20 summits and climate change talks, both India and China coordinate their strategies. Here in these forums both unite in the name of third world solidarity against the first world. In Copenhagen summit on climate change in 2009, the world took notice of close Sino-Indian cooperation. This brightened the prospect of improved Sino-Indian relations. It has been described as Copenhagen spirit. Brazil and South Africa have also joined China and India and thus forming a powerful bloc of developing countries against the developed countries. In Doha round multilateral trade talks, India and China are cooperating on the contentious issues of agriculture subsidy and Non-Agriculture Market Access (NAMA). The same Sino-Indian cooperation has been witnessed in G-20 summits also.

Nehru visualized close Sino-Indian relationship. Nehru courted China, seeing it as a benign neighbour that had like India emerged from the ravages of colonialism. New Delhi even opposed a discussion in the UN General Assembly in November 1950 on Tibet's appeal for international help (Chellaney, 2006: 159). Nehru was also offered permanent membership of the Security Council from Asian quota, which was given to China but then was being held by Nationalist China (Taiwan). Nehru declined the offer and urged the US to give it to Communist China, which was the true successor state of China and not Taiwan. But because of geopolitical reality of the Asia, Nehru's vision of the close Sino-Indian ties could not make much headway and Nehru later regretted his trust on China.

However, despite several setbacks including Sino-Indian war in 1962, there is a large group of scholars both in India and China who advocate close partnership between the two most populous countries of the world for the rise of Asia and ushering in of the Asian Century. North America and Europe is declining and global distribution of power is shifting to Asia. This process of shifting of power from the west to the east can be expedited by the close partnership between these two Asian giants.

Asian Century

India and China relate to each other as immediate neighbours, linked by geography, history and age-old civilisational ties of religion, culture and people to people interaction. Sino-Indian relationship has grown in range, depth and vitality in the past two decades. China and India are widely seen as the rising powers set to steer the US dominated international system towards Asian ascendancy in this century. Mostly seen as rivals and sometimes even as adversaries, India and China are presently trying to embark on a new path where their combined strength and joint cooperation can take on the West and force a change in the rules of global engagement such that it would benefit both the countries and third world.

In the post-Westphalian world, oriental world have had to observe norms and practices formulated and articulated by the West. The global order crafted by the West kept oriental powers including India and China away from accessing sophisticated technologies and slowed down their growth and preserved western monopoly over the wealth and power. Foreign Minister S.M. Krishna echoed this sentiment, while addressing China Institute of International Studies in Beijing on April 6, 2010, 'India and China have only begun to impact seriously on the world. Today, we are striving to rewrite the rules of the world a little more in our favour' (Krishna, 2010: 50).

Sino-Indian Geopolitical Rivalry

By following the age-old principle of enemy's enemy is friend, Pakistan and China have befriended each other against the common enemy India. Sino-Pak relationship, one Pak diplomat observed, is higher than mountain, deeper than ocean and sweeter than honey. If growing Sino-Pak friendship is creating anxiety in India, then growing India-US strategic partnership is creating anxiety in China. China treats the evolving India-US strategic partnership primarily directed against it. The US, Japanese and Indian interests lie in ensuring that Asia is not dominated by china and that the overall balance of power remains in favour of the liberal democracies and not autocracies. There are only two alternatives before the Asian countries: either accept Chinese hegemony or take steps to balance Chinese power. New Delhi hopes and believes that the latter will be more acceptable to China's neighbours (Malik, 1995: 322).

China's attitude towards India is not different from that of the US attitude towards China. China is a status-quoist power in relation to India whereas the US is a status-quoist power in relation to China. Beijing's unwillingness to accommodate India's rise is similar to the US's reluctance to accommodate China's rise. The future of the Asian and global politics will be determined by the triangular United States-China-India relationship.

India's historic quest for strategic autonomy, its self-identity as a great civilization and the great power ambitions of its own mean that it will never be the kind of junior ally the US had during the Cold War. Unlike Great Britain and Japan, India is rising and not retiring great power. India's quest for strategic autonomy and Japan's fear of strategic abandonment by Washington will bring India and Japan closer to each other to forge common strategies vis-à-vis China (Malik, 2009: 185-86).

China is one of the bitterest critics of India's nuclear and missile program. In the wake of Pokharan-II explosion in 1998, China along with the US and others demanded the roll back of India's nuclear weapon program and joining of the NPT as non nuclear weapon state. China's attitude further hardened when the US government made public the confidential letter written to President Clinton by the Prime Minister Vajpayee explaining the reasons for Pokharan-II explosions. In this confidential letter India has singled out China not Pakistan as the main threat to India's national security and for safety against nuclear China India needed its own credible nuclear deterrent. China was also critical of Indo-US Civil Nuclear Cooperation Agreement. China's role was not very cooperative in IAEA and NSG while granting waiver to India. In response to a question, Anil Kakodkar then Chairman of Atomic Energy Commission termed Chinese role as unfortunate (Hindu, September 8, 2008).

Contested Borders

Sharing one of the world's longest and most rugged frontiers, China and India are the only two countries today without a fully defined border. In the longest continuous border-negotiating process between any two nations in the history, China has held fifteen rounds of dialogue since 1981 with India to settle the border disputes. Yet, after more than a quarter century of continuous talks, the two have not been able even to agree on a mutually defined line of control separating them (Chellaney, 2006: 169). Bharat Karnad feels, 'something is radically wrong not just with the Indian government's thinking about what constitutes vital national interests and about ways to secure them, but also with the Indian negotiating style. How else to explain the usual outcome of negotiations with China which invariably favours that country' (Karnad, 1998: 1435).

The border dispute is a colonial legacy. China is not recognizing McMahon Line. China claims that this line has been arbitrarily drawn by Colonial British India, when China was weak and unilaterally imposed upon China against its wishes by the British-Indian government. Since most of this disputed area is not inhabited by the people, the option of ascertaining the views of people is not available. Even where people live such as inhabited areas of Arunachal and Ladakh, China is not in favour of ascertaining the views of people. China has forcibly occupied 38,000 sq. km. of Aksai Chin area and claiming the whole of Arunachal Pradesh. Pakistan has ceded large part of Kashmiri territory under its occupation to China despite Indian objections. Bilateral relations are adversely affected by allegation and counter-allegations of encroachment in each others territory in Ladakh and Arunachal regions.

Tibet occupies the central position in Sino-Indian border dispute. India-China border is basically Indo-Tibetan border. Till the occupation and annexation of Tibet in 1950-51, India had no common border with China. Sino-Indian relation has been taken hostage by the Tibet imbroglio. Without resolving the Tibet issue, Sino-Indian ties cannot be stabilised. Resolution of Tibet issue to the satisfaction of Tibetan people, China and India is the pre-condition for better Sino-Indian relation (Singh, 2012: 13). China accuses India of instigating Dalai Lama to indulge in anti-China activities from the Indian soil. India has recognized Tibet as integral part of China but China is not ready to extend the same favour regarding Kashmir and Arunachal. China has accepted British drawn McMahon line as border between China and Myanmar but withholding the same recognition to Sino-Indian part of McMahon line. India is willing to accept status quo but China has become more aggressive and is demanding more territory in Arunachal particularly Twang, which it claims to be religiously and culturally important for Tibet. If religious and cultural significance of a place can be the basis for claim then India has greater claim to Kailash-Mansarovar as this is more scared to Hindus. Will China give Kailash-Mansarovar to India on this ground? Then how can India cede Twang to China?

Since neither China nor India would ever give up the areas they occupy at present, the most feasible settlement would be the acceptance by both sides of the existing LAC, with some minor adjustments in the eastern and western sectors. After all the possession of Aksai Chin in the western sector is as vital for China as possession of Arunachal Pradesh is for India in the eastern sector (Malik, 1995: 318).

Of late, rich and powerful China has become very assertive in its territorial dispute with its neighbours be it Japan, Vietnam or Philippines in South China Sea or India in Tibet. Chinese nationalism or Han chauvinism could prove to be more threatening to its neighbours than Chinese communism (Malik, 1995: p.322). China has made visa a tool of its foreign policy to put pressure on India. China keeps on needling India by issuing stapled visa to Kashmiri Indians and denying visa altogether to the people of Arunachal Pradesh. Now China has resorted to new tactics of stamping visa with the Chinese map showing all disputed territory as part of China, which includes Aksai Chin, Arunachal Pradesh and disputed islands in the South China Sea. This time India in its tit-for-tat action against China has started stamping its map on visas issued to the Chinese showing Aksai Chin and Arunachal as part of India (Hindu, November 24, 2012).

Sino-Indian Maritime Rivalry: String of Pearls?

Beijing aspires to have command over vital sea lanes between the Indian and Pacific

Oceans through a string of bases, naval facilities and military ties. This has been described by the strategic community as 'String of pearls' strategy. The term 'string of pearls' was first used by an American scholar Booz Allen Hamilton in a report titled 'Energy Futures in Asia', prepared for the Pentagon. Since then it has become popular in strategic parlance in South Asia. The report says, 'China is building strategic relationship along the sea lanes from the Middle East to the South China Sea in ways that suggest defensive and offensive positioning (not only) to protect China's energy interests, but also to serve broad security objectives' (Chellaney, 2006: 142).

China has built or in the process of building ports at Sittwe in Myanmar, Chittagong in Bangladesh, Hambantota in Sri Lanka and Gwadar in Balochistan of Pakistan. All these Indian neighbours have some sort of bilateral differences with India and have roped in extra-regional power China in their hedging strategy against India. The emergence of Chinese facilities on each flank of Indian Peninsula represents a major challenge to India's command of the sea in its own backyard. China critics have accused China of pursuing the policy of encirclement against India and so India should also pay back China in the same coin by forging close strategic partnerships with Japan, Vietnam, Taiwan, Mongolia and countries of ASEAN who are feeling threatened by the rise of Chinese power. China's strategy for a forward naval presence in places like Myanmar, Sri Lanka and Pakistan represents a direct challenge to India's national security interests in the Bay of Bengal, the Arabian Sea and the Indian Ocean-all critical areas for world trade and oil shipments (Chellaney, 2006: 135).

Rise of China has alarmed the countries of Southeast and East Asia and so countries of this region want the presence of the US and Indian navy to counterbalance the Chinese power. They do not feel threatened by the Indian navy, because India has enormous goodwill and soft power in this region. India's 'look east policy' began by Narasimha Rao government has also helped in bringing India closer to the countries of this region. India's look east policy is not being liked by China. Over the years Japan, Singapore and Vietnam have emerged as the great supporter of increasing Indian naval presence in the region.

Pakistan, Sri Lanka, Bangladesh and Burma have denied that deep sea ports being built by the Chinese are military ports. China has claimed that it has no strategic interests in these sea ports and has rubbished the whole idea of string of pearls or encirclement of India. This is canard spread by the anti-Chinese strategic community both in India and the US, who still suffer from cold war mindset and cannot think beyond the strategy of containment and encirclement. Regarding Chinese built deep-sea port at Hambantota, Sri Lankan Foreign Minister G.L. Peiris dismissed Indian concerns that the port was part of Beijing's policy to expand its strategic footprint in the Indian Ocean, describing it as a purely commercial venture. 'There is absolutely no military dimension to this at all. This was never conceived of as a military port', asserted Sri Lankan Foreign Minister. He also claimed that Indian government had never raised any questions or concerns about the Chinese intentions in constructing deep-sea port. 'There is simply no military aspect to this port operation altogether. It will never be a military port', asserted Lankan Foreign Minister. He also claimed that Sri Lanka, in fact, first offered the port project to India, which was turned down by the India and then it approached China (Hindu, August 13, 2010).

Sino-Indian Rivalry in Myanmar

New Delhi saw itself losing out to China in Myanmar. Realists argued that India's pro-democracy stance had driven Myanmar into China's lap. Starting in the mid 1990s, a course correction was affected by India with the announcement of 'look east policy' in 1992. New Delhi began engaging Myanmar and dropped its support for jailed Burmese leader and Nobel laureate Aung San Suu Kyi. Though China has made spectacular inroads, it remains wary of Indian influence in Myanmar. Taking advantage of Sino-Indian rivalry for influence in Myanmar, the Military junta used Beijing and New Delhi against each other. Both the rising powers China and India are insecure enough about the other that they pandered to the endless demands of the Myanmar Generals for economic assistance and political legitimacy. However, this is also true that it was never in Myanmar's interests to choose China over India. The best policy for Myanmar is to befriend both India and China and not playing India against China and China against India (Bhatia, 2010).

In strategic terms, China is interested in Myanmar as a cargo and energy transit route along a south-north axis running from Sittwe in the Bay of Bengal to Yunnan province. For India the west-east transit axis is crucial since Myanmar is a crucial link both for better connectivity with north-eastern states and with the wider ASEAN region. Unless Myanmar speeds up the completion of trans-Asian railroad and highway projects, India's aspiration of closer economic integration with Southeast and East Asia will remain incomplete. China, which has been opposed to India's closer integration with Southeast and East Asia, has a stake in disrupting this east-west connectivity.

China and India compete for Myanmar's energy assets. However, India lost out to China in 2006 not only because of Chinese competition but also because Delhi's inability to work out a transit plan through Bangladesh. Today, given Myanmar's potential in both natural gas and hydroelectric power, there is enough to keep both Indian and Chinese companies gainfully occupied in harnessing Myanmar's energy resources for the benefit of their respective economies. There is no reason for energy to become a zero-sum game between India and China (Vardarajan, 2010).

Southeast and East Asia

China is opposed to India's increasing role in Southeast and East Asia. China was not in favour of India being included into East Asian Summit, but because of strong ASEAN and Japan support India was included. China is also opposed to India becoming member of the evolving East Asian community mooted by Japan and Asia-Pacific Community by Kevin Rudd former Prime Minister of Australia. The ideas of East Asian Community and Asia-Pacific Community have been conceived by Japan and Australia on the pattern of the European Union. China is opposed to increasing presence of the Indian navy in South China Sea and naval exercises with Vietnam and Japan. China is also opposed to increasing role of Indian navy in protecting the sea lanes in Asia-Pacific in general and Malacca strait in particular. Malacca strait is critical for energy security of China, Japan, South Korea and other Northeast Asian economies. At its narrowest point, Malacca is only 2.5 km. wide and so maritime terrorist can block this strait by sinking any oil carrying super-tanker. Chinese Premier Hu Jintao has called it 'Malacca dilemma' and has proclaimed the safety of Malacca for navigation as top Chinese security priority.

Pakistan Factor in Sino-Indian Relations

Pakistan is of immense strategic significance to the Chinese geopolitical interests. Pakistan is a market for China's exports, and a vital link in China's new communication chain connecting the oil-rich Persian Gulf, Middle East and Africa. On top of all this, Pakistan is a sanctuary for Islamist militants from Xingjian. Security cooperation with Islamabad has assumed highest priority for Beijing. The government owned *China Daily* newspaper underscored the complexity of the Sino-Pak relationship, 'An increasing number of members of the East Turkistan Islamic Movement (ETIM), which led the riots and is labelled a terrorist group by the U.N. Security Council, are reportedly fleeing to Pakistan and settling down there for future plots' (*Hindu*, July 17, 2010).

China is the 'all weather friend' of Pakistan and China has taken the place of the US in helping Pakistan in attaining parity with India. Sino-Pak geopolitical interests converge in South Asia against India. China perceives India as a regional rival and to contain India, China is bolstering Pakistan. Chinese economic and military assistance has sustained the Pak quest for parity with India (Singh, 2011: 72-73).

Indian strategic community tend to view Sino-Pak relations in a zero-sum game perspective. Sino-Pak bonhomie has always caused much apprehension in India. China's reported plans to build two more nuclear reactors at Chashma and proposed rail link from Kashgar in China's Xinjiang region across the Karakoram Mountains to Havelian in Pakistan's North West Frontier Province are causing concerns in India. This railway line will run parallel to the Karakoram Highway, the highest paved road in the world, built with Chinese assistance. Karakoram

Highway has proved an expensive link to maintain and the proposed railway line would prove far more expensive. This has dampened Chinese enthusiasm in the proposed rail link.

India has voiced concerns over China undertaking infrastructural projects in Pak occupied Kashmir (PoK). New Delhi's argument is that by carrying out infrastructure projects, China is affirming its support to Pakistani claims over land it views as disputed. China has opposed infrastructure projects funded by the Asian Development Bank (ADB) in Arunachal Pradesh on the similar grounds, arguing that the ADB was legitimising India's claims to the state, which China considers as disputed territory (*Hindu*, July 10, 2010).

Sino-Pak relations have withstood the strain of shifting international relations for more than 60 years. However, it is by no means a problem free relation. There have been differences over alleged training camps for separatists Xingjian militant groups in Pakistan's North West frontier region. But Sino-Pak friendship has solid foundations and India must recognise that it cannot alter the dynamics of the Pakistan-China relationship to suit its own strategic interests. National Security Advisor Shivshankar Menon has rightly observed that Sino-Indian relationship has its own logic. Linking it with another bilateral relationship would be self-defeating (*Hindu*, July 12, 2010).

The trend for quite some time has been of Beijing trying to keep a balance between its relations with India and Pakistan. India's National Security Advisor Shivshankar Menon has observed that India is looking forward to forging a relationship with China which is 'not externally driven'. India needs to view Sino-Pak ties in new perspective and with new thinking. China's close relationship with Pakistan should have no bearing on the momentum of New Delhi advancing the impetus of Sino-Pak ties. It is high time to de-hyphenate India-China-Pakistan relations. India and China are no longer in an 'either-or' or 'zero-sum game' kind of situation. Sino-Indian relationship is not dependent on the state of Sino-Pak relationship or vice-versa (Bhadrakumar, 2010).

The fact that China has also been hit by terrorists in Xingjian province has opened up a new area where India feels the two countries can cooperate to address the common concerns related to growing menace of Islamic jihadism and resultant problem of separatism, extremism and violence. Out of the box thinking or thinking the unthinkable, it has been suggested by Wu Jianmin, a senior advisor to the Chinese Foreign Ministry, that China and India could think of a concerted initiative to ensure the stability of volatile Pakistan and Afghanistan. While this informal non-official proposal requires much dressing up, in a positive diplomatic sense such bold new thinking is the stuff of futuristic regionalism. Wu Jianmin said,

The rise of Asia requires peace and stability in this region. So, you can see that China's interest and the Indian interest coincide....We (in China) do not regard Pakistan as a counterweight to India. It is not propaganda: you have to put yourself in China's shoes....For the first time since 1840, we have a chance to modernise China. To achieve our goal, what we need is peace abroad and stability at home....Trust-building is now going on between China and India. Despite some obstacles, China and India, at the leadership level, are very clear that they need each other (Jianmin, 2010: 61).

Sino-Indian Trade and Commerce

Trade and commerce has brought India and China closer to each other. Despite numerous problems, Sino-India trade is flourishing. Main concern, however, is huge trade imbalance in favour of China. Moreover, Chinese are not opening their markets in IT (Information Technology) and pharmaceuticals sectors, where India has edge over China. Chinese investment in India and ban on certain Chinese Telecom companies such as Huawei are other sticky points. China accused India for carrying out 'under the table' and unfair competition against Chinese companies. China alleged that out of the twenty-six telecom companies blacklisted by India because of security concerns, twenty-five are Chinese companies. China demanded that India should provide 'a fair, open and transparent investment environment for Chinese companies.' Chinese state controlled media accused the Indian government of discrimination against Chinese companies. Chinese media went to the extent of saying, 'India should realise that it was unwise and impossible to try to contain the growth of its neighbour.' *The Global Times*, a state controlled English newspaper of China, claimed in its editorial that while China respected India 'as an admirable Asian neighbour', India 'has not reciprocated with due respect or trust.' 'Most disputes in recent years have started with suspicion or hostility on the Indian side, and China was forced to respond,' the editorial accused. New Delhi played down the Chinese media criticism and asserted that the ban was not country-specific. Chinese telecom giant Huawei, which is under the scanner in India, also lost a bid to sell equipment for a major United States mobile operator because of security concerns in Washington. In 2008 also, Huawei lost a $2.2 billion bid for a U.S. firm on security grounds (Hindu, July 10, 2010). In view of these facts, hysterical Chinese reaction against India is unjustified.

Energy Cooperation or Competition

Today energy and security are inseparable. Energy is getting increasingly intertwined with geopolitics. China's China National Petroleum Corporation (CNPC), China National Offshore Oil Corporation (CNOOC) Limited, and India's Oil and Natural Gas Commission (ONGC) are locked in stiff competition to acquire overseas energy assets. India owned ONGC Videsh Limited (ONGCVL) has lost to Chinese oil companies in most of the places in Angola, Nigeria, Sudan in Africa, Venezuela and Ecuador in Central America, Iran, Kazakhstan, Russia and Myanmar in the neighbourhood. Chinese bidding has been very aggressive for these energy assets and moreover China offered economic assistance and arms, ammunition on favourable conditions ignoring the human rights concern of autocratic regimes, which India was not in position to offer. Popular global perception is that Chinese and Indian companies are engaged in fierce bidding wars to acquire energy assets; the reality is that Chinese companies have beaten Indian competition wherever it has arisen (Chellaney, 2006: 107).

Rapidly rising Indian and Chinese economies are hungry for energy resources. Both have been competing and collaborating in this area. The two are working out arrangements where they don't hike up international oil prices unnecessarily in their attempt to outbid each other (Sharma, 2010: 52). China is willing to cooperate with India in the energy sector only if the following three conditions are met:

- Indian oil companies are willing to play the role of junior partner to Chinese state-owned oil companies.
- Energy resources do not lie in India's immediate neighbourhood (Burma, Bangladesh, Central Asia and Iran).
- Energy resources lie in countries or regions, where Sino-Indian cooperation would cause a wedge between India and the US such as Syria, Sudan, Venezuela, etc. (Malik, 2010: 181).

Dragon Vs Elephant

China hates being compared to India as India hates being compared to Pakistan. India wants to be de-hyphenated with Pakistan but loves to be hyphenated with China and China loves to be compared and hyphenated with the United States but the US hates to be compared with any nation and wants to maintain its pre-eminent global position (Singh, 2010: 40). Chinese find the growing global tendency to compare their country with India as offensive and demeaning. Chinese claim that their country is competing with the US and not India. China has never looked at Indian as an equal nor can Beijing comprehend the idea of India being China's equal in the future. Chinese are dismissive of India's claim as the world's largest democracy. From the Chinese point of view, India is an emerging South Asian regional power rather than a potential global player. Beijing's attitude towards the expansion of the UN Security Council and India's nuclear programme is an indication that China will not countenance the emergence of an Asian peer competitor (Malik, 2010: 164-65).

China and India are caught in a classic security dilemma. They view their own actions as defensive but view others action as offensive. Beijing insists New Delhi abide by 'Five Don'ts' that laid the basis for the Sino-Indian rapprochement in the 1990s:

- Don't peddle 'the China threat theory'.
- Don't support Tibet or Taiwan's independence.
- Don't counter the Sino-Pakistani 'all weather friendship' or Sino-Burmese 'special relationship'.

- Don't align with the US and/or Japan to contain China.
- Don't see or project yourself as an equal of China or as a nuclear and economic counterweight to China in Asia.

As long as New Delhi subscribes to these 'Five Don'ts' or 'Five Principles', both in words and deeds, Beijing is willing to develop its relations with India as part of its strategy to have good relations with all its neighbours (Malik, 2010: 169-70). This is a new 'Panchsheel' of China for good neighbourly relations.

China is also blocking India's membership in regional and international institutions. It created hurdles in India's membership to the ARF (ASEAN Regional Forum), APEC (Asia-Pacific Economic Cooperation), ASEM (Asia-Europe Summit Meeting), SCO (Shanghai Cooperation Organisation), the UN Security Council, etc. Beijing also resents India-led regional initiatives such as the Mekong-Ganges Cooperation (MGC) and BIMSTEC (Bangladesh, India, Myanmar, Sri Lanka, Thailand Economic Cooperation).

Why should China's rise cause 'concern' to the rest of the world while India's ascent does not? The commonly heard argument is that India's policies and practices are far more 'transparent' than those of China (Suryanarayana, 2010: 61). Global community feels more comfortable while dealing with India because of its democratic and transparent political system, whereas the non-democratic and opaque Chinese political system causes concerns.

Kanti Bajpai has identified four pillars of interactions evolved by India and China after the famous visit of Rajiv Gandhi in 1988 to stabilise their bilateral relations. These four pillars are border negotiations, high level summits, confidence-building measures and bilateral trade. Both sides have agreed that both governments must remain engaged in discussion despite no possibility of border settlement in the foreseeable future. There have been more summits between the presidents, prime ministers/premiers and foreign ministers of the two countries than in the previous forty years. Among the CBMs, there are two areas where the two sides have to pay urgent attention-nuclear weapons and naval CBMs. China has so far refused to discuss nuclear weapons with India but as India nuclearises, China has to engage India in nuclear talks for sake of military stability. Increasing Chinese naval presence in Indian Ocean and Indian in China Sea makes it imperative for the two to put in place the naval CBMs to prevent unnecessary naval confrontations. Rapidly rising trade is the fourth pillar of Sino-Indian relations. Trade has the potential of stabilising bilateral relations but asymmetric trade is problematic. Two must address the trade asymmetry for the healthy enduring relations otherwise asymmetry instead of stabilising can lead to trade war. (Bajpai, 2011: 19-22).

Bharat Karnad, however, does not share the optimism of Kanti Bajapi and treats 'Confidence Building Measures as liability' for India. China realises that CBMs can promote its concept of 'mutual and equal security'. India has jumped on CBMs bandwagon without any clear ideas other than the hope that they will do for Indo-Pak and Sino-Indian relations, what they managed to do in Europe (Karnad, 1998: 1429). Booming bilateral trade is no guarantee for improved Sino-Indian relations as Germany and Britain went to war against each other despite having a very high volume of trade. Summit meetings are more a photo-opportunity rather than transacting any serious business. Prolonged border negotiations without any prospects of settlement are irritating and disappointing.

Conclusions

In the history, two rising regional powers have never been on good terms. They have always engaged in the stiff competition to march ahead of the other and to achieve this objective they have also tried to contain and counter-balance each other. The weaker of the two has always roped in the extra regional powers to counter-balance the rival. Precisely because of this reason, India is trying to rope in the US against China in its hedging strategy. Since China is potential challenger to the superpower status of the US and so the US also needs India to contain China. On all bilateral and regional issues, India and China usually adopt diametrically opposite positions, which preclude any possibility of meaningful cooperation between the two Asian giants.

Rising Sino-Indian trade, commerce and investment diminishes the possibility of war or conflict. Market forces compel the nations to maintain peace and stability, which is conducive to trade, commerce and prosperity. At present, China is the largest trading partner of India. Their bilateral trade has exceeded $70 billion. Any dispute between them will adversely affect their rapidly growing trade, which will harm the interests of both the nations. Though, India is not the largest trading partner of China, but the balance of payment (BOP) is hugely in favour of China. Moreover, India exports mainly natural resources needed by the Chinese industries and imports finished products from China, promoting Chinese industries at the cost of indigenous industries as per classical 'dependency theory' of the international trade. Import of cheap Chinese products is adversely impacting the growth of labour intensive industries in India. The present Sino-Indian trade is more beneficial to China rather than India. If this is the scenario then why China will unnecessarily provoke any conflict with India to vitiate the present atmosphere of peace and stability.

I argue in this paper that primarily India and China are rivals and their bilateral relationship is characterised by the zero-sum game. The limited Sino-Indian partnerships on certain global issues such as climate change, multilateral trade talks (Doha round), restructuring/democratisation of Bretton Woods institutions, etc., where their short term interests converge against the developed west are peripheral. Their partnership on these global issues is dictated by short-term gains and is not adequate enough to pave the way for enduring Sino-Indian partnership. This partnership can be characterised as symbolic or tokenism devoid of substance. However, these symbolic partnerships bode well for their future relations as both can build upon this partnership to overcome the mutual trust deficits and augment their cooperation for the mutual benefits of their people as India and China face similar problems of poverty, underdevelopment, nation-state building, where they can learn from the experiences of each other. Sino-Indian relations in the foreseeable future will be characterised by tactical cooperation for short term gains and peaceful geopolitical rivalry and competition for prestige and influence. Richard K. Betts has called this kind of relationship as 'containment without confrontation- polite containment which need not preclude decent relations' (Betts, 1993/94: 54).

Coming together of the two Asian giants China and India will definitely expedite the process of dawning of Asian century. But because of intense geopolitical rivalry between Beijing and New Delhi, this is definitely a difficult proposition. Sino-Indian geopolitical rivalry is adversely impacting the advent of Asian century/renaissance. Following former US National Security Advisor Brzezinski, who has suggested G-2 US-China summit meetings to address global problems, some analysts have suggested Asian variant of G-2 summit meetings of China and India to fix the problems of Asia. However, this kind of G-2 summit diplomacy will create more global and regional problems rather than addressing it.

REFERENCES

Bajpai, Kanti, India and China: Can the Giants of Asia Cooperate? The Second Y.B. Chavan Memorial Lecture organized by the IDSA, New Delhi, on November 30, 2011, www.idsa.in/system/files/2ndYBChavanMemorialLecture.pdf accessed on 25 November 2012.

Bhadrakumar, M.K., "De-hyphenating: Sino-Indian ties", *The Hindu* (Chennai), July 17, 2010.

Betts, Richard K., "Wealth, Power and Instability", *International Security*, Vol. 18, No.3, Winter 1993/94.

Chellaney, Brahma, *Asian Juggernaut: The Rise of China*, India and Japan (New Delhi: HarperCollins Publisher India, 2006).

China Daily report cited by M.K. Bhadrakumar, "De-hyphenating" Sino-Indian ties", *The Hindu* (Chennai), July 17, 2010.

Jianmin, Wu cited in P.S. Suryanarayana, "Rising Status", *Frontline*, Vol. 27, No. 16, August 13, 2010, p. 61.

Karnad, Bharat, "Getting Tough with China: Negotiating Equitable not Equal Security", *Strategic Analysis*, January, 1998, pp.1429-1441.

Krishna, S.M. cited by Pranay Sharma, "Masons to the Wall", *Outlook* (New Delhi), Vol. L, No.15, April 19, 2010, p. 50.

Krishnan, Ananth "Faith against odds", *The Hindu* (Chennai), August 8, 2010.

Krishnan, Ananth "Hambantota will never be a military port", *The Hindu* (Chennai), August 13, 2010.

Malik, Mohan, "China-India Relations in the Post-Soviet Era: The Continuing Rivalry", *The China Quarterly*, No.142, June 1995, pp. 317-355.

Malik, Mohan "India and China: As China Rises, India Stirs", in Harsh V. Pant (ed.), *Indian Foreign Policy in a Unipolar World* (New Delhi: Routledge, 2009).

Mearsheimer, John J., "India Needs The Bomb", *The New York Times*, March 24, 2000.

Pentagon's "Energy Futures in Asia" Report quoted by Brahma Chellaney, p. 142.

Bhatia, Rajiv, "Crafting a Richer India-Myanmar Partnership", *The Hindu* (Chennai), August 11, 2010.

Sharma, Pranay, "Masons to the Wall", *Outlook* (New Delhi), Vol. L, No.15, April 19, 2010.

Singh, Tej Pratap, "India-China: Eternal Enemies or Future Allies", *Defence and Security Alert,* Vol.2, issue 2, November, 2010, pp. 38-42.

Singh, Tej Pratap, "Pakistan: Unending Quest for Parity", *Defence and Security Alert,* Vol. 2, Issue 7, April, 2011, pp. 71-73.

Singh, Tej Pratap, "Tibet Factor in Sino-Indian Relation", *Uday India,* Vol. III, No. 20, April 28, 2012, pp. 13-15.

Suryanarayana, P.S. "Rising status", *Frontline,* Vol. 27, No. 16, August 13, 2010.

The Hindu (Chennai).

Varadarajan, Siddharth, "Facing up to the Myanmar Challenge", *The Hindu* (Chennai), July 27, 2010.

Index